I0125153

J. T. Walker

General Report on the Operations of the Great Trigonometrical

Survey of India

During 1873-1874

J. T. Walker

General Report on the Operations of the Great Trigonometrical Survey of India
During 1873-1874

ISBN/EAN: 9783744622059

Printed in Europe, USA, Canada, Australia, Japan

Cover: Foto ©Suzi / pixelio.de

More available books at **www.hansebooks.com**

GENERAL REPORT

ON THE OPERATIONS

OF THE

GREAT TRIGONOMETRICAL SURVEY OF INDIA,

DURING

1873-74,

Prepared for submission to the Government of India.

BY

COLONEL J. T. WALKER, R.E, F.R.S., &C.,

SUPERINTENDENT OF THE SURVEY.

Dehra Dun:

PRINTED AT THE OFFICE OF THE SUPERINTENDENT G. T. SURVEY.

M. J. O'CONNOR.

1874.

THE OPERATIONS OF THE

GREAT TRIGONOMETRICAL SURVEY OF INDIA

IN 1873-74.

~~~~~~~~~~~~~~~

The following is a summary of the several operations of the year under review, given in the order in which they will be found described in this report.

(2.) The operations carried out during the year under review have produced the following out-turn of work;—of Principal Triangulation, with the great theodolites of the Survey, 70 triangles, embracing an area of 7,190 square miles, and disposed in chains which, if united, would extend over a direct distance of 302 miles, and in connection with which 3 astronomical azimuths of verification have been measured;—of Secondary Triangulation, with vernier theodolites of various sizes, an area of 5,212 square miles has been closely covered with points for the topographical operations, an area of 3,650 square miles has been operated in *pari passu* with the principal triangulation but exterior thereto, and in an area of 12,000 square miles—in the ranges of mountains to the north of the Assam Valley which are inhabited by independent tribes—a large number of peaks have been fixed, many of which have already been found serviceable in the geographical operations now being carried on with the Military Expedition against the Dufflas;—of Topographical Surveying, an area of 534 square miles has been completed in British portions of the Himalayas, on the scale of one inch to the mile, an area of 2,366 square miles in Kattywar on the two-inch scale, and areas of 690 and of 63 square miles respectively, in Guzerat and in the Dehra Dún, on the scale of 4 inches to the mile;—of Geographical Exploration, much valuable work has been done in Kashgharia and on the Pamir Steppes, in connection with Sir Douglas Forsyth's mission to the Court of the Atalik Ghazi, and several additions to the geography of portions of Great Thibet and of Nepaul have been obtained through the agency of native explorers.

(3.) The principal triangulation has been executed with the great theodolites, whose azimuthal circles have a diameter of 24 inches and are read by 5 equidistant microscopes. The average theoretical ' probable error ' of the angles, as deduced from the observations, and the average geometrical error of the triangles—or the amount by which the sum of the three observed angles of each triangle differs from 180° + the spheroidal excess—are shown in the table given in the margin. In the course of the operations of the present year the northern section of the Brahmaputra Meridional Series has been completed, whereby two important circuits of triangulation formed by it with the Assam and East Calcutta Longitudinal Series to the north and south, the Calcutta Meridional and the Eastern Frontier Series to the

Series.	Probable Errors of Observed Angles.		Geometrical Errors of Triangles.	
	Number.	Amount.	Number.	Amount.
I	60	±0″·14	20	0″·40
III	42	·25	14	·83
IV	78	·14	26	·14
V	30	·54	10	·70
Average,...	...	±0″·22	...	0·43

west and east, have been closed. The Straits of the Gulf of Manaar have been reconnoitered, with a view to connecting the triangulation of India with that of Ceylon, which has been found to be feasible.

(4.) But the most important features in the operations of the principal triangulation of the present year are the resumption of the chain of triangles in Burma, and the completion of the Bangalore Meridional Series, for the revision of the southern section of the Great Arc. The triangulation in Burma was suspended in 1870, during the financial difficulties of the Government, for reasons which are set forth in my Report for 1869-70; it is now urgently required, in order to furnish a basis for topographical and revenue survey operations which are about to be commenced in Burma; but to enable it to be undertaken without increasing the normal expenditure of this Department, one of the parties employed on the principal triangulation has been broken up, and thus instead of the *five* parties so employed last year there have been only been *four* this year. The completion of the revision of the Great Arc concludes the revisionary operations for certain important triangulations which were originally executed at the commencement of the present century with very inferior instruments, and are specified in my Report for 1864-65 as requiring to be repeated with the best modern appliances; thus I have now much gratification in expressing my conviction that no portion of the principal triangulation remains which will ever require to be revised, and that the last of the old links, in all the great chains of triangles, which might with any reason have been objected to as weak and faulty, have now been made strong and put on a par with the best modern triangulation.

(5.) The pendulum observations have been completed, and the final results are now being computed and prepared for publication.

(6.) Considerable assistance has been rendered to Colonel Tennant in the operations connected with the observations of the Transit of Venus; several astronomical instruments have been lent to him, and the services of an officer of this Department, Captain Campbell, R.E., have been placed at his disposal for an entire year. The Transit was independently observed by Mr. Hennessey at Mussooree, near the Office at which the Head Quarter's of this Survey are established during the recess season; Mr. Hennessy's account of his observations is given at the end of the first appendix to this report.

(7.) Owing to the absence of Captain J. Herschel R.E., from India, and to the services of Captain Campbell having been placed at Colonel Tennant's disposal, the operations for astronomical determinations of latitude, and astro-telegraphic determinations of differences of longitude, have been suspended.

(8.) The operations for determining the tidal constituents at certain stations in the Gulf of Kutch, with a view to the investigation of the supposed variations in the relative levels of the land and sea, have been fairly initiated, as will be reported on in full detail in Section XI.

(9.) The final reduction of the triangulation and of the pendulum operations, the preparation of the results for publication, and the printing of such results as are prepared, have made good progress, though not as great as I could have wished, owing to so much of my time having been taken up with other matters that I have frequently been obliged to set aside my own share of the work for months together.

(10.) During the recess of 1874, the Surveyor General, Colonel Thuillier C. S. I., went to England for three months, and I was directed to officiate for him in addition to performing my own duties. It so happened that just at that time I was called on, as officiating Surveyor General, to report on several matters of great importance, viz., the results of the recent reorganization of the several branches of the Survey Department, working under the direct orders of the Government of India, which had been carried out with effect from the commencement of the financial year 1874-75; the reorganization of the Madras Revenue Surveys, with a view to arranging for the preparation of complete maps of the Madras Presidency by topographical surveys of the unsurveyed tracts lying between the revenue paying districts; the Cadestral Surveys in the North West Provinces, &c. These duties absorbed almost the whole of my time while I was acting for Colonel Thuillier, and have led to correspondence which has taken up much of it since his return; but as the subjects under discussion will presumably be dwelt on in his Administration Report for the present year, any further notice of them here is unnecessary.

(11.) I have also had to render assistance to Captain Bailey, R.E., the Superintendent of the newly formed Department of Forest Surveys, in organizing his establishments and training them in such a manner that their work may, on the one hand, satisfy all the requirements of their own department, for the purposes of forestry, and on the other hand be so conducted as to be suitable for combination with the operations of this Department. There were large tracts of forest in the Dehra Dún which required to be surveyed by the Forest Department, and Captain Bailey was directed to commence his operations by surveying them, as they are situated within a convenient distance of my Head Quarters. The additional trouble which this has caused me has not been little, but it has been more than repaid by the pleasure I have experienced in assisting an officer so anxious to learn all that is needed to enable him to do his work thoroughly well, as is Captain Bailey.

(12.) I now proceed as usual to describe the operations of the several Survey Parties and Offices. Further details, and accounts of various matters of general interest, which have been brought to notice during the year, will be found in the first appendix, which gives "Extracts from the Narrative Reports of the Executive Officers"; while the second appendix gives accounts of certain Trans-Himalayan Explorations, in Great Thibet, &c., the details of which have not yet been published.

NO. I.—TRIGONOMETRICAL.

THE SOUTHERN SECTION OF THE BANGALORE MERIDIONAL SERIES.

(13.) Of the southern portion of the Great Arc—the portion situated between the parallels of 8° and 18°, which was measured by Colonel Lambton at the commencement of the present century—a revision has long been deemed an essential desideratum for geodetic purposes, and the execution thereof has been regarded as an object to be carried out whenever the general triangulation of the country had sufficiently approached completion to permit of the employment of one of the trigonometrical parties thereon; the revision has been proceeded with from time to time of late years, by triangulations emanating from the Bangalore base-line, which were carried on whenever opportunity offered, so that at the commencement of the present year about five-sixths had been revised; the gap remaining to be finished lay near the Cape Comorin base-line and was about 108 miles in length. This gap has now been completed by Major Branfill and his assistants; and thus the triangulation of the entire arc, from Cape Comorin to the Himalayas, has at last been brought to the same stand-

PERSONNEL.

Major B. R. Branfill, Dy. Supdt. 2nd Grade.
Mr. G. Belcham Asst. Sur. 1st Grade.
Mr. C. D. Potter „ „ „
„ J. Bond „ 3rd „
„ E. W. Laseron „ 3rd „

ard of accuracy as that secured for the northern section, by the operations of Colonel Everest, in 1833-41.

(14.) The revision was last taken in hand in the year 1870-71, when it was brought down from the north to the Palanei mountains, which flank the great plain of Coimbatore. Here great difficulties were met with in extending the triangulation southwards, in a symmetrical manner; the country had to be minutely examined, and many a promising design had to be abandoned before a practicable one was discovered. Colonel Lambton had met with similar difficulties, and they had baffled all his attempts to secure a station of observation at an obligatory point on the Palanei mountains, and he had been obliged to content himself with erecting a flag on that point—the Permaul Hill—and taking observations to it from the surrounding stations, and thus he was only able to measure two of the three angles in all the triangles (five in number) of which it forms a station. In the present instance the difficulty was surmounted, but only by giving one of the triangles a side of which the length is 64 miles, exceeding the longest side of any principal triangle yet measured in India; on so long a side observations can only be taken when the atmosphere is unusually clear, and this was fortunately the case when Major Branfill commenced operations this year, though when he first attempted the observations, at the end of the season of 1870-71, the atmosphere was unfavorable and he was compelled to return to his recess quarters leaving the work incomplete.

(15.) The operations of this year were intended to close on a side of the polygon around the Cape Comorin Base-line which had been completed in 1868-69, immediately after the measurement of the base-line; but it was found that one of the two stations on the side of junction had disappeared. This station was situated on a remarkable group of Red Sand Hills, where, in 1808, Colonel Lambton had constructed a station by driving long pickets into the drift sand; in 1869 Major Branfill, finding no trace of these pickets, had caused a masonry well to be sunk to a depth of ten feet, where it reached what was believed to be firm soil below; but during the interval of 4 years this well had been undermined,

SKETCH
of the Proposed Connection of the
TRIANGULATION
of INDIA and of CEYLON
——

N D I

• Ramnad .

Paumben H.ᵉ

Gandamadaua Parvat
• Ramiseweram

Erukkam. I.

MANAR ISLAND

Bridge
Adam's
Ramis R.
or 4 & 5/6 above water

GULF OF MANAR

• Mandodde.

• Thoppukhadaroi

Madurinhora. I.
Kateracheru. I.
Pungersavu.

Frederics I.
Kadarava. I.
Palletiva. I.

• Pallasarapakadin

• Punakari

CARKILS or HORSES

JAFFNA
• Surchachehari

N O Y

Tomb Pedro

G. G. BURNTHA, Pram.

G. G. OLDMAN, Extra.

Polotinographed at the Office of the Superintendent Great Trigonometrical Survey, Dehra Doon, August 1874.

Remarks

The ruled lines shew triangles to be measured on the side of India
The dotted lines   Dᵒ   Dᵒ   Dᵒ   Ceylon

Scale 1 Inch = 8 Miles

Scale 1 Inch = 8 Miles

and nothing remained thereof but some scattered *debris.* It would appear that the sand hills travel progressively in the direction from west-north-west to east-south-east, which is that of the prevailing winds in this locality ; if Colonel Lambton's station was situated on the highest point of the hills and in a similar position relatively to the general mass as Major Branfill's, then the hills must have travelled a distance of about 1,060 yards to the E.S.E., for the results of the triangulation show that this is the distance between the positions of the two stations ; thus the rate of progression would be about 17 yards per annum. From Major Branfill's Notes on the Tinnevelly District, which are appended to the General Report for 1868-69, it appears that certain measurements of the eastward drift had made it as much as 440 yards in the four years 1845-48 ; but the distance between the trigono-metrical stations of 1808 and 1869 probably affords the most accurate measure which has hitherto been obtained of the rate of progress of this remarkable sand-wave, which gradually overwhelms the villages and fields it meets with in its course, and has never yet been effectually arrested ; numerous attempts have been made, by growing grass and creepers and planting trees on the sands, to prevent the onward drift, but they have hitherto been unsuccessful.

(16.) During the field season Mr. Bond had the good fortune to encounter a couple of the wild folk who live in the hill jungles of the Western Ghâts ; he has written an interesting description of them, which will be met with in the extracts from Major Branfill's report, at page 5—, of the first of the appendices to this report.

(17.) On the completion of the principal triangulation, Major Branfill proceeded to the Straits of Manaar, with a view to ascertain the practicability of carrying a triangulation across them, to connect the survey of India with that of Ceylon ; the connection was found to be feasible, and the sketch facing this page was prepared by Major Branfill to show how it may be accomplished. The Straits were first examined at Adam's Bridge, where they are narrowest ; but the islets composing the bridge were found to be sand-hillocks which for the most part are covered by the sea at high-water, and are only accessible at low-water during fine weather ; they are thus most unpromising positions for the construction of suitable stations, and it was soon found necessary to abandon all idea of crossing over them. Higher up, on the line between Rameswaram and Jaffna, there are several islands which are composed of coral and sandstone and on which stations can therefore be erected. Of these the nearest to the Indian coast is Kachi-tivu, a small island not more than a mile in diameter, but standing well out of the water, and visible from the island of Ramesweram on one side and that of Neduven-tivu on the other ; here it will be quite feasible to construct two stations—which need not be high ones—at a distance of about a mile apart, and to fix their positions by obser-vations at them and at the Ramesweram stations ; they will then serve as a base from which to determine the positions of the two next stations, which will have to be erected at the extremities of the island of Neduven-tivu. This island belongs to Ceylon and is about 7 miles in length ; it is covered with a dense growth of palm trees, and the Ceylon Government has undertaken to construct towers of a suffi-cient height to overlook these trees, and to command the requisite view all round, and serve as stations of the triangulation. It has been proposed that the positions of these towers, as well as of the stations on the island of Kachi-tivu, should be fixed from the side of India by Major Branfill, with one of the first class theodo-lites of this Survey, as the acuteness of several of the angles which are involved in the triangulation necessitates the employment of the best instruments which can be provided for the measures of the angles, and the instrumental equipment of the Indian Survey is much superior to that of Ceylon ; on the other hand the more symmetrical triangles, beyond the towers on Neduven-tivu, will be measured by the officers of the Ceylon Survey. Colonel Fyers, R.E., the Surveyor General of Ceylon, has taken great interest in the proposed operations, and done all in his power to co-operate with me in the matter ; and arrangements are now being made by Mr. Twynam, the Government Agent of the Northern Province of Ceylon, who resides at Jaffna, for the construction of the two towers on Neduven-tivu.

(18.) On the completion of his reconnoissance of the Straits, Major Branfill proceeded to lay out a longitudinal chain of triangles on the parrallel of 9° 15', which will run eastwards from the Great Arc to the coast, and thence across to Neduven-tivu, and from which a chain of triangles must eventually be carried up the Coast of Coromandel to Madras.

(19.) The general out-turn of work has been excellent. The principal triangulation, by which the revision of the Great Arc has now been completed, extends over a direct distance of 108 miles, is polygonal throughout, and covers an area of 3,239 square miles. Star observations, for determining the azimuth, were taken at a station at which the latitude had been determined astronomically by Captain Herschel, and pendulum observations had been made by the late Captain Basevi. An important chain of secondary triangles, 62 miles in length, fixing 51 secondary points, some of which are high and important hill peaks, was executed, in continuation of a series which had been commenced at Mangalore, and carried down the Malabar Coast for some distance, and was then diverted eastwards and brought through the Pálghát gap in the Western Gháts, and has now been made to close on the triangulation in Coimbatore.

(20.) On returning to recess quarters Major Branfill and his assistants took in hand the reduction of the observations and the calculations of the usual preliminary results. The difference between the measured value of the base-line at Cape Comorin and the computed value brought down by the triangulation from Calcutta, viâ Madras and Bangalore, was found to be barely appreciable, being slightly more than a quarter of an inch in 1·7 miles, or more exactly 2·23 millionth parts of the length measured. Geodesists will be gratified to learn that no serious errors have been met with in the values of the three sections of the Great Arc comprised between the parallels of 8° 9' and 18° 3', which were deduced from Colonel Lambton's observations at the commencement of the present century; the final values will be greater, in each section, than those hitherto adopted, but probably by not more than 160 feet in any section, nor than 320 feet in all.

(21.) Major Branfill's duties during the recess have been much increased by his having had to take temporary charge of the two extra parties at Bangalore, during the absence of the officers in permanent charge who had been transferred elsewhere, and pending the arrival of other officers to take their places. I have much reason to be satisfied with the excellent manner in which Major Branfill performs every duty assigned to him, the interest he takes in all parts of his work, the training he gives to his assistants, and the constant supervision which he exercises over them.

NO. II.—TRIGONOMETRICAL.

THE OPERATIONS IN THE ASSAM VALLEY.

(22.) A full account of the history of these operations, and the difficulties which have been met with in their prosecution and have so greatly retarded their progress, was given in my report for last year. In the present year the triangulation has been advanced a distance of 47 miles, through the forest clad plains on the south bank of the Brahmaputra river, the operations terminating within a few miles of the Civil Station of Sibságar.

PERSONNEL.
W. G. Beverley Esq. Offg. Assistant Superintendent 1st Grade.
Mr. G. A. Harris Surveyor 4th Grade.
Mr. W. G. O'Sullivan Surveyor 4th Grade.
Mr. J. O. Hughes Assist. Surv. 4th Grade.

(23.) The amount of progress made would be considered small in most parts of India, but for this difficult country, where every line has to be cleared of trees and thick jungle with great labor, and the population is so scanty that laborers are rarely met with on the spot and have usually to be imported from a

(9)

distance, and where food for the surveyors and laborers and materials for the construction of the stations have also to be imported from a distance, it is as much
as could well be expected, and it is materially greater than the progress which
was made in either of the two preceding years.

(24.) Considerable advantage was derived from a modification in the
construction of the stations which I had directed Mr. Beverley to introduce;
instead of the usual central masonry pillar for the theodolite, surrounded by a
platform (generally of solid earth work) for the observer, both raised to a sufficient
height to overlook all irremoveable obstacles in the lines, a small pillar has been
built, which is merely sufficient to indicate the site of the station permanently,
and over it a tripod stand has been erected for the theodolite; the stand is formed
of three stout logs firmly braced together, with the ends buried in the ground, and it
is made sufficiently high to give the required command; around and isolated from
it, a platform is constructed, of bamboos or timber, for the observer; these have
been found to suffice very well for all practical requirements, and Mr. Beverley
reports that "from the rapidity with which they can be constructed they have
helped materially to advance the survey". Hitherto the signals under observation
have also been set up on these tripods; but as their mounting does not require to
be as firm and rigid as that of the theodolites, I have directed a further modification
to be introduced in the construction of the stations, whereby the signals will be
set up at a considerable height above the theodolites, and will thus be visible over
the top of the long grass and jungle, the clearance of which has usually been
found to be a very formidable task; I trust that this expedient will be found practicable, and that in future the line clearing will be restricted to the cutting down
of such trees as are too high to be looked over.

(25.) During the season Mr. Beverley was able to fix several additional
points in the Duffla Hills to the north of the valley, which will be most valuable
aids to the officers who have been attached to the Duffla Expedition in order
to make a survey of the country. A number of points were also fixed on the
Naga Hills, to the southeast, which should be of much value to the officers
now engaged in making a topographical reconnoissance of those hill tracts.
Connections have also been made with the stations of the Revenue Survey in the
valley. The aggregate length of the lines which had to be cleared, in course of
the construction of the principal chain of triangles, was 178 miles.

(26.) Towards the conclusion of the field operations Mr. G. A. Harris was
compelled by failing health to return to the recess quarters at Shillong; he had
suffered much from fever, against which he struggled bravely, remaining in the
field—far from medical aid—longer than he should have done, in order to complete
his share of the operations; at last he was obliged to desist from work and to
return to Shillong, where he died a few days after his arrival. He was a very
painstaking and worthy member of the Department, and his loss is much regretted.

NO. III.—TRIGONOMETRICAL.

THE BRAHMAPUTRA SERIES, MERIDIAN 90°.

(27.) This important meridional chain of triangles lies wholly between the
Calcutta and the Assam Longitudinal Series. It was commenced at the south
end, in 1867-68, and was completed during the present year, having been executed
throughout as a chain of successive polygonal figures. Lying almost wholly in
alluvial plains, lofty towers have had to be erected as stations of observation, in
nearly every instance, and almost all the lines between these towers have had to

be cleared of trees and jungle; thus though the labor entailed has been very considerable the progress has been comparatively slow, averaging 30½ miles per annum, the entire length of the series being 220 miles.

(28.) At the commencement of the present year a gap of 54 miles remain-

PERSONNEL.
Captain Carter, Officiating Deputy Supdt. 2nd grade.
Mr. L. H. Clarke, Surveyor 2nd grade
„ Collins, Asst. Surveyor 4th grade.

ed to be completed, in order to connect the principal triangulation from the south with that to the north; all the intermediate stations had however been select-ed and built, and the lines between them had been cleared, and thus during the present year there was little to be done in the way of preliminaries before the commencement of the principal triangulation; at a few of the stations bamboo scaffoldings had to be erected for the support of the observatory tent, and a few lines, in which jungle had grown up since they were first cut, had to be re-cleared.

(29.) Captain Carter took the field at an early date, being anxious to complete the triangulation before the month of March, when the villagers usually begin to burn the grass and bamboo jungles, and the atmosphere is so pervaded with smoke and haze that all distant objects are altogether shut out from view for weeks together, until the periodic rains commence to fall and clear the atmos-phere. Fortunately he was successful in finishing the requisite observations by the 6th March, but he found the field season a particularly trying one, for though it was short he was all the while working against time.

(30.) Captain Carter deputed Mr. Clarke to execute secondary triangula-tions for the purpose of fixing the positions of points of importance in the vicini-ty of the series which could not be seen from the principal stations. Mr. Clarke was more particularly instructed to fix as many as possible of the stations of the Revenue Survey which had been completed in the Rungpore and adjoining dis-tricts before the triangulation was commenced; but no station marks were met with, presumably because the reasonable procedure of constructing permanent pillars at the points of junction of three or more villages—which prevails in the North-West Provinces and the Punjab, and furnishes a certain number of permanent marks for future reference which are invariably incorporated among the stations of the Revenue Survey—has only commended itself to the approbation of the Bengal Government very recently, and at the time when the surveys of Rung-pore and the adjoining districts were being carried on, no such pillars were erect-ed; thus the only means of making a connection between the trigonometrical and the revenue operations was by fixing the positions of all the temples which were met with, and also of the banyan trees under which the villagers hold their markets. On entering the Goálpára District 25 permanent marks were fixed by Mr. Clarke, and these should be of much use to the Revenue Surveyors who are now em-ployed in that district.

(31.) The connection of the triangulation of the Brahmaputra with that of the Assam Series has completed a chain of triangles—between the Calcutta and the Sonakhoda base lines—of which the length is 420 miles, and which forms with the Calcutta Meridional Series a circuit of 660 miles. The errors at the close of the circuit were only 0·″18 in latitude and 0·″23 in longitude, and may be considered immaterial. On the other hand the linear error generated between the base lines was as much as 4·4 inches per mile, which is larger than any linear error hitherto met with at the close of either of the principal chains of triangles of this Survey; it is probably due to the circumstance that the triangulation was wholly carried over plains which were covered with jungle and tropical vegeta-tion, and consequently the necessity arose for opening out lines in every instance, in order to secure mutual visibility without incurring the expense of raising the sta-tions to a great elevation; there is always a tendency to lateral refraction in rays which graze the surface of the ground or the sides of glades, and this may effect the observations very sensibly. But errors arising from lateral refraction tend to cancel each other in the long run, and the small errors at the close of the circuit indicate that in the present instance this has probably happened.

NO. IV.—TRIGONOMETRICAL.

THE JODHPUR SERIES, MERIDIAN 72¼°.

(32.) This chain of triangles—which was commenced last year at a side on the north flank of the Karáchi (Kurrachee) Longitudinal Series, by Lieutenant M. W. Rogers—has this year been advanced a considerable distance northwards, by Lieutenant (now Captain) Hill, who succeeded Lieutenant Rogers on his departure to Europe on furlough.

PERSONNEL.

Capt. J. Hill, R.E., Offg. Deputy Superintendent, 3rd grade.
Mr. W. C. Price, Asst. Surveyor, 1st grade.
Mr. C. P. Torrens, Asst. Surveyor 3rd grade.
Mr. W. Oldham, Asst. Surveyor 3rd grade.

(33.) The operations of the present year lay in the desert of Marwar and Jesalmer, through the tract which is called " the region of death," in Greenough's General Sketch of the Physical and Geological features of British India; happily it was this year found to be undeserving of so dire an epithet, for the survey party enjoyed excellent health, on the whole. The region is however much dreaded by the people of the surrounding more favored districts, probably, as Captain Hill reports, " on ac-
" count of its desolate appearance, the frequency of its famines, and the distress
" and disease that are generally prevalent among the poorest classes of its inhabi-
" tants, owing to the miserable food and unwholesome water on which they are
" compelled to subsist".

(34.) The desert is covered with sand hills "which are generally flat
" topped, low, and of about equal altitude, so that the advantages of a hilly
" country are lost, and short sides are unavoidable." On the other hand however the absence of vegetation relieves the surveyor of the necessity of building tower-stations and clearing the lines between them, which is a great advantage, and enables the operations to be carried on far more rapidly and economically than would be possible in Eastern Bengal, in Assam or in Burma. Special arrangements have to be made to provide the surveyors with food and wholesome water, in this region where neither the one nor the other is procurable; but camels are plentiful and readily obtained, and thus, with a little forethought and at a slight expense, there need be no risk of failure in the supply of the necessaries of life. Occasionally observations are delayed when the atmosphere is pervaded with dust and sand, but not to any thing like the extent which happens in the forest and jungle tracts of India, when the grasses are fired and a thick pall of smoke and haze obscures the atmosphere, sometimes for weeks together.

(35.) The out-turn of the field season's work is very good and creditable to Captain Hill and his assistants. The principal triangulation was carried a distance of 90 miles along the meridian, by a series of consecutive polygonal figures which embrace an area of 1,552 square miles. An astronomical azimuth of verification was measured at one of the principal stations. The preliminary operations for the selection of the sites of the stations were carried over a distance of 102 miles and have been kept well . ahead of the final triangulation. And secondary chains of triangles have been extended from the main series, in the course of which the positions of upwards of 80 points, and the heights of 29 of these points, have been fixed.

(36.) When the net work system of triangulation, which had been adopted by Major Lambton for the operations in southern India, was superseded by the method—introduced by Colonel Everest—of meridional and longitudinal chains of triangles, it was intended that the meridional chains should be placed at about 1° apart, and tied together by longitudinal chains at convenient intervals ; and this intention was carried out over the entire extent of country lying to the north of the parallel of Calcutta and between the meridians of 74° and 89°. Of late years however it has been deemed unnecessary to execute so large an amount of principal triangulation, and consequently the intervals between the main meridional chains have been made about twice as great as formerly : thus between the

Indus Series and the Gurhágarh there will be only two principal series—the Jodh-púr and another on the meridian of 70°—instead of five, the number originally contemplated. But this reduction in the amount of the principal requires an increase in that of the secondary triangulation, otherwise a sufficient number of fixed points of reference will not be provided for the use of topographical and fiscal surveyors and the public generally. Arrangements are therefore being made to run longitudinal chains of secondary triangles, at intervals of about 1° apart, from the Indus to the Jodhpúr Series; these will be carried on rapidly with light and portable instruments, as soon as the stations have been selected and perma-nent marks built at them for future reference.

NO. V.—TRIGONOMETRICAL.

THE EASTERN FRONTIER SERIES, IN BURMA.

(37.) This chain of triangles emanated from the Assam Longitudinal Series, near Gowhatti, in the year 1861-62; in the following years it was carried through the Kasia and Tipperah Hills, and then down the east coast of the Bay of Bengal, through the districts of Chittagong, Akyab and Arracan, to the vicinity of Toangoup and Sandoway; it was then diverted eastwards, into British Burma, over the range of hills which intervenes between Arracan and Prome; and by the year 1869-70 the principal triangulation had been completed to a short distance beyond Prome, and stations had been selected in advance across the northern portions of the British districts and down the eastern frontier, to the vicinity of Moulmein. The operations were then suddenly arrested, in conse-quence of the financial embarrassments of the Government of India, which neces-sitated large reductions of expenditure in all directions. The expenses of the triangulation—as well as of all operations requiring a large amount of local labour, though only for a short time—are vastly greater in Burma than in any part of India proper; as the country is very thinly populated, the wages of common daily laborers are increased fourfold, and those of the regular native establishments have to be more than doubled; the country is covered with dense forests, up to the very tops of the hills, and consequently extensive clearances have to be made and long lines cut, and that frequently in uninhabited or very sparsely inhabited localities, to which laborers have to be brought from great distances; local allowances are necessarily granted to all the surveyors; and all this raises what may be called the contingent expenditure, or the excess above the normal pay of the surveyors, to about three times what ordinarily prevails in India proper. Thus when reduc-tions of expenditure were called for in 1870, the series in Burma was naturally selected as the one to be stopped, for thus the largest savings which could be made with the least injury to private individuals were effected.

(38.) This year I was directed by the Government not only to resume the triangulation in Burma but to push it on with all possible vigour, though without any increase of ex-penditure over the amount provided in the Budget. Happily the services of Messrs. W. C. Rossenrode and H. Beverley, who had been carrying on the tri-angulation when it was suspended, were available for its resumption, without detriment to the operations in other quarters; for the Bilaspúr Meridional Series, on which these gentlemen had latterly been employed, was completed last year, by the junction of its two sections, one of which had been brought up from the south by Mr. Rossenrode and his party, and the other carried down from the north by the party under Mr. Keelan. In order to meet the expenses which would now be caused, Mr. Keelan was transferred to do duty at Head Quarters, his party was broken up, and the funds which had been provided for its employment elsewhere were placed at Mr. Rossenrode's disposal.

PERSONNEL.

W. C. Rossenrode, Esq., Deputy Superintendent 3rd grade.
Mr. H. Beverley, Surveyor 1st grade.
„ J. W. Mitchell, „ 4th „
„ J. C. Clancey, Asst. Surveyor 4th grade.

(39.) The first thing Mr. Rossenrode had to do was to induce a sufficient number of the trained native subordinates to re-engage for service in Burma, and to fill the places of the large number of men who were unwilling to commence a life of banishment from their native country. These difficulties surmounted, and a party formed which promised to be efficient, Mr. Rossenrode embarked with it on board a steamer at Calcutta, and reached Rangoon on the 7th November.

(40.) Meanwhile arrangements had been made to obtain a supply of elephants for the party, as without the aid of these serviceable animals the operations could not be carried on. Ten were procured at Moulmein, under the orders of the Chief Commissioner, and they arrived at Rangoon a few days after the party; they were found to be very fine animals but untrained and shy, and they had never carried loads; they were immediately put under training by the mahouts whom Mr. Rossenrode had brought with him for the purpose from Bengal. But it was long before they could be made use of, and in the interim a few elephants were obtained on loan from the Commissariat Department, and then Mr. Rossenrode commenced his march northwards, and on the 4th of December reached one of the stations in the plains of the Henzada District, down to which the principal triangulation had been brought in previous years.

(41.) I may here observe that in the original design of the triangulation provision was made for the measurement of a verificatory base-line in the plains of the Henzada District, on the same parallel of latitude as the base-lines already measured at Bider and Vizagapatam; a suitable line was selected and cleared, and towers were built at its extremities as stations of the principal triangulation. But this is almost the only instance in which the principal triangles have been brought down from the hills into the plains, for the plains are invariably covered with luxuriant vegetation and frequently with dense forests, and consequently high towers have to be built and heavy line-clearances made to render the stations mutually visible; and the less there is of this sort of thing the better, everywhere, and in Burma more particularly.

(42.) Mr. Rossenrode commenced operations by clearing the lines of the jungle that had grown up on them during the four years which had elapsed since they were first cut. During the months of January and February he took the necessary observations at three stations on the plains and at four hill stations. On the 10th March he reached the hill station of Kaneingdong, which is about 50 miles north of Pegu. The sides of the triangles which converge on this station are of various lengths, ranging from 22 to 43 miles, longer sides than usual having been introduced in order to cross over the Sittang valley by a single span, and thus avoid bringing the operations down into a flat and densely wooded country. Unfortunately the burning of the jungles had commenced, and the thick haze and smoke shut out all view of the surrounding stations; even hills which were only five miles distant were entirely obscured. For nearly two months Mr. Rossenrode had to remain at the station, watching 'by night and day' for glimpses of the lamps and heliotropes, but in vain; eventually, in the first week of May, a shower of rain fell and cleared the atmosphere, after which the observations were speedily completed. Mr. Rossenrode then proceded to his next station, Myaya-bengkyo, where, on the 11th May, the monsoon set in with such violence that during the breaks he was only able to complete the angles to the back stations, which were comparatively near and low; the forward stations were far off, and one of them was so elevated that it was constantly capped with clouds or enveloped in mist, and so the signals could not be observed. He had therefore to close work and proceed to his recess quarters at Moulmein. The march was performed "with "much inconvenience and difficulty, owing to the whole country being submerged, "the depth of water varying from one to four feet, throughout each stage".

(43.) What has been stated will suffice to show the great difficulties of carrying on the triangulation in Burma. When the stations are situated in the plains, at comparatively short distances apart, the progress of the work is much less dependent on the condition of the atmosphere than when they are on hills far apart from each other, and the final observations can be completed with greater rapidity; but, on the other hand, the preliminary operations of selecting sites, building towers and clearing lines, are very laborious and expensive and cause great delay; thus, as a matter of economy of time and money, the plains are never entered when they can be avoided. Even the hills present many difficulties, as they are always covered with forest and are frequently flat topped and do not afford a commanding view all round from a single point; thus on one occasion it cost even so skilful and practised an officer as Mr. H. Beverley three weeks of hard labor to find a suitable site for a station, on the low and undulating ranges to the south of Shoaygheen.

(44.) The out-turn of work comprises a double polygon, covering an area of 1,294 square miles, by which the principal triangulation has been advanced a direct distant of 50 miles. The preliminary operations were carried over a distance of 112 miles, in which the stations have all been selected and built in readiness for the principal triangulation of the next year. Stations have also been selected for a secondary chain of triangles, to connect the important towns of Rangoon and Pegu. Considering all the difficulties with which Mr. Rossenrode had to contend in this first year of the resumption of operations in Burma, that he had to form a new native establishment for the work, that much of the best time of the year was necessarily devoted to preliminary arrangements, and that the operations were seriously retarded by causes which were altogether beyond his controul, I think that he is entitled to much credit for what has been done; his arrangements have been very judicious and satisfactory, and I believe he has done his best to carry out my instructions to economize the funds placed at his disposal for the prosecution of the operations.

NO. VI.

SPIRIT LEVELLING OPERATIONS IN THE MADRAS PRESIDENCY.

(45.) A suspension of the astronomical and geodetic operations in the Madras Presidency, which are described in Sections X and XI of my Report for 1872-73, having been rendered necessary because of Captain Herschel's departure to Europe, Lieutenant Harman, R.E. was placed in charge of Captain Herschel's party, and employed in in spirit levelling. His operations were carried on in a manner precisely similar to those in Sind, the Punjab, the North-West Provinces and Bengal, which have been briefly described in previous reports, and in full detail in the introduction to the *Tables of Heights in Sind &c.* Calcutta 1863, and also in Volume XXXIII of the *Memoirs of the Royal Astronomical Society;* and their object was the same, *viz.*, to connect together and reduce to a common datum the several lines and systems of levels executed for Railways, Canals and other Public Works, and to check the values of height of the principal stations of this Survey which have been determined by the trigonometrical method.

PERSONNEL.
Lieut. H. J. Harman, R.E., Offg. Asst. Supdt. 1st Grade.
Mr. O. V. Norris, Asst. Surveyor 2nd Grade.

(46.) This is the first year that I have been able to employ a party, in the Madras Presidency, solely on levelling operations; arrangements had been made to form a special party for that Presidency in 1869, but they fell through in consequence of financial difficulties; and thus hitherto the work of this nature which has been done there, by this Survey, consists of short lines of levels, to connect the Cape Comorin base-line with the tidal station at Tuticorin, and the Bangalore base with the railway levels from the sea at Madras.

(47.) The several systems of levels for the Public Works in the Madras Presidency are so numerous that it was difficult to decide where to commence our operations. Major Branfill had, at my request, obtained from the officers of that

Department a Skeleton Map of Southern India, showing the lines of levels which had been taken by the several Railway Companies and the Canal Officers, each of which was referred to a separate datum. It was necessary to refer them all in turn to the mean sea level, as deduced at stations where systematic tidal observations, continued over a long period, had been or would be taken. There was then, and still is, only one such station, Tuticorin; but the establishment of others, at various points on the east and west coasts, was contemplated, and the first of these would probably be at Karwar, the well known port on the west coast. A line from Tuticorin would not have been immediately useful for combining the several existing systems of levels; consequently Lieutenant Harman decided on commencing operations at Gútí (Gooty) and working westwards through Bellary, Dharwar and North Kanara to the port of Karwar.

(48.) This line was completed very satisfactorily, and is 304 miles in length. One of the sections traverses the Arabail Ghát, and was found to be "almost intolerably hilly for the work," the sum of the rises and falls aggregating 11,251 feet. Two trigonometrical stations, and thirteen points on the railway and irrigation lines were connected; sixteen bench-marks were laid down, and upwards of three hundred other points were fixed for future reference.

(49.) A site was selected and marked for the future tidal station at Karwar. Every effort was made to ascertain whether the tidal observations which had been taken several years previously at this post, by officers of the Indian Navy, had been referred to some permanent point of reference on the coast; but none such could be found, or Lieutenant Harman would have connected it with his line of levels. Under the circumstances it was necessary for him to make an approximate determination of the mean sea level by a few days observations of the tides; these, when reduced to the "mean of the year" with the aid of the local tide tables, will furnish a very fair preliminary determination of the mean sea, to serve for immediate requirements, pending the completion of the systematic observations to be taken hereafter with a self-registering tide-gauge.

(50.) Lieutenant Harman has labored with great energy and self devotion during this his first year of independent employment. He was unfortunately unable to complete the bringing up of his field books and the preparation of the results for publication, for before he could do so I was obliged to send him away, with scant notice, to a part of India very distant from the scene of his operations. He is now conducting the Assam Valley Triangulation, with orders to join the Survey Party attached to the military expedition against the tribe of Dufflas; this tribe occupies a tract of hills to the north of the valley, which has hitherto appeared on the maps as a *terra incognita*, but which I trust will soon be thoroughly explored and mapped.

NO. VII.—TOPOGRAPHICAL.

THE SURVEY OF KATTYWAR.

(51.) The operations of this important topographical survey have been carried on during the present year under the executive superintendence of Captain Pullan. Good progress has been made, both in the field work and the mapping, and the completion of the survey of the entire Province of Kattywar, within the next five years, may be confidently looked forward to.

PERSONNEL.
Capt. A. Pullan, S.C., Offg. Deputy Superintendent 3rd Grade.
J. McGill, Esq., Assistant Supd. 2nd Grade.
Mr. F. Bell, Surveyor 3rd Grade.
„ J. Wood, „ 4th „
„ N. C. Gwynne, Asst. Surveyor 1st Grade.
Mr. E. Wyatt, Assist. Sur. 2nd Grade.
„ W. A. Fielding, „ 3rd „
„ H. Corkery „ 4th „
Visaji Ragonath and 12 Native Surveyors and Apprentices.

(52.) The final topographical operations embraced an area of 2,201 square miles, which comprises portions of the Districts of Hallar, Machu Kanta and Jhalawar and of the principal Native States—Nawanagar, Morbi, Rajkot, Wakanir and Gondal—which are included in those Districts.

The entire area was surveyed on the scale of 2 inches to the mile, by the usual method of plane tabling on a trigonometrical basis, but with the addition of a large amount—1,235 linear miles—of traversing, to lay down the boundaries of the talukas and furnish checks on the operations of the plane tablers. A survey of the town and cantonments of Rajkot was made on the scale of 12 inches to the mile, in doing which all the principal roads were traversed with chain and theodolite and stone bench-marks were fixed at a number of important points on the traverses, for future reference.

(53.) The triangulation executed in advance, for the topographical operations of next year, covers are area of 2,174 square miles, in which 578 points have been fixed, and the heights of 309 of these points have been determined.

(54.) The mapping comprises 20 sections, each 32 × 17 inches, on the 2-inch scale, drawn for reproduction on full scale and also for reduction by photography to the 1-inch scale, and a degree sheet on the ½-inch scale, drawn for reduction by photography to the ¼-inch scale, for incorporation into the Indian Atlas;—also a map, 44 × 35 inches, of the Rajkot Town and Cantonments, on the 12-inch scale. Owing to an unfortunate oversight which has been made in the mapping, the breadth of the talúka boundary lines has been very unnecessarily increased on one of the 2-inch maps, the appearance of which has been much deteriorated in consequence.

(55.) The delays attendant on the demarcation of the boundaries of the Native States, prior to survey, have in some instances been so great that the survey of the country had to be carried on without waiting for the demarcation of the boundaries, the directions of which could therefore only be shown approximately on the maps; Captain Pullan reports that most of these detached bits of boundary have now been definitely settled and marked out, and that they will be surveyed next year.

(56.) The Kattywar Survey Party has been much weakened this year by the deaths of two of the assistants, and the loss of a third who has become lunatic. Mr. J. Wood died suddenly, and most sadly, shortly after his return to recess quarters in May; he had served in the Department for nearly fourteen years, was very intelligent, and had always worked willingly and well, and given every satisfaction to each of the officers under whom he had been employed. Mr. E. Wyatt had been compelled by ill health to take leave of absence at the close of the field season; he was never able to rejoin, and died in the following November; he had served for nine years, and had become a very skilful draftsman, as well as a useful surveyor, and his loss is much regretted.

NO. VIII.—TOPOGRAPHICAL.

THE SURVEY OF GUZERAT.

(57.) In section VIII of my report for 1872-73 I have shown that, from the very commencement of our operations in Guzerat, the importance of endeavoring to effect a combination of our work with that of the Revenue Surveyors who had preceded us in that Province, with a view to utilizing their work to the utmost possible extent, had been fully recognized; I indicated the attempts which had been made

PERSONNEL.

Major C. T. Haig, R.E., Deputy Supdt. 3rd Grade.
Lieut. J. E. Gibbs, R.E., Assistant Supdt. 2nd Grade.
Mr. J. Peyton, Surveyor 1st Grade. (During the recess only)
" A. D'Souza, Surveyor 2nd "
" A. D. L. Christie, Surveyor 4th Grade.
Mr. C. H. McA'Foe, Asst. Surveyor 1st Grade. (During a portion of the field season only)
Mr. E. J. Connor, Asst. Surveyor 1st Grade.

Mr. J. Hickio, Assistant Surveyor 2nd Grade.
Mr. G. D. Cusson, Asst. Surveyor 3rd Grade.
Mr. A. Bryson, Asst. Surveyor 3rd Grade.
Mr. G. T. Hall, Asst. Surveyor 4th Grade.
11 Native Surveyors and Apprentices.

REVENUE SURVEYORS.
Mr. T. A. LeMesurier.
5 Native Surveyors.

to do so, and showed that they had met with such varying results that while some officers pronounced the combination to be impossible, others thought that it might be effected, and with very great advantage as regards the general value and utility of the maps.

(58.) I myself had from the first been inclined to take the more favorable view, on the general grounds that it appeared impossible that the myriads of measures which had been made for the purpose of defining the areas of all landed properties, down to the minutest fields, and which had been plotted together so as to form village maps on the large scales of 8 inches and 16 inches to the mile, could not be utilized to some extent in the course of the execution of a professional survey of the country.

(59.) Moreover utilization appeared to me to be most desirable, in that, if feasible, it would tend to improve the character of the professional survey. That survey was about to be undertaken by an establishment which had been formed on the old and long standing scale of establishments for the production of rapid preliminary maps, and consequently contained a much larger proportion of the European than of the Native element; for the object to be accomplished was the attainment of a rapid but only fairly accurate survey of the country; the method to be adopted was that of plane tabling, and each plane tabler was expected to turn out a much larger area in a given time than could possibly be obtained, of minute and close survey, in the time allowed; thus an out-turn of about 100 square miles *per mensem*, during each month that the plane tabler is actually on the ground under survey, is even still considered a fair average out-turn for the scale of 1 inch = 1 mile, and formerly a much larger out-turn was expected. But the country of Guzerat is a rich and fertile plain, covered with trees and fences and habitations, and consequently very ill suited for a rapid survey by the method of plane tabling. Thus it appeared to me to be most probable that if the professional surveyors did not utilize the facts of measurement which they might obtain from the revenue surveyors, either they would have to do over again, at great expense, a large portion of the work of minute measurement which had already been done at great expense, or their maps would be found wanting in accuracy of detail in those parts of the country which are most densely inhabited and most rich and valuable. In the latter case the expectations which would naturally be formed of a professional survey of the "Garden of Western India", executed at the present time and upwards of a century after the country had become a British possession, might be grievously disappointed.

(60.) For the last two years the survey has been under the executive superintendence of Major Haig, who has shared my belief in the practicability of utilizing the fiscal measurements, and has labored earnestly and patiently in working out the best method of doing it. He soon found that a certain amount of co-operation on the part of the Revenue Surveyors was essential to success; this was reported to the Bombay Government, who readily acceded to the proposals submitted for sanction, and sent a small but sufficient party of native surveyors—at first under Mr. A. Dalzell and afterwards under Mr. T. A. LeMesurier—to assist Major Haig; this they were to do by giving him full details of the fiscal measurements, and indicating the positions of the principal pillars and marks of reference, the fixing of which by Major Haig's surveyors was a necessary preliminary to the incorporation of the fiscal details into their maps.

(61.) The Survey of Guzerat had originally been commenced on the same scale as that of the adjoining Province of Kattywar, namely 2 inches to the mile, or $\frac{1}{31680}$; but it was clear from the out-set that this scale, though well suited for the portions of Guzerat which are under Native States, and are not directly administered by the British Government, and have not been brought under fiscal survey—as is the case with by far the greater portion of Kattywar—might not be sufficiently large for the districts which are directly under British administration and have been fiscally surveyed. What scale should be adopted was a matter on which no conclusions could be arrived at, until the problem of the practicability of utilizing the fiscal measurements at all, and if so to what extent, had been satisfactorily solved. In my last annual report I had to acknowledge that, owing to circumstances which are there fully explained, it was still premature to form any positive conclusions on the subject. I am now in a position to state that the scale of 4 inches to the mile may be adopted with advantage, and that Major Haig has succeeded in executing several excellent maps on that scale.

(62.) The reason why an equal measure of success was not attained previously is that, originally, a comparatively small number of the fiscal marks had been fixed, and an attempt had been made to join entire village maps together by their peripheries; the maps however are often of considerable size, and it so happens—from the system of operation in the field measurements—that the peripheris are the parts where there is greatest accumulation of error; thus when contiguous maps were juxtaposed, large discrepancies were occasionally met with, more particularly on lines of considerable length, and they were found to be unmanageable. But Major Haig has ascertained that, by fixing a sufficient number of the fiscal marks to enable the village maps to be cut up into triangles with sides not exceeding three quarters of a mile, the details can be fitted on his maps without any sensible inaccuracy. The greater number of the marks are fixed by the triangulation and the traverses, and the remainder by the plane tablers, who are required to pick up all obligatory points which had not been fixed by the surveyors preceding them.

(63.) The village maps show with accuracy all the walls, fences and hedges which form the boundaries between contiguous fields and properties in enclosed tracts of country, and the narrow strips of uncultivated land which form the boundaries in open country; but, as is well known, they do not give topographical features at all, nor do they give the roads and water courses which are exterior to the cultivated and cultivable fields with any attempt at accuracy. The system of operation which Major Haig introduced last year was to have the fitting in of the details which are given in the village maps effected on the ground, by the plane table surveyors, *pari passu* with the survey of the topographical details. This year however he has found it preferable to restrict the plane tablers to the survey of the topographical details, and to the fixing of such additionrs points as may be necessary to enable the details of the village maps to be subsequently plotted on their tables, under his immediate supervision.

(64.) With the object of obtaining a fair practical test on his system of combination, he carried on operations in two parts of the district, at some distance from each other; in the Ahmedabad Collectorate, where the Revenue Survey operations had been carried out nearly a quarter of a century ago, and in the Surat District, where they had been done recently. The old work was known to have been much more roughly executed than the modern, but the errors of the sections into which it is now subdivided, as already explained, were found to be easily manageable; on the other hand in the new work the errors almost entirely disappeared, and Major Haig is of opinion that the new work is suitable for reproduction even on the 8-inch scale, should this be required.

(65.) If the whole of Guzerat consisted of lands which have been fiscally surveyed, I should have no hesitation in concluding that the whole ought to be surveyed on the 4-inch scale, as Major Haig has been doing, whereby a series of maps would be available for this neglected portion of India, on the same scale as those which have long ago been constructed for the British Districts in Bengal, the North-West Provinces, the Punjab, and Oudh. But the fiscal operations do not cover more than a third of the area of the province. The lands subject to the British Government are held under three kinds of tenure, known as Khálsa, Tálukdári, and Inámi; in the Khálsa villages every field has been surveyed fiscally, for the owner of each field pays his rent directly to the Government; in the Tálukdári villages a Tálukdár pays the rent for the whole village, and consequently the fiscal maps usually give only the boundary lines and the roads, and occasionally a little partition into fields; while of the Inámi villages generally no maps are forthcoming. Thus the value of the fiscal work for topographical purposes is almost solely restricted to the Khálsa lands. Consequently it is of these lands alone, with as much of the others as are interlaced with them, that 4-inch topographical maps should be made; the remaining portions of the province, comprising the British Táluk⁴⁶ri and Inámi villages, the villages belonging to Native States and the Dáng Forests, should be surveyed on the 2-inch scale, as is being done in Kattywar.

(66.) The triangulation of the field season under review embraces an area of 1,650 square miles, in which the positions and heights of 237 points, and the positions (without heights) of 337 points have been fixed, in advance, for the topographical operations. And this triangulation has been supplemented by 848 linear miles of traverses, furnishing a large number of traverse stations, of 1,268 of which the co-ordinates have been computed.

(67.) The area embraced by the topography is about 690 square miles, which is a smaller out-turn than was accomplished in former years, when the scale employed was only half as great; but being the first season of work on the 4-inch scale, and of successful combination with the fiscal materials, I consider it very satisfactory and creditable to Major Haig and his assistants. Major Haig expects that with a little more practice, and a slight increase to his grant for contingent expenditure, the party will be able to turn out nearly as much work annually on the 4-inch scale, as could be accomplished, in those portions of the district which have not been operated in by the Revenue Surveys, on the 2-inch scale.

(68.) Eight maps on the 4-inch scale, each measuring 32 inches by 17, and embracing 7′ 30″ in longitude and 3′ 45″ in latitude, have been completed and sent in to this office, and are now being photozincographed. They show all the walls, fences and other divisions between the fields; they also show the 'numbers' by which the fields are registered in the fiscal records, and which have thus come to be popularly used, by the owners and villagers and the public generally, as the names of the fields. They give all the details which are given on the fiscal map, and all the topographical information which is required to supplement those details. They cannot but be most useful to the local officials in the administration of the country, to engineers employed in laying out lines of roads, canals, and railroads, and more particularly for local irrigation works, when it is a matter of great importance to have a map showing the fields which are brought under irrigation, and the owners of which have to be taxed in proportion to the benefits they receive. The only regret I have felt in looking at these maps is that the excellent fiscal work which has been done by the Revenue Surveyors was restricted to the Khálsa lands, instead of being carried over the entire province. Thus while some portions of the maps are elaborately detailed, other parts—as for instance where a Tálukdári or Inámi village comes in among a cluster of Khálsa villages—are comparatively meagre and deficient in detail. This is somewhat detractive from the artistic appearance of the maps; but I am content to waive appearances, and be satisfied with the practical gain secured by utilizing the work which was done before we came into the field, and which we have found ready to our hands; I would not advocate the securing of uniformity and superior artistic finish, either by assimilating the Tálukdári and Inámi to the Khálsa villages, which would cause much additional expense, or by suppressing the results of the fiscal surveys in the Khálsa villages, which would be to abandon all the fruits of the laborious and expensive operations carried out by our predecessors.

(69.) Major Haig makes prominent mention of the services of Lieutenant J. E. Gibbs R.E., who was employed in triangulating a portion of the Dáng Forests, and whose interesting notes on the manners and customs of the inhabitants, &c., will be found at page 32—ₐ of the appendix,—of Mr. T. A. LeMesurier, of the Bombay Revenue Department, whose intelligent and cordial co-operation has much contributed to the success which has been attained in combining the fiscal with the topographical details;—and of Mr. A. D'Souza, who was of great assistance in training the native surveyors and supervising their operations.

NO. IX.—TOPOGRAPHICAL.

THE SURVEYS IN DEHRA DUN.

(70.) The Himalayan Mountain ranges may, for geographical purposes be broadly divided into two portions, one lying to the east the other to the west of meridian 81°. The eastern portion includes the Nepaulese territories, Sikkim, Bhútan, and the ranges to the north of the Assam Valley which are occupied by independent hill tribes ; in this portion most of the prominent peaks have long since been ' fixed ' by the operations of this Survey, but only a very small area has been regularly surveyed, and under existing political conditions any considerable extension of survey operations is impossible. The western portion, on the other hand, has long been freely accessible to Europeans, and regular surveys of the entire area included between the plains of Hindostan on the south, the frontiers of Eastern Turkestan and China on the north, and the tracts occupied by independent hill tribes in the Valley of the Indus on the west, have now been all but completed. These surveys have been executed on various scales, and at various times, by members of this Department.

(71.) First the districts of Kangra, Lahaol and Spiti, and the Native States of Chamba, Tíri and Garhwál, which embracing an area of 26,700 square miles, were surveyed during the years 1849-54; the maps were drawn in the field on the scale of ¼ inch = 1 mile, but evidently with a view to publication on the ¼-inch scale of the Atlas Sheets and with the object of exhibiting the general geographical rather than the exact topographical features, for the average area turned out every field season by each person employed exceeded a thousand square miles ; the operations were carried on under the direction of the late Surveyor General and Superintendent of the Trigonometrical Survey, Sir Andrew Waugh, and furnished a series of valuable preliminary maps of regions, including three British Districts, which had hitherto been unsurveyed. Then the survey of the territories of the Maharajah of Kashmir was commenced, and an area of about 21,800 square miles was completed in Kashmir and Jammú on the ½-inch scale, but with much more topographical detail than had been given in the preceding survey ; and after this the operations were extended over the remainder of the Maharajah's territories, but on the smaller scale of ¼ inch to the mile, which was adopted for an area of about 52,000 square miles, comprising the whole of Ladakh, Little Thibet and the regions up to the northern boundary line, and a portion of Chinese Thibet beyond; these operations were carried on during the years 1854-64,. and were initiated by Sir Andrew Waugh and carried out by Major Montgomerie, mostly under his directions. Lastly a survey of the British District of Kumaun and Garhwál was commenced in 1865, on the scale of 1 inch = 1 mile, and it is now nearly completed ; the western frontiers of Nepaul have been reached and surveyed to the furthest points visible from our own side of the frontier; the area completed amounts to 9,520 square miles within, and 270 outside, the districts; the area remaining may be roughly estimated as amounting to 3,200 square miles; it is situated for the most part in the higher ranges and regions of perpetual snow, which lie to the north towards the frontier of Chinese Thibet, and much of it may be surveyed on a smaller scale.

(72.) Thus when, in May 1873, I replied to a call from the Government to sketch out a programme of operations for each of the Trigonometrical Survey parties for the next five years, I suggested that, as it would not be possible for us to operate in the interior of Nepaul nor in any portion of the Eastern Himalayas, the Kumaun and Garhwál party should be employed in re-surveying the districts of Jaunsár-Báwar, Kangra, Kúlú and Spiti, which are under the direct adminis-tration of the British Government, making a detailed survey on a scale suitable for local requirements, to supersede the original small scale geographical survey. My proposals were approved of by the Government, and by Her Majesty's Secretary of State for India ; and the operations will be commenced as soon as is practicable.

(73.) They will however necessitate some important modifications in the method of survey hitherto employed, and in the personnel of the surveyors. Until the year 1865 the object in view was to obtain rapid and skilfully generalized sketches of the principal topographical features of the country, and therefore none but European surveyors were employed. The surveys subsequent to that year were executed on a larger scale, and are very much more minute and elaborate; so much so that it has been necessary to publish the results in two sets of maps, one shewing all the hills and general topographical features and the principal villages, the other in a skeleton form, omitting all hill shading, but showing the water courses and the whole of the villages and hamlets and various details which could not be introduced into the shaded maps;—these surveys have likewise been done by a purely European agency. But it has been shewn to be clearly advantageous to employ native agency also to a certain extent, and to introduce as many native surveyors into the party as can be efficiently supervised, in order that the cost of the operations may be reduced as much as may be practicable without impairing the value of the results. Steps had therefore to be taken to train a certain number of natives for the future operations.

(74.) An excellent opportunity for so doing occurred during the present year. When Captain Bailey, the Superintendent of the newly formed Department of Forest Surveys, was temporarily affiliated with this Department, for the reasons already mentioned in para (11.) of this report, it was at first intended that he should make a survey of the whole of the Dehra Dún District, a re-survey of which has long been much wanted, owing to the great increase of cultivation and the formation of extensive tea-plantations since Major Brown's survey in 1840. As the forest tracts are much interlaced with the cultivated tracts and the tea-plantations, a survey of both was necessary to complete the map of the District; and as the area of the former considerably exceeds that of the latter, Captain Bailey might have surveyed both, without his own operations being very materially retarded; and this was at first intended, for it would have afforded an admirable opportunity for imparting the requisite training to his establishment, to fit them for their work in other parts of India. After a few months however the calls on Captain Bailey from all quarters became very numerous, so that it seemed uncertain whether he could even be permitted to remain to complete the forest tracts, and quite certain that he ought not to undertake anything exterior to them. Consequently I directed Captain Thuillier to withdraw a portion of his assistants from the Survey of Kumaon and Garhwál, and employ them in the non-forest tracts of the Dehra Dún, and also to commence training a body of native surveyors, to be employed on measurements of boundary lines and road traverses, and in various other matters for which an expensive European agency is not desirable.

(75.) Commencing operations in the month of November, Captain Thuillier was able to avail himself of the services of almost the whole of the Kumaon and Garhwál party—the exceptions being Mr. Peyton who was employed in mapping, and Mr. Low who was still in the higher ranges, working up the valley of the Gori towards the passes above Milam—for it would have been useless at that time of the year, with the winter fast setting in, to send men into the unsurveyed portions of Kumaon and Garhwál, which were all at such great elevations as to be only accessible during the comparatively warm months immediately preceding and following the summer monsoon. Thus Mr. Ryall and two assistants were employed in the Dún until the end of the month of March, when they proceeded to resume the operations in the higher ranges, as will be described hereafter.

PERSONNEL.

of the Kumaon and Garhwál Party.

Captain H. E. Thuillier, R.E., Offg. Depy. Supdt. 1st Grade.
E. C. Ryall Esq. Offg. Asst. Supdt. 2nd Grade.
Lieut. St. G. Gore, R.E. Offg. Assist. Supdt. 2nd Grade.
Mr. J. Peyton, Surveyor 1st Grade.
" J. Low, " 3rd "
" L. Pocock, Asst. Sur. 1st "
" J. Macdougall, Asst. Surveyor 2nd Grade.
Mr. H. Todd, Asst. Sur. 2nd Grade.
" T. Kinney, " 2nd "
" E. Wrixon, " 3rd "
" E. Litchfield, " 3rd "
" I. Pocock, " 4th "
And 18 Natives under training as Surveyors.

(76.) The work in the Dún being the survey of the non-forest tracts, the same scale had to be employed as that which had already been adopted for the *pari passu* survey of the forest tracts, *viz.*, 4 inches = 1 mile*. This is the scale which has long been used for the British districts in the plains of the Bengal Presidency; it is sufficiently large to show the boundaries of the smallest villages, the lines of demarcation between cultivated and uncultivated tracts, and all topographical details required for the purposes of the district officer and the engineer. The numerous surveys which have been made on this scale have almost invariably been executed by native surveyors, working under close European superintendence, and Captain Thuillier's first duty was to collect a number of intelligent young natives, who could read and write, and to train them, as it was impossible for him to obtain trained men excepting on prohibitorily high salaries.

(77.) Captain Thuillier has described his operations so clearly and minutely, in the portions of his narrative report which are pointed at pages 36—ₐ and 37—ₐ of the appendix, that it is only necessary for me to remark that, though there is no great show of topography—as was scarcely to be expected under the circumstances—much good work has been done, the fruits of which will be more apparent hereafter than they are at present. An area of 529 square miles has been well covered with trigonometrical points as a basis for the future topographical operations, 1,372 points in all—or about 2·3 per square mile—having been fixed, of 156 of which the heights were also determined. The aggregate length of the boundary lines which were traversed amounts to 848 linear miles. The topography embraces an area of 63 square miles.

(78.) In running the traverses, and in other portions of the operations which are rather mechanical than artistic, the native lads soon become fitted for rendering serviceable aid; but to teach them the art of delineating the features of the ground by the method of plane-tabling was of course a far slower matter. While this was being done some portions of the district were plane-tabled by the European surveyors, and it was found that skilful draughtsmen, who had turned out their 100 square miles per mensem in the hills of Kumaon and Garhwál, on the 1-inch scale, were not able to accomplish more than 15 square miles, in the same time, on the 4-inch scale, in the Dún. Thus—though the scale for the future operations which are mentioned in para (72), will probably not be the 4-inch but the 2-inch, which has already been employed in the Revenue Surveys of the

* I may here be permitted to observe that the fixing of a scale, at the outset, for the Forest Surveys, was a matter of no small difficulty; the opinions of a considerable number of forest officers, employed in different parts of India, were taken on the subject, and there was a general concurrence of opinion that two classes of maps were required, namely,

(1.) Working or detailed maps on a large scale;
(2.) General maps on small scales.

But there were considerable differences of opinion as to the proper scale for the working maps; several scales were recommended, varying from 4 to 12 inches to the mile, the 8-inch being the favorite.

It was doubtful whether the officers whose opinions had been received were sufficiently cognizant of the technicalities of surveying and mapping to be able to appreciate fully all that is involved in the question of scale, when the answer to that question has to govern future procedure, and to decide whether the operations to be carried out are to be rough, quick and cheap, or elaborate, slow and costly, or some thing intermediate between these two extremes. Thus it was clearly necessary that I should endeavour to ascertain the purposes of forestry for which the maps were wanted, and to find out what details of the configuration and general facts of the ground were expected to be shown on them, that I might decide on the scale which would be most suitable. Captain Bailey drew up a *precis* of the opinions of all the officers who had been consulted on this point, from which the following enumeration of the requisite details is taken.

"The formation of the ground as accurately as possible, chains of mountains, valleys, plateaux, precipices, dells,— " the altitudes of peaks, valleys and other important places—railways, tram-ways, roads, metalled or otherwise, timber " roads and slides, cattle paths and foot paths, milestones where erected,—rivers, canals, brooks, lakes, ponds, wells, " springs, drainage cuts, with weirs, dams, bridges and fords,—the perennial flow of rivers, the points from which naviga- " tion, rafting and log floating, can be carried on,—bogs, marshes, rocks, fields of boulders, sand, gravel or kunker, old " village sites, stone quarries,—towns, villages, houses, fields, meadows, grazing grounds, gardens, wood depots, camping " grounds, rest houses,—places where water may collect, and other obstacles to division and export roads,—areas subject to " inundations,—all levels which are necessary to artificial inundation. The maps are also required to form an official record " of the boundary lines and marks, and areas of forest divisions, blocks and compartments; also of the exterior and " interior boundaries of divisions, circles, ranges, blocks and compartments; the positions and distinguishing numbers " of all pillars on the boundaries of fiscal divisions and jurisdictions of private property or private rights in the forest: " the positions of seed and planting nurseries, and all blanks of any considerable extent, say from 1 to 5 acres."

This is a very formidable list of forestry requirements, and it illustrates what a variety of things may be asked for when the proposers have only to exercise their brains in stringing together a number of requisitions, and not their bodies in giving practical effect to their suggestions by lending a hand to obtain what is wanted.

The questions of scale and detail are still undecided, and they will have to be disposed of on financial considerations, and with due reference to the capabilities and value of each of the several forests; "the cost must be cut according to the cloth;" but these are matters which are not in my province. The operations in the Dún being of a tentative nature, and required for the purpose of organizing and training the forest surveyors rather than for pure forestry, I recommended the adoption of the 4-inch scale, the smallest of all suggested; this scale was approved of by the Government, and has been employed up to the present time, and all details have been shown which it is capable of representing.

Hill Districts of Hazara in the Punjab—it is clear that the introduction of a cheap native agency, into a party which has hitherto been framed on the old topographical organization of European surveyors only, is essentially necessary to secure economy in the future;—and it is a well known fact, from the experience which has been gained by the Bengal Revenue Survey parties who have employed natives largely, that the requisite economy may be secured without impairing the quality of the results, provided always that the number of native surveyors is not greater than can be efficiently supervised by the Europeans.

NO. X.—TOPOGRAPHICAL.

HIMALAYAN SURVEYS IN KUMAUN AND GARHWAL.

(79.) For the reasons already stated in para (75), it was not desirable to resume operations until the commencement of the spring of 1874. Early in April Mr. Ryall marched from Dehra Dún with four assistants, and proceeded *vià* Almora to the ground to be surveyed, which lay among the upper valleys of the Rámganga, Sarju, Gori and Rálam rivers. Operations were carried on until the beginning of July, by which time Mr. Ryall had triangulated an area of about 460 square miles, and his assistants had completed the topography of about 534 square miles, much of which was closely supervised by himself. By this time the rainy season, which this year commenced at an unusually early date, had set in with such persistence that it was useless to remain out in the field any longer, for even in the breaks of rainfall the ground was mostly hid from view by mist and cloud-caps. The party consequently returned to Almora and recessed there, as that was the nearest point to the field of operations at which houses were to be met with. Immediately after the cessation of the rains they returned to their field duties, and made excellent progress; but as the subsequent operations appertain to the year 1874-75, and must therefore be described in the next annual report, they need not be further noticed here.

PERSONNEL.
E. O. Ryall Esq.
Mr. Mc A'Fee.
„ E. Litchfield.
„ I. Pocock.
„ Mc. Carthy.

NO. XI.—TIDAL OBSERVATIONS.

DETERMINATIONS OF MEAN SEA LEVEL IN THE GULF OF KUTCH.

(80.) In my last report I described the arrangements that were being made for carrying out the Tidal Observations which I had been directed to undertake in the Gulf of Kutch, with a view to ascertaining whether secular changes were taking place in the relative level of the land and sea at the head of the gulf. The coasts had been carefully reconnoitered by Lieutenant (now Captain) Baird, who, after long searching, had found three places which appeared to be well adapted for the erection of tidal stations, being situated at points near which there is always a considerable depth of water and to which the tide has free access; the foreshores of the gulf had been found to be generally far from promising, consisting mainly of long mud banks, which often stretch for miles out into the sea and are left bare at low water, when they are intersected by innumerable tortuous and shallow creeks whose shifting channels would be very unfavorable positions for tide-gauges. But at Hanstal Point—near the head

PERSONNEL.
Captain Baird, R.E., Offg. Deputy Superintendent 1st grade.
Mr. T. Rendell, Assistant Surveyor 1st grade.
Narsing Dass and three other Sub-Surveyors, &c.

of the gulf,—at Nowanár Point—half way up, on the northern or Kutch coast,— and at Okha Point, on the southern coast—opposite the Island of Beyt and on a line with the entrance to the gulf,—positions had been found which fulfilled the requisite conditions for tidal stations, and were believed by Captain Baird to be the only suitable points to be met with on the coasts of the gulf.

(81.) It happens however that none of these points are situated in ports or harbours, where the piers, jetties, landing stages or docks, which have been constructed for the requirements of the shipping, present great facilities for setting up tide-gauges in the vicinity of deep water, so that it is almost invariably the custom to erect them in such places; these points on the contrary are all situated at some distance from the nearest inhabited localities, and present no facilities whatever; for not only building materials and food for the workmen but fresh water also have to be brought to them from considerable distances. It was thus imperative that the plan of operations should be of the simplest nature possible, so as to be carried out with the least cost and greatest expedition.

(82.) A tide-gauge may either be set up on a staging in the sea, over deep water, or on shore, over a well which is connected by a system of piping with the deep water. Cœteris paribus the former position is decidedly the best of the two, and if any jetties or piers had been available for the operations I would certainly have had the stations erected on them. But under existing circumstances it was only possible to set up the tide-gauges over deep water by erecting stagings for them in the sea; and they would have had to be very strongly built, for they would be required to withstand the full force of the sea, without undergoing any displacement whatever, and that not for a short time only but for several years, so as to include both the first series of tidal registrations, taken to determine the present relations of the land and sea, and the final series, which will have to be taken to determine the future relations several years hence. The stagings would moreover have had to be connected with the land by piers, in order to permit of ready access to the instruments at all times. The cost of such stagings and their connecting piers would however have been very considerable and have far exceeded the funds available for the operations; I was therefore compelled, though with some reluctance, to decide on having the tide-gauges set up on shore, over wells sunk near the high water line and connected with the sea by piping.

(83.) Captain Baird spent the recess of 1873 at Bombay in preparing for the operations of the field season of 1873-74. The several self-registering instruments which were to be employed—the tide-gauges, the aneroid barometers and the anemometers, or anemographs—were overhauled and put into good working order. The gauges were tested by being employed to register the tides in the harbour of Bombay for several weeks continuously, and were set up over wells connected with deep water by piping, in order that the experimental observations should be taken under precisely similar circumstances to the actual observations.

(84.) The wells are iron cylinders, with an internal diameter of 22 inches which slightly exceeds the diameter of the float; the cylinders were made up in sections of 50 inches in length, the lowest of which is closed below with an iron plate, and the whole, when bolted together, forms a water-tight well, into which water can only enter through the piping for effecting the connection with the sea. The piping is of an internal diameter of 2 inches, which has been computed to be sufficient to permit of the transmission of the tidal wave to the well without sensible retardation. Iron piping is laid from the well to the line of low water; it is brought vertically up from the bottom of the well nearly to the surface of the ground, and is then carried down to the sea, where flexible gutta percha piping is attached and carried into the deep water. The outer piping terminates in a 'rose,' which is suspended a few feet above the bed of the sea by a buoy, in order to prevent the entrance of silt as much as possible, and it can be readily detached from the iron piping whenever it has to be cleaned.

(85.) The level of the water in the well should obviously always coincide with that of the sea, and if it does not do so the registrations of the gauge are worthless; thus an imperative necessity arises for comparing the inside and outside levels, from time to time, in order to remove all doubt as to the efficiency of the communication between the well and the sea. For this purpose an ordinary gauge was attached to a pile driven into the bed of the sea, and its zero was connected with that of the self-registering gauge over the well, by spirit levelling, and thus a comparison of the levels could be readily made whenever desirable. On taking these comparisons during the trial observations at Bombay, Captain Baird was surprised to find that, while the levels were generally identical, there were occasional large differences which at first could not be accounted for; eventually however he succeeded in tracing them to the accidental presence of air inside the piping. He soon devised a simple method of expelling the air and restoring the requisite identity of level, by fixing a stop-cock, for the exit of the air, at the vertical bend, where the iron piping—after rising from the bottom of the well to within a few inches of the surface of the ground—begins to slope downwards towards the sea; this bend has necessarily to be made at a point a little below the level of the lowest high water tide, and consequently, on opening the stop-cock at high water, all the air inside the pipe is of course immediately expelled, and then the water inside the well at once assumes the same level as that of the sea. But for this expedient it would have been impossible to carry on the operations continuously for any length of time, as there was found to be a decided tendency for air to collect in the pipes. It is most fortunate that this was discovered during the experimental observations at Bombay, for there stop-cocks could be readily constructed and attached to the piping, whereas at either of the stations in the gulf it would have been impossible to have had this done.

(86.) While in Bombay Captain Baird also constructed three portable observatories, for erection at the tidal stations, which were made in such a manner as to be readily put together, or taken to pieces and re-erected at any other place where they might afterwards be required.

(87.) On arrival at the stations where the tide-gauges were to be erected, the first thing to be done was to make an excavation for the iron cylinder. At Hanstal firm soil was met with, which permitted of the hollowing out of a hole of sufficient depth, without any measures to prop up the sides and prevent them from falling in. But at Okha and Nowanár, where the soil is sandy, it was necessary to sink small masonry wells of a sufficient diameter to receive the iron cylinders and the vertical shaft of the piping; they were sunk in much the same manner as the wells which are so frequently used in this country for the foundations of bridges and aqueducts; the operations were considerably facilitated by the employment of Bull's patent dredgers, for scooping out the soil under the sinking masonry, which had been found so useful in the construction of the Oude and Rohilcund Railway that Captain Baird had been directed to provide himself with some for his operations.

(88.) Okha Station—being near the mouth of the gulf and the nearest to Bombay, where all the preliminaries were made—was selected as the first to be taken in hand. There all the instruments and stores, and the European assistants—including Mr. Peters a skilled artificer employed on the Bombay Harbour Works, whose services had been obligingly placed at Captain Baird's disposal for a short time—and the native establishment, were sent direct from Bombay in a pattimar (or native sailing vessel). Meeting with contrary winds, the "Kotia Romani" took such a long time to perform the voyage that Captain Baird began to fear that she must have gone down with all hands on board; at last however she arrived, with her passengers and crew nearly starved, for they had taken with them only a week's provisions for a voyage which lasted fourteen days. On the 5th November the landing of the stores and the sinking of the masonry well was commenced; the well had got down to the requisite depth, 25 feet, by the 4th December, and by the 20th the cylinder had been set up, the piping connecting it with the sea had been laid out into deep water, the observatory was erected, and the several self-registering instruments—a tide-gauge, an anemometer and an aneroid barometer—were all in position and ready for the preliminary trial of their performances. By the 23rd every thing was complete, the instruments were all working well, and Captain Baird was about to proceed to the next station, when an unanticipated mis-adventure occurred which, though intensely annoying at the time, was useful in indicating that it was essentially necessary to take special precautions for the protection of the piping.

(89.) About 3 A.M. on the morning of the 24th, a large native boat was seen drifting from her anchorage towards the station; the crew were all asleep, and before they could be aroused by the sentry on guard, the boat had dragged her anchors across the flexible piping, broken it in two places, and carried away the buoys and the anchor to which they were attached. Being on the spot and provided with spare piping, Captain Baird was able to rectify the damage in a few hours; he also made arrangements for protecting the piping by laying out and anchoring hawsers around it, to intercept passing boats and prevent them from drifting into mischief. Similar measures were carried out at the other stations, and these precautions were essential to the success of the operations; for each station would ordinarily be left under the charge only of the native subordinate employed in winding the clocks of the tide-gauges and the other self-registering instruments, in changing the papers on their barrels and in generally looking after their performances; consequently any injury to the piping would cause a suspension of the tidal registrations for probably a fortnight or more, until Captain Baird could either come in person or send a European assistant to repair the damage, and the break of continuity thus occasioned would greatly impair the value of the observations.

(90.) While engaged in completing what had to be done at Okha, Captain Baird sent his assistants in advance to Hanstal and Nawanár to sink the wells, erect the observatories, and get every thing ready for him to set up the instruments. The extracts from his report, which will be found in the appendix, give full details of the operations at each station, and I need not dwell on them, as they were generally similar to those at Okha of which I have given the principal out-lines.

(91.) The operations were carried on under many and great difficulties. No small amount of risk was incurred by Captain Baird and his assistants when crossing the gulf in native sailing vessels, which had to be done frequently, whenever their presence was needed at either of the stations, both during its construction, and afterwards when accidents occurred, or defects in the working of the instruments had to be rectified, which needed European supervision. On one occasion the pattimar, while under full sail with a stiff breeze, struck on a sand bank and heeled over, and would probably have capsized altogether but for the vigorous action of Mr. Peters, who immediately took command and directed the nacoda and crew to do whatever was necessary for the protection of the vessel. These risks would have been avoided had I assented to a proposition frequently urged on me by Captain Baird, to accept the loan of a small steamer belonging to the Department of Public Works in Bombay, which had been offered, on the condition that we should pay the wages of the Captain and crew and the cost of the coal;—but this would probably have trebled the cost of the operations and therefore the proposal could not be entertained.

(92.) Huts had to be built and iron water tanks provided at each station, for the native surveyor and the underlings who were placed in charge of the instruments, and for the men of the guard furnished by the Durbar of the Native State in which the station is situated. Arrangements had also to be made to supply these men with food and drinking water, which at Hanstal was no easy matter, for the nearest point whence these necessaries of life could be obtained was about 25 miles off. At each station a line of post runners had to be established, to the nearest point on the main postal lines of cummunication, as it was essentially necessary that Captain Baird should receive daily reports from the men in charge of the observatories.

(93.) A singular political difficulty arose at Hanstal. The station is situated in lands which are claimed by both the Rao of Kutch and the Chief of Náwanagar; each of the Durbars vied with the other as to which should be the first to supply the requisite guard, hoping thereby to establish an acknowledgement on the part of British Officers to its claims; the guard from Náwanagar was first in the field; but not long afterwards, and during the absence of Captain Baird, some armed men landed from Kutch, apparently with the intention of ousting the Náwanagar men; but after much altercation and a slight scuffle, they re-embarked and gave no further annoyance.

(94.) At short distances round each station three blocks of stone were sunk in the ground, to serve as bench-marks for future reference, and each of them was carefully connected with the zero of the tide-gauge. Bench-marks were also placed in position on the lines over which, next year, the levels will be carried which are required to connect the tidal stations together and determine their present differences of level, and again hereafter, when a sufficient interval has elapsed to allow of the rising or sinking of the surface of the ground to an appreciable extent.

(95.) The regular tidal registrations were commenced at Okha by the end of December, at Hanstal by the end of March and at Nawanár by the end of April. It was hoped that they might have been carried on continously for at least a year, or perhaps longer, at each station, in order to furnish the requisite data for investigations of the separate influence of each as well as the combined of all of the principal tidal constituents, and the least that is needed for this purpose is a series of observations extending over a year. During this time the errors of the clocks for driving the barrels of the self-registering instruments would have to be frequently determined and the clocks corrected; the instruments would also have to be examined and cleaned, and possibly repaired also, and the relations between the curves on the diagrams and their zero times would have to be carefully redetermined, from time to time; and all this would have to be done either by Captain Baird or by his assistant Mr. Rendell.

(96.) A programme was therefore drawn up for the periodic inspection of the tidal stations, and Captain Baird arranged that he and Mr. Rendell should make tours of inspection in turns. It was calculated that the time required for a tour, embracing all three stations, would be about a month, from the date of leaving to that of returning to the recess quarters; these had been established at Rajkot, the nearest town to the gulf where house accomodation, suitable for Europeans, could be obtained. Anticipating that during the monsoon months the weather at the tidal stations might be found too cloudy to permit of astronomical observations for determining the clock errors, Captain Baird provided himself with two portable chronometers (a siderial and a mean-time) which were rated at Rajkot and carried about on the tours of inspection, for comparison with the clocks.

(97.) The inspection of the observatories necessitated a great deal of hard marching, and entailed much exposure and privation. Even so early as in the month of May, before the setting in of the monsoon, the Runn of Kutch was covered with water, from six inches to a foot in depth, which had to be waded through for many miles distance to reach the station at Hanstal. At such seasons travellers usually cross the Runn by riding on the camels of the country; these animals are bred in large numbers along the borders of the gulf, and are accustomed from their birth to wonder about the swamps, browsing on the mangrove bushes, and thus they learn to walk with ease, and keep their feet, on ground which would be impassable to most other camels. Of his journey with Mr. Rendell to Hanstal in the month of May, Captain Baird writes, " our only " land marks in the whole of the last 14 miles were two small mounds of earth " thrown up—when there were postal chowkees there—at 4 or 5 miles apart, and " the observatory itself; we both felt a curious sensation as if we were being " carried out to sea, which was occasioned by seeing small branches of scrub " floating on the surface of the water and being driven by the wind inland; and " once, with the exception of one of the mounds above mentioned in the distance, " there were no fixed objects visible to destroy this optical illusion." Later on, when the monsoon set in, the difficulties of locomotion were greatly increased; direct communication with Nawanár, by crossing the gulf in a sailing boat, became impossible, as none but native vessels were available for the purpose, and they could not venture to cross in the strong gales of wind which then prevailed; thus to reach the tidal station at that place it was necessary to make a very long detour round the head of the gulf, crossing the Runn at its narrowest point, opposite to Wawania. Moreover the common unmetalled roads in a black soil country, as is the western portion of Kattywar, become all but impassable during the rains; and thus Captain Baird was often unable to get over the ground more expeditiously than at the rate of a mile an hour. Between the 7th July and the 8th September he was actually 38 days in the field, and marched nearly 800 miles, under most adverse circumstances.

(98.) I will now notice the general working of the tide-gauges at the three stations. At Okha the registrations have gone on most satisfactorily up to the time of the latest report received from Captain Baird; there appears to have been only a single break in the continuity of the record, and it only lasted for five hours and is consequently quite immaterial. At Hanstal there have been several short breaks, caused, sometimes by the driving clock getting out of order, but more frequently by the deposit of fine mud in the well and in the piping, notwithstanding the precautions which had been taken to keep the rose at the extremity of the piping high above the mud banks; this necessitated the occasional suspension of operations while the mud was being removed, and care was always taken to make the break between the times of high and low water, whenever possible; thus the record of the highest and lowest points of curves has been secured in almost all instances, the breaks may usually be interpolated between them, and the instances in which this has not happened are so few that Captain Baird believes they will not sensibly influence the final results. The foreshore at Okha being sand and rock without mud, there has been no tendency there for the piping to become choked. Both at Okha and Hanstal air was found to enter the iron piping, whenever the latter was laid bare by the action of the surf, which frequently happened; but it was readily expelled at high water, by opening the stock cock which has already been described as having been attached to the piping for that purpose.

(99.) At Nawanár however matters went on less prosperously. At the July inspection of this station, Captain Baird found every thing apparently in good order; the curves on the diagram of the tide-gauge seemed at first to be all that could be desired; but it was soon evident that they were erroneous, for the level of the water in the well differed very sensibly from the sea level. On examining the piping, the extreme end was found to be buried in sand above the low water line, at a spot where, a few weeks before, there had been a depth of 20 feet of water at low tide, and which was now left bare for some time daily. On further examination it was ascertained that the configuration of the foreshore had entirely changed, and an extensive sand spit had formed on the line of the piping; this had been caused by the drift from a belt of sand hills to the south, under the influence of the strong winds which blow from the south-west during the monsoon, the registered velocities of which were as much as 860 to 890 miles daily, for several days preceding the misadventure. There is reason to expect that the original configuration of the foreshore may be restored, within a few weeks after the cessation of the monsoon. But the position has been clearly proved to be unsuitable for continuous tidal observations, extending over a long period; for it is only during the months of fine weather, between November and May, that observations can be carried on there, otherwise than by setting up the tide-gauge on a staging erected for it out in deep water, the cost of which would be inadmissible.

(100.) The preliminary results of the observations up to the end of September have been worked out by Captain Baird, and it appears that the greatest range of the tide is

14·8 feet at Okha
19·6   ,,   Nawanár
and 21·2 ,, Hanstal,

(29)

or 2 to 4 feet more in each instance than the ranges given in the Marine Charts. Very fairly approximate values of the progress of the tidal wave, up and down the gulf, have been obtained, shewing that

High water occurs at Nawanár 1*h* 5*m* after Okha
     ,,   Hanstal 1 40   ,,
Low water occurs at Nawanár 1 36   ,,
     ,,   Hanstal 2 53   ,,

(101.) The curves of the self-registering aneroid barometers were compared four times daily with a mercurial barometer, and the differences met with—after allowing for index errors—were usually so trivial and unimportant that every confidence may be felt in the general accuracy of the curves. The aneroids are of a delicate construction and are liable to get out of order, but as spare ones were available no break of importance occurred at either station.

(102.) The anemometers were less satisfactory in their working, probably because they were so much more exposed to the vicissitudes of the weather. The long continuance of winds coming from the same quarter caused the direction gear to clog, and until this was discovered the recorded directions are to some extent incorrect. On the other hand the velocity gear was kept in constant action by the strong winds which were prevalent. Several severe gales were recorded. The greatest velocities registered in 24 hours were

620 miles at Okha on the 20th June
890 ,, Nawanár 26th ,,
1130 ,, Hanstal 5th August;

on the latter date the anemometer at Hanstal recorded 270 miles in three hours, between 9 A.M. and noon. Captain Baird is not entirely satisfied with the performances of these instruments ; but, considering their small size (for the sake of lightness and portability), and their exposure to fierce winds, to rain and, worse than all, to the constant oxidising influence of the sea, I think it improbable that any instruments would, under similar circumstances, have given much better results.

(103.) Rain gauges were set up at each station ; the total rainfall during the monsoon was

10·75 inches at Okha
13·61 ,, Nawanár
18·40 ,, Hanstal
21·91 ,, Rajkot (40 miles inland).

(104.) It will be seen that, so far, a greater range of tide, a greater velocity of wind and a greater rainfall, have been registered at the head than at the mouth of the gulf, and intermediate values at the midway station of Nawanár.

(105.) The scientific value of the tidal observations will be greatly increased by the contemporaneous observations of the barometric pressure, the velocity and direction of the wind, and the amount of rainfall. I am not aware of any series of tidal observations which are better furnished than these with the requisite data for separating local atmospheric influences from the true tidal constituents, which are caused by the varying positions of the sun and moon.

(106.) Captain Baird has laboured most heartily and skilfully in carrying out the operations and doing all that could be done to secure their success ; they have proved to be so arduous, and have entailed so much exertion and exposure that I am almost disposed to regret that they were ever undertaken. The most trying of his duties was the inspection of the stations during the monsoon, which was done entirely by himself, as he generously gave his assistant leave of absence, on urgent private affairs, at that time.

(107.) The latest reports state that all was going on well, at Okha and Hanstal ; Captain Baird had proceeded to Nawanár to rectify matters there, after which he was to commence the line of levels for connecting the three stations. He has been instructed to dismantle the three observatories before the commencement of the monsoon of 1875, by which time it is hoped that upwards of a year's observations will have been taken at Okha and Hanstal, which will suffice for an investigation of all the principal tidal constituents at those stations ; and some months observations will probably have been completed at the intermediate station of Nawanár, which should be of considerable value, though inferior to that of the observations at the two other stations.

NO. XII.—GEODETIC.

THE PENDULUM OPERATIONS.

(108.) When my last report was sent in, Captain Heaviside was in England, taking observations at the Kew Observatory, with the Royal Society's and the Russian pendulums, in order to complete the original programme of operations, and link the work done in India, by the late Captain Basevi, with that done in Western Europe, Russia and other parts of the globe. General Sir E. Sabine, to whom the initiation of Captain Basevi's operations was in great measure due, took much interest in the work which was being done at Kew and rendered much assistance to Captain Heaviside.

PERSONNEL.

Captain W. J. Heaviside, R.E., Deputy Superintendent 3rd Grade.
Mr. H. E. T. Keelan, Surveyor 3rd Grade.

(109.) As the results by the pendulums of the Royal Society are differential only, and do not afford a value of the length of the second's pendulum—the originally adopted Imperial Standard for British measures of length—Sir E. Sabine proposed that such additional 'experiments' should be made at Kew, as would be requisite for the conversion of the several comparative results, in India and elsewhere, into absolute values. He pointed out that hitherto there were in Britain only two localities—No. 2 Portland Place in London and the Royal Observatory at Greenwich—in which the absolute length of the seconds pendulum had been determined ; the first of these had been sold into private hands, and was no longer available for public purposes ; and the second had been appropriated for other purposes, so that the Astronomer Royal could not surrender it, nor indeed arrange to have the pendulum experiments conducted in any part of the Greenwich Observatory, and consequently he proposed that a temporary building should be erected for them, in the grounds of the surrounding Park, and pulled down on their completion. But at Kew provision had long been made for such experiments ; the room was available in which the Royal Society's differential pendulums had been swung before they were taken out to India, and were then being re-swung on their return. Sir E. Sabine suggested that the absolute pendulum, which had been employed by Captain Kater in his determination of the length of the seconds pendulum, and which was then at the Kew Observatory, should be swung by Captain Heaviside on the completion of his own operations. I felt bound to assent to a suggestion emanating from so high an authority, and consequently directed Captain Heaviside to take the requisite swings with Captain Kater's pendulum, and these he has duly completed.

(110.) It remained however to compare the unit of length thus determined with the Standard Yard, the present national standard of length ; and this could be no where done better than in the Ordnance Survey Office at Southampton, where special operations have been carried on for some years past for comparing the several national standards of length, and all the requisite apparatus is available. Lieutenant Colonel A. R. Clarke, R.E., by whom the comparisons of standards had been conducted, kindly undertook to measure the distance between the knife edges of the Kater pendulum, in the condition in which it was made over to him on the completion of the swings at Kew, and this has relieved Captain Heaviside of what might have been a very troublesome and tedious duty.

(111.) On the completion of his operations Captain Heaviside gave back to the Royal Society the invariable pendulums, the clock and other instruments which had been lent for the experiments in India, and—with the approval of the Secretary of State—he presented the Society with the air-pump and vacuum apparatus and other instruments which had been subsequently obtained at the cost of the Indian Government. He was asked by the Astronomer Royal to accompany the expedition which was about to be sent to Kerguelin Island, for the observation of the Transit of Venus, and take pendulum experiments on that island; but, believing that the Indian Government had done quite enough for pendulum science, and being anxious for Captain Heaviside's speedy return to complete the reduction of his and Captain Basevi's observations, I demurred to his being sent to Kerguelin Island, and suggested that an officer might be deputed by the Home Government for the purpose, with the pendulums and apparatus which had been used in India, the practical manipulation of which might readily be taught him by Captain Heaviside. The proposal however appears to have fallen through, for I have heard no more about it.

(112.) After taking a short leave of absence in England on the completion of his operations, Captain Heaviside returned to India and arrived at the Head Quarters in October last; he has ever since been employed in reducing the observations, and preparing them and the results for publication, with the assistance of the Computing Office. This work will entail a considerable amount of labour, but great care is being taken to eschew all theoretical refinements, however tempting, which are liable to increase the number of the calculations without sensibly affecting the accuracy of the results, and in printing the observations to restrict the details to what is essentially necessary for the verification of the deductions.

(113.) The Secretary of State for India having expressed a desire to be furnished with the results of the operations as soon as possible, a table is given, on the following page, of the results of the whole of the observations with the Royal Society's pendulums. Comparisons of the actual with the theoretical values—the latter computed with an assumed ellipticity of $\frac{1}{300}$—are given in the right hand column. It will be seen that at the ocean station and at most of the coast stations, the actual number of vibrations exceeds the theoretical number, and that an increase has invariably been met with in proceeding, along a parallel of latitude, from the interior of the main land to the ocean; conversely a marked decrease is met with in proceeding up the main land to the Himalayas, and it is very considerable at the station of Moré, on the table-lands of the Himalayas, at an altitude of 15,427 feet above the sea; there is thus incontestible evidence in confirmation of the hypothesis of a diminution of density in the strata of the earth's crust which are under continents and mountains, and an increase of density in the strata under the bed of the ocean, and it is clear that elevations above the mean sea level are accompanied by an attenuation of the matter of the crust, and depressions by a consolidation.

(114) The reductions of the swings with the Russian pendulums and Captain Kater's pendulum are not yet sufficiently advanced to enable any conclusions to be drawn regarding the results.

Preliminary Abstract of approximate mean results with the Royal Society's Invariable Pendulums Nos. 4 and 1821.

Number	Stations	North Latitude	East Longitude	Height in feet above sea level	By Observation	By computation in terms of Punnæ with an ellipticity = $\frac{1}{300}$	Observed – Computed
	Base Station.						
1 {	Kew Observatory, (1865) / " " (1878) }	51 28	– 0 19	15 {	86114·03 / 14·38 }	86113·55	+ 0·66
	Indian Arc Stations.						
2	Punnæ, ...	8 10	+ 77 41	44	85978·29	...	...
3	Kudankulam, ...	8 11	77 45	166	78·44	85978·32	+ 0·12
4	Mallapatti, ...	9 29	78 3	343	78·83	79·89	– 1·06
5	Pachapáliam, ...	11 0	77 40	971	80·13	82·00	1·87
6	S. W. end Bangalore Base, ...	13 1	77 37	3116	81·64	85·27	3·63
7	N. E. "	13 4	77 42	3007	82·35	85·40	3·05
8	Namthabad, ...	15 6	77 36	1219	86·36	89·19	2·83
9	Kodangal, ...	17 8	77 41	1972	91·23	93·52	2·29
10	Dámargída, ...	18 3	77 43	1934	91·16	95·64	4·48
11	Somtánn, ...	19 5	77 42	1711	95·70	98·12	2·42
12	Badgáon, ...	20 44	77 39	1120	86000·18	86002·35	2·17
13	Ahmadpur, ...	23 36	77 43	1681	08·00	10·34	2·34
14	Kalfánpur, ...	24 7	77 42	1765	10·29	11·85	1·56
15	Pahárgarh, ...	24 56	77 44	1641	10·58	14·31	3·73
16	Usira, ...	26 57	77 40	812	18·81	20·64	1·83
17	Datairi, ...	28 44	77 41	719	23·66	26·51	2·85
18 {	Kalíánø, (1966) / " (1870) / " (1875) }	29 31	77 42	826 {	24·36 / 24·01 / 24·44 }	29·16	4·88
19	Nojli, ...	29 53	77 43	881	24·94	30·45	5·51
20	Dehra Dún, ...	30 20	78 6	2289	24·71	31·98	7·27
21	Mussooree, ...	30 28	79 12	6920	25·67	32·42	6·75
	High Table-land Station.						
22	Moré, ...	33 16	77 54	15427	86019·24	86042·43	– 23·19
	Coast Stations.						
23	Alleppy, ...	9 30	76 20	6	85981·25	85979·90	+ 1·35
24	Aden, ...	12 47	45 2	5	87·35	84·88	2·47
25	Mangalore, ...	12 52	74 49	7	84·29	85·01	– 0·72
26	Madras, ...	13 4	80 17	27	84·47	85·37	0·90
27	Cocanáda, ...	16 56	82 18	9	93·58	93·09	+ 0·49
28	Coláha, (Bombay) ...	18 54	72 51	35	86000·64	97·66	2·98
29	Calcutta, ...	22 33	88 24	18	8·14	86007·29	0·85
	Ocean Station.						
30	Minicoy, ...	8 17	73 2	6	85982·33	85978·43	+ 3·90
	Other Stations.						
31	Mcean Meer, ...	31 32	77 25	706	86031·78	86036·18	– 4·40
32	Ismailia, (Egypt) ...	30 36	32 16	32	31·48	32·90	1·42

The first observations at the Kew Observatory were by Mr. Lüevy; the observations marked thus* were by Captain Heaviside, and all others by Captain Basevi.

The results 'by observation' are the corrected results, after the application of the usual reductions to the observations, *viz.*, 1st the reduction to an infinitely small arc, 2ndly that to a standard temperature (72° Fahrenheit) 3rdly that to a vacuum, and 4thly that to the mean sea level. The 2nd and 3rd of these reductions have been made with preliminary values of the factors of temperature and pressure, which may differ somewhat from the final values: consequently all the results are preliminary only and will have to be corrected, but the corrections cannot materially affect the differential results in the right hand column.

NO. XIII.—GEOGRAPHICAL.

TRANS HIMALAYAN EXPLORATIONS.

(115.) The second appendix to this report contains three papers, the 1st a narrative of an exploration of the Namcho or Tengri Núr Lake, by a native explorer, during 1872, drawn up by Lieutenant-Colonel Montgomerie; the 2nd a memorandum, by the same officer, on the results of the same exploration; and the 3rd some extracts from the narrative by a native explorer of his journey from Pitoragarh (in Kumaun) *viâ* Jumla to Tadum, and then down through Nepaul, along the Gandak river, to British territory.

(116.) Of these papers the two first, which are illustrated by a map, were prepared by Colonel Montgomerie in England, from the original journals which he took with him for the purpose, as mentioned in para. (111.) of my report for last year; they describe an exploration, through an almost unknown portion of Great Thibet, from Shigatze across the Brahmaputra river to the northern shores of the great Namcho Lake, the furthest point of which lies about 100 miles to the north of the town of Lhása. The third, which is also illustrated by a map, gives an account of journeys through regions some of which were unknown and others known only from the information contained in rude itineraries; thus the route from Pitoragarh to Jumla was over new ground; that from Jumla to Muktináth and Tadum over ground of which rude information was already forthcoming, but it required additions and rectifications; the route through Nepaul, from Muktináth down the Gandak river to British territory, was practically new also, and is a useful contribution to our knowledge of the geography of the Nepaulese Dominions.

(117.) But the quarter in which the most extensive and valuable geographical acquisitions have been made, during the present year, is in Kashgharia and the western portions of Eastern Turkestan, in the Pamir or Bám-i-dunia (Roof of the World), and in the regions of the Upper Sources of the Oxus. In my last report I stated that, having been called on to depute an officer to accompany Mr. (now Sir Douglas) Forsyth on his mission to the court of the Atálik Gházi, I had selected Captain Trotter for the purpose, supplied him with all the requisite instruments, sent four of the Pandits—the trained native explorers—with him, and done all else that was in my power to secure the success of the mission from a geographical point of view. And the result has been that considerable additions and rectifications have been obtained; and Captain Trotter may well be congratulated on the success with which his labours have been crowned, notwithstanding that they were carried on under numerous and great difficulties, in consequence of their having been necessarily conducted in mid-winter, a most inclement season of the year for travellers in the highly elevated plateaux of Central Asia.

(118.) To the north of Kashghar Captain Trotter carried a survey through the Artysh valley up to the Russian frontier, at Lake Chadyr Kul, and, though he was disappointed in his expectation of being able to strike off eastwards to the Terekty pass and return by the road from there to Kashghar, he has satisfactorily succeeded in connecting his work with that of the Russian geographers. He subsequently made a survey of a considerable portion of the road towards Úsh-Turfán, to the north-east, and reached the Belowti pass, which is 150 miles from Kashghar and about 90 miles from Úsh Turfán. Meanwhile Captain Biddulph surveyed the road from Kashghar eastwards to Marálbáshi. But no opportunities were afforded for reconnoitering any portion of the long belt of almost unknown country at present ruled by the Atálik Gházi—which extends eastwards for a distance of probably over 700 miles beyond the points reached by Captains Trotter and Biddulph—nor the road to the west leading into Khokand *viâ* the Terek pass.

(119.) Captain Trotter afterwards made a survey of the route which proceeds from Yangi Hissár south of Kashghar to Tashkurghán, and then westwards *viâ* Aktásh over the Little Pamir, and ascertained that the lake on this table-land, called Barkut Yassin by the Mirza in his journals—extracts of which are given in my report for 1869-70—is one of the sources of a river which is here called the Aksú and afterwards the Murghábi, and which joins the Oxus near Wámur, and is in all probability the principal source of that river, as has already been conjectured by Colonel Yule. Captain Trotter continued his survey down to Kila Panja, the little town in Wakhán from which one of the principal sources of the Oxus derives its name. This was the furthest point reached by Captain Trotter to the west; but fortunately he was able to send one of his native surveyors down the Panja river for a considerable distance. The man first went to Ishkashim, so far travelling a route which is well known from the journals of Wood and the Mirza; and then he struck northwards into a region that was altogether unknown, and followed the downward course of the Panja river for a distance of nearly 100 miles, finding its direction to be in reality very different from what has hitherto been conjectured and represented on the best maps of these regions; he reached Kila Wámar, in Roshán, but was unable to go down the river any further. An exploration has however been since made from Fyzabad and Koláb up the river, to a point which is believed to be at no great distance from Kila Wámar, by Colonel Montgomerie's Havildar, who is now returning from Kábul with his journals; he writes that he has suffered great hardships and lost some of his papers; but if enough evidence is forthcoming to determine the course of the Oxus from Kila Wámar down to the plains of Koláb, a problem which is of the highest importance, both politically and geographically, will be solved.

(120.) From Panja Captain Trotter returned to Aktásh, *viâ* the Great Pamir, passing the lake which was discovered in 1838 and named Victoria by Lieutenant Wood of the Indian Navy. From Aktásh he returned to Yarkand by almost the same route that he had already travelled. The Pandit who accompanied Captain Trotter as far as Tashkurghán, on the outward journey, returned thence by a more direct route to Yarkand, carrying a traverse survey along an entirely new piece of road.

(121.) It was not considered desirable to send the (Hindú) Pandits into localities inhabited solely by a Mahomedan population, and hitherto they had been chiefly employed in surveying various lines of routes between Ladakh and Yárkand, some new, others old but requiring rectification. But while Captain Trotter was absent in Wakhán one of these men, Krishna, was sent *viâ* Sanju to Khotan, with instructions to penetrate as far eastwards as possible. He traversed the ancient road to China, as far as the Sorghák gold fields, and then, returning to Keria, struck southwards along the road to Rudok, crossed the Kuen Luen range and the great table-lands of the higher Himalayas on the western confines of Chinese Thibet, and reached the village of Noh, which is about 20 miles to the north of Rudok; here he was stopped by the Chinese officials and nearly turned back again by the road he came, but eventually he was permitted to go direct to Leh by the Pangong Lake. His work was very carefully executed, and has stood the usual tests, furnished by comparing the route survey with the astronomical and trigonometrical determinations of position, most satisfactorily; and this is all the more important in the present instance, in that large corrections have been shown to be needed in the work of 1865-66, which has hitherto been accepted, though with some misgivings.

(122.) Captain Trotter is now at my Head Quarters, preparing a geographical memoir for Sir Douglas Forsyth's Report of the Mission, which will contain full details of his operations and those of the officers associated with him who had opportunities for visiting places which he could not go to. The report will probably be published a few weeks hence, and therefore any further notice of Captain Trotter's labours is here unnecessary.

NO. XIV.—THE COMPUTING OFFICE.

EXAMINATION, FINAL REDUCTION AND PUBLICATION OF THE OBSERVATIONS.

PERSONNEL.

J. B. N. Hennessey, Esqr., Deputy Supdt. 1st Grade.
W. H. Cole, Esqr., M.A. Asst. Supdt. 1st Grade.
Lieutenant St. G. C. Gore, R.E., Asst. Supdt. 2nd Grade.

COMPUTING BRANCH.

Mr. C. Wood, Surveyor 3rd Grade.
„ H. W. Poychoss, Asst. Surveyor 1st Grade.
Mr. J. W. Macdougall, Surveyor 2nd Grade.
Baboo Gunga Pershad, Computor.
„ Cally Mohun Ghose, Computer.
„ Kally Onomar Chatterjee Computor and 11 other Computers,

PRINTING BRANCH.

Mr. M. J. O'Connor, Printer.
21 Compositors and Apprentices.

PHOTOZINCOGRAPHIC BRANCH.

Mr. C. G. Ollenbach, Zincographer.
„ C. Dyson, Photographer.
1 Apprentice, „
2 Native Draftsmen and a map keeper.

DRAWING BRANCH.

Mr. G. W. E. Atkinson, Surveyor 4th Grade.
Sheik Snidudeen, and 5 other Draftsmen.
5 Assistant draftsmen, also some apprentices and map colorists.

(123.) The Computing Office has been employed in its usual duties of carefully examining and reducing the observations, and of publishing the ultimate results of such portions as have been finally treated, and preliminary results of the portions which await further materials before they can be finally disposed of. The 3rd volume of the "*Account of the Operations &c.*" has been printed and is ready for publication, the 4th is all but complete; but as these volumes contain little else besides the numerical details of the observations and calculations and their results, I have decided to postpone their publication until the completion of the 2nd volume, which is intended to give a brief history of the operations, and a full description of the procedure which was adopted at the outset and of its subsequent modifications, of the instruments employed from time to time, and of the formulæ and methods of computation by which both the preliminary and the final results have been obtained. Of this volume about 250 pages quarto have been printed, but much more remains to be done; its preparation necessarily devolves in great measure on myself, and has to be held in abeyance when I cannot find time to devote to it; but I am in hopes that the volume will be finished by the end of 1875.

(124.) Good progress has been made with the publication of the Synoptical Volumes which give all the data required by surveyors and geographers and the public at large. Of these the following have already been issued, No. 1, the Great Indus Series; No. 2, the Great Arc, section 24° to 30°; and No. 3, the Karáchi (Kurrachee) Longitudinal Series; three more volumes are nearly ready for publication.

(125.) Considerable assistance was rendered to Captain Trotter, whose geographical operations have been reviewed in the preceding Section; all his very numerous observations for absolute and differential longitudes, and for latitudes, heights &c., have been reduced in this office, and much other work has been done for him, whereby he has been enabled to prepare his maps and reports far more rapidly than would otherwise have been possible. The completion of the pendulum operations has likewise necessitated the rendering of a large amount of assistance to Captain Heaviside, in reducing and printing the observations. In these and all the other duties of this office Messrs. Hennessey and Cole have laboured with the same skill, assiduity and zeal, which it has been my pleasing duty to bring to prominent notice in previous reports.

(126.) On the death of Captain Basevi—from exposure incurred on the high table lands of the Himalayas, while he was engaged in the pendulum operations—a subscription was raised among his brother officers and associates for a memorial of him; a sum of over R. 2,000 was subscribed, and then the question arose how it should be expended, whether in a monument or painted window to be erected in a church, or—as had been suggested—in a clock to be erected at the Head Quarters Office. His widow was consulted on the subject, and she was altogether in favour of the clock, as best serving to perpetuate his name among those by whom his labours would be best appreciated. A memorial clock, with a suitable inscription, was therefore obtained from England and it has been erected over the office portico; it strikes the quarters as well as the hours, and keeps admirable time, and it has altogether superseded the hand-struck gong by which, for very many years, the office hours have been regulated.

No. XV.—CARTOGRAPHY.

(127.) An important series of Final Charts has been prepared to illustrate the several synoptical volumes which have been specified in para. (124). These maps are drawn on the scale of ¼ of an inch to the mile, for publication by photozincography on half that scale, and great care is taken to assimilate the spellings of the names in the charts to those in the volumes, and to do all that is necessary to enable them to serve as aids to a correct understanding of the data of the triangulation of former years. Five preliminary charts, of the triangulation of the current year, have also been prepared, giving full numerical data to satisfy immediate local requirements.

(128.) Re-prints, with additions and corrections, of two of the four sheets of the 2nd edition of the Map of Turkestan have been made. Preparations have also been made for the publication of a 3rd edition of this map at an early date; each of the four sheets has been entirely re-drawn; a large amount of valuable and recent information, with which I have been favoured by Colonel Stubendorff, the Director of the Topographical branch of the Russian War Office, is being incorporated into them, and also the results of Captain Trotter's surveys; and I am only awaiting the return of Colonel Montgomerie's Havildar, now daily expected, to have the maps completed and sent to press.

(129.) In addition to the above, some progress has been made with the series of Level-Charts on which the systems of levels for Railways, Canals and other Public Works are shewn, after having been connected with the main lines of levels of this Survey and reduced thereby to the datum of the mean-sea level. The maps of Mussooree and Landour have had the recently re-demarcated boundary lines shown on them, which has been a very tedious and troublesome business, and has been protracted over several years. A map of Kumaun and Garhwál has been specially prepared for the Gazetteer of that district which is now being compiled by Mr. E. T. Atkinson, c.s., but the delays caused by having to alter the spellings of the whole of the names, in conformity with the recent orders of the Government on the orthography of Indian names, have prevented the publication of the map hitherto. Much assistance has been rendered to Captain Trotter in the compilation of his new geographical information, the maps of which have all been drawn in this office.

(130.) In the typographic office 1,220 pages, mostly quarto, have been composed and 320 copies (on an average) of each have been printed. And in the photozincographic office, 61 maps have been photographed and put on zinc, and the number of prints which have been 'pulled' is 9,207 of maps, 2,027 of charts, 3,557 of diagrams, and 28,125 of professional and office forms.

(131.) It now only remains for me to acknowledge the valuable services which have been rendered by my Personal Assistant, Mr. H. Duhan, who has relieved me of much official routine work, which would otherwise have taken up time I could ill spare for it. Of Mr. Robert Scott—whose good services in the correspondence office and as general store-keeper, it has always been a pleasure to me to acknowledge in my annual reports hitherto—I regret to have to state that this must be my last notice; he died on the 12th September, after a long and painful illness; he had served in the Department for nearly 30 years; hard working, simple minded, and ready to oblige everybody, 'good old Robert' will long be affectionately remembered and respected by all who knew him.

(132.) An abstract of the out-turn of work executed by each of the Survey parties, the results of the operations of which can be exhibited in this form,

(37)

is given on the following page. I consider the amount of progress which has been made during the year on all sides, by the Survey Parties while in the field and also in recess, and by the Offices at Head Quarters, to have been generally very satisfactory.

J. T. WALKER, COLONEL, R. E.,

Supdt. Great Trigonometrical Survey.

DEHRA DUN,
Dated 15th February, 1875.

(38)

Abstract of the out-turn of work executed by the Great Trigonometrical Survey Parties, during the Survey year 1873-74.

DESCRIPTION OF DETAILS.	1 Bangalore Meridional Series 24-inch Theodolite.	2 Assam Triangulation 12-inch Theodolite.	3 Brahmaputra Merl. Series 24-inch Theodolite.	4 Jodhpur Meridional Series 24-inch Theodolite.	5 Eastern Frontier Series 24-inch Theodolite.	7 Kattywar Topographical Survey.	8 Guzerat Topographical Survey.	9 Dehra Doon Topographical Survey, 4-inch=1 mile.	10 Kumaon and Gurhwal Topographical Sur, 1-inch=1 mile.	TOTAL.
Number of Principal Stations, newly fixed, ...	13	...	11	19	8	...	...	...	..▲	51
Number of Principal Triangles, completed, ...	20	...	14	26	10	...	...	...	...	70
Area of Principal Triangulation, in square miles,	3,239	...	1,105	1,552	1,294	...	...	...	...	7,190
Lengths of Principal Series, in miles, ...	108	....	54	90	50	...	...	...	...	302
Average Triangular error, in seconds, ...	0·40	...	0·83	0·14	0·70	...	...	...	...	...
Average probable errors of Angles, in seconds,±	0·14	...	0·25	0·14	0·54	...	...	...	...	...
Astronomical Azimuths of verification, ...	1	...	1	1	...	...	...	...	...	3
Number of Secondary Stations whose positions and heights have been fixed,	51	93	81	29	...	309	227	158	120	1,026
Number of Secondary Stations whose positions only have been fixed, ...	...	...	.	...	...	132	337	619	...	1,088
Number of Secondary Triangles of which all 3 angles have been observed, ...	13	17	17	24	...	164	335	174	29	793
Length of Secondary Series in miles, ...	...	47	37	116	...	...	...	...	...	200
Area of Secondary and Minor Triangulation square miles, ...	1,413	281	280	1,667	...	3,174	1,550	529	650	8,862
Area embraced by Triangulation to hill peaks square miles. ...	...	12,000	...	...	...	...	...	...	...	12,000
Number of Points fixed by intersection, but not visited, ...	61	95	21	54	...	626	369	597	...	1,823
Length of boundary lines and check lines traversed in linear miles. ...	...	...	...	...	...	1,235	982	848	...	3,065
Area topographically Surveyed on scale of 1-inch=1 mile,...	...	...	...	...	...	...	...	...	534	534
„ topographically surveyed on scale of 2 inches=1 mile in square miles,	...	...	...	...	...	2,366	...	...	...	2,366
„ topographically| surveyed on scale of 4 inches=1 mile in square miles,	...	...	...	...	...	690	63	...	...	753
Number of Revenue Survey Stations and boundary junction pillars, fixed by Triangulation,...	...	1	8	1	...	P	P	51	...	61P
„ of Principal Stations selected in advance, ...	10	...	...	14	10	...	...	...	...	43
Lengths of Approximate Series, Principal in miles, ...	64	...	...	102	112	...	...	...	...	278
Lengths of Approximate Series, Secondary in miles, ...	...	30	...	...	...	...	...	...	...	30
Number of Towers constructed, ...	5	...	...	...	...	...	...	...	...	5
Do. of Pillars and Platforms for Principal Stations, ...	6	...	...	18	8	...	...	...	...	32
Do. of Pillars constructed Secondary Stations, ...	12	14	20	10	2	...	...	46	...	104
Do. Miles of Rays cleared, ...	173	178	26	5	70	...	...	P	...	452P
Do. Miles of path-way made, ...	6	...	...	...	225	...	...	...	...	231
Do. Hill tops cleared of forests and jungle,	...	3	...	3	22	...	...	37	...	65
Do. Principal Stations whose elements were computed,	21	...	11	12	15	...	...	...	...	59
Do. Secondary and traverse Stations whose elements were computed,	90	115	32	...	...	P	1,478	P	P	1,715P
Do. Preliminary Charts of Triangulation,	2	2	1	3	...	...	...	...	...	...
Do. Of Topographical maps, ...	...	...	...	...	...	22	8	...	4	34
Do. Principal Stations placed under official protection,	16	13	11	19	8	...	...	...	...	67
Do. Stations protected and closed, ...	12	9	14	20	5	...	...	...	...	60
Do. Points fixed by traverse, ...	...	...	23	...	...	P	P	P	P	23P
Aneroid Determinations of height, ...	...	...	...	172	...	P	P	P	P	172P

APPENDIX.

EXTRACTS FROM THE NARRATIVE REPORTS

OF THE

EXECUTIVE OFFICERS IN CHARGE

OF THE

SURVEY PARTIES AND OPERATIONS.

Extract from the Narrative Report—dated 16th July 1874—of MAJOR B. R. BRANFILL, Deputy
Superintendent 2nd Grade, in charge Madras Party.

(2.) The proposed work for the field season 1873-74, just concluded, was the comple-
Proposed field work 1873-74. tion of the Great Arc (revision), Southern Section, which had
been in abeyance for two seasons, and the commencement of
the Rámnád Longitudinal Series in latitude 9° 30'.

(4.) The party marched from Bangalore on 1st November and reached Kutipárei S., the
Field work begun 2nd December. first station for observation, on 2nd December, when operations
were begun with a set of circumpolar star observations for azi-
muth, this being a Zenith Distance (latitude) and also a Pendulum Station. Owing to cloudy
weather it took ten days to complete the observations, nearly double the usual time.

(5.) It may be remarked here that one of the rays observed at this time, that between
Kutipárei S. and Perumál H.S., is the longest side of any principal triangle yet observed in the
Great Trigonometrical Survey of India, being 63·944 miles in length. It is probably due to
the unusually clear atmosphere of the cloudy weather, that the Perumál signal-lamp, with a re-
flector only a foot in diameter, could be bisected at so great a distance. In March 1871, when
the corresponding observations were made on this ray at Perumál H.S., a similar signal-lamp
was not once visible in the course of several weeks, and even the heliotrope signal, with a full
aperture of 8 inches diameter was scarcely capable of being observed through the hazy air of
that season.

(6.) Final observations were continued without interruption, and with little delay, at
S. Section of the Great Arc Series the twelve stations remaining, until the series was completed
completed. before the end of February, by closing upon the stations which
had been connected with the Cape Comorin Base-line in 1868-69.

(7.) In consequence of the disappearance of one of the two stations forming the side
Loss of former station on the red of junction between the Ráthápuram and Valanád polygons, it
sand hills. was necessary to re-observe at three of the stations already
observed at and fixed. It had been necessary to occupy a point
on the red sand hills or "théri" (for an account of which I may refer to the notes on the
Tinnevelly district appended to the general report of the G. T. Survey operations for 1868-69).
Mr. Mitchell who built the station there, had been directed to construct it of masonry, like a
well, which he was to sink through the sand to the firm soil below, which he reported was
reached at ten feet below the surface of the highest sand hillock. This depth however proved
insufficient, for during the interval of four years it had been undermined and nothing remained
but the debris to mark the spot.

(8.) No other suitable spot being available for a station it was necessary to re-occupy
Spot re-occupied with a temporary the site again this year: and this was done by means of a tem-
station. porary station consisting of wooden piles driven deeply into the
sand.

(9.) Colonel Lambton in like manner about the year 1808-9 used a similar temporary
Relative site of Colonel Lambton's station, presumably on the highest part of the "théri", or
Red Hill Station of 1808-9. sand waste; but it appears (from the computations) to have
been about 1,061 yards to the W.N.W. ¼ N. of the present
(1874) station and 13 or 14 feet lower.

(10.) From this it seems as if the highest part of these sand hills had shifted about
Probable secular motion of the 1,060 yards to the E. S. E. during the sixty years elapsed, or
"théri" to the eastward. nearly 17 yards a year. Moreover, the point occupied by Mr.
Mitchell in February 1869 was the highest point of this particular
sand ridge, and of the sand hills in general. Whereas the highest point of this particular sand
ridge now (February 1874) is about 30 yards farther to the eastward than it was in February
1869, having thus only travelled at the rate of 6 yards a year, but in the same direction, to the
E. S. E., and it still appears to be the highest point of the "théri." Some banian stakes have been
planted on the chance of their taking root, and so marking the locality for future reference.

(11.) All the stations on and around the Cape Comorin Base-line were examined and
Base-line stations put into good found generally in a good state of preservation. The towers and
order. observatories received the little repairs they seemed to require
and the closing piles of stones and earth were restored after
the five years' weathering they had sustained since first left.

(12.) As soon as the final observations of the Great Arc were finished, I proceeded to
Reconnoissance of the Straits of Manár. utilize the little clear weather that remained at the end of
February by reconnoitering the Straits of Manár with a view
to the practicability of a trigonometrical connection with Ceylon. The results of this reconnoissance which I reported to you met with your approbation.

(13.) The next work to be done was the Rámnád Longitudinal Series which I now took up in person. I had sent Mr. Belcham at the end of December to reconnoiter the country along the parallel of 9° 30′ and to commence laying out the Approximate Series. After a very careful and detailed examination he reported this line of country very unsuitable for the great triangulation, it being an unbroken plain of black (cotton) soil, generally under cultivation, with high standing crops, and plentifully wooded by groves of fruit trees (Tamarind, Mango and Palm), the view being also every where obstructed by long lines of high banks of tanks and irrigation channels. It was evident that every ray must be tediously traced and cleared in the regular manner, and that high towers would be required even for comparatively small triangles.

Commencement of the Rámnád Longitudinal Series.

Unsuitable nature of the country on 9° 30′.

(14.) It was impossible to lay out and prepare any stations of the new series in time for observation this season. I therefore abandoned the intention, and sent the large theodolite into store, whilst I proceeded to lay out the series myself, directing the assistants, after finally closing the Great Arc stations, to build the new stations as soon as selected.

Principal observing closed for the season.

(15.) After a careful examination of the country I found that, taking the most favourable line, namely that bordering the coast-line and on the parallel of 9° 15′, where advantage of the coast-line sand hills could be taken, I could not reach Rámnád, distant only 64 miles, by less than 16 triangles forming a single series. The addition of three stations made this into a double series, which I propose for observation next season. A number of towers or high masonry pillars with temporary wooden platforms will be necessary.

Rámnád Series approximately laid out on parallel of 9° 15′.

(16.) The party returned to recess at Bangalore on 26th May after a tolerably healthy and successful season's work.

Close of field season.

(17.) The out-turn of field work this season consists of 13 principal stations newly fixed by 20 triangles forming 8 quadrilaterals, a hexagon and two fifths of a pentagon, covering 3,289 square miles and extending the (Great Arc) series, which is now complete, 108 miles to the southward, executed at a cost of Rs. 12-15 (or about 26 shillings) per square mile. A set of star observations for azimuth has been taken as usual, and 51 secondary points and minor stations have been fixed, chiefly within the area of the principal triangles above mentioned; but an area of 1,413 square miles is embraced by the secondary triangles exterior to the main series, besides some 20 high and important hill peaks.

General statement of the field season's work accomplished.

The Rámnád Longitudinal Series has been approximately laid out for a distance of 64 miles by 19 stations forming two quadrilaterals and three hexagons, 6 of the high masonry pillars required for which have been built.

The Mangalore and Paniáni Minor Series has been completed and connected with the Coimbatore Minor Series of 1869-70, by a longitudinal branch, through the Pálghát gap in the Western Ghâts, thus completing a circuit for verification. The length of these series is altogether 212 miles, of which 62 has been done by Mr. Laseron this season. Mr. Mitchell laid out and observed about 120 of it during the two previous seasons, the remaining 30 having been done by myself in March and April 1870.

(18.) The object of this triangulation, was to provide reliable trigonometrical points in a part of the country which had not previously been triangulated and thus fill up the great gap left in previous charts of the old (Col. Lambton's) and recent trigonometrical surveys.

Object of the Malabár Minor Triangulation.

(19.) The field season has been an uneventful one, but the following particulars may be thought worthy of mention:—As was to be expected, on quitting the vicinity of the Western Ghâts for the flat lowlands of the South-East Coast, we met with instances of terrestrial refraction such as we had not seen for some years. The heliotrope signals near the sea shore, in cases when the rays passed too near to the ground, or *grazed* over low vegetation, reminded me of the signals I had seen in Sind and the Panjáb. Sometimes an afternoon heliotrope appeared like a pillar of fire, in height 6 or 8 times its width; and the same signal would in a little while appear as two or more distinct, separate signals, puzzling the observer which or which part to intersect.

(20.) On entering the black soil country, morning mirage was to be seen nearly every day about sunrise, such as I was familiar with in the Indus valley and also in the Kistna and Godavery river deltas, but have seldom seen elsewhere. The more common afternoon, or heat mirage was a matter of daily occurrence.

Mirage common.

(21.) Some of the strangest instances of these phenomena were witnessed and noted on the spot by Mr. Boud, who writes as follows :—

"I was surprised to see the curious phenomenon of mirage, the apparent unusual elevation and nearness of distant objects with an inverted image suspended in air immediately above them, whole villages appearing thus and also as if built on an island. One very close morning, about 6-30 A. M., in May, on looking out for the heliotrope I expected to see on the tower station (a masonry pillar 19 feet high) about 5½ miles distant to the southward, I noticed a curious sight and called Mr. Belcham's attention to it. The entire pillar was visible with an inverted image of it apparently suspended above, and instead of one heliotrope, five distinct images were seen—one at the top and base of each image of the pillar and one in the space midway between their tops. In a little while the signals became vertically lengthened until they coalesced into a pillar of light. In about half an hour the whole (signal and pillar) had disappeared below the ground horizon some 3 miles off". I anticipate great inconvenience from this source in the future.

Instance of peculiar mirage.

(23.) Mr. Bond had the good fortune to procure an interview with a couple of the wild folk who live in the hill jungles of the Western Ghâts, to the south-west of the Palanei hills, and took the opportunity to observe and note on the spot some of their peculiarities. We had often heard of the existence of some strange dwarfish people who occasionally frequented the jungles near our station of Pémalei, a few miles west of Strivilliputtúr, at the north-west corner of the Tinnevelly district, but none of us, when visiting the Pémalei hills for the purpose of selecting, building or observing at this station, had seen any trace of them, except that whilst observing the final angles we noticed some fires burning at night far off in the distant valleys, commonly stated to be entirely devoid of villages, and civilized inhabitants. When returning afterwards to Pémalei, in order finally to close and deliver over charge of the station to the local officials, Mr. Bond having heard that the wild men of the woods occasionally came to Strivilliputtúr with honey, wax and sandalwood to exchange for cloth, rice, tobacco and betelnut, induced three of the "*Kávalkárs*" or hill watchers, through whom principally this barter is carried on, to attempt to catch a specimen of this strange folk. What follows is Mr. Bond's account :—

Wild jungle folk.

(24.) "Knowing a locality they frequented, whence they could easily steal the remains of food and pots left by the herdsmen, the three Kávalkárs went there to look for them, and on the second day sighted a couple, who at once made off through the jungle for the rocks, with great fleetness and agility, using hands and feet in getting over the latter.

Mr. Bond's account of them.

(25.) "After a difficult and exciting chase and a very careful search they were again caught sight of, crouching between two rocks, the passage to which was so narrow that it cost their captors a severe scratching to reach them and drag them out one at a time by the legs. They were brought to me in a state of great fear—a man and a woman—as I was descending the hill, and began to cry on being led to my camp at a large village a few miles out in the plains. After some coaxing however, with promises of rice and tobacco, they consented to accompany me willingly. On reaching my tent in the evening I gave the man some clothes, and offered them a little money in small silver and copper coins. Each of them selected the latter, refusing the silver pieces of ten times the value, saying that they could get rice with the copper, and apparently had no idea of the value of the former. I gave the woman some pieces of cloth and a few small things, for which they both showed their thanks by repeated prostrations on the ground before me.

Capture of a couple of them.

(26.) "The rest of the day was spent in taking notes on this strange pair and in getting from them all the information I could through the hill watchers, who were able to converse with them to a slight extent. They seemed as great a curiosity to the villagers themselves as to myself; and a crowd assembled to watch them, expressing their surprise at the ease and freedom with which they sat in my tent without shewing any fear or any desire to run away. The following observations were noted on the spot :—

Their peculiarities noted.

"The man is 4 feet, 6½ inches in height, 26¼ inches round the chest and 18½ inches horizontally round the head over the eyebrows. He has a round head, coarse black, woolly hair and a dark brown skin. The forehead is low and slightly retreating ; the lower part of the face projects like the muzzle of a monkey and the mouth, which is small and oval with thick lips, protrudes about an inch beyond his nose ; he has short bandy legs, a comparatively long body and arms that extend almost to his knees : the back just above the buttocks is concave, making the stern appear to be much protruded. The hands and fingers are dumpy and always contracted, so that they cannot be made to stretch out quite straight and flat ; the palms and fingers are covered with thick skin (more particularly so the tips of the fingers), and the nails are small and imperfect ; the feet are broad and thick skinned all over ; the hairs of his moustache are of a greyish white, scanty and coarse like bristles and he has no beard.

Description of the male.

6—a

"The woman is 4 feet 6½ inches in height, 27 inches round the chest (above the breasts)
and 19½ horizontally round the head above the brows; the colour
of the skin is sallow, or of a nearly yellow tint; the hair is black,
long and straight, and the features well formed. There is no difference between her appearance and that of the common women of that part of the country. She is pleasant to look at, well developed and modest.

Description of the female.

(27.) "There are said to be five or six families living about the Pémalei hills, men and women being about the same height, all the men having the same cast of features and being built as the specimen above described.

Number and general appearance.

"The dress of the man consists of a "*langoti*" or small piece of cloth tied round the loins. The women when they cannot procure cloth wear only a skirt of leaves.

Dress.

"They both believe themselves to be 100 years old, but judging from their appearance I suppose the man to be 25 and the woman about 18 years of age. They say that they have been married 4 years, but have had no children.

Age.

"Their marriage custom is very simple; a man and woman who pair off, mutually agree to live together during their life time, the conditions being that the man is to provide food and the woman to cook it, and the marriage is considered to be binding after these conditions have been carried out for the first time, *i.e.* after they have eaten their first food together.

Marriage custom.

(28.) "They eat flesh, but feed chiefly upon roots and honey. The roots, of which the man next morning went to the jungle and fetched me two kinds, are species of wild yam. I tasted both when cooked and found them far from unpalatable.

Food.

"They have no fixed dwelling places but sleep on any convenient spot, generally between two rocks or in caves near which they happen to be benighted. They make a fire and cook what they have collected during the day, and keep the fire burning all night for warmth and to keep away wild animals. They worship certain local divinities of the forest,—Rákas or Rákári, and Pé (after whom the hill is named, Pé-malei).

Dwelling.

"When one of them dies the rest leave the body exposed and avoid the spot for some months. Whenever the herdsmen, wood-cutters or hill watchers come across a corpse and tell the "*grám munsaf*", or head village official, he sends men to bury it and reports the circumstance to the Tahsíldár. The grám munsaf of this place (Mamsápuram and Shiventipatti) told me that six had been buried under his orders.

Neglect of their dead.

(29.) "As I detained this couple in my camp till late in the evening, they begged to remain all night, as they were afraid to enter the jungles so late for fear of wild beasts unless they had a torch with them. I then offered them food if they would cook it near my tent, and gave them what they asked for, rice; but when a fowl and curry stuff were suggested they took them also. The man would have killed the fowl by cutting off its head between two stones, but I told my people to give him a knife and shew him how to cut its throat, which they did, but he evidently disliked to use the knife and begged my servant to do it for him, and turned away his head as if he did not wish to see it done.

Cooking and feeding.

"Whilst the woman cooked the rice, the man cut up the fowl, by placing the knife between his toes and drawing the meat along the edge of it. They seemed ignorant of the use of salt and curry stuff as they did not use the condiments till told to do so. Moreover they wanted to eat the food when only half cooked.

"The man having washed his hands remained squatting on the ground till his wife served him, which she continued to do, without eating anything herself, till he signed to her that he had had enough: she then brought him water to wash his mouth and hands and afterwards ate her own food.

"The fingers alone were used in eating: some rice mixed with the curry was collected into a lump and thrown into the mouth, and I noticed that they did not mix any of the meat with the curry. What remained of their food was put carefully away and carried off next day into the jungle.

(30.) "Next morning I sent the man to fetch specimens of the roots they ordinarily feed on whilst the woman remained at my camp. On his return soon after midday I dismissed them apparently not ill pleased with their involuntary visit."

Dismissal.

(31.) I am happy to report that all my assistants have worked willingly and well, sending in their weekly diaries and their monthly abstracts and returns with regularity. A brief account of the work done by each assistant taken from his own narrative report is given here.

Assistants of the party.

(32.) Mr. G. Belcham, Assistant Surveyor 1st grade, was transferred to this party
Mr. G. Belcham.   from No. 1 Extra Party (Astronomical) in order to practise the
                           usual field duties of a triangulating party, of which he had
hitherto had little or no actual experience. During the first month of the field season, he remained with me as observatory recorder and office assistant, occasionally using a small theodolite for practice. During the next two months, January and February, he was employed in
a reconnaissance of the country along the parallel of 9° 30', with a view to the Rámnád Longitudinal (approximate) Series. He carried out this duty well, undergoing a great deal of exposure and thoroughly examining the country, without however being able to lay out any definite
regular series, although he made a general scheme of triangulation, possible at the cost of
tracing and clearing nearly all the rays and building high towers. He also, during this time,
visited and observed at several points about the island of Rámésweram with a view to the Ceylon
connection.
        He next took up a little minor triangulation with the 12-inch theodolite for the determina-
tion of the position of Pandalagudi, Zenith Distance (Lat.) Station. The results of this, his first
essay in independent triangulation, are satisfactory. The rest of the field season (seven weeks)
was spent in building two masonry pillar stations, one with solid platform 16 feet high, and the
other 19 feet high.
        (33.) Mr. J. Bond, 2nd grade Assistant Surveyor, has been temporarily attached to
Mr J. Bond.   the party, joining my camp on 19th December, when he took
                           up the duties of observatory recorder and office assistant, in
performing which, during the ensuing two months, he gave me entire satisfaction. He next
undertook the final closing and delivery of 8 of the principal stations, which he accomplished
in 5 weeks, marching over 200 miles. He was next engaged, during the last six weeks of the
field season, in station-building and ray-clearing on the Rámnád Series, and nearly completed
two stations.
        (34.) Mr. C. D. Potter, Assistant Surveyor 2nd grade, has done a good season's work,
Mr. C. D. Potter.   having built two (23 feet) masonry pillar stations, 4 large plat-
                           forms, and finally closed and delivered over 4 stations, besides
inspecting and repairing or restoring the closing piles, &c., of 9 stations about the Cape Comorin
Base-line. He also traced and cleared some 90 miles of rays carrying out my instructions with
diligence.
        (35.) Mr. E. W. Laseron, Assistant Surveyor 3rd grade, has been employed throughout
Mr. E. W. Laseron.   the field season in the completion of the Malabár Minor Tri-
                           angulation. This triangulation was begun by Mr. Mitchell in
1871-72, starting from a side of the principal triangles near Mangalore and has closed at Coimbatore, on the closing side of the Coimbatore Minor Series, a short series which was done by
myself with a 14-inch theodolite in March and April 1870, emanating from a side of the Great
Arc Series. The total length of this series, between the sides of these two principal series, is
about 212 miles. Mr. Laseron's triangulation appears to be as good as could be expected and his
portion of the entire work compares favourably with the rest of the work.

        Extract from the Narrative Report—dated 1st August 1874—of W. G. BEVERLEY, Esq. Officia-
        ting Assistant Superintendent 1st Grade, in charge Assam Valley Triangulation.

        (2.) The rains having ceased earlier than usual, the party was able to resume field
work by the middle of November.
        (3.) In order to give time for advancing the approximate work and constructing pil-
lars, I visited Selá and Kurwá principal stations to fix peaks in the Bootan Himalayas and fill
up the gap to the west of Long. 92° 30'. The weather was however very unfavourable, and the
atmosphere unusually thick for the time of the year, and no distant peaks were observed. The
position and height of the obelisk in the river were determined, also the heights of the Church
in Gowhatty and of a remarkable temple in the neighbourhood, all of which had been overlooked at the commencement.
        (4.) On my way to Nikorí-Chaprí T.S. to commence final observations, I visited the
hill stations of Kandalí, Kholá (a station in Nowgong) and Púraparbat in Tezpore, and
was able to fix the civil station of Nowgong, the permanent mark being the S.W. corner of
the Jail wall. Several new peaks were also added and heights taken to nearly all. A better
value was also obtained for the side from which Tezpore Church had been fixed.
        (5.) During December and part of January, I took final observations from Madaigñon
T.S., Nikorí-Chaprí T.S., Rodongá T.S., Belaguri T.S. and Nigrí Ting T.S. and carried 5 final
rays. I also reconnoitred the country about Jorhát, to take steps for fixing it, and then ascended the Brahmaputra up to Dibrúgarh to examine the nature of the country on either bank.

On my return I found the station of Majhulia ready, and I took final observations from it, and from Bor Bhiti T.S., Bor-Chaprí No. 2 P.S. and Phakwadol T.S.

(6.) The advance stations not being built I marched to Sibságar on the 18th February, and examined the ground about with a view to fixing points in the civil station and the Revenue Survey permanent mark, either by traverse or triangulation. On returning I visited the selections of Gauriságar, Bor-Alí P.S. and Sintamunigarh T.S. and took up the trial and final rays between them.

(7.) While these were in hand I took secondary observations to peaks, whenever weather permitted, from them. I completed the principal angles remaining at Phakwadol T.S. and one angle at Noe Alí T.S. by the end of March. During April, I completed the principal observations at Noe Alí T.S. and Sintamunigarh T.S. and took secondary observations at Gauriságar Temple S., selected and built Gohaingáon P.S. and observed from it the Revenue Survey station and 3 points in the civil station.

(8.) Sibságar has been fixed by direct triangulation but the values are for the present dependent on a base-line measured in the station. These values will be corrected in the ensuing season, when the principal side Gauriságar to Gohaingáon P.S. has been directly obtained.

(9.) By the 24th April the low ground was all under water from the continuous heavy rain, and I closed work and marched to Dikú Mukh, and left by steamer on the 30th on return to recess quarters.

(10.) Mr. Harris left Shillong on the 20th October, and marched to Gowhatty. He was employed in entertaining Khlassies, masons &c. for his establishment and in looking after repairs of tents &c. during his stay there. He left by steamer on the 8th and arrived at Nigrí Ting on the 14th November, where he commenced work by renewing the scaffolding at that station and sending men and materials across the Brahmaputra river. By the end of December he had completed and built the pillars at Rodongá and Belagurí and the masonry portion of that at Phakwadol.

(11.) Mr. Harris had 3 parties at work. By the end of March he had completed and built all the pillar and post stations that had been allotted to him. His progress was slow, from his inability to visit and superintend the different parties at work owing to repeated attacks of fever and enlargement of the spleen. He was to have selected and built Borghup station, and cleared the ray from Bor-Alí to Gauriságar, but was so prostrated by illness that he was at last unable to undertake any work and had therefore to retire from the field in the beginning of April.

(12.) I had repeatedly desired Mr. Harris to obtain a medical certificate and retire, but he was anxious to push on the work and advance the progress of the Survey, and continued in the field longer than advisable.

(13.) Mr. Harris returned to recess quarters at Shillong on the 24th April. His constitution however was quite impaired, and he suffered from repeated attacks of fever and dysentery, and died on the 12th May. The Department has lost in him a very useful and valuable member.

(14.) Mr. O'Sullivan arrived at Gowhatty on the 30th October and soon after completed all his arrangements for the field. While waiting for the steamer he visited Mairangká principal station to take secondary observations to peaks, but was unable to do any work because of the unfavourable state of the weather.

(15.) Mr. O'Sullivan left on the 8th November and met his establishment at Nigrí Ting on the 15th and commenced work at once. By the end of the month he had cut and cleared 2 final rays, selected a station on the right bank, and taken a large number of horizontal and vertical angles at Nigrí Ting. In December he carried 5 trial and cut 5 final rays, selected 2 stations and took some secondary observations from Belagurí and Rodongá on the Majhili.

(16.) At Belagurí Mr. O'Sullivan tried what is known as a post station, and found it succeed remarkably well. These stations consist of three stout logs buried in the ground, and carefully braced together. They have been used at Belagurí, Majhulia, Bor-Chaprí No. 2, Túramúra, Raunápukrí, Soathol and Bor-Alí, and from the rapidity with which they can be constructed have helped materially to advance the Survey. The stations are denoted by the usual dot and circle engraved on a large rock imbedded in the ground, or on a slab let into a masonry pillar 2½ to 3 feet in diameter, and 1 to 2 feet in height.

(17.) The south flank stations were all selected by Mr. O'Sullivan during the previous season on the left bank of the Brahmaputra. I have visited them all, and am able to state that better selections could not have been made. Mr. O'Sullivan was therefore employed to select stations on the north flank in connection with these. To avoid the frequent crossing of the river and to save time, he was directed to select and build the stations required on the right bank, to carry and cut the trial and final rays, and also to take the principal observations with a 12-inch theodolite.

Mr. O'Sullivan has ably and energetically executed the instructions given him, and the following is his out-turn of work :

Miles of trial and final rays cut	180
No. of stations selected	6
Do. do. built	2
Do. principal angles observed	10
Do. do. stations at which secondary observations were taken	7

(18.) Mr. Hughes commenced work in renewing and repairing the scaffolding and pillars at Madaigáon T.S. and Nikorí Chaprí T.S. He was then employed in building the pillar and scaffolding at Bor Bhiti, and in collecting materials for building at Noe Alí and Phakwadol up to the end of December.

(19.) Mr. Hughes was afterwards employed in carrying and cutting rays for the rest of the season, both on the north and south banks of the Brahmaputra, occasionally under Mr. O'Sullivan, but latterly entirely by himself. He has shown zeal and energy in carrying out his duties, and is becoming a good Surveyor. His out-turn of work during the season comprises—

Miles of trial and final rays cut	48
No. of stations selected	1
Ditto. built	2
In conjunction with Mr. O'Sullivan	
Miles of trial and final rays cut	31
No. of stations built	2

(20.) The triangulation has been carried a direct distance of 46·5 miles ; a further advance might have been made had Mr. Harris continued in health. This extent of triangulation is in excess of that of the preceding season, and is due to there having been a good number of stations in advance on one flank. No rays had been carried but the sites were selected after reconnoisance on isolated mounds, old roads and embankments. The rays were carried and cut last field season.

(21.) The country traversed is generally low and subject to inundations. On the north bank, on the Majhuli island, the forest was heavy and the reed jungle very thick, which caused considerable delay in carrying rays through. On the south side the country was more open, large open low grass plains being met with, which very much facilitated ray cutting. These plains are called *Pathars* and are grazing grounds for cattle during the cold weather, being submerged during the rains. Numerous villages also exist both to the north and south of the country over which the triangulation was carried. This tract is one of the healthiest in the Sibságar District. From Noe Alí T.S. to Dibrúgarh, the country again gets very unhealthy from the heavy jungle on both sides of the river, and swamps, for which reason probably scarcely any villages are found except a very long way from the river, and hence the absence of ferries also, between Salmárra Ghát and Dibrúgarh.

(22.) The weather throughout has been somewhat unfavourable. At the commencement of the season, owing to the early cessation of the rains, the atmosphere was very thick and prevented a good view being obtained of the peaks, while the heavy fogs also interfered with the observations being obtained at proper times. At the end of December rain set in, and the season was an unusually wet one.* The ground was thoroughly saturated with moisture, and much inconvenience and sickness resulted from pitching on damp ground. By the 24th April all the low ground was quite under water, in some places to a depth of 3 feet; ray cutting had therefore to be given up and the work closed.

(23.) There was a large percentage of sick in each camp during the past season, but only 2 deaths took place in the field. Every member of the establishment however has suffered more or less from the unhealthiness which prevailed towards the end of the season; several have scarcely yet recovered from the effects.

(24.) Every assistance has been afforded to the Survey party by the Deputy Commissioner of Sibságar ; a little inconvenience was experienced from the absence of some Mauzadárs, who were reported to, and dealt with by, the district officers at once.

(25.) In March Captain Samuells the officer in charge of the Revenue Survey party requested me to make a connection with the initial points of his Survey at Jeypore, south-east of Dibrúgarh. The only means of effecting this, was by carrying a Secondary Triangulation along the low hills, starting from the side Sintamunigarh to Gauriságar of the Assam Valley Triangulation. I applied to the Deputy Commissioner for permission, and sent him a rough chart shewing how far into the Lotha Nága territory it would be necessary to penetrate. My letter and chart were submitted to the Chief Commissioner, who desired that every assistance should be given me for the work, and that the District Superintendent of Police should be directed to accompany the party. The reply was however received too late for the work to be undertaken last season; the country at the foot of the hills was represented to be very dangerous from the malaria, and owing to the sickness in the camps, I was unable to get up a party for the work; besides the observations had not advanced sufficiently to give the required data.

* Rain fell on 83 days or nights between 30th December 1873 and 30th April 1874.

Extract from the Narrative Report—dated 1st September 1874—of Captain T. T. CARTER, R.E., Officiating Deputy Superintendent 2nd Grade, in charge of the Brahmaputra Series.

The Native Establishment of the Brahmaputra Series had been ordered to rejoin at Bogra on the 1st of November, and accordingly Mr. Clarke, as senior assistant in the party, was directed to arrive there by that date taking with him Mr. Collins who had just joined the department; I myself arrived at Calcutta on the 1st of November and after taking over charge of the 24-inch Theodolite from the Mathematical Instrument Depôt Calcutta and making other arrangements proceeded on the 4th November to join my camp at Bogra.

By the 10th November the whole party had collected.

Since the previous field season the staff of the party had entirely changed. Mr. A. W. Donnelly, Surveyor 2nd Grade, had succumbed during the recess to an affection of the liver, probably of long standing though doubtless aggravated by the trying work of the previous field season. Mr. C. J. Neuville, Surveyor 2nd Grade, was considered by the medical officer of the department as unfit for work in Lower Bengal and Mr. Healy, Assistant Surveyor 4th Grade, had resigned. Mr. L. H. Clarke, Surveyor 2nd Grade, an officer of long standing in the department and whose services were for disposal on the completion of the Biláspúr Series and Mr. D. Collins, who had just joined the department, were the new staff.

After the usual preliminaries had been settled Mr. Clarke was deputed on the 14th of November to proceed to the tower station of Kánchipára and erect the scaffolding there for the observatory tent, on completion of which he was to proceed to the tower stations of Káshdoho, Boreil, Narsingbanj, Gobindpur and Alangjáui in turn, clearing the rays to be observed from the same and erecting the bamboo scaffoldings for the observatory tent, and at the same time to fix by traverse any pakka buildings or revenue survey marks within a radius of 4 miles round these stations, and failing these, the háts, that is, places where the bazar or rather market is held once or twice a week; these háts have been held in the same places for years, their locality is seldom changed and they are generally the site of some fine old Banyan or other tree which affords protection from heat and rain to buyers and sellers; so that their position when fixed would probably approximate closely to that shown in the revenue survey maps of the district. I had previously addressed the Superintendent of Revenue Surveys, Lower Circle, as to whether there were any revenue survey pillars or other marks which could be connected with the operations of the G. T. Survey in that portion of the Rungpore district through which our line of triangulation lay; a set of survey maps of the Rungpore district on scale of 1 mile to the inch was forwarded but no descriptions of stations were forthcoming; however 23 points, 8 of which were temples and 15 háts or market places as shown on the revenue survey maps were fixed in the vicinity of the tower stations named, and a mark has been left in each hát for future reference, vide description of traversed points, season 1873-74.

Having despatched Mr. Clarke on this work on the 14th of November, I left Bogra in company with Mr. Collins on the 17th, arriving at Kánchipára tower station on the 20th: the machan or scaffolding of bamboos, was ready for the observatory tent and the instrument set up on the 24th. It was the 4th of December before observations were completed owing to haze and clouds which continued during the whole of the first week; this combined with a bad form of fever which had carried off two of the heliotropers, prostrated the native doctor, my own servants and several of the men, and in some parts of the Bogra district was almost an epidemic, was not a promising commencement of the field season; besides which the series lay, on its western flank, in the Rungpore district where already the price of rice was high and it was most desirable to expedite the work and complete the series before any real scarcity came on, which was to be anticipated and did occur later in the season. The district of Goálpárá too, in which lay the hill stations on the eastern flank of the series, is none of the healthiest; water is scarce in the hills and the previous year the men employed in building the platform stations had been laid up with fever to a man, though they were clear of the district by the 1st of April; the rays too on the closing side were long, the side Rangira H.S. to Sámding H.S. being over 21 miles, that from Singimári H.S. to Alangjáui T.S. about 20 miles, and the difficulties I had in seeing my signals the previous season with sides never over 12 miles told me what to expect from these long sides when the inhabitants began burning the bamboo jungle on the low Gáro hills about the middle of March, and unless therefore the series was finished early in March there was the chance of its not being completed during this season, as delays of 6 weeks have been known to occur before now in similar ground and for similar reasons. It was therefore a hard and anxious time from the day I began work to the day I finished, the 6th of March, and though the field season was short it was a particularly trying one working as it were against time.

After completing observations at Kánchipára T.S., they were continued at the tower
stations as per margin. It was now necessary to cross over in-
to the Goálpárá district and observe from the hill stations, my
object being to complete the work there during the months of
January and February (the two healthiest) and then cross back again and complete observations
at the tower stations on the west flank of the series.

Káshdoho T.S. Dec. 5th to Dec. 11th
Boroil T.S. Dec. 12th to Dec. 19th

The hill stations were taken up and completed in the order as shown in the margin. On
the whole the weather was favorable with the exception that
from the 4th to the 13th of January, at Rangira H.S., not a
single observation was taken owing to a dense haze which
was not dispersed till heavy rain fell on the night of the 13th
of January. The delay at Singimári was owing to the ray to
Alangjáni being obstructed, which was not found out till I proceeded to take observations.

Gáropára H.S. Dec. 20th to Dec. 26th
Peskárbhita H.S. Dec 27th to Jan. 2nd
Rangira H.S. Jan. 3rd to Jan. 16th
Singimári H.S. Jan. 17th to Feb. 1st
Sámding H.S. Feb. 2nd to Feb. 5th

On completion of observations at Sámding H.S., they were taken up at the tower stations
as per margin (an azimuth being observed at Alangjáni T.S.)
and on the 6th of March the junction was completed with the
Assam Longitudinal Series.

Alangjáni T.S. Feb. 7th to Feb. 19th
Gobindpur T.S. Feb. 20th to Feb. 26th
Narsingbanj T.S. Feb. 27th to Mar. 6th

The result of the connection shows an error of 4·4 inches per mile in the side of junction Alangjáni T.S. to Sámding H.S. : though this is large, yet the elements of Latitude, Longitude and Azimuth, as deduced from both series, approximate very closely, and it does not appear to me that the agreement of the linear value of the common side is a severer test than the
agreement of Latitude, Longitude and especially of the Azimuth at the terminal stations.

The positions of the two stations as obtained from each series are as follows :—

		By Brahmaputra Series.	By Assam Longitudinal Series.
Alangjáni	T.S.	Lat. 25° 59' 7"·817	25° 59' 7"·648
		Long. 89 48 6 ·029	89 48 6 ·818
		Azmth. 293 0 47 ·700	293 0 46 ·225
		Log. distance in feet, 4·9962011	4·9962313
		Height in feet 96	feet. 102
Sámding	H.S.	Lat. 25° 59' 42·"000	25° 59' 42·"801
		Long. 90 4 45· 719	90 4 45· 979
		Azmth. 113 8 4· 608	113 8 3· 161
		Height in feet 368	feet. 367

I will now proceed to report on the work of the assistants attached to the party.

Mr. L. H. Clarke, Surveyor 2nd Grade, completed the building of the bamboo scaffolding for the 6 tower stations on the western flank of the series by the 1st of February; he had
also at the same time connected, with a rigorous theodolite and chain traverse, 8 paka buildings
and 15 háts or bazars in the vicinity of the same, marking each station of the traverse with
two mark bricks and a mound of earth raised above them, the terminal station of each traverse (where it was not a paka building) was subsequently marked by a masonry pillar. Mr.
Clarke had also to carry a ray trace between the tower stations of Gobindpur and Narsingbanj
T.S. and Alangjáni T.S., and clear the final ray between the same. Subsequently, from the
1st of February till the 2nd of April, he was engaged in the Goálpárá district building the protecting pillars over the hill stations, in accordance with Departmental Order No. 1 of the 15th
of January 1866, and also on secondary triangulation.

The secondary triangulation was executed in the first place to lay down points for the
Revenue Survey of the Goálpárá district, a narrow strip of which extends from the vicinity of
the hill station of Sámding, south between the Gáro Hills and left bank of the Brahmaputra
river till it touches the Meymensing district; the survey of this portion of the Goálpárá district
as well as the laying down of a definite boundary line between it and the Gáro hills will, I am
led to believe, be taken up in the ensuing cold weather, and the points laid down by Mr. Clarke
will I hope, be of great service to the officers employed thereon; of these points 11 are at the
foot of the hills of which 5 are masonry buildings (3 temples, 1 old indigo factory, and 1 well)
and of the others 6 are well known háts, kachahrís, or Police Stations at the foot of the hills,
the remaining 14 points are on the lower spurs of the Gáro hills. The stations at the foot of
the hills have been marked by paka masonry pillars and from the descriptions given by Mr.
Clarke should be easily recognized.

In executing the secondary triangulation a connection was made with the Gáro Hill
Survey, executed by Lieutenant Woodthorpe R.E. in the season 1872-73, the stations of Sámding, Rangira, Borchi and Shekarpára being common to both works.

Mr. Clarke's total out-turn of work during the season was as follows and I think deserving
of commendation.

No. of miles of theodolite traverse fixing 8 masonry buildings and 15 hâts or market places 46
" " ray trace traverse and ray clearing 26
" machans erected at the tower stations for the observatory tent .. 6
" secondary stations visited 11
" secondary points fixed 25
" " heights " 23
" hill stations protected in accordance with Departmental Order No. 1 of 1866 5
" platforms built for secondary stations 20

Mr. Collins, Assistant Surveyor 4th Grade, was appointed to this Department on the 6th of October and consequently was entirely new to the work. He was employed during the whole season as office recorder and in the current duties of the office. There were few opportunities for training him but he was instructed in the use of the 7 inch theodolite and after a short time he was able to compute out observations for time : he gives promise of turning out well with training. I have every reason to be pleased with his application.

It will hardly be necessary for me to enter into the physical aspect, cultivation, natural history &c., of the Gáro Hills, the whole of which have been traversed by Lieutenant Woodthorpe R.E. and fully described by that officer, vide the "General Report of the Topographical Surveys of India for the season 1872-73."

The portion of the Rungpore district through which our work lay this year was very populous; being higher than the country described in my last year's report, it was not so much cut up with bhils or swamps and consequently locomotion was easier. The rice crop having failed there was a certain amount of distress on the high land, on the low land the villagers had sown a considerable quantity of wheat as an intermediate crop before the "Aus" or early rice crop would come in June and July; the cases of distress met by myself were chiefly where the person had no means wherewith to buy and whose credit was bad.

In concluding this report I beg to record the assistance rendered by Captain Williamson the Deputy Commissioner of the Gáro Hills.

The health of the party was not good, it suffered a great deal from fever from which 5 men died.

In my last year's report I stated that I had not been able to inspect the tower stations built by Mr. Healy, Surveyor 4th Grade, or the platform stations built by Native Surveyor Narsing Dás, the former's work was very good, and the platform stations and isolated pillars erected by the latter were of very good workmanship, and considering the circumstances under which they were built he deserves much credit.

Extract from the Narrative Report—dated 13th July 1874—of Captain J. HILL, R.E., Officiating Deputy Superintendent 3rd Grade, in Charge Jodhpur Series.
....

(2.) Lieutenant Rogers having been granted furlough to Europe, I was ordered to Poona to relieve him, and received charge of the party from him there on the 28th October 1873. After opening out the axis of the 24-inch theodolite and cleaning it in my presence, and after giving me full information regarding the manipulation of the instrument, Lieutenant Rogers started for England, and the party proceeded to the field viâ Ahmedabad and Palee, and thence across country to Dugur H.S., where I commenced my observations on the 10th December.

(3.) The country from Dugur H.S. northwards, over which the series had to be carried, is a sandy desert. The sand hills are generally flat topped, low, and of about equal altitude, so that the advantages of a hilly country are lost, and short sides are unavoidable. When I commenced my work the weather was good for observing; but unfortunately it did not long remain so; and the season on the whole was, as regards weather, decidedly unfavorable. There was a great deal of cloud and mist, without rain; and except at the commencement of the field season the lamps were almost useless as signals. I closed work on the 3rd April, and during the period of my observations, which was a little less than four months, I find that by adding up the various mornings, afternoons and evenings when work was stopped by bad weather or bad signals, the days so lost amount to the large number of thirty-four. At one station alone I was detained eleven days. Having finished my observations on the date above mentioned, I marched southwards, closing with the help of Messrs. Price and Torrens the stations at which I had worked during the season, and arrived at Mount Aboo on the last day of April.

(6.) The following is a general statement of the season's work:—Observations were taken at 21 Principal Stations, forming 3 hexagons and 2 quadrilaterals, which embrace an area of 1,552 square miles and extend a distance of 90 miles along the meridian. An azimuth was observed at Jambo H.S., in Lat. 27° 16', to two circumpolar stars. The approximate series was extended 102 miles. The positions of the cities of Jodhpúr and Jesalmer, of the towns of Phalaudi and Pokran and of several villages were fixed. The area of secondary and minor triangulation external to the principal series was 1,667 square miles.

General Statement of Season's Work.

(8.) Mr. Price was in charge of the Approximate Series, and extended it well into Bikanír through a very desolate and arid tract. He had very great difficulty in selecting sites for stations and was often obliged to contract the sides of his triangles until they approached the minimum limit allowable. To build towers in such a country, destitute as it is of lime and almost destitute of water and of labour, would swallow up so much money and time that it would only be permissible as a last resource. Mr. Price worked hard and intelligently : the amount of his work, especially when the difficulties he had to overcome are considered, is I think very creditable to him.

Mr. W. O. Price.

(9.) Mr. Torrens was employed on Minor Triangulation. He has determined the positions of Jodhpúr, Jesalmer, Pokran, and of several villages, temples and other intersected points. He has worked very satisfactorily and energetically and has a good out-turn to show for his season's work.

Mr. C. P. Torrens.

(10.) It may be as well for me to explain my reasons for directing Mr. Torrens to fix the position of Jesalmer, as that city lies nearer to the future series which will be carried along the meridian of 70° than to the Jodhpúr Series. The position of the town of Pokran which lies in about the latitude of Jesalmer, had to be determined from the Jodhpúr Series. The distance from Pokran westwards to Jesalmer is about the same as from Jesalmer on to the meridian of 70°. The strip of country between Pokran and Jesalmer is exceptionally populous for that part of the desert: it has the advantage of being hilly and adapted for triangulation, and a minor series carried over it would necessarily fix several useful points, and could be conducted without much trouble or expense. On the other hand, from Jesalmer westward to the meridian of 70° there is by all accounts nothing but an uninhabited wilderness of the most desolate kind. Mr. Torrens verified his triangulation by observing an azimuth in the vicinity of Jesalmer.

(11.) Mr. Oldham acted as my recorder and office assistant during the field season, and in both capacities rendered me very efficient assistance. After my observations were completed, and while I was closing stations he made a recorded plane-table traverse of that portion of the Jodhpúr and Jesalmer boundary which crosses the series. The boundary unfortunately is a disputed one, so Mr. Oldham could only carry his traverse along what seemed to him the most probable line in the strip of country claimed by both States. This piece of work will enable me to show an approximate boundary on my Preliminary Chart.

Mr. W. Oldham.

(12.) With the exception of the approximate work, which extended into Bikanír, the field operations of the season were confined to the states of Jodhpúr and Jesalmer. In the Jodhpúr desert the triangulation traversed a sandy country, but towards the close of the season the series entered a part of Jesalmer where the ground is hard and strewn with dark shining stones. The reflection from these stones is sometimes like the reflection from water, and for this reason vertical observations to certain of the heliotropes gave a good deal of trouble. Mirage was frequently observable in the mornings; but, except in one or two instances, did not retard my work.

General Observations on the Desert.

(13.) All over the country triangulated, and especially in Jesalmer, water is scarce and in general brackish. In many cases, according to the statement of the people, well water which is drinkable in the cold season becomes actually poisonous in the hot weather. The villages and wells are few and far between. The former generally consist of a collection of circular thatched wigwams, the inhabitants of which are a primitive, dirty and good-humoured people, given, however, to highway robbery and other forms of thieving. The wells are very deep. I measured one at the village of Akhadna near Nok in Jesalmer (said by the people to be 80 *purush* in depth) which is 5 feet in diameter and 374 feet deep. The water arrived at after such a laborious excavation was unfortunately bitter and quite unfit for use. The deepest well I have seen is at the village of Bákri in Jodhpúr. It has been bored through rock and I found it to be 5 feet 4 inches in diameter, and 450 feet in depth. Its water is good, and I know of no other well so deep in Rajpootana.

(14.) A remarkable thing is that one sees herds of antelope living in districts which are totally without water, except what is drawn from deep wells or village tanks. The people affirm that these animals in common with the rats, which exist in myriads in the sand hills, never drink.

(15.) It is at first strange to come across villages here and there in a wilderness which seems fitted to produce nothing but stunted, thinly-scattered bushes and coarse grass. Wheat has to be imported from Sindh; but near the villages millet *(jawári)*, and Indian corn *(bájra)* may sometimes be seen, and in a few favoured localities a little barley. The people also collect a kind of grass (which they call *bhrút*), from which they obtain flour. The grain of this grass is about the size of a pin's head, and is enclosed in a prickly husk which causes a great deal of discomfort to both man and beast, as it sticks in the clothes of the former and the hair of the latter and is very difficult to get rid of. Although most of the villages in the vicinity of the season's operations are sufficiently wretched looking, several seemed to be fairly flourishing and are presided over by substantial Thákurs.

(16.) The town of Phalaudi is an interesting place to come across in such a desert country.

Phalaudi. The stone tracery of the houses in its principal streets is very beautiful, and it possesses a large and well built fort, the walls of which are over 40 feet high. This fort has a small garrison and its armament consists of a few antiquated field pieces which seemed quite unserviceable from rust and general neglect: in the centre of it there is a deep and capacious reservoir for water. The fort is commanded, but at a distance of 6,600 yards, by the Ekka hill, on which one of my stations is situated. Mr. Torrens has furnished notes (which I append) on the country over which he carried his Minor Triangulation. These notes include notices of the cities of Jodhpúr and Jesalmer and of the town of Pokran.

(17.) The natural productions of the part of the desert where my work lay are very few. There are salt works on the boundary between Jodhpúr and Jesalmer near the village of Agar. Near Phalaudi fuller's earth is obtained, and at a place in the same vicinity a natural cement is found which is much prized, and used in the best class of buildings. The chief trade seems to be in sheep and salt. The *banjáras* who bring corn from Sindh load their bullocks for the return journey with salt; they also carry away loads of the fuller's earth just mentioned. The most useful animal in the desert, the camel, here seems to be little if at all in the market. The people breed their own camels and keep them for their own use. Good, serviceable blankets, which are made in every village, also seem to be kept for home use, and are not a general article of sale.

(18.) The desert is very heartily dreaded by the people of the surrounding districts, probably on account of its desolate appearance, the frequency

Health of the Party. of its famines, and the distress and disease that are generally prevalent among the poorest classes of its inhabitants, owing to the miserable food and unwholesome water on which they are compelled to subsist. Such causes of disease occurred among the native establishment; but the party, on the whole, enjoyed excellent health. In order, however, to attain this result great care had to be taken to supply the men with good food and water, the latter often having to be brought on camels from very remote wells. The coolness of the weather, which was probably due to the great amount of cloud and mist, may also have contributed to the healthiness of the party.

(19.) In conclusion, it only remains for me to acknowledge gratefully the assistance given by the Jodhpúr, Jesalmer and Bikanír Durbars to myself

Conclusion. and my assistants. The Jodhpúr and Jesalmer Durbars furnished me with guards of sepoys and sowars, and the former sent an excellent vakeel with me who was of the greatest service to me all through the season. Mr. Price reported to me that every help was given to him in Bikanír, and Mr. Torrens bore testimony to the cordial assistance he received while working in Jesalmer. Without such assistance progress in such a region would have been almost an impossibility; but with it, all trouble was removed except what was inseparable from the work itself.

Notes by Mr. C. P. Torrens.

The city of Jodhpúr lies at the foot of the hill on which the fort is situated, and at its southern side; the greatest length from north to south is about

Jodhpúr City and Fort. 2½ miles, and the greatest breadth ¾ of a mile. It is closed in on the north side by the fort, and on the east, south, and west by a high wall, capable of mounting guns, having six gateways. It is a good specimen of a native city and is kept fairly clean; there are many wells, and three tanks, one of the latter, an artificial one (only completed last year) is very fine and large, its bed and sides being of "paká" masonry.

The fort is built on a hill, the highest in the neighbourhood, rising 420 feet above the surrounding country. There are two roads leading up to the fort, which unite a few yards distant from the gateway, and turn a sharp corner before reaching the gate; both roads are well protected by guns; besides this there are two other gates to be passed before the fort is gained, the first a small yet strong one in a narrow pass between two rocks, and the second a large one approached by a steep ascent, well commanded by guns, and like the outer one made difficult by being placed round a corner. Access to the fort from any other direction would be impossible, as the sides are sheer precipices of from two to three hundred feet. The country below is commanded on all sides by the guns of the fort. There is a good sized tank in the fort.

The city of Jesalmer is much smaller than Jodhpúr, its reported number of inhabitants

Jesalmer City and Fort.   being 10,000; but from all I could see and hear, the place was once in a far more flourishing state, and the ruins of its former greatness are yet to be seen. The water supply for the city is obtained from an adjoining lake, and when this fails, which is generally the case early in June, good water has to be brought from the small village of Kisan Ghát which is about 3 miles distant. There are numerous wells in the city but the water is not good. The city used to be closed in by a rampart, now useless, as the wall is rapidly crumbling to pieces, and has fallen in in many places.

The fort, once strong, is now in a dilapidated state and would ill stand an assault; it contains no tank but many wells. The Jain temples in the fort are very fine, the carving in stone being exquisite; in fact this may be said of most of the houses in the city, the doors, windows, and walls having more or less carving about them. The greater number of the inhabitants, who reside within the walls of the fort, consist chiefly of a mixture of Bháti Rajpoots and Jains, and are as a rule great opium eaters.

The town of Pokran is on low ground, closed in by hills to the north, south, and west;

Pokran.   and high ground to the east. Water is very plentiful in the neighbourhood, and very good; the town possesses three tanks, fine large ones, reported to contain water throughout the year; besides these there are many wells. There is a small fort in the town well built, and strong in appearance; but quite commanded by the adjacent hills.

Close to the town is a large salt marsh about 5 or 6 miles in diameter, into which the drainage of the surrounding hills finds its way during the rains. From the water of this marsh as also from that of another somewhat larger in dimensions, near the village of Lowah (8 miles S.E.) a small quantity of salt is reported to bo obtained.

The entire tract of country through which the Jesalmer Minor Series passes, with the

Nature of Country.   exception of a few square miles of fairly cultivated ground round Pokran and Jesalmer, is nothing but an arid sand waste, consisting of low sand hills covered with scanty brush-wood. Villages, small and few in number in the eastern portion, get yet smaller and fewer as you proceed west. Vegetation also decreases rapidly, and at 15 or 20 miles west of Pokran, even the *bhrút* grass refuses to grow; its place being taken by a kind of shrub (peculiar to the desert) called by the natives *lona*; the seed of which is collected after the rains and stored away for the year's consumption; it is far inferior to the grain of the *bhrút*, and is very brackish; so much so that it is only eatable after being well washed in fresh water, and even then, only when mixed with twice its quantity of good flour. From the appearance of the grain, and from what I could learn from the natives, there is not much nutriment to be derived from it; and it appears to be used but to increase the quantity of food taken by each individual. Most of the villages have small ponds in which the rain water collects, in a good season sufficient to last for 7 or 8 months, but as a rule, owing to the scanty fall of rain, the supply fails in from 4 to 6 months; the villagers then have to get water from long distances (16 to 18 miles). I have also been informed that some of the poorer classes who cannot afford to get the water from a distance, drink the brackish water (a well or two of which every village possesses) mixing with it a little *dahi* (curds) the acidity of which in a measure counteracts the brackishness of the water. The average depth of wells is about 250 feet, and the water in all more or less brackish, good fresh water having been procurable but twice in the series, at Pokran and Jesalmer.

Extract from the Narrative Report—dated 4th August 1874—of W. C. ROSSENRODE Esq., Deputy Superintendent 3rd Grade, in Charge Eastern Frontier Series.

(2.) In compliance with your request I proceeded to your Head Quarters, after completing the Southern Section of the Biláspur Meridional Series G. T. Survey of India, with the party attached thereto.

(3.) All the Principal computations of the above series were brought up at your Head Quarters, and a good portion of the Secondary work had been completed when I closed office and left for Burma, to resume the field operations of the Eastern Frontier Series.

(4.) Agreeably to instructions, I left your Head Quarters; and proceeded to Chunar, took charge of all the Government property appertaining to the Sambalpur Series, deposited there, and then started by rail to Calcutta.

(5.) I arranged for the passage of the men and the transport of the Government property by steamer, and sent them under charge of Mr. Henry Beverley. I followed by the next steamer, and on my arrival was informed that cholera had broken out among the Native Establishment, that 2 men had already succumbed, and a third man had been attacked that very morning and was immediately removed into the Rangoon Hospital. He died there that same night. The men were then removed into tents some distance from their former locality, and no fresh cases occurred.

(6.) On arriving at Rangoon I made enquiries for the 10 elephants which were, at your request, to be purchased in the Province, for the use of the party, and heard that they were at Moulmein and that orders had been issued directing them to be sent on to Rangoon to join me. The elephants reached Rangoon on the 17th, and on the 18th November they were made over to me.

(7.) These animals had never been laden. They were shy and timid of strangers, and were accustomed to the Burmese words of command, and could only be controlled by the men of the Province. Acting on the Chief Commissioner's suggestions, I had brought drivers from Upper India for the elephants. These men had no control whatever over the animals; in fact, they could not approach them. The men who had driven them from Moulmein to Rangoon could not be induced to remain a few days with the elephants, until my men became used to the animals and learned the Burmese words of command, which the animals understood and obeyed. I now had no other alternative but to engage Burman mahouts at once. I succeeded in employing two men at 14 rupees each per mensem, and failing to obtain others, I wrote to Colonel Duncan, and he, through the Deputy Commissioner, sent me two others after I had left Rangoon. These men were employed by the Deputy Commissioner on 25 rupees each per mensem, and as these rates were preposterously high, I returned them to Rangoon the day that they arrived, adopting this precaution to avoid any intercourse between my men and them, for fear of the former becoming discontented.

(8.) Being convinced that the new elephants would be useless to me for some months, I applied for and obtained the consent of the General commanding in British Burma, to my being supplied with five Commissariat elephants on hire for a couple of months until the cattle attached to the party became more tractable and were trained to carry loads.

(9.) With the Commissariat elephants and country carts, I was able to leave Rangoon on the 25th November, a week after the newly purchased elephants had joined me from Moulmein. During this week their pads and saddles were made, the former at the Rangoon Jail, and the latter by the elephant attendants. The new elephants carried nothing. For a month or more they were a source of great anxiety to me. They were constantly throwing their drivers and bolting into the forest, and were recaptured at much expense, after long intervals. Two men were severely hurt from falls, one died about a month after, and the other still complains of pains in his back from the injuries he received six months ago.

(10.) The grand trunk road from Rangoon to Prome, the only road made road in the Province, brought me to the West End of the Base-line. Here the carts were discharged, as they could not proceed further, owing to the country being still too wet. Carts are used in the interior in the dry weather, only from the middle of January to the end of April. The jungle requires to be cleared annually from the cart-track, and fallen trees, and other obstructions are not removed but avoided by fresh clearances of the jungle : there are no made roads in the interior. The forest is cleared to the extent of 5 or 6 feet in width, the most level country is selected and the carts soon make tracks and wind, turn and twist through this cut path, avoiding ravines, swamps, and all such impediments which wheeled conveyances are unable to surmount. These cart-tracks are made from village to village, and are most circuitous and tiresome.

(11.) I arrived at my first station, the West End of the Base-line, on the 4th December. After inspecting the station and arranging for coolies for Mr. Mitchell, I left him with instructions to reclear the ray to Kedau Pillar Station, and proceeded with Mr. Clancey to the East End Station of the Base-line, arranged for coolies, and started Mr. Clancey on the ray from it to Kedau Pillar Station. I personally took up the two rays from the East End Base to Keingbingyee and Tongtalung Pillar Stations, and commenced the construction of the wooden scaffolding for the observatory tent and the observer at the latter station, as the ray to it approached completion. The next scaffolding I took up was Kedau, and I then proceeded to Keingbingyee, and completed the scaffolding and the ray to that station from the East End and began my final observations on the 1st January 1874.

(12.) Messrs. Mitchell and Clancey after completing their respective rays, took up the ray Kedau to Tongtalung, one at each end. I ordered Mr. Clancey to join me at Keingbingyee to record in the Observatory, and Mr. Mitchell continued the ray and had it ready when I reached Kedau Pillar Station, after completing my observations at Keingbingyee Station.

(13.) The paddy crop was uncut, the harvest had just commenced when I took up the ray cutting. Coolies were obtained with difficulty, but the coolie contractors, who had worked with me when I was before in Burma, hearing of my arrival, offered their services, and I gladly employed them on the same terms as they were formerly paid on ray clearing. These contractors received 8 annas each per diem for superintending the cutters they had provided, and an additional anna for every man they supplied. I made over one contractor and his men to Mr. Mitchell, another to Mr. Clancey, and retained two others myself. As it was the interest of each contractor to provide as many men as he could, receiving as he did an anna for each man, he supplied the full complement, and no delays occurred in clearing the rays and constructing scaffoldings surrounding the pillar stations. The coolies were paid 8 annas each per diem, and came readily so long as the rays were near their villages; but, although I tried my utmost to induce the contractors to accompany me to the hills, to clear the roads to the stations for conveying the theodolite and for the baggage elephants, I could not tempt them to undertake the cutting of these roads.

(14.) The Burmans are convinced that the block, extending over 40 miles of direct distance, of the Pegu Yoma hills is exceedingly unhealthy. They believe that the men of the plains who work on the hills, are sure to contract fever or lay in the germs of serious diseases. Captain Alexander, the Assistant Commissioner of the Tharrawaddy district, in which I was working, says in his letter to me, dated the 5th December 1873, "I could not send you a man "I could trust on 12 Rs. a month to act as peon, he would only be a common coolie if he did go "into the hills &c. away from his friends and exposed to fever &c. unless he was remunerated "highly.

"I know by experience that in the villages away from the road and east of it, the people "have nothing in the shape of provisions for sale, they only grow and buy sufficient for their "own consumption."

(15.) From the above it will be seen, that Captain Alexander alludes to this unhealthi-ness, and from the great sickness in camp this season I found it to be the case, for there were a greater number of sick when working on the hills than in the plains.

(16.) Owing to the contractors and their coolies refusing to accompany me, much delay was experienced in cutting the roads to the hill stations for the elephants and theodolite, and especially for the former, which required not only the overhanging branches to be removed, but all overhead up to 15 feet in height to be cut.

(17.) Although the roads were taken in hand early in December, they were not ready when required in February. I and Mr. Clancey had to superintend the road cutters, and to hurry them on, followed by the elephants and baggage. The paths were difficult and very trying to the elephants, but with light loads they got on better than I expected. This hard work of carrying loads up and down hill for 8 and 10 consecutive hours daily, proved the best training school for the new elephants.

(18.) I am dependent entirely on my elephants in this series, and they have to do all the work; it is impossible to obtain the large number of men a survey party requires, to take up the baggage and tents to the hill stations when elephants cannot ascend them, when too steep or rocky. The cattle in such cases are taken as far as they can go, and the property is carried up in driblets by the establishment assisted by the few coolies I may succeed in procuring.

(19.) The elephants of the party have hard work, they are seldom idle, they are either carrying baggage or conveying provisions. The country is devoid of resources, and Surveyors have to exercise their ingenuity and forethought in conducting their operations. To expect assistance, to calculate upon it or to wait for it, ends only in disappointment, disaster and failure. The motto here holds good "every man for himself"; you must do, and be doing; you must work, and have all about you working; you can rely upon no aid or assistance. The free trade and free labor system prevails throughout the Province, and the inhabitants, having the option to work or not, drive the best bargains they can when their services are needed. The Officials are powerless, and recommend the employment of permanent bands of coolies on monthly pay.

(20.) The final operations progressed rapidly during the favorable weather, until the 9th March, when the haze set in and the hills were fired. The atmosphere then became so impregnated with the haze and smoke, that nothing whatever could be seen; even hills 4 and 5 miles distant were entirely obscured. I could not leave the station I was then at until the beginning of May, when partial showers cleared the atmosphere and enabled me to complete the observations. I then proceeded to Myaybengkyo, where the monsoon broke on us with such violence on the 11th May, that during partial breaks I was able to obtain my angles to the back stations only.

(21.) One of the forward stations, The-ye-khu, was so elevated, about 5,000 feet, that it was generally capped with clouds or was enveloped in mist; the observations to it could not be taken, as neither day nor night signals were seen continuously for 15 minutes. I was under these circumstances compelled to close work, and return to recess quarters at Moulmein.

(22.) I am glad I did close work, for I found the country daily getting more and more under water, from Shoaygheen to Moulmein. I marched with much inconvenience and difficulty, owing to the whole country being submerged, the depth of water varying from one to four feet, throughout each stage. From the day I closed work to the day the camp reached Moulmein, it rained daily; there were, certainly, breaks for a few hours every day, but for hours together we were never without rain. The signal-men who left their respective stations after me, were able only to rejoin at Moulmein, by engaging boats for the whole distance. Between Pegu and Martaban the country is one extensive swamp for seven months each year. Mr. Beverley found great difficulty in marching last year in the first week of December. He attempted to go across the swamp, but failing to do so retired to the high ground at the foot of the hills and then ascended Kaneindong and Myayabengkyo Hill Stations, and after selecting The-ye-khu and Kuladong, he found the route he had first taken practicable.

(23.) There was much difficulty this season, about collecting supplies at the different stations, owing to insufficiency of carriage. I had only one spare elephant for this purpose, I have already represented this to you, and I trust you will be pleased to sanction the 4 additional elephants I have applied for. With these 4 and the spare one already alluded to, I shall have 5 elephants for maturing my commissariat arrangements, and I shall be quite independent of the country, where carts are procured with difficulty at exorbitantly high rates; I had to pay 5 rupees a stage for a cart. The demands of the owners of carts must be complied with in this Province, as well as the demands of coolies and guides.

(24.) The season has been unusually sickly. I had an average of 18 sick in camp when I ascended the hills; there were 9 casualties in my camp, and one in Mr. Beverley's, and two men lost their sight. They suffered from ophthalmia, which owing to the intense heat, terminated in total blindness. One was attended by the Hospital Assistant of the party, and the other was sent to the Shoaygheen Hospital, but both cases proving unsuccessful I was obliged to send the men to their respective homes, paying their passage and the passage of a third man to see them safe to their respective villages.

(25.) The work accomplished this season has been the completion of the double figure containing the Base-line. Owing to the long sides and adverse weather, the out-turn has been small, but, I trust I shall be more successful during the ensuing season.

(26.) Mr. Henry Beverley, Surveyor 1st Grade, has been engaged the whole season on approximate work. He had to visit two of the old stations, Kaneindong and Myayabengkyo; in the former station he found the upper mark and a portion of the pillar destroyed by wild elephants. He excavated the structure until he came upon the lower mark, and rebuilt the pier to its original height and secured it from being again destroyed by wild elephants, by digging a trench round it. At Myayabengkyo he found the pillar and platform totally destroyed: this was done by the Burmans from the plains or by the Kareus of the adjoining hills. Every stone was removed and flung to some distance from the station. A large deep pit was dug, with the intention of appropriating the treasure which they suspected was secreted there; finding none, they returned to their villages without being detected. Both Mr. Beverley and I instituted enquiries, no clue however could be obtained regarding the perpetrators of the mischief. A new station was constructed on the debris of the former, and as this station had not been connected with the back stations of the old work, it entailed no revision of angles.

(27.) Mr. Beverley next selected The-ye-khu and Kuladong Hill Stations, forming a quadrilateral, in order to break up the compound figure with several centres which was formerly selected. These new stations entailed the revision of the former work, and owing to bad weather and difficult ground, he did not progress at the rapid rate he usually advances the triangulation. Jungjungia Hill Station situated on a low undulating densely wooded range, extending over a great distance, caused considerable delay; he had to search for the highest spot by erecting several scaffolds on this deceptive undulating ground. His search extended for three weeks of daily labor, until Jungjungia H. S. was selected. The rays then required clearing, which for want of labor and the difficulty of removing the thorny bamboo jungle, interlaced and entwined together, added considerably to the delay. All the rays from the station were successfully cleared, but the one to Sittang proving impracticable after the completion of the ray trace, owing to the undulating hilly ground between the stations being about here and there very nearly the same elevation as the stations themselves. The ray was abandoned, Sittang station rejected, and Kúmbúngán, a station in the plains, fixed by the tedious process of ray tracing, and the rays from it to the connecting stations were cleared, but owing to the rains having set in he was unable to make arrangement for the materials for constructing the pillar, which will require a height of 15 feet.

(28.) In addition to the above, Mr. Beverley selected the stations of Suplitong, Chaiteo, Shoayouugbia, Chaideo and Kathabatong; of these the first three were visited, cleared and constructed in 1869-70, by Messrs. Connor and Bryson. Suplitong H. S. (formerly called

Monthamatong) pillar was dug up by villagers in search of treasure, and as the original site of the station could not be used, owing to the excavation, the new station has been constructed 5 feet from the old spot.

(29.) The pillar of Chaiteo Hill Station was also found to be tampered with; the upper mark-stone was removed, and the pillar partially destroyed by pilgrims, who frequent the pagodas and monasteries on the hill during the annual festivals. This station was rebuilt. Shoayoungbia Pillar was visited and found in good preservation. Chaideo H. S. was selected in lieu of Keylatha, and is on the eastern extremity of the same range. A large pagoda occupies the highest portion of Keylatha hill, and as no suitable site could be found for a station on its summit, Chaideo was substituted. The hill station of Kathabatong was selected and prepared. The following is the out-turn of approximate triangulation :—a quadrilateral, a compound figure and a tetragon; of these the two eastern are proposed stations, and have not been visited. The above figures number 10 stations, selected and prepared over a direct distance of 112 miles. Mr. Beverley's progress has been satisfactory.

(30.) Mr. J. W. Mitchell, Surveyor 4th Grade, joined me at Rangoon on the 6th November 1873, from the Madras Party. He accompanied me from Rangoon to the West End Base-line Station and took up the clearing of the ray from it to Kedau Pillar Station, which he completed on the 15th December. He then began the ray Kedau to Tongtalung. While he was thus engaged, he was taken ill with fever, and was completely prostrated by the severity of the attack; he continued at his post, treating himself, and on regaining health and strength after a fortnight's illness he personally attended to the ray, which during his illness, was continued by the head man of his detachment.

(31.) After completing the clearance of his portion of the ray, from Kedau to Tongtalung Pillar Station, and forming the junction with the remaining portion brought up by Mr. Clancey from the Tongtalung end, he joined my camp at Kedau Station on the 11th January 1874, and after receiving my instructions both written and verbal he left on the 13th January to begin his secondary triangulation, based upon a side of the principal operations to fix the important towns of Rangoon, Pegu and Henzada.

(33.) Mr. Mitchell's secondary series exhibits 11 stations, forming 13 triangles; of which, he has visited 9, the other two are cleared and marked but not visited, he was encamped in the vicinity and owing to weakness and bad state of health at the time, he was unable to ascend them.

(34.) Mr. Mitchell joined me at Moulmein, by steamer from Rangoon; he was still suffering in health. I hope with better health he will be able to shew a larger quantity of work next year after this season's experience in a difficult country.

(35.) Mr. J. C. Clancey, Assistant Surveyor 4th Grade, has been employed clearing rays during the early part of the season. He completed the entire ray from the East End Base-line Station to Kedau Pillar Station, and half the ray from Tongtalung to Kedau, Mr. Mitchell having cut the other half from the Kedau end. After the completion of the above rays, he joined me, and continued the whole season in camp, recording in the observatory and assisting generally in all office duties. He has learned the use of the 7-inch theodolite, and was instructed to observe the sun for time. He has been of great assistance to me in the observatory and office.

(36.) To make himself more efficient for this series, he devoted much of his leisure to acquiring the Burman language, and could read pretty well when he returned to recess quarters; as he is still continuing his studies, he will soon acquire as much knowledge of Burmese as is necessary for communicating personally with the inhabitants in their own language.

(37.) Mr. Clancey afforded satisfaction, and promises to become a valuable assistant.

Extract from the Narrative Report—dated 9th July 1874—of Lieutenant H. J. HARMAN, R.E., Officiating Assistant Superintendent 1st Grade, In charge No. 1 Extra Party.

(1.) The camp and natives of the party left Bangalore for Gútí in the Bellári Division, by march, on October 23rd 1873. Mr. O. V. Norris, Assistant Surveyor 2nd Grade and myself joined the camp on its arrival at Gútí travelling by rail from Bangalore.

Movements of party and its operations.

The main line of levels was opened on November 7th 1873 from a rock *in sitû* at Gútí on the Gútí-Bangalore high road; thence the line was carried through Bellári, Hospetta and Hampságram, across the Túngábadra River at Hesarúr to Gadak; then on by way of Behatti and Húblí (near Dhárwar) it was continued to Múndagod in North Kanara, from which place it was taken due west to Yellápur, and down the Aribail Ghát by the new cart road to the sea at the port of Kárwar, North Kanara District.

This main line was completed on May 10th 1874, and on May 12th tidal observations, for determining the mean sea level at Kárwar approximately, were commenced and were extended over a period of 5 days.

(2.) The season was throughout a hot one, for the work; instances of being able to read the staves at greater distances than 4 chains (88 yards) between 9 A. M. and 3·30 P. M. were rare: over the black soil in the Bellári District the weather was reputed unusually warm for that time of the year (Decr. and Jany.)

Weather and Health Statement.

We experienced many windy days, while working between Bellári and Dhárwar entailing extra labor and loss of time.

From November 7th 1873 to May 1874 work was stopped only on three occasions by rain; between May 1st and 6th we had storms of wind from the N.E. accompanied by torrents of rain; subsequently, and very fortunately, the weather held up fair until May 18th. Down the coast at places south of Kárwar, much rain fell during the month of May.

I am happy to say that the camp suffered but little from sickness during the 7 months it was out on the work; the season in North Kanara was considered a healthy one.

(3) For many stretches the whole line, water was. scarce, and this proved very annoying, as the camp had to be pitched in situations, remote from the favorable positions for carrying on the work. The 200 miles of country, from Bellári to Húblí is principally of black (cotton) soil, red soil and rock outcropping on the higher portions.

Nature of the country passed over.

Black soil is indescribably bad for Levelling work in every way; the red soil gives a good foundation for the instrument, and the air is always much steadier over it than over black soil, but peg driving becomes a troublesome operation.

The above mentioned piece of country is undulating, in places very wavy, and occasionally hilly.

The remaining portion of the line from Húblí to Kárwar was found almost intolerably hilly for the work, as may be seen on reference to the "Sum of Rises and Falls passed over by the Staves" given in the table at the end of this Report; only 14 miles of the main line led across country.

The River Haggri was crossed at Páramadavenhalli, there was little water in it, but its sandy bed stretches from bank to bank over a width of nearly ¾ of a mile.

The River Túngábadra was passed at Hesarúr on February 1st 1874, then it had a width of water of 11 chains, and was 10 feet deep in midstream.

(4.) Work used to be closed between 10 and 10½ A. M. and resumed as soon after 2 P.M. as the state of the air permitted, so that the number of stations observed before and after noon were about equal.

Hours of work and arrangement of the same.

The lengths of line observed in a "Forward" direction (towards Kárwar) balance in amount the lengths of line gone over in a "Back" direction (from Kárwar) in the 20th mile from Kárwar: in the last 20 miles to the sea, the length of the forward section is a little in excess of back section.

(5.) The temporary Tide Gauge apparatus used at Kárwar consisted of a hollow iron Telegraph Standard, put down at the head of Kárwar pier: the distance of the surface of the water from the zero of the Gauge, was measured by means of a large float, inside the post. Readings were taken at equal intervals of time (solar and lunar, hourly) of a solar and lunar day, extending over 4 complete days : also sets of observations were taken on each side of the High and Low Water. As the rise of tide at Kárwar is small, it is probable that the result obtained by taking the arithmetical mean of the series, observed after this method, will, when corrected by the " mean of the year" be found to be very approximate to the truth.

Tidal work at Kárwar.

(7.) The following Tables show the out-turn of work in detail.

	Length in miles.	Number of sections.	Number of stations.	Sum of rises and falls passed over by the staves.
Main Line.				Feet
Double line of levels Gútí to Húblí	200	75	1,962	7,774
Do. do. do. Húblí to Kárwar	104	45	1,930	11,251
Branch lines, also double	19	..	239	845
Totals	323	120	4,131	19,870

The G. T. Stations of Namthabad near Gúti and Kúndgorl near Dhárwar were connected. The height of top of rails in the Gúti, Gúndakul, Virápur and Bellárí Stations on the "North Western Line" of Madras Railway was determined.

Six points of the Kárwar-Bellárí Railway Survey were picked up, also 3 points on Irrigation Lines of Levels.

	Number of imbedded B. M. S.	Number of paká points and rocks duly prepared and inscribed.
Gúti to Húblí	13	217
Húblí to Kárwar	3	98
Total	16	315

Mark mounds of stones set in cement were erected in the vicinity of some 50 of the above points.

Extract from the Narrative Report—dated 29th July 1874—of Captain A. PULLAN, S.C., Officiating Deputy Superintendent 3rd Grade, in charge Kattywar Survey Party.

PERSONNEL.
Captain A. Pullan, S. C.
John McGill, Esq., Asst. Supdt.

Surveyors and Asst. Surveyors.
Mr. F. Bell.
„ J. Wood.
„ N. C. Gwynne.
„ T. Rendell.
„ E. Wyatt.
„ W. A. Fielding.
„ H. Corkery.

Head Sub-Surveyor.
Visaji Ragonath.

Sub-Surveyors.
Govindji Mahalay.
Narsu Dinkar.
Krishna Govind.
Shridhar Sassaram.
Vishnu Moreshwar.
Bholaji Dhosokar.
Nilkant Vital.
Keshu Vital.
Tookaram Chowdry.

Apprentices.
Ganesh Ramchandra.
Vishnu Bulwant.
Mahadeo Ragonath.

The Party was constituted as per margin. Of the Surveyors Mr. F. Bell joined me in the field during February 1874. Mr. T. Rendell was transferred to the Tidal and Levelling Party from the 1st of March 1874 and Mr. Corkery joined me from Poona on the 6th of December 1873.

During the recess of 1873 fair copies of Sheets 10, 11, 20, 21 and 22 were prepared on the 2-inch scale for reduction and publication on the 1-inch scale.

Recess work, fair copies.

Degree Sheet No. VI, comprising Sheets 15, 16, 17, 18, 25, 26, 27 and 28 of Kattywar, was fair drawn on the ¼ inch scale; this work was commenced by Mr. N. C. Gwynne during recess and completed in the field. The map will be found in my opinion highly creditable to Mr. Gwynne.

Degree Sheet No. VI.

The out-turn of work during the past field season has been very satisfactory. 2174 square miles of country have been trigonometrically surveyed preparatory to next year's topographical operations, while 2201 square miles of country, exclusive of overlap, have been topographically surveyed and 1234 linear miles of Traverse Survey have been run over that area, demarcating the boundaries of States and checking the details of the Plane Table Survey.

Out-turn of Field work.

The Party started for the field on the 22nd October. The subordinate Native Establishment marched from Poona to Bombay, which place they reached on the 27th. On the 28th they sailed by "patimar" (native boat) for Gogo and landed at that port on the 7th and reached Wadwan on the 15th November. With the Native Establishment was the heavy baggage together with the horses of myself and my assistants. The rest of the Party proceeded by rail to Wadwan in Kattywar and I opened office there on the 18th November 1873.

Departure of the Party for the Field.

Five or six days were spent in completing the projection of plane tables, mending perambulators, testing chains, &c., and at the end of that time the various plane table and traverse parties dispersed to their different boards. Mr. McGill, Assistant Superintendent,

proceeded on the 20th of November to take up the triangulation which I had assigned to him.
He was accompanied by Lieutenant Gibbs, R.E., of the Guzerat
Lieut. Gibbs, R.E., Asst. Supdt, Party, as Major Haig was anxious that Lieutenant Gibbs should
Guzerat Party. have the advantage of some weeks' training under an observer
of Mr. McGill's skill and experience. Lieutenant Gibbs, remained with Mr. McGill for a
month and at the end of that time he proceeded to Wadwan and thence to Sanand to join the
Head Quarters of the Guzerat Party at that place.

As I had received instructions from you to make a survey of the city of Rajkot together
with the British cantonment, on the scale of 12 inches = 1 mile,
Captain Fullon. I proceeded from Wadwan to Rajkot and took the necessary
measures for commencing the survey of Rajkot, examining the ground, ascertaining the position
of existing boundary stones, and comparing the map of cantonments as issued by the Quarter
Master General's Department with the station as it now stands.

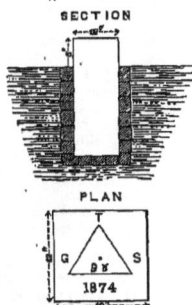

Bench-marks were erected at important points of the
Survey. These bench-marks were of stone 12 in. × 12 in. at top,
6 inches of dressed stone appearing above ground and 2 feet being
firmly built in below. On the margin is a diagram of one of these
bench-marks. The figures below the central dot denote the number
of the station in Guzerati.

Besides superintending the progress of this survey and
personally examining the projection of the field chart, I surveyed
the environs of the town of Rajkot, with the plane table, on our
usual topographical scale and also examined, in the field, the work
of Native Surveyors Govindji Mahalay, Shridhar Saccaram, Vishnu Moreshwar, Nilkant Vital, and Keshu Vital who were working
in adjoining boards. In the month of March I moved northwards,
examining the work of the plane table surveyors *en route* to Jhin-
jura on the border of the Gulf of Kutch. Here finding the
"mangrove" swamp and treacherous sand offered considerable
obstacles to the plane tabler, I took up L. P. Table, N. W. Section,
Sheet 32, myself and surveyed the edge of the gulf accompanied
by Ganesh Ramchandra, a very intelligent lad, whom I thus trained
to this half land half water surveying, so that next year he will be
able to work alone. Besides turning out this plane table I examined the work of surveyors in
adjoining boards and continued my inspection until the 25th of April, when the season's work
being with the exception of two check traverses completed, I moved in the direction of Wadwan,
which place I left on the 6th of May *en route* for Poona, after having seen the field stores and
equipment carefully housed for the rainy season.

Mr. McGill on leaving my camp at Wadwan on the 20th November proceeded northwards towards the Rann of Kutch to complete the triangulation
J. McGill, Esq., Assistant Supdt. of Sheet 31, left unfinished by Mr Wyatt, as he found that
Mr. Wyatt had in many cases not taken reciprocal vertical angles. Mr. McGill was obliged
to visit the major portion of Mr. Wyatt's stations over again. On the 27th of December he
was able to proceed and take up the triangulation of Sheets 42, 43, 44, and 45; this triangulation,
in many places difficult and irksome, owing to the mud banks and salt creeks which intersected
the western half of the work, Mr. McGill successfully completed by the 20th of April, and
as he was then quite knocked up by the exposure of the last ten days of work I requested
him to proceed to Poona and be ready to open office there on the arrival of those assistants
who completed their work first. I may here mention that Mr. McGill fixed the position of
the Tide Gauge building at Hanstal and erected a station
Tide Gauge building at Hanstal. on the bench-mark west of the building. He also fixed a bench-
mark on Somartar Island in the Rann of Kutch. It is unnecessary for me to comment on
the work of so able a triangulator as Mr. McGill further than to say that his work is as accurate and good as that of former seasons.

Mr. Bell was transferred to the Kattywar Party on the 1st of March from the Bombay
Tidal and Levelling Party, and proceeded to take up the
Mr. F. Bell, Surveyor 3rd Grade. triangulation of Sheets 40, and 41. Mr. Bell worked very well
until the 20th of April, when he wrote to me that the heat was very severe and the refraction
and dense haze rendered it almost impossible to observe satisfactorily; whereupon, as the work
he was engaged on was not of an urgent nature, I directed him to close work. Mr. Bell
requires some practice at supplying points for topographers.

Mr. J. Wood left Poona on the 25th October in charge of the Native Establishment
Mr J. Wood, Surveyor 4th Grade. and heavy baggage of the party. He executed this charge
(deceased). successfully and worked steadily through the field season and
turned out his plane table in a very neat and workmanlike manner. On the 24th of April he
proceeded to Poona, and on the 8th of May I received a telegram from Mr. McGill giving me,

the news of Mr. Wood's sudden and violent death. I have already had the honor of communicating with you as to the circumstances of Mr. Wood's sad end; I would here merely record
my deep regret for his loss and add my testimony to that of other executive officers as to his
steady industry and devotion to his work.

Mr. Gwynne was employed from the middle of November until the 8th of January in
Mr. N. C. Gwynne, Assist. Surveyor completing the fair drawing of Degree Sheet VI, of Kattywar;
1st Grade. this work he did to my thorough satisfaction. On the comple-
tion of the Degree Sheet Mr. Gwynne took up topographical work and turned out 3 plane
tables in a thoroughly good and artistic style. Mr. Gwynne also trained Ganesh Ramchundra,
Sub-Surveyor, and this lad's subsequent work has proved that Mr. Gwynne is a clever and
painstaking instructor.

Mr. Rendell was employed on topographical work until the middle of February and
Mr. T. Rendell, Assistant Surveyor completed 2 accurate and neatly executed plane tables. Mr.
1st Grade. Rendell was on the 1st March 1874 transferred to the Tidal
and Levelling Party under Captain Baird.

Mr. Wyatt was employed on topographical work during the entire season and completed
Mr. E. N. Wyatt, Assistant Surveyor 3 plane tables of good quality both for accuracy of detail and
1st Grade. artistic drawing. Captain Trotter, R.E., my predecessor,
particularly mentioned Mr. Wyatt to me as a very hardworking assistant and I can thoroughly
endorse this opinion.

Mr. Fielding was employed on topographical work during the entire season. He executed
Mr. W. A. Fielding, Assist. Surveyor 4 plane tables and instructed Sub-Surveyors Vishnu Balwant
2nd Grade. and Mahadeo Ragonath in the use of the plane table. Mr.
Fielding always turns out a considerable amount of work and it is always accurate. He is very
painstaking and his style of drawing is now very good.

Mr. W. Oldham, Assistant Surveyor   Mr. W. Oldham was transferred to this party on the
3rd Grade. 1st of June last. He has worked very steadily and well since
he joined me.

Mr. Corkery was appointed to the Department on the 20th November 1873 and joined
Mr. H. Corkery, Assistant Surveyor my camp on the 6th December 1873. As it was necessary that
4th Grade. he should be trained, I sent him in the first instance to Mr.
Fielding, and afterwards to Mr. Wood, for instruction, and when the latter officer reported
him fit for independent work I sent him on the 18th of January to take up R. P. Table, N. W.
Section, Sheet 33; Mr. Corkery finished this plane table on the 29th March. He has worked
steadily and well, and on the whole his progress has been good.

Visaji Ragonath, senior Sub-Surveyor, was employed in projecting plane tables, com-
Sub-Surveyor Visaji Ragonath. puting points, and also in the survey of Rajkot on the 12-inch
scale; he worked during this season in the same satisfactory
way in which he has always done hitherto.

Govindji Mahalay worked very well throughout the season executing 3½ plane tables
Sub-Surveyor Govindji Mahalay. in good style and very correctly. For honesty and energy
Govindji Mahalay is a pattern to the rest of the Sub-Surveyors.
 *   *   *   *   *   *   *

Having in view the area triangulated by Mr. McGill, covered as it is by a very large number of well selected intersected points, and the very considerable area of country topographically
surveyed, supplemented as it is by the 12-inch survey of the town and cantonments of Rajkot,
on which the smallest details are plotted to scale, also having consideration to the small
triangular error of the triangles and the inconsiderable chain error of the traverses, I think, I may
fairly say that the out-turn of work for season 1873-74 is very creditable to all hands.

Towns.   The principal towns contained in the sheets surveyed this
season are as follows.

1st. Rajkot on the bank of the Aji River, the residence of a 2nd class chief and the official capital of the peninsula. The Political Agent for the state of Kattywar resides there and it
is also a military station for a small British force. 2nd. Morbi on the banks of the Machu, the
principal town of the Morbi State and residence of the Thákur. Under the able superintendence
of Mr. Sambu Pershad, the Extra Assistant Political Agent, the town with its well kept roads and
neat public offices is an example to the other states. The roads throughout the state of Morbi
are in excellent repair. 3rd. Wánkaner the Capital of the state of that name on the bank of
the Machu is a strongly fortified town and the residence of the Thákur. Other towns of lesser
note are Kotra Sángáni, Pardhari, Lodika, Látipur and Tankaria.

Worthy of mention is the little feudal village of Khirasra standing on a high plateau
about 10 miles S.W. of Rajkot: the village is surrounded by a strong bastioned wall, behind
which nestle the houses of the "Bhayad"—or blood relations and connections of the Thákur—
and over all towers the "Keep" of the Thákur, grim and loopholed; outside the walls and
close beneath them are the houses of the cultivators and low caste artisans, these also with a
strong wall breast high to protect them.

This village vividly recalls the not very remote times of Surashtra, when every man's hand was against his neighbour, when cattle lifting was the honored occupation, and the popular dictum was that "they may *take* who have the power and they may *keep* who can."

Of the small rivers which water the tract of country surveyed, the principal are the

Rivers. Machu, Aji, Demai and Únd. The Machu river, which is the most considerable, rises among the Wánkaner Hills, and flowing under the walls of Wánkaner and Morbi discharges itself into the Rann of Kutch near Málía. This river is remarkable for its rugged and rocky channel and precipitous sides; many a long detour has to be taken along its banks ere a place is found passable for carts.

Aspect of the Country. Sheet 35, the most southernly portion of the ground surveyed, is hilly, the hills being low steep and bare of vegetation, the valleys between being well cultivated and very fairly productive. This sheet is traversed from east to west by the very peculiar range known as "Sirdhári", which runs for over 30 miles in a long low narrow ridge, varying from 40 to 100 feet in height and from 12 to 8 feet in breadth; no bends or sinuosities occur throughout its length, and it has the appearance of having been "ruled" across the country. The geological formation of the range is basaltic. The ground in sheet 34 is irregular, rising into plateaux with rugged steep sides about 40 or 50 feet high, notably so near Rajkot. The high ground is not however broken up into ridges as in sheet 35. Sheets 33 and 32 are level, the country becoming, as one nears the Rann, an almost unbroken flat, richly cultivated and supplied with water from many large tanks and ponds.

The scenery at the head of the Gulf of Kutch is very peculiar; first, there is the distinctly marked line of cultivation, cotton, wheat, "bajri", making a pleasant variety of color and outline; trees are dotted about, and villages stand out in relief against the sky, or show white against the green masses of the "tope" of trees which almost invariably surrounds them. Next comes the dry, salt impregnated surface of the Rann, half sand half black earth; here and there a stunted bush or two dot the waste, but as a rule it is utterly bare and desolate. A low range of sandy hills shuts in this Rann from the wide spreading swamps, which extend as far as the eye can reach and are covered with a dense thicket of almost impassable mangroves, and intersected with a close network of salt streams. The sea itself is away beyond the mangrove swamps, and at high tides the waters of the gulf roll up, covering the morass and washing up to the very foot of the sandy hills. A white sail dots the horizon here and there, and the observer is cheated for the time into the idea that he is on the sea shore; but a few hours after the illusion is dispelled and the sea might be far away save for the cool salt breeze that pours through the tents, and brings a reminder of the vicinity of the ocean. While surveying the country bordering on the gulf I witnessed some very beautiful effects of "Mirage"; at midday more especially the surface of the soil, glittering with saline particles, seems changed to a glassy sheet of water, the scattered villages assume larger proportions, houses and walls appear gigantic, trees gain double height and bulk, while all appears reflected as in the waters of a placid far stretching lake; but, while the observer gazes in admiration and wonder, the beautiful vision fades, or rather passes on to light up another portion of the coast in like manner. On another occasion the smooth salt surface of the ooze became a still summer sea, such as Vandevelde loved to paint, and on its bosom lay old dismantled boats, white gulls flitted here and there, and a far away grey line of coast closed the picture in the extreme distance. Had I not known that the gulf was six miles off, and hardly accessible at all from land, I should have thought myself within a few minutes walk of the sea, so perfect was the illusion. Nothing grows on these salt morasses except mangrove and a long coarse grass in scattered patches. Various sea birds feed at will, over the slimy ooze and along the edges of the salt streams that wind their way through the swamp; and in the early morning herds of antelope may be seen hurrying back to the borders of the cultivation, after having eaten their day's allowance of salt on the edge of the Rann.

I may notice here the beautiful crystals and agates which abound over the portion of Kattywar which I have visited; masses of crystal white and amethyst together with "fortification" and other agates are scattered broadcast over the ploughed fields or sparkle among the *debris* of the river's bed.

Cultivation. Cotton is largely cultivated over all this part of Kattywar and is a source of certain income to the cultivators; the principal grains grown are Wheat, "jowari" and "bajri" and near some of the villages are fields of vegetables and patches of sugarcane; wild indigo is found all over this part of Kattywar and I should say might be cultivated with advantage. A noteworthy feature in the country under review are the dense belts of toddy palm which occur at Ságália, Sanosra, Chela, Jodpur and Jodpur Rohisala; there are distilleries at all these places.

Temperature. The climate of this part of Kattywar is dry and warm away from the sea coast, but as one nears the gulf, is sensibly affected by the cool sea breeze which blows nearly all day. The minimum temperature near Rajkot at 12 o'clock during the month of January, was 66°·9 and maximum at 12 o'clock 89°·0; during February in the same part of the country, minimum 72°·5, maximum 90°·0; during March in the Morbi district, minimum 79°·9, maximum 100°·8; during April at the head of the gulf of Kutch, minimum 87°·6, maximum 103°·0.

I was agreeably surprised to find that drinkable water is procurable even during summer
Water. all along the borders of the Rann. Here and there the Sur-
veyor has to send several miles for good water, but as a rule a
little care and arrangement is all that is required to enable the traveller and his people to obtain
drinkable water all the year round.

A very large number of camels are bred along the borders of the gulf between Juria
Animals. and Malia; droves of them may be seen wandering here
and there over the swamps, browsing on the mangrove; inured
from their birth to the treacherous slippery ground, they pass along safely over the ooze and
swamp where a Bikaner or Hissar camel would slip and fall before it had gone fifty yards, in
fact where any camel but this peculiar breed would refuse to go at all. Great horse breeding
country as Kattywar is, not many horses are bred in the part of Kattywar of which I am now
speaking. Sheep are very plentiful and their meat is particularly juicy and good.

The rural population of this part of Kattywar are principally Kolis and Kanbis under
Population. the rule of Jhareja Rájputs; a sprinkling of wandering Waghérs
along the river banks, and the usual complement of low caste
Dhérs to each large village. In the towns there is a large admixture of the Mahomedan
element, and along the border of the gulf and in the northern part of Morbi, towards the
Rann, many of the villages are inhabited solely by "Miana" Mahomedans, strongly built
black bearded fellows, good fishermen and boatmen, but unwilling to work, save for themselves
and at their own craft; they have also the reputation of being accomplished thieves.

Proposed arrangements for next   I propose that the work of next season shall em-
season.   brace.

1st. The triangulation and topographical survey of the small portion of Kutch required
to complete sheets 42 and 31.

2nd. The triangulation of the northern half of sheet No. 10$_A$ on the Index Chart.

3rd. The triangulation of sheets 52, 53, 58 and 59.

4th. The topographical survey of sheets 43, 44, 45 and 31.

5th. As there are still many small detached bits of boundary shown *approximately* on
the various published sheets of Kattywar, and as these boundaries have now
been for the most part definitely settled and marked out, I purpose sending an
experienced traverse Surveyor to take them up and survey them correctly; the
boundaries when completed will be laid down on the office copies of the
different sheets and thus no boundaries will remain approximate on our
sheets.

TABULAR STATEMENT OF OUT-TURN OF WORK IN KATTYWAR DURING THE FIELD SEASON 1873-74.

Triangulation.

No.	Observers' Names.	Instrument used.	Area triangulated in square miles.	No. of Points Heights fixed.	No. of Points Position fixed.	No. of stations visited.	Triangles, 3 Angles Observed. No. of triangles.	Triangles, 3 Angles Observed. Mean triangular Error.	Triangles, 3 Angles Observed. Discrepancy per mile.	Triangles, 2 Angles Observed. No. of triangles.	Triangles, 2 Angles Observed. Average discrepancy per mile.	Remarks.
1	John McGill, Esq., ...	Cooke and Son 7-inch	1780	280	650	105	155	" 10·6	Feet 0·6	996	Feet 0·9	Employed for 3 months on the Rajkot Survey.
2	Mr. F. Bell, ...	Troughton & Simms' 6-inch	894	23	108	27	29	11·2	0·6	148	1·0	Recorder with Mr. Bell from 1st Mar.
		Totals, ...	2174	309	758	132	184	Mean 10·9	Mean 0·6	1142	Mean 0·95	

Topography.

No.	Plane-tabling.	Area surveyed, Scale 2 inches = 1 mile.	Average No. of plane table stations per square mile.	Remarks.
1	Captain A. Pullen, ...	56	5·7	
2	Mr. J. Wood, ...	216	10·3	Empl. for 2 months
3	„ N. C. Gwynne, ...	167	5·7	on Degree Sheet VI
4	„ T. H. Rendel, ...	144	9·0	Transferred from March 1st.
5	„ E. N. Wyatt, ...	225	8·4	
6	„ W. A. Fielding, ...	255	7·0	Joined on 6th December 1873.
7	„ H. Corker, ...	72	8·6	
	Native Surveyors.			
8	Govindji Mahalày, ...	255	8·9	
9	Sridhar Sucaram, ...	343	9·5	
10	Vishnu Moreshwar, ...	230	9·9	
11	Nilkant Vittal, ...	250	10·6	
12	Keso „	80	8·0	
13	Ganesh Ramchandra,...	153	9·4	
14	Vishnu Balwant, ...	8	8·7	Very good work for a beginner
15	Mahadeo Baggomath,	22	9·0	
	Total number of square miles surveyed inclusive of overlap,	2366	...	

Traverses.

No.	Names.	No. of Linear Miles Traversed. Thuka Boundary.	No. of Linear Miles Traversed. Check Line.	Average error per 1000 links.	Remarks.
1	Naru Dinkar	187·2		0·63	
2	Krishnaji Govind	202·0	19·6	0·88	
3	Bholoji Bhoosehar	416·9	22·2	0·59	
	Tukarum	236·6	150·3	0·94	
	Totals, ...	1042·7	192·3	Mean 0·74	

Extract from the Narrative Report—dated 23rd October 1874—of Major C. T. HAIG, R.E., Deputy Superintendent 2nd Grade, in charge Guzerat Survey Party.

(2.) Owing to rather a large amount of mapping I did not leave my recess quarters at Poona for Guzerat till the 1st December; the party then consisted of the strength as per margin.

Date of taking the field.

PERSONNEL.

Major C. T. Haig, R.E.
Lieut. J. E. Gibbs, R.E.
Mr. A. D'Souza.
„ A. D. L. Christie.
„ C. H. McAfee.
„ E. J. Connor.
„ J. Hickie.
„ G. D. Cusson.
„ A. Dryson.
„ G. E. Hull.

Native Surveyors.

Gopal Vishnu.
Ganesh Bapuji 1st.
Rooji Narayen.
Laximon Ghorpuri.

Balwant Govind.
Mukund Dinkur.
Ganesh Narayen.
Ganesh Bapuji 2nd.
Bhow Govind
Monajon Aboo.
Trimbak Sudnaeo.

Revenue Survey.

Mr. T. A. LeMesurier.

Native Surveyors.

Kubur Parbhudass.
Parbhu Kissor.
Lalu Ambaram.
Jogul Manaukram.
Gopal Ganesh.

At Surat I was joined by Mr. T. A. LeMesurier, Assistant Superintendent Guzerat Revenue Survey, as successor to Mr. A. Dalzell in charge of the Revenue Survey Establishment attached to my party, the latter gentleman having been transferred to the Nassick Revenue Survey.

(3.) On the 16th March 1874 Mr. McAfee left my Party and proceeded to join the Kumaon and Garhwal Party and from the 1st of March 1874 till the end of the field season Mr. Cusson was absent sick.

(4.) During the season one sheet and a quarter, *i.e.* about 690 square miles, have been

Work done.

topographically surveyed on the scale of 4 inches to the mile. Two sheets have been prepared for topography, by triangulation and traversing, connecting all the village trijunctions and other important points on the Revenue Survey Maps with our triangulation. Two sheets, of which the triangulation had been previously done, were completed as above with traversing and one sheet was covered with a net-work of triangles without any traversing and also the triangulation for the Survey of the Dáng Forests in sheets 52, 59, was commenced by Lieutenant Gibbs, who covered an area of about 500 square miles with triangles of 10 mile sides besides fixing a number of intermediate points which can be made stations of a triangulation of smaller sides.

(5.) The area topographically surveyed is much smaller than usual, and smaller than

Topography.

I had hoped to have completed; but as it was our first season of working on the 4-inch scale it cannot be considered unsatisfactory, especially as it throws on the hands of the party a larger amount of mapping than they have hitherto been able to attempt in one recess.

(6.) I proceeded direct from Poona to Ahmedabad and thence I marched with my

The start.

whole staff of topographers to Moria, a convenient village about 13 miles on the road to Gogo, and in plane table No. 16 of sheet 80. On this plane table we commenced work, all the Surveyors being for a time spectators, so that they might, when they separated, all work on the same system, which was somewhat different from that to which they had been accustomed; and they then distributed themselves over the 12 easternmost plane tables of sheet 80 so as to be all near at hand, and I visited them all to see that they understood the plan of working.

(7.) I will now describe in detail the mode of working which was finally adopted and

Mode of procedure.

which all the Surveyors now quite understand, though we took some little time in maturing it, during which the work progressed rather slowly.

(8.) I have stated in my last year's report that in designing the project of the traversing, the end I kept in view was to determine the position of a point close to every village site and the positions of all the village boundary trijunctions. Besides these obligatory points the traverses of course give us others, as for instance the traverse stations between the obligatory points and many crossings of roads and nallas. Additional measurements when necessary are also taken to enable all the obligatory points and all the traverse stations to be plotted on the Revenue Survey village maps.

(9.) On distributing the topographers I provide each with a plane table on which is a graticule $3\frac{3}{4}$ minutes longitude by $3\frac{3}{4}$ minutes latitude, and all the triangulation and traversing stations and data points, and along with this a copy of the Revenue Survey Map of every village (wholly or partly included within the graticule) reduced on semitransparent paper to the scale of 4 inches to a mile. On these village maps are also marked all the triangulation and traverse data points.

(10.) A Surveyor thus provided, having made all his points on the ground conspicuous with poles and brushes, where necessary, sets up his table at the given point near some village site from which he traverses round the village with his plane table and lays down the actual limits of the ground occupied by houses and the emanations of all roads; then if the village is a small one he sets up his table at one of the data points on the boundary and traverses round the boundary, laying down all points where roads cross it; he then has two points on each principal road, one at the village and the other at the boundary, and with the aid of a piece of black leaded transfer paper he traces in the road on to his plane table from the village map. If the distance between the village site and the boundary exceeds three quarters of a mile he traverses round an intermediate circuit, and such of his plane table stations as are important as being near to roads or other topographical features he plots on the village map (by means of measurements to the nearest corners of fields) as well as plotting them on his plane table. He also sets up his plane table at every tank and works along the banks of all streams, such items not being shewn on the village map with much accuracy of detail but merely as non-assessed spaces. In the course of this procedure he will notice any roads which may have recently sprung up and are not shewn on the village maps, and he sketches in the undulations of the ground, and indicates its character whether wooded or open. From the village authorities he borrows the local copy of the village map on which all the hedges are shewn, and ascertains how much of the land is assigned or " Wánta" as it is termed, and who the assignee or Wántawála is, and what portions are lying waste; and this information he indicates on his own copy of the village map.

(11.) Then when he sends his plane table to my Office completed and accompanied by the village maps I have not merely a topographical survey of the country on the scale of 4 inches to a mile, but I have the means of laying down on it all the fiscal details shewing which parts are hedge-bound and which open. The village maps also give the positions of all the wells and the names of all the tanks.—I say I have the means of laying down these minutiæ, but it still requires a little method to accomplish, because if the village map be superposed in its place on the plane table it will not always fit into its correct limits; in fact we may say that if we take any two points in the village map and place them on their correct positions on the plane table we shall find a discrepancy between any third point and its correct position; but if the three points are not far from each other, say ¾ of a mile apart, the discrepancy will be so small that it can readily be adjusted by an ordinary draftsman and the necessary correction applied to the intermediate detail. But from what I have just stated, in regard to the process of working in the field, it will be at once understood that, what with triangulation stations, traverse stations and plane table stations, there will be a net-work of points common to both maps by which they can be divided up into triangles always having sides less than three quarters of a mile. Thus by taking a triangle at a time the fiscal details of the village map are easily transferred to the plane table map, and in this way we have a topographical map on which the lands of every village have assigned to them their correct limits and the interior fiscal details being added it becomes a cadastral map of the country. Of course properly speaking a cadastral map is one which shews all the buildings in the towns to scale, but all that I have been able to do in that direction has been to survey the principal thoroughfares through the villages and fill in the spaces with conventional blocks of buildings.

(12.) I must now state in what particulars we in practice deviated from the above
Deviations in practice. detailed method. In the first place during the execution of the first 12 plane tables I directed the Surveyors to transfer the fiscal details from the village maps, each on to his own plane table, as he progressed with his topography. This was found by some hands a very difficult and tedious job, and some of them executed the job in such a way that it had to be done over again; consequently I directed them only to furnish me with the *means* of transferring the details from the village maps to the plane tables in my office.

(13.) Then as I had no separate staff of draftsmen in my Office I had to let the work of transference of fiscal details from the village maps to the plane tables stand over till we returned to Poona, when I found it more advantageous not to transfer these details on to the original plane tables at all, but on to the fair copies, and for the following reasons.

(14.) Before returning to Poona I represented to Colonel Prescott, Superintendent Guzerat Revenue Survey and Assessment, that it would greatly accelerate the publication of the large scale maps if I had the original plane table maps photozincographed in pairs in blue, and so save the labor of having them all traced by hand with the aid of a tracing glass, and I also represented that my contingent grant would not admit of my paying for this at the ordinary rates, and I therefore asked him to apply for permission to have this work regarded as part of the legitimate assistance that should be rendered by the Revenue Survey in the utilization of their maps and charged to the account of the Revenue Survey. This was at once acceded to. Then the Officer in charge of the Photozinco. Office asked me to let him undertake the job as speedily as possible as he then had but little work in hand but expected soon to have his hands full. I therefore sent him the plane tables as they were, without waiting to transfer the fiscal details on to them.

(15.) But to return. The topography of sheet 80 was not completed until nearly the
Progress of topography in sheets 80 and 14. end of March, after which I moved into the Surat District and took up a portion of sheet 14. I was anxious to take up

a portion of this district because in sheet 80 the Revenue Survey detail with which we had to deal was the result of operations undertaken nearly a quarter of a century ago, whereas the detail in sheet 14 is the result of very recent work, and, as might have been expected, the forcing which was necessary in sheet 80 to get the details into their proper relative position almost entirely disappears in sheet 14.

(16.) The country along the eastern margin of sheet 80 and extending a few miles into the sheet is thickly wooded and closely hedge-bound; but as we advanced west we got into a very open and bare looking country, the trees and hedges being almost entirely confined to the village sites or their immediate vicinity. This sheet includes a very remarkable lake called the Nal (popularly spelt Null) covering an area of about 18 square miles. The water I believe nowhere exceeds 10 feet in depth and for the most part it is capable of being crossed by wading; during the monsoon the depth of water increases and I am told there is then a water connection between the Gulf of Cambay and the Rann of Kutch *via* this Nal. The water of the Nal is sweet during the monsoon and early cold weather but as the hot weather advances it becomes more and more brackish.

Description of sheet 80.

(17.) There are a number of islands in the Nal near its margin. Most of these, and many parts of the banks of the Nal, are covered thickly with reeds which are used by the natives for thatching their houses, and the poorer classes live on the roots, which they clean, dry and grind into flour called "Bir" : on the adjoining tracts of salt waste there is a short kind of grass the root of which is also eaten by the natives.

(18.) The country in the east half of the sheet is very level and wooded; the western portion is open, and from the low level many plateaux rise from 5 to 15 feet, to which the cultivation is mostly confined.

(19.) The sheet comprises portions of the Sanand, Dholka, and Viramgam Tálukás of the Ahmedabad Collectorate and small portions of petty states under the Kattywar Political Agency. It is traversed by the Ahmedabad and Gogo and the Ahmedabad and Viramgam roads.

(20.) In sheet 80 there are four different kinds of tenure under which the land is held, *viz.* Khálsa or Senja, Tálukdári, Inámi, and Foreign territory under the jurisdiction of the Political Agent in Kattywar. There is an interesting and lucid explanation of the different land tenures under British rule in Guzerat in the General Report on the Administration of the Bombay Presidency for the year 1872-1873. Here it is sufficient to state that in the Khálsa villages the ryot or tenant of each field pays his rent direct to the British Government; in the Tálukdári villages a Tálukdár pays a rent for the whole village; while in the Inámi villages no rent is paid at all to Government. It is necessary to mention this because of the consequent difference in the village maps. In the map of a Khálsa village we find the land divided into a host of fields, sometimes almost too small to be properly shewn on the 4-inch scale, but of course sometimes as large as 10 or 12 acres, and every tank or unassessed space is indicated. A Tálukdári village map presents very little partition into fields, the roads forming frequently almost the only division of the map and often they are not all shown nor are all the tanks. Of the Inámi villages generally there are no maps forthcoming at all, but sometimes a map exists giving merely the periphery or boundary of the village. There are no maps at all of the villages in Foreign territory. The Khálsa village maps are therefore by far the most valuable to us and next to them the Tálukdári.

(21.) Khálsa villages are also very frequently divided into Wánta (a share) and Talpat (the remainder), the Wánta land being held by some Tálukdár; but the British Government let out the fields, collect the rents, and settle the account with the Tálukdárs. I mention this, not that there is any difference in the map from that of a village not so divided, but because it is an important division, and one that I am therefore indicating on our final maps.

(22.) The S. E. section of sheet 14 which was also surveyed during the past season comprises a portion of the Ulpár (spelt also Ulphár and Orpád) Táluká of the Surat Collectorate, and of the Káthor Pargana of the Nowsaree Máhal in Gaikwári Territory. It is a flat country, fairly wooded, but the trees are for the most part small, babool trees predominating. The principal towns in this section are Ulpár, Káthor, Sáudhir and Variao. The river Tapti enters this section at the S. E. corner and passes close along its southern margin ; in the vicinity of the Tapti there are many ravines 50 feet deep and more, several of which are utilized as roads. The B. B. and C. I. Railway also crosses this section, entering it at about 170 miles from Bombay and leaving it in the 180th mile. There are also several made roads traversing this section, *viz.* the Surat and Dándi road (Dándi is the village on the coast from which the mail boat crosses the Gulf of Cambay to Gogo), the road from Surat to Ulpár and on to Hánsot in the Broach Collectorate in sheet 13 (published), and the road from Ulpár to the Sayen (Sion) Railway Station.

Description of sheet 14.

(23.) The villages in this part of the country are much more numerous than in the Ahmedabad District ; there the areas of some of the village lands exceed 10 square miles, here one square mile is a common area for a village, and the holdings are small in proportion. There is also an absence of Tálukdári villages in the Surat

Comparison between the materials of the Revenue Survey in sheet 80 and in sheet 14.

District, and only very few Inámi villages, so that sheets 80 and 14 present the extremes of
the gain to be derived from the Revenue Survey Maps, and while even in the Ahmedabad
District we may obtain a very satisfactory map on the 4-inch scale, shewing all the holdings,
bye-roads, foot-paths, wells &c., in sheet 14 it would be quite possible to produce as satisfactory a map on the 8-inch scale, if it were necessary.

(24.) The right plane tables in sheet 14 were completed about the end of April, and
I opened Office in Poona on the 1st May.

Close of the field season.

(25.) I will now proceed to report in detail on the work performed by each of my
assistants. As it was imperative that I should myself attend
to the topography at the opening of the field season, it was
impossible for me to ground Lieutenant Gibbs in the departmental method of triangulation,
so I directed him to accompany Mr. McGill, Assistant Super-
intendent in the Kattywar Party, who left Poona on the 7th
November. After keeping with him until he had acquired the knowledge of the practical details
of triangulation that was necessary, he re-joined me near Sauand near the end of December,
and on the 7th January he left with a party to run a longitudinal series of triangles across
the middle of degree Sheet II, emanating from side Warsora-Dhámanwa of the Aboo Meridional Series and to close on the Kattywar net-work triangulation.

Assistants.

Lieutenant Gibbs.

(26.) This turned out to be a work of great difficulty on account of the flatness of the
country and the denseness of the forest, so that Lieutenant Gibbs had not even completed one
triangle before I had to call him away to commence the triangulation of the Dángs, which
was a work of first importance but which could not be taken up till the end of February, on
account of the deadly fever which closes the Dáng jungles to strangers throughout the cold
weather.

(27.) Had I anticipated the difficulties with which Lieutenant Gibbs met in degree
sheet II, I would have reserved that work for my most experienced triangulator who perhaps
might have achieved a little more success; but it gave Lieutenant Gibbs an opportunity of
seeing some of the greatest difficulties with which a trigonometrical surveyor has to contend,
and it was owing to no want of energy on his part that greater success was not achieved.

(28.) His initial side Warsora-Dhámanwa lay through a dense jungle which, in the
22 years since the ray was cleared and observed by Lieutenant Rivers, had grown up so as not
to leave a trace of its having ever been cleared.

(29.) After several ineffectual attempts to select a couple of stations by mounting
high trees, Lieutenant Gibbs was obliged to proceed to fix his stations by means of ray trace
triangulation, and he had run a chain of 23 such triangles, of sides varying between ¼ a mile
and 3¼ miles and extending over a distance of about 16 miles, when on the 19th February
he had to close his work and proceed to take up the Dáng triangulation.

(31.) On the side Pilwa-Ghoutwál he laid out and observed a double series of triangles
closing on Rúpgarh h.s., using a 10-inch theodolite by Troughton and Simms and observing
his angles on one pair of zeros. A reference to the tabular statement of the out-turn of
work will shew how successful Lieutenant Gibbs was in point of accuracy in this work. In
this series he fixed 8 new stations and 32 intersected points. These latter are all on hill tops;
he tried to fix points in the valleys but did not succeed, on account of the thick state of the
atmosphere which rendered the observations of opaque objects backed by trees impossible.

(32.) Lieutenant Gibbs anticipates that there will be great difficulty in the topographical survey of this district, for not only does the haze and smoke impede the view down from
the hill tops into the ravines, but the ravines themselves are so precipitous and tortuous that it
will be very difficult to find spots in them from which the hill stations will be visible, and
the amount of iron in the rocks will render the magnetic compass useless. I attach a very
interesting report by Lieutenant Gibbs on this district.

(33.) Lieutenant Gibbs, after completing this work, determined the position of the new
Light House on " the Prougs," a shoal of rocks in continuation of the Kolaba promontory in
Bombay.

(34.) Mr. D'Souza was employed early in the season in instructing new hands in
plane tabling and afterwards in supervising and examining the
work of the native Surveyors, and I found him so useful in
this work that I contemplate employing him in a similar way next season. He instructed two
native Surveyors, Monajee Aboo and Trimbak Sudaseo, in the use of the plane table, in the course
of which he with his own hands completed one plane table and nearly half of two others or
about 44 square miles on the 4-inch scale. Mr. D'Souza had under him 5 plane table parties,
each in charge of a native Surveyor, and he exercised a rigorous supervision over them all,
examining each plane table on the ground. The total area of the plane tables which he examined amounts to 360 square miles.

Mr. D'Souza.

(35.) Mr. Christie started on his work from Broach on the 15th November and in the
course of the season covered sheet 31 with a net-work of
triangles averaging 2 to 3 miles sides, which he executed with a

Mr. Christie.

6-inch theodolite by Troughton and Simms.

(37.) Sheet 31 comprises about 140 square miles of the Broach Collectorate and the remainder is Gaikwári territory. Mr. Christie took pains to connect all his stations in British territory with the Revenue Survey "Bánds" at the corners of the fields in which they were situated. This completed the triangulation of the Broach Collectorate; the traversing which is still required to connect all the village sites and trijunctions will be taken up by the Revenue Survey Party under Mr. LeMesurier next month. Mr. Christie progressed much more rapidly over the western half of the sheet than over the eastern, as the former is open the latter very woody, but he very satisfactorily covered the sheet with points.

(38.) Mr. McAfee instructed Mr. Bryson and Ganesh Narayen in the use of the
Mr. McAfee.
plane table and exercised a supervision over Raoji Narayen when working on his first plane table, and afterwards completed one whole plane table and half of another and a portion of a third which he had to give up on being ordered to join the Kumaon and Garhwal Party.

(39.) Mr. Connor, assisted by native Surveyors Gopal Vishnu, Ganesh Bapuji 1st and
Mr. Connor.
Ganesh Bapuji 2nd, prepared sheets 78, 79 for topography with triangulation and traversing. Mr. Connor himself executed the triangulation and gave the necessary instructions to his three native Surveyors—each of whom was provided with a traversing party for the running of traverses starting from and closing on his triangulation stations. Mr. Connor did not cover these two sheets with a net-work of triangles but ran a circuit of triangulation round the margin of the two-sheet-space and ran a meridional chain across the centre of the space, and so gave out the traverses as to fix the positions of the sites of all the villages and of the trijunctions of all British village boundaries as well as of conspicuous trees and other points useful to the plane-table Surveyors. There is in these two sheets a considerable portion of Gaikwári territory in which the village boundaries not being demarcated, the traverse Surveyors fixed the village sites and a sufficiency of useful points for plane tabling.

(40.) Mr. Hickie was employed the entire season in my Office, chiefly in projecting
Mr. Hickie.
plane tables and charting and miscellaneous current work of which there was an unusual amount, so much so that his hands were always full as well as those of the two native surveyors I also kept in my Office.

(41.) Mr. Cusson was employed in plane tabling and he altogether turned out 58
Mr. Cusson.
square miles very neatly; illness compelled him to abandon his plane table on the 20th February, and he came to my camp where I employed him in my Office until 1st March, when it became apparent that he would not be fit for hard work for some time and therefore for the remainder of the field season he went on privilege leave.

(42.) Mr. A. Bryson was employed all the season in plane tabling. Having always
Mr. Bryson.
before been engaged in triangulation, I placed him under Mr. McAfee for instruction for a short time. His draftsmanship was not good, and I am sorry to say he did not inspire me with much confidence as to the accuracy of his work as I had to reject one of his plane tables.

(43.) Mr. Hall was also employed the whole season in plane tabling, and I am well
Mr. Hall.
pleased with his diligence and accuracy, it was only his second field season but he has now become a valuable assistant.

(44.) The tabular statement appended to this report will show in detail the amount and
Tabular Statement.
relative value of work turned out by each of my Assistants and by the native Surveyors.

(45.) I have now to mention the Revenue Survey Establishment under Mr. T. A.
Revenue Survey Establishment under Mr. LeMesurier.
LeMesurier; he joined me at Surat on the 3rd December and at once proceeded with me to Ahmedabad, and after receiving his instructions he took his Establishment into sheet 82 the traversing of which he took up, connecting every village site and trijunction with the triangulation. He finished this about the middle of January, and then took his Establishment into sheet 14 and completed the traversing in the northern portion of the sheet which it had not been possible to finish during the previous season, and then he took up the traversing of sheet 15 which he finished about the middle of April and then proceeded to Poona.

(47.) During the past recess Mr. LeMesurier, who is a very good draftsman, has been rendering valuable assistance in the drawing of the maps; six sections (double elephant sheets) have been drawn by him. His Surveyors were employed during the first part of the recess in the reduction of their traverses in sheets 82, 14, 15, computing the rectangular co-ordinates of the stations with reference to the centres of the respective sheets, and afterwards in transferring the field details from the Revenue Survey village maps to the blue photozincographs of the plane table sections. These blue photozincographs are furnished me in duplicate; on one copy the native Surveyors transfer the field details in bold black lines, the other is taken up as the final map for submission to your Office, and on it the field details are traced with the aid of a tracing glass from the first copy.

(48.) In a few days I hope to be able to send you some of the sections of sheet 80 for publication, when I have no doubt you will be thoroughly satisfied as to the advisability of completing the Survey of British Guzerat on the 4-inch scale. We are not in full working trim, yet but I expect that with but very little more assistance (in the shape of an increased grant for contingent expenditure), besides what has been already given me in the Revenue Survey Establishment under Mr. LeMesurier, to be able to turn out annually nearly as much work on the 4-inch scale as was expected from us on the 2-inch scale.

(49.) I should perhaps here mention that the scale of Survey being the same as that of the published maps, and the large scale of 4 inches requiring a softer general tone than maps on the 1-inch scale, my draftsmen have been required to draw in a style altogether different from that to which they have hitherto been accustomed. The drawing of the maps on the 2-inch scale for reduction by photography to the 1-inch scale had to be coarse and bold, whereas in the maps I am now preparing every thing has to be drawn as finely as possible. Doubtless it will be noticed that there is room for improvement in the maps but I cannot but think that considering that they are the first of the kind produced in this Office they must be considered very satisfactory.

Notes on the portion of the Dángs visited in March—May 1874 *by Lieutenant J. E. Gibbs, R.E.*

(1.) The portion of country, to which my report refers, comprises parts of the Dharampur, Bánsda, Baroda and Sulgána native states, and of the Dángs which are for the present under the charge of the Collector of Khandeish.

(2.) The general aspect of the country is a mass of wooded hills and valleys.

(3.) The hills are for the most part isolated, rugged and steep. Towards the east
Hills.   however they become more and more connected, plateaux being
                      formed, which are again sometimes surrounded by higher
masses. In the line of the Gháts, to the east and south of the Dángs, huge and fantastic masses of rock tower above the rest. The spurs of the hills almost invariably rise in steps, and the summits are generally flat.

(4.) The valleys till they reach the open country are narrow and very winding, with
Valleys.   steep sides, countless short steep ravines running into them
                      down the hills. The beds of the streams are rocky, and the
streams are during the dry season naturally bunded up in many places, without which provision the water supply would soon run short. During the rainy season they become torrents.

(5.) The water of the streams is very bad for drinking purposes, as is often the case in
Water.   thick jungles; but here the inhabitants make matters worse
                      by throwing in poisonous bark to stupify the fish, which then
rise to the top, and are shot with arrows if large, or caught in the men's clothing if small. The people in consequence always take care to drink from springs, or from excavations at the sides of the river beds. Towards the end of the hot weather most of the water gets putrid. There is a deep well with good water at Wagai, another at Gárví. At Rúpgarh there is a perennial spring at the top of the hill, supplying a tank in the old fort and a hollow in a cleft in the northern scarp, with water which is at any rate better than what is obtainable at the foot of the hill. At a few other places the water was palatable, but in most varied from the nasty to the nauseous. At Unáe Mátá there is a celebrated hot spring, which according to my informants cools sufficiently once in 15 days for people to bathe in it; Captain McRae tells me that it is cool only on one day in the year, during the annual fair. When I visited it the temperature was 128¼° F. that of the air in the shade being 89°; an analysis of some of the water I brought away with me gives however nothing abnormal in its composition. It would be interesting to detect the means by which the priests divert the hot water on bathing days before it emerges from the shrine.

(6.) The slight amount of information as yet collected about this hill country leaves a wide field for research in ethology, zoology, botany, and geology; and as it is unlikely that any one, whose duties do not compel him to enter the country, will do so, except perhaps for a few weeks' sport, it would be well if those who have to enter could be induced to take note of, and report on the many points of interest that must necessarily fall under their notice.

(7.) The far greater number of the inhabitants, and all that live in fixed villages belong
Inhabitants.   to the Kumbí, Warlí, or Rajpút castes, all those in one village
                      generally belonging to the same caste. These villagers till the
ground to a small extent, and for food supplement the small animals, which they shoot with

arrows, with fruit, coarse rice and nágli. Though their food is scanty, they drink very hard, the Parsees having a good trade in toddy and mahwa liquor. This latter tastes and smells somewhat like Kirsch-wasser, and the first batch of each brew is above proof, the second quality being about as strong as ⅓ gin and ½ water. Such is the liquor of which a man will consume large quantities in a day, with the thermometer rising above 100° in the shade. While the mahwa flowers are falling, the people distil for themselves, but have no idea of collecting a private store. The people wear very little clothing, except in the neighbourhood of the larger villages of the plain. Every man carries a small sickle shaped knife in the string of his *langoti*. Their huts have wattle walls of the tall boru grass stalks with a roof of the same covered with "pullies" of hay; the latter they seem invariably to place stalk ends down-wards, while the fan shaped part lies above; this arrangement looks as if it must hinder the rain from running off; indeed I do not think the people attempt to keep out the wet effectually. They are a miserable looking lot, ugly and weak, with stringy limbs and potbellies, that made my khalasies remark with contempt that all the men had "aurat ke pet" (thereby showing a profound ignorance of what often takes place in the ranks of luxury). Lung and chest complaints, and the skin diseases, due to poverty of blood and dirt, seem common among them. Fevers too are of course very prevalent. The statistics I have collected about the villages I visited seem to point out that the population is rapidly decreasing, the proportion of children to adults being as 34 is to 59. Indeed the small number of children met with is striking. In practice the people seem to be monogamous. They are very shy of strangers, occasionally flying as if panicstricken, but as a rule they soon come back, and are very civil and obliging. Their curiosity in some matters is as remarkable as their apathy in others. A crowd of men have frequently sat and gazed at me steadily, watching my every movement, but of that crowd several probably had never been 10 miles from their village, except in the direction of the nearest town. Sometimes however they will suddenly desert their villages and migrate after the manner of the Bhíls. The aboriginal Bhíls are now very few in number, and rarely met with except in the retinue of their chiefs, since if warned of the approach of a stranger they will desert their habitations at once, and if surprised in the woods will flee and hide almost before one is aware of their presence. They are slighter and smaller than the other races, and are chiefly noticeable for their extreme blackness, wild appearance, and scantiness of clothing. They live chiefly in bough huts, which may often be met with deserted. The Bhíls having strange superstitions, and at once migrating if they think their locality is unlucky or haunted. They will seldom remain a fortnight in one place. They feed on all sorts of vermin and garbage—many roots, and all fruits coming with them under the head of food. They are a dirty and most degraded race, having no notions of equity or honour. Their one happiness is to get drunk. At Pimprí I saw the Bhíl Rájá or naique of that Dáng. He is said to be the best of the lot, but even he is only sober in the early morning; he possesses an elephant, but the state he keeps up is very small. Besides the inhabitants proper there are parties of Hindoo and Mussulmán traders, called Banjárás, who are continually bringing in salt and taking out rice, nágli, and the like, carried in double bags by large droves of bullocks. The whole of a family marches together, and they encamp at night within walls built up with the bags. The women are very well dressed and have a sort of head dress peaked at the back over which the sárí passes. Also there are the people employed by the Forest Department. All the cartmen I met with were Musulmáns.

(8.) The language spoken on the western edge of the hill country is Guzerathi, but
Language. soon changes to a corrupt Marathi which is very difficult to understand.

(9.) Any one who has plenty of spare time may amuse himself very well here. Tigers,
Animals. panthers, bears, boars, bison, sámbar, bekre, and in the low ground hares are all to be met with if suitable arrangements be made.

(10.) The birds, are in large numbers, and of all sizes and colours from the large black
Birds. and white eagles to the tiny humming birds. A very interesting collection might be made, and I regret that I am unable to give the names of the many varieties that I was able to notice. A list of the local birds would without doubt be of great value to the ornithologist.

(11.) I saw some very fine rock snakes, one couple about 9 feet long. Lizards, small
Reptiles. and large, are in great variety.

(12.) Scorpions and centipedes are common, especially the latter, so that one has always
Insects. to be on one's guard against them. The small black centipede seems to be the most common. Of *insects proper* the lepidoptera make a beautiful show. Often during the heat of the day pairs of gaudy butterflies have chased each other round and round my observatory tent on the hill top, and rested on the ropes within my reach. Beetles too of every colour and size, locusts, tree suckers (which drive their long proboscos through the soft white bark of certain trees) and two or three sorts of mantis are very common. I saw some very fine spiders, notably one large variety of a light grey colour with handsome black markings on the body and along the thighs.

(13.) The trees that strike the eye most are :—the tall Saouwar or Red Silk cotton
tree, *Bombax Malabarica* (Hooker), with its magnificent show
Botany.   of crimson flowers, followed by seed pods containing the silk
cotton; the Bhíls gather this when the pods are half ripe to make into tinder; it also makes
good stuffing for pillows.

The Khandol *(Sterculia urens)* a bare white tree with gaunt leafless arms, looking
ghostlike by moonlight; it has tufts of velvety, puce-coloured, star-shaped flowers; the
soft white wood is used for making into platters, as it does not warp in drying.

The Sagwan or Teak tree *(Tectona grandis)*, with tall straight trunk.

There were few large trees in the parts I visited, the Pimprí valley having been cleared of
them for building the Bombay navy. Towards the interior of the Dángs there are very fine trees.

The Sisoma or blackwood tree *(Dalbergia latifolia)* I found in large quantities in the
neighbourhood of Ghusmáe Mátá, and to the northeast, growing to a thickness of 18 inches;
for upholstery and cabinet work it is of course very valuable.

The Khair tree *(Acacia catechu)*, valuable owing to the terra japonica obtained by
boiling the heartwood and unripe seeds. The heartwood is cut into chips by the men, and
the boiling is superintended by the women; each woman has in front of her two rows of 6
pipkins each in which the chips are boiled; in the centre are two larger pots, into which the
concentrated 'káth' from the smaller pots is collected; here it is allowed to thicken still more,
and finally is extracted in portions as large as can be taken up in the fingers, and left to dry
in the sun. There are several manufactories in the Dángs; the people who make the káth
are of a low race, and filthily dirty; there is supposed to be some secret in the process. The
terra japonica is used in betel chewing, and also exported for tanning purposes.

The Am *(Mangifera Indica)*, the Jungle Mango.

The Amlí *(Tamarindus Indica)*, valuable for its fruit and giving good wood for building
purposes.

The Panas, or Jack Tree *(Artocarpus Integrifolia)*, with its huge fruit with peculiar
shagreen exterior.

The Bar *(Ficus Benghalensis)*, the well known banyan tree.

The Mahwa *(Bassia latifolia)*, from the flowers of which the 'daru' liquor is made.

The Dharí *(Grislea tomentosa ?)*, a low tree with thorny stem, and beautiful bunches
of tubular scarlet flowers.

The Waras *(Heterophragma Roxburghii)*, a small tree with bunches of scalloped and
crimped white flowers.

There were several kinds of trees from which, if wounded, red sap exudes, from which
strange sight the idea of the enchanted wood of Tasso, and of other similar wonders probably
sprang.

(14.) The whole of the hill country consists of 'Deccan' trap. The hills are all
capped with thick strata of dark basalt, varying in texture
Geology.   but generally finely crystalline, and containing much iron.
It is occasionally slightly columnar in structure. The sides of the hills below the precipitous
capping are covered with debris of the rocks above; but where rock masses project from
the loose stuff, they generally appear to be less compact than those above. As I have already
mentioned, the spurs of the hills rise in the characteristic steps. In the beds of the rivers
I generally noticed that the rock was considerably speckled with small felspar crystals,
and also showed much hornblende when fractured. The boulders were of many different
kinds, most of them close grained and crystalline; some however being very porphyritic,
some full of the magnetic oxide of iron which rusts in the cracks into the peroxide, and
some very full of slender prismatic crystals of what I believe to be natrolite. However I
had not the means by me for determining the mineralogy, and I could not afford to carry
about specimens with me.

Looking down from a high hill, it is at once evident that all the configuration of the
ground is simply due to the erosion of water, but at the same time the stupendous result is
almost bewildering; no other natural agent could have carved out the steep, deep, and narrow
valleys through the horizontal strata; but the amount of power and time required for the process
cannot be calculated. This does not of course refer to the strangely tilted peaks in the gháts,
above referred to, which show unmistakeable signs of the immediate proximity of volcanic force.

Having been warned previously to my entering the hill country that the water, even if
boiled and filtered, would be unfit for drinking purposes, and that those who drink it would be
sure to suffer from fevers and diarrhœa, I took with me a portable still, which with very little
trouble supplied me and the Christians and Mahomedans of the party with water for drinking
and cooking purposes. The Hindoos objected to using it, and it would have been of little
good giving it to them, as on the march they drink from any pool near. I believe that it is
principally owing to the use of the distilled water, that my servants and I were very free from
sickness, while all the peons and khalasies had several attacks of fever and diarrhœa, although
I made them take quinine almost every day. I therefore strongly recommend the use of a
portable still in districts where the water is known to be bad.

INDEX CHART OF THE GUZERAT TOPOGRAPHICAL SURVEY

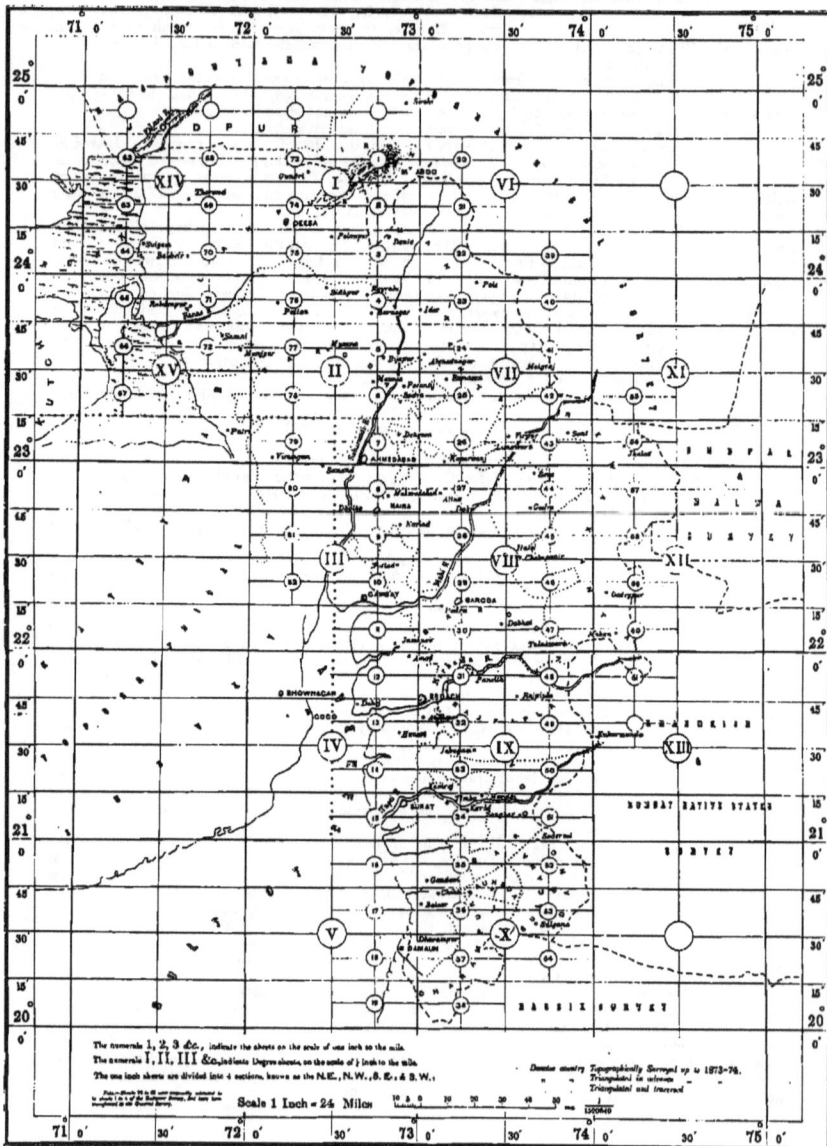

The numerals 1, 2, 3 &c., indicate the sheets on the scale of one inch to the mile.
The numerals I, II, III &c. indicate Degree sheets, on the scale of ¼ inch to the mile.
The one inch sheets are divided into 4 sections, known as the N.E., N.W., S.E., & S.W.

Denotes country Topographically Surveyed up to 1873-74.
Triangulated in extreme
Triangulated and traversed

Scale 1 Inch = 24 Miles

TABULAR STATEMENT OF WORK IN GUZRAT, DURING THE FIELD SEASON 1873-74.

Triangulation.

Observer's Names.	Instrument used.	Area triangulated, miles.	No. of Stations visited.	3 Angles Observed.				2 Angles Observed.				Remarks.
				Triangles.	Triangular error.	Error per mile.	No. of Heights.	Triangles.	Error per mile.	No. of Points.	No. of Heights.	
Lieut. J. E. Gibbs, ... Do.	10" by Troughton & Simms. do.	20* 490	24 11	23 16	17·1 2·8	Not computed 1·1 inch	22 11	14 59	Not computed 4·0] inch	7 32	... 32	*Approximate. [rays cut. Ray Trace Triangulation 45 Dlugs. Δ n† mean diff. of 8 common sides.] Mean diff. of 20 common sides. Net-work Δn over sheet-31—96 miles of my cutting—22 rays.‡ Mean diff. of 60 common sides.¶ Mean diff. of 60 common sides.
Mr. A. Christie, ...	6" by	600	79	125	19·7	9·1? "	58	333	5·1? ft.	200	...	One long], and two meridl. series in sheet 78 and part of sheet 79.§ Mean difference of 52 common sides.
" E. J. Connor, ...	Do.	640* 120	125	171	12·7	5·7? "	114	251	Not computed	130	...	210 stations have had their elements computed.
Total, ...		1660 234	835	...	...	205	667	...	869	32	

Plane Tabling 4 in. = 1 mile.

No.	Names.	Plane Tabling sq. miles.	Stations per sq. mile.	Remarks.
	Native Surveyors.			
1	Mr. A. D'Souza*	44	9·5	*Also instructed Native Surveyors in the new method of surveying, and new men in the use of the plane table, and generally superised and examined their whole work. The other assistants also examined some work.
2	" C. H. McAfee,	93	13·4	
3	" G. D. Cannon,	51	5·7	
4	" A. H. Bryson,	78	12·9	
5	" G. Hall,	112	16·4	
	Native Surveyors.			
1	Reoji Narayen,	111	18·1	†Joined Head Quarters for office work on 3rd of January and returned to plane tabling on the 13th of February.
2	Bhao Govind,	100	16·6	‡Resigned on the 10th of February, re-engaged 11th May.
3	Balwant Govind,†	61	14·5	§Joined Head Quarters for office work on 7th of February being too ill for work in the field and returned to plane tabling on the 21st March.
4	Laxmon Ghorpurey,‡	34	9·9	
5	Mohand Dinkar,§	44	9·2	
6	Ganesh Narayen,	63	18·8	||See also Traversing.
7	Ganesh Bapuji 1st,||	21	21·6	
	Total, ...	746¶	average 13·5	¶Including overlap.

Traversing.

No.	Names.	Linear miles of Traverse.	No. of Points.	Hypothenusal error per 1000 links.	Remarks.
	Native Surveyors.				
1	Gopal Vishnu,	215·933	107·097	0·9 links	In all 1288 Traverse Stations have had their elements computed.
2	Ganesh Bapuji 1st,	74·179	89·890	1·8 "	
3	Ganesh Bapuji 2nd,	296·547	106·633	2·4 "	
	Recruse Surveyors.*				
1	Kubar Purbhu Dass,		106·633	1·5 "	*Not including Ganesh Bapuji 1st whose days employed &c. are under 'Plane Tabling.'
2	Purbhu Kisor,		71·058	1·0 "	
3	Jugal Monsukram,		92·997	0·7 "	
4	Gopali Ganteb,			0·7 "	
5	Lalu Ambaram,			1·4 "	
	Total, ...	981·645		average 1·2 links	

Extract from the Narrative Report—dated 20th November 1874—of Captain H. R. THUILLIER, R.E., Officiating Deputy Superintendent 1st Grade, in charge of the Kumaun and Garhwal and the Dehra Dun Survey Parties.

(1.) During the recess of 1873, while Lieutenant J. Hill, R.E. was in charge, the party
Recess of 1873. was employed on computations and in preparing the fair maps
of Kumaun, surveyed during the previous field season. Four shaded and two skeleton sheets were completed and sent for publication before the party took the field.

(2.) On the 1st October 1873, I received charge of the Kumaun and Garhwál Party from Lieutenant Hill, R.E.

(3.) The only portions of Kumaun and Garhwál which then remained to be surveyed,
Portions of Kumaun and Garhwál embraced some of the highest ground in the great Himalayan
remaining to be surveyed. range. To attempt surveying such elevated regions during the
winter months, would in all probability end in failure. Such ground can only be attempted with a fair prospect of success during the autumn and spring months. I was therefore instructed to postpone the prosecution of the Kumaun and Garhwál Survey until the spring of 1874, and in the interim to employ the party in making a survey, on the scale of 4 inches to a mile, of such portions of the district of Dehra Dún, as are not included in the Government Forest lands which were being surveyed independently by Captain F. Bailey, R.E. of the Forest Department.

Dehra Dún Survey.

(4.) As there was no separate demarcation establishment to precede the Survey, the Superintendent of the Dún was referred to for assistance regarding the demarcation of the village and other boundaries, as soon as the Survey was determined on. The last settlement of the district was completed in the year 1864, and though the boundaries are tolerably well demarcated with permanent pillars, they are not sufficiently numerous to define the boundaries for the purposes of a Survey. The Superintendent promised cordial support and assistance, and orders were promptly issued to Zamíndárs and Grant holders to define their boundaries by temporary marks at bends and turns, where not otherwise defined by natural features, and to have the lines cleared between them ready for the Survey.

(5.) On assuming charge of the Kumaun and Garhwál Party, the organization consisted
Organization of the Party. entirely of European Surveyors. For the large scale Survey
of the Dún, the system of plane-table surveying which had been the only method made use of for the small scale Surveys on which this party had hitherto been employed, required modification. For the flat ground, of which there is a considerable amount in the Dún, in which boundaries are the chief object, the ordinary method of chain surveying had to be resorted to. For this process it was necessary to employ native agency, otherwise the cost of such operations, which involve considerable additional labour, would be materially enhanced.

(6.) One of my first duties therefore was to change the organization by having a pro-
Reorganisation. per proportion of Native Surveyors to the Europeans. I found
however it was impossible to obtain trained men, and I was therefore forced to entertain men who were entirely ignorant of surveying and to have them instructed in the special work which we required. The labours and difficulties attendant in training a large number of men need not be expatiated on; it is sufficient to say that without an exception all the men were perfectly ignorant of the rudiments of surveying, and were generally unacquainted with English, which increased the difficulties of instruction. To teach such men the use of delicate instruments would have been a labour involving considerable delay and in many cases perhaps failure; and as the working season was passing on, it was an object of importance to utilize as far as possible the services of these men while the field season lasted.

(7.) I decided therefore to have them taught the use of the simplest instrument for tra-
Method of Surveying. versing, *viz.*, a circular protractor (ordnance pattern) mounted on
a plane-table. This method of traversing had been introduced by Lieutenant Hill with success in the Bhábar and Taráí tracts of Kumaun. A circular cardboard protractor, graduated to quarters of a degree from left to right, commencing from the south, is mounted on an ordinary plane-table, and the magnetic meridian line, found in the usual way at a trigonometrical station, is marked on it. For traversing, the plane-table is set up by the long magnetic needle, the azimuths of back and forward stations are taken by placing the edge of the sight rule over the centre of the circle, intersecting the objects, and then reading the bearings off the graduated circumference. The azimuths having been read off a circle of large diameter, are susceptible of considerable accuracy, and being referrible to the true meri-

dian are all the more quickly plotted on an ordinary graticule, than magnetic bearings, and require no correction if it is necessary to compute the traverse. The observations also can be taken more quickly than with the prismatic compass, as it is not necessary to wait between them for the needle to come to rest.

(8.) The field operations commenced early in November and the members as per margin were employed for various periods during the season in the Dún work. Lieutenant Gore R.E. was deputed on special work to fix trigonometrically two stations at Roorkee, selected by Colonel Tennant, R.E., for the observations of the Transit of Venus. Mr. Ryall was entrusted with the duty of training the Native Surveyors and superintending the boundary surveys; Messrs. L. Pocock and Kinney with triangulation, and to Messrs. Litchfield, Wrixon and I. Pocock were consigned the main circuit traverses.

E. O. Ryall Esq.
Lieut. St. G. Gore, R.E.
Mr. J. Low.
  „   L. Pocock.
  „   J. Macdougall.
  „   H. Todd.
  „   T. Kinney.
  „   I6. Wrixon.
  „   E. Litchfield.
  „   I. Pocock.
16 Native Surveyors.

Out-turn of work.

(9.) Owing to our taking the field late, the new nature of our work and the difficulties and delay in training the whole of the Native Surveyors, the out-turn of work has been small, but I trust will be considered satisfactory, considering that we had to initiate a new system and teach all the Native Surveyors in a body. The area topographically surveyed on the scale of 4 inches to a mile was 40,051 acres, or about 63 square miles; the triangulation has covered an area of 529 square miles: 271 linear miles of main theodolite traverses and 577 miles of boundary traverses have been run.

(10.) The East End Dehra Dún Base-Line Station was adopted for the initial or starting point of the Survey, and being well and centrically placed will be maintained as the origin for the whole of the Dún Survey.

Origin of Survey.

(11.) The traverses, including those of the boundaries, were all reduced in the field and found to stand the usual tests in a satisfactory manner. Every precaution was taken to insure accuracy of results. The lines were in all cases traversed with two chains of a different unit, whose lengths were from time to time tested with the standard, and corrected accordingly. The directions of the main traverse lines were laid out with the object of connecting boundary pillars at sufficiently close intervals so as to form proper checks on the village boundary traverses. It was found that this could be done in most cases by running them along the main roads, streams, &c. so that in addition to establishing check points for the minor traverses, they include a large amount of topographical detail which was plotted on the plane-tables before they were sent out to the Plane-Tablers. In addition to these checks, 51 boundary pillars were fixed trigonometrically, so that the boundary traverses are in all cases well tied in. The main theodolite traverses were in all cases run between trigonometrical stations. On reference to the tabular statement at page 41—a it will be seen that in 55 traverses, the united lengths of which amount to 271 miles, the average difference from the corresponding trigonometrical values is 0·74 per 1000, and the average closing angular error 21″ per station.

Theodolite traverses and their errors.

(12.) The boundary traverses comprise 184 villages and estates. These were done entirely by the Native Surveyors, whom we had trained at the commencement of the field season, and considering their inexperience, and the delays met with in prosecuting their work owing to the want of demarcation of the boundaries, the result I think is as much in quantity as could be expected, and in quality very creditable, considering the rough ground which a large portion of the Dún consists of. I have classified these traverses under two heads according to the nature of the ground traversed. It will be seen from the tabulated statement that in fair level ground in 124 traverses, the united lengths of which amount to 403 miles, the average closing error is 1·97 per 1000. In the rough and hilly ground, in 58 traverses with a united length of 174 miles, the average closing error is 4·71 per 1000. This error, though apparently large, is wonderfully good for the nature of the ground traversed over. As the Dún chiefly consists of broad plateaus intersected by deep ravines, it is a natural arrangement that the boundaries of villages &c. should be defined by such natural features. This is the case in the majority of boundaries, and in the northern portion of the valley at the foot of the Himalayas, the ground is very hilly, rugged and broken. Chain measurements in such ground, unless reduced to the horizontal level, would be quite untrustworthy. I therefore provided the Surveyors with rough wooden clinometers, graduated to degrees, by which they observed and registered the angles of inclination. In many cases inclines of from 20° to 50° have been chained over; adding to this the roughness of the ground, especially in the ravines where large boulders are met with in great abundance, the error of the work in land of this character will not be wondered at. To show the intricacies of the boundaries, I have appended a column in the detail of work, giving the number of traverse stations, as they increase the labour of the work and add to the probabilities of error. This gives the average distance between each station to be only 6½ chains.

Boundary traverses and their errors.

(13.) The boundary work, owing to the delay in training the Native Surveyors, cannot be said to have been fairly started till the end of December, and as these preliminary traverses were required to be surveyed,

Obstructions and delays.

reduced and plotted before the topography could be taken up, the plane-tabling was not commenced till the beginning of March, and the out-turn of topography therefore has been necessarily very small. The progress of the boundary traverses also was considerably retarded from
causes beyond our control; the chief cause of delay being due to inefficient demarcation.
Although orders were issued on the subject by the Superintendent of the Dún in October, it
was found that they had not been carried out and consequently the non-attendance of the
Zamíndárs or properly qualified men to point out the boundaries was a source of much trouble;
complaints were constant and progress slow. The Surveyors in many cases found that no steps
whatever had been taken for preparing the boundaries for the survey, and in order to prevent
further delay, often had to clear their own lines. They were generally entirely dependent on
the attendance of the Patwáries for marking the boundaries at the actual time of survey, a
system which naturally would cause delay under the most advantageous circumstances, but when
combined with the ignorance and indolence which most of the Patwáries of the Dún evinced,
proved fatal to the rapid progress of the work, and much valuable time was thereby lost. Boundary disputes, which were numerous, tended to cause further delay. Some of these were
however amicably settled at the time of the survey through the aid of the Peshkár or Cánúngo,
whose services had been kindly placed at my disposal by the Superintendent of the Dún;
others however were beyond his powers, and as there was no settlement officer at hand to adju-
dicate and adjust them, they had to be abandoned. Such disputed portions I, at one time, had
surveyed as claimed by each owner, but this I found was waste of time, as generally neither of
the claimants were right.

(14.) The amount of triangulation and traversing completed in advance of the portion
topographically surveyed, covers an area of 198 square miles.
Triangulation and traversing in ad-
vance of the detail Survey.   This embraces 18 plane-table sections which are therefore quite
ready to be topographically filled in, and will be taken in hand
at the commencement of the field season.

(15.) I now proceed to report separately on each Officer's work, the details of which
are tabulated on page 41—a

(16.) Mr. Ryall was entrusted with the duty of training the Native Surveyors for the
E. O. Ryall Esq.   boundary traverses, and took the field on the 10th November.
Messrs. Litchfield, Wrixon and I. Pocock were also attached
to him temporarily for the purpose of being employed in main circuit traverses. As previously
stated, the natives were thoroughly ignorant of any kind of work connected with surveying;
the assistants also were inexperienced both in this method of field work and in the reductions,
and the task of instructing some of them and the whole of the Native Surveyors devolved on
Mr. Ryall, who was consequently not able to take any very active share in the actual survey
operations. Early in December, five of the Native Surveyors who had been trained, were transferred to Lieutenant Gore, R.E., for employment under him. With the remaining men, Mr.
Ryall was instructed to take up the village boundaries in the Western Dún, north of the main
road running from Dehra to Ambári.

(17.) He reports that no actual boundary work was commenced till the first week in
December, and that owing to the inexperience of the Native Surveyors, much that was done
during that month had to be revised, so that the out-turn of work in December was very small,
only three or four villages being successfully surveyed. The work done by the Native Surveyors
in January, though still unsatisfactory, was found to be an improvement on their former attempt.
On 14th February, Mr. Ryall transferred seven of the Native Surveyors to Messrs. Kinney and
Litchfield to assist them in filling in the interior details, and proceeded further west carrying
on the boundary traverses. At the end of March, Mr. Ryall was relieved from his duties
connected with the Dún Survey, in order to carry on the Kumaun and Garhwál Survey which
had been suspended during the winter. I am much indebted to Mr. Ryall for his exertions in
training a large number of men and rendering them practically useful in a few months in a
difficult country.

(18.) Lieutenant Gore, R.E. was posted to the party on 1st August 1873, and was sent
Lieutenant St. G. O. Gore, R.E.   at the commencement of the field season on some triangulation to fix points at Roorkee, in anticipation of the observations
of the Transit of Venus. Lieutenant Gore started on this duty on 6th November. Two stations selected by Colonel Tennant, R.E. were fixed by observations to and from the principal
stations of Chándipahár and Doíwála, which are situated in the Siwálik Hills; other permanent
objects viz. the Dome of the College, Foundry Chimney, &c. were also fixed.

(19.) On the completion of this undertaking, early in December, I sent Lieutenant
Gore with a party of five Native Surveyors who had been trained by Mr. Ryall, to take up the
survey of the village boundaries, commencing from the Dehra and Shorepur road and working
westwards. Lieutenant Gore continued on this duty during the remainder of the field season,
and by his energetic and systematic arrangements produced a large amount of boundary work
out of his natives. In addition to this he made a large scale survey of the Harbanswála and
Arcadia Tea plantations, on the scale of 20 inches = 1 mile, comprising an area of about 640
acres. He closed work on 27th May. Lieutenant Gore has become thoroughly acquainted

with the practical operations of the Survey and has rendered me much valuable assistance.
    (20.) Mr. Peyton was not employed in the field, his services being required in the draw-
ing branch of the Head Quarters' Office where he also supervis-
Mr. J. Peyton.
ed the Native Draftsmen belonging to this party, who remained
in Quarters preparing the skeleton sheets of Kumaun and Garhwál. Mr. Peyton was transferred
to the Guzerat Party from the 1st May.
    (21.) Mr. Neuville was appointed to this party on 1st November, but owing to the state
of his health which the Civil Surgeon of Dehra certified was
Mr. O. J. Neuville.
quite unequal to out-door work of any nature, and that any
exposure would be attended with considerable risk, his services were utilized in the head camp
in carrying on the current Office work and in the computations of the triangulation and traverses
which involved a considerable amount of labour.
    (22.) At the end of the field season of 1872-73, Mr. Low had received orders from
Lieutenant Hill, who was then in charge of the party, to con-
Mr. J. Low.
tinue his field operations in Kumaun throughout the summer
and autumn months. This portion of his work will be reported on under head of the Kumaun
and Garhwál Survey. He returned to Dehra about 20th December, and after a few days' rest
commenced operations in the Dún. Up to the middle of February he was employed in traversing and though his progress was not rapid at first, owing to want of experience in work of this
nature, the results were good. He was afterwards employed on triangulation in the Siwálik
Hills, east of the Mohan Pass. This undertaking was taken up chiefly for the purpose of
furnishing points for Captain Bailey's Survey of the Siwáliks. Mr. Low commenced observations on the 7th March and closed work on 27th May, completing an area of 83 square miles.
The details of his work will be found in the tabulated return at page 41—n. His observations
were much hindered by the hazy weather which invariably prevails during April and May, and his
progress was further retarded by the physical difficulties of the Siwálik Hills, the precipitous
nature of which caused much delay in moving from point to point. Mr. Low had thus been
for 18 consecutive months on field duty and has worked hard and well.
    (23.) Mr. L. Pocock took the field on 8th November and was employed throughout the
season in triangulating. He executed a net-work triangulation
Mr. L. Pocock.
covering 267 square miles, consisting of 104 points visited and
451 fixed by intersection, the heights of 103 of which were determined by vertical observations.
Mr. Pocock is a rapid and excellent observer and has throughout given me every satisfaction.
Unfortunately his health is far from good and he cannot stand much exposure. His progress
was somewhat retarded on this account, but he worked hard till the beginning of May when
his health broke down, and on submitting a medical certificate, he was permitted to proceed to
recess quarters where he was employed in bringing up the computations of his work.
    (24.) Mr. Macdougall was transferred to this party on 1st January, but as his services
were required in the Computing Office, he did not join till the
Mr. J. W. Macdougall.
end of that month. He was employed till the end of April in
the office in computations. I was much pleased with his steady application and industry. He is
very energetic and hardworking, but his want of accuracy is a great drawback to his usefulness
as a computer. During May he was employed in traversing in and about the station of Dehra.
The results of his work were very satisfactory and will be found detailed in the tabular statement.
    (25.) Mr. Todd was employed in quarters till 23rd February in preparing one of the
degree sheets of Kumaun and Garhwál, and in the current work
Mr. H. Todd.
connected with the publication of the one inch sheets. He
joined my camp at the end of February, when I instructed him to take up the topography of
section 17 and the western half of section 28. He commenced plane-tabling on the 12th
March and completed the above sections single handed, there being no Native Surveyors available at that time to assist him. On 4th May he took up the topography of section 16 with two
Native Surveyors, each with a plane-table, one of whom however had received no instruction in
plane-tabling. Mr. Todd had therefore to train him ab initio. With the exception of a small
portion in the S. W. corner, this section was also completed. The portion of country in which
Mr. Todd worked is a level plain, partly cultivated and partly waste and forest land, with a fair
amount of detail which had to be delineated principally by the laborious process of chaining.
At the end of March, I inspected Mr. Todd's work and found it very carefully done. His total
area comprises 22,507 acres, which was executed at the rate of 16 square miles per mensem.
Mr. Todd is a very careful and accurate Surveyor and though his health was not good towards
the end of the season, he continued assiduously at his work till 23rd May and has proved himself to be a valuable assistant both in the field and in office.
    (26.) Mr. Kinney took the field on 25th November and was first employed in triangula-
ting in the neighbourhood of Dehra. On the 15th December,
Mr. T. Kinney.
on the completion of this piece of work, I attached him to Mr.
Ryall to assist him in the training of the Native Surveyors and in the reduction of the boundary
traverses. On 16th January, he was deputed to connect certain boundary pillars with trigono-

metrical stations so as to furnish checks for the village traverses. He was employed in this way with Mr. Ryall till the middle of February, by which time the preliminary work was sufficiently advanced for the topography to be taken up. To Mr. Kinney was allotted the western half of section 38 and the eastern half of section 28; he was provided with three Native Surveyors, all of whom however he had to train in plane-tabling, their previous work having been confined to boundary traverses. He commenced the topography on 10th March and on closing work for the season on 27th May, had completed an area of 13,530 acres which was at the rate of 14¼ square miles per mensem. The greater portion of this piece of country is very highly cultivated and with a large amount of detail, and considering that a great portion of his time was taken up in training three Sub-Surveyors, his out-turn may I think be considered very creditable.

(27.) Mr. Wrixon was transferred to this party from 1st October and was employed throughout the greater part of the field season in carrying main traverses for fixing trijunction pillars, so as to form proper checks on the boundary traverses. He subsequently, for the same object, executed some minor triangulation near the foot of the hills where the ground would not admit of traverse lines being run between trigonometrical stations. His work will be found detailed in the tabular statement and stood the usual test very satisfactorily. I am glad to be able to report favorably of Mr. Wrixon's exertions. He still requires a good deal of supervision, but his system of working has considerably improved since he has been attached to this party.

Mr. E. P. Wrixon.

(28.) Mr. Litchfield took the field on 24th November and after a few days' instruction in traversing, he was sent to carry on main circuit traverses over ground to the N. W. of Dehra. These circuits embraced comparatively very rough ground, the traverse lines running into and over numerous deep ravines. Under the circumstances, the results of his labour which will be found in the tabulated return, are very creditable. On the completion of this piece of work, he was employed for a month and a half in assisting Mr. Ryall in the reduction of traverses, and subsequently in the beginning of March, took up the topography of section 37 which he was employed on till the 4th April, when, on account of his services being required for the Kumaun and Garhwál Survey, he closed work in the Dún. He completed an area of 4,014 acres at the rate of about 11 square miles per mensem. His ground was much more intricate than the portions surveyed by Messrs. Todd and Kinney, hence the slower rate of progress.

Mr. E. Litchfield.

(29.) Mr. Pocock had hitherto done no independent field work, having been employed in the Office during the previous (his first) field season; he had therefore to be instructed in the method of traversing and connecting traverses together. In the beginning of December, he was deputed to carry a series of traverses from the E. End Base-Line through the valleys of the Asan and Jumna. His progress, owing to his inexperience, was at first slow and was further much retarded by the bhábar grass and khyr jungle through which his lines had to be cleared. Mr. Pocock applied himself very diligently to his work and promises to become a useful member of the Survey. Having been told off to accompany the party proceeding into Kumaun for the continuation of the survey there, he closed work in the Dún on 4th April. The detail of his work will be found in the tabulated return.

Mr. I. Pocock.

(30.) The Native Surveyors have as a body done well and worked diligently, and considering they were all new hands, have done as much as could be expected of them. In flat even ground some of them have already done independent work in putting in the features, and with more practice, I have no doubt will improve and turn out good work. A few of the more intelligent men, I am in hopes, may be utilized in surveying the more rugged and hilly ground near the foot of the hills, but I fear it will take sometime to train them for work of this nature, which cannot be tested by the system of *partál* lines.

Native Surveyors.

(31.) As the topography had to be taken in hand during the season, and check points furnished for the village boundary traverses, a very large amount of calculation had to be done in the field. I at first thought that the system of plotting the boundary traverses by protraction would have answered every purpose, but as the Native Surveyors were all unpractised hands and not good at the work, and the boundaries as a rule were very intricate, it was found that time would be saved by reducing all these traverses in the first instance. This laborious duty devolved chiefly on the Head Office and occupied a very considerable portion of my time. I have now however four natives thoroughly trained in these computations, which will relieve the European assistants of this irksome task.

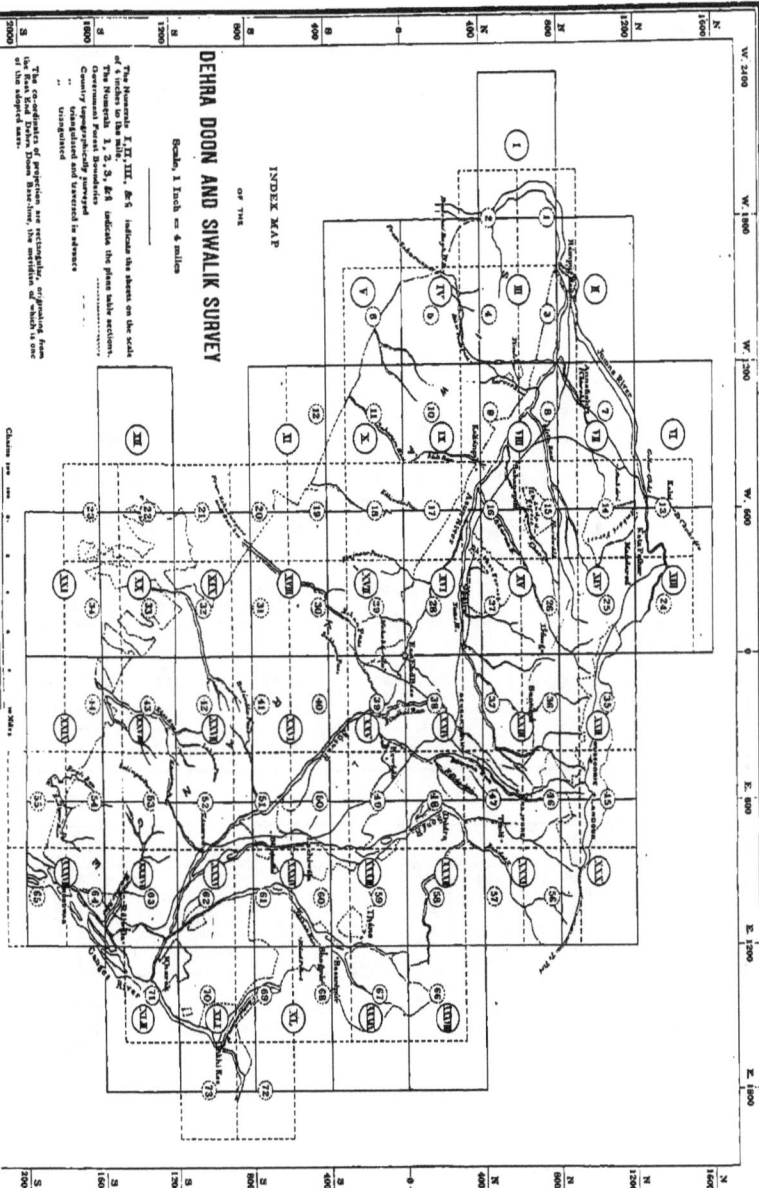

DEHRA DOON AND SIWALIK SURVEY

INDEX MAP

OF THE

Scale, 1 Inch = 4 miles

The Numerals I.,II.,III., &c of 4 inches to the mile, indicate the sheets on the scale.

The Numerals 1, 2, 3, &4 indicate the plane table sections.

Government Forest Boundaries

Country topographically surveyed

triangulated and traversed in advance

triangulated

The co-ordinates of projection are rectangular, originating from the East End Dehra Doon Base-line, the meridian of which is one of the adopted axes.

Chains

Miles

W. 2400 W. 1800 W. 1200 W. 600 0 E. 600 E. 1200 E. 1800

DEHRA DUN SURVEY.

Tabular statement of out-turn of work. Season 1873-74.

Details of Triangulation.

Observer's Names.	Instrument used.	Area triangulated in square miles.	No. of stations visited.	No. of points fixed by intersection but not visited.	No. of stations whose positions and heights have been fixed.	No. of stations whose positions only have been fixed.	No. of hill tops cleared of forest.	Average number of trigonometrical points per square mile.	Average area in square miles to each trigonometrical height.	No. of triangles of which all three angles have been observed.	Mean triangular error.	No. of triangles of which only two angles have been observed.	No. of trijunction boundary pillars fixed.
Lieut. St. G. C. Goro,...	Inch. 14	158	4	4	0	8	0	0·05	...	4	1·5	4	
Mr. J. Low, ...	8	83	44	106	58	92	37	1·75	1·8	68	8·9	221	
„ L. J. Pocock, ...	12	287	104	451	108	452	0	2·08	3·0	69	15·5	782	15
„ T. Kinney, ...	7	11	13	38	0	47	0	4·27	...	16	50·4	60	7
„ E. P. Wrixon, ...	7	10	22	0	0	20	0	2·00	...	17	24·3	15	29
Totals, ...	...	529	187	597	156	619	37	...	...	174	...	1082	51

Details of topography. Scale 4 inches = 1 mile.

Names.	Area in acres.	No. of Plane Table Stations.	No. of acres per Plane Table Station.	Out-turn of work in acres per diem.
Mr. H. Todd,	22,507	2,447	9·2	831
„ T. Kinney,	13,530	1,220	11·1	301
„ E. F. Litchfield,	4,014	622	6·5	228
Totals, ...	40,051	4,289	9·0	...

Details of traversing.

THEODOLITE TRAVERSES.				
Names.	Linear miles of traverse.	No. of stations.	Average error per 1,000 links.	Average angular error per station.
Mr. J. Low, ...	18	84	0·63	16
„ J. Macdougall, ...	26	87	0·78	16
„ E. P. Wrixon, ...	129	292	0·60	28
„ E. F. Litchfield, ...	11	70	0·89	11
„ I. S. Pocock, ...	87	149	0·81	34
Totals, ...	271	682	Mean 0·74	Mean 21

PLANE TABLE AND PROTRACTOR TRAVERSES.			
Nature of ground.	Linear miles of traverse.	No. of stations.	Average error per 1,000 links.
Native Surveyors { Fair, ...	403	4,404	1·97
Rough and hilly, ...	174	2,666	4·71
Totals, ...	577	7,070	

KUMAUN AND GARHWAL SURVEY.

(32.) The extent of country which remained to be surveyed in Kumaun and Garhwál
was estimated at about 3,600 square miles and consists of ground
Arrangements for the continuation of the Survey. of very great altitude, physically the most trying and formidable to Surveyors. A considerable portion of this tract about
the high ranges, probably one half, may be said to be simply impracticable and can really be
only reconnoitred. It was arranged that this unsurveyed portion should be placed under the
charge of Mr. E. C. Ryall, who by his long and varied experiences in mountain surveying was
specially fitted for such an arduous undertaking.

(33.) The period during the year in which actual field operations can be carried on in
Limited period of field operations. such high altitudes being very short, it was arranged that the
party should recess close to the scene of its operations, in order
to avail itself of as much of the clear and mild weather as possible. The probable working
period was estimated at 45 days before the rains and about the same number afterwards, though
this of course depends a great deal upon the nature of the season. Almora being the nearest
station to their operations, was selected for recess quarters.

(34.) The members as per margin were told off for the operations in Kumaun and
Garhwál, Mr. McA'Fee having been transferred to this party
E. C. Ryall Esq.
Mr. McA'Fee.
„   Litchfield.
„   I. Pocock.
„   McCarthy.
from the Guzerat Survey in April and Mr. McCarthy from the
Head Quarters' Office in February. The party assembled in
Dehra early in April and after making their necessary arrangements for the campaign, started for Almora on 12th April.

(35.) At the close of the field season of 1873-74, Mr. Low was directed by Lieutenant
Mr. J. Low.
Hill, R.E. who was then in charge of the party, on the completion of his topographical work, to carry a minor series of
triangles from the base Húm H.S. to Punya H.S. up the valley of the Gorí to the Passes
above Milam. Mr. Low however owing to unavoidable delays, as stated in Lieutenant Hill's
narrative report for last year, did not finish his plane-tabling work till the end of June. It
was not till the beginning of July therefore that he could commence his observations, which
proved to be too late; for owing to clouds and bad weather Mr. Low after remaining one month
at his first station Húm H.S. did not succeed in getting half a day's work. The state of his
health then compelled him to apply for a month's privilege leave to proceed to Naini Tal for
medical treatment. He recommenced his observations at his first station on 27th September,
and from that time till 1st December he was steadily engaged in pushing on the triangulation.
During this time he visited 24 stations ranging in height from 4,000 to 13,800 feet above sea
level. The season was a particularly severe one, the first heavy fall of snow taking place so
early as the 10th October. The establishment all suffered more or less in consequence, and six
of the natives were severely frost bitten, one of whom I regret to say, lost all the toes of one
foot; the other men recovered. Mr. Low had severe weather to contend with and his work
involved a good deal of exposure. Although his area embraced a portion that had been previously triangulated, he fixed a number of additional points which rendered matters more easy
for the plane-tablers.

(36.) Mr. Ryall has submitted the following report of the operations under his charge
Out-turn of work. up to the time of returning to recess quarters at Almora in
July.

"My camp left Dehra on 12th April reaching Káládúngi on 26th and Almora on 2nd
of May where I was detained till the 7th. In the meantime I was pushing on with the computations, while the Assistants under me were going on with the projection of their boards.
At Bagesar, two marches out of Almora, I thought it advisable to split up my camp into two
and march to our ground in separate detachments by different routes. By the time I got to
the ground I had finished all the computation of the triangulation required for our work. When
marching from Naini Tal to our ground the party suffered somewhat from the great heat in
the valleys.

"Of the four Assistants, *viz.*, Messrs. McA'Fee, Litchfield, I. Pocock and McCarthy,
none, with the exception of Mr. Litchfield, had had any training in hill sketching; it devolved on
me therefore to train these three. In this duty Mr. Litchfield helped me greatly by taking
Mr. I. Pocock in hand. I deputed Mr. McA'Fee to finish up about 14 square miles of P.T.
section No. 57 and Mr. Pocock about 28 square miles of the same section lying to the northeast. After these portions were completed, Mr. McA'Fee was directed to take up P.T. section
No. 63 and the western parts of section No. 62. I anticipated that the trigonometrical points
lying to the west of these sections would not perhaps be sufficient to extend the sketching in
them much to the eastward. I provided Mr. McA'Fee therefore with a 7-inch theodolite to
enable him to lay down some additional points should he deem it necessary to do so and could
find the time to extend the triangulation in that direction. Mr. Pocock, I arranged, should
assist Mr. Litchfield by taking up the eastern parts of P.T. sections Nos. 56, 48 and 40. To

Mr. McCarthy I allotted the sketching of the Rálam valley, being a part of P.T. section No. 55. "Having made the above dispositions, I proceeded to extend the triangulation taken in hand by Mr. Low last year. At first sight the conducting of a series of triangles into the Milam valley appears impracticable, but a few days' reconnoitring convinced me that it was feasible. I lost no time therefore in extending it. I found however that I could make no progress till 8 days after on account of unseasonable weather.

"The incessant rains that besieged the whole of Kumaun from 30th May up to 13th July with the exception of one day the 19th June, was an unusual circumstance and tended greatly to retard the progress of the work. After the 12th June however the weather, without apparently abating in the daily amount of rainfall, became so far favorable as to give to the Surveyors employed in sketching a few hours of the early morning. It became apparent therefore to all of us that encamping on the heights was necessary to enable one to take advantage of the few clear hours during the earlier parts of the day.

"I pressed on with my triangulation up to the Uttar Dhurra Pass. I found it impossible to observe at some of my stations and deferred visiting them to a future and more favorable time. The ascent to some of these stations is very steep the entire way; in others it is gradual for about half the distance only and none of those peaks I was informed had so much as 6 square feet of flattish ground for encamping on. It was clear that to visit these places it would be necessary to go up in one day, finish the observations and return again the same day. This the weather would not admit of my doing, for it generally takes me about 4 hours climbing to accomplish 6,000 feet, beginning at an altitude of 10,000 feet above sea level. It is not an easy matter to climb up precipitous ascents of rock, ice and snow in the day time and doing so at night is simply out of the question.

"The extent of triangulation finished by me covers an area of 460 square miles comprising 14 stations visited, of an average height of 15,500 feet above sea level. I closed work on 2nd July and got out of the Milam valley on the 7th when I was joined by Messrs. Pocock and McCarthy. I arrived at Almora on 14th July.

"Mr. McA'Fee began work on 24th May and having finished up the portion of P. T. section No. 57 allotted to him, proceeded with the sketching of P. T. section No. 68. Up to the 11th June Mr. McA'Fee was only able to accomplish in all 34 square miles of sketching, the weather being too unfavorable to do more. He unfortunately fell ill on that day and halted on his ground for 9 days with the hope of recovering, but as no improvement took place in the state of his health, he marched to Almora for medical advice. Mr. McA'Fee showed throughout great willingness and but for his falling ill, I have no doubt, he would have brought in a large quantity of work. The average height at which he worked, is about 8,500 feet and the highest point visited by him is 11,300 feet.

"Mr. Litchfield after training Mr. I. Pocock commenced work on his own ground on 26th May and notwithstanding the badness of the weather, pushed on with his sketching in a very creditable manner and completed 238 square miles of topography. The highest points visited by Mr. Litchfield are about 17,000 feet and the average height at which he worked is about 12,500 feet. Mr. Litchfield closed work on the 30th June and marched back to Almora where he arrived on 9th July.

"Mr. I. Pocock commenced his work on the 15th May under the supervision and training of Mr. Litchfield. In 6 or 7 days Mr. Pocock was sufficiently advanced to get on with his work independently. Considering all things and the badness of the weather Mr. Pocock made very fair progress completing the sketching of 149 square miles. The highest point visited by Mr. Pocock is about 16,000 feet above sea level, and the average height at which he worked is about 10,000 feet. Mr. Pocock closed work on 5th July and joined my camp on its way back to Almora on the 7th.

"Mr. J. McCarthy after being duly trained by me, commenced his work on 27th May. At first Mr. McCarthy got somewhat confused on account of the intricate disposition of the snowy peaks about him. I had an opportunity on the 12th June of meeting him and putting him all right. Mr. McCarthy did very well, turning out an area of 128 square miles. He worked at an average height of 15,000 feet above sea level, the highest point visited by him being about 18,000 feet. Mr. McCarthy closed work on 5th July and joined my camp on the 6th idem.

"It now remains for me to deal with such points in connection with the work as appear to me not to be irrelevant in a report of this kind. It is a generally received opinion among those who have not had experience of the hardships of moving about in mountains of considerable altitude that the undertaking is somewhat akin to a pleasure trip; that so far as regards health it is the finest thing; that the sight of glorious mountain scenery, the hard walks, the bracing air, &c., are changes that promote in every way the physique of those who go through those "pleasures." Having had a good deal of experience among mountains, I will give a rough sketch of what I think about the realities of mountain travelling in very high altitudes.

"The traveller who goes only to gratify his taste for sport and the traveller who goes with the double object of seeing strange places and enjoying mountain scenery, have easy times of it compared to what the Surveyor has to undergo. The Surveyor goes under an obligation and is naturally anxious about his work. He has to visit places and climb mountains that an ordinary traveller never attempts. The former has to pass most of his nights on high ridges; the highest point that the latter ever visits is a Pass, and to that he has invariably a fair road and seldom passes a night at what one would call a very great elevation. Survey officers while working at very great elevations are much exposed to the distressing influences of rarified air and a cold temperature, which I cannot help thinking must be injurious to the constitution. To the hardships that they are exposed might be added the risks they constantly incur when journeying from mountain top to mountain top, for they very rarely have the luxury of using foot-paths. The work of carrying loads therefore becomes singularly harassing to the inhabitants who are summoned to act as coolies; and at elevation averaging over 12,000 ft. it becomes impossible for them to carry the standard weight of 20 seers per cooly. Guides of the district of Bhot in Kumaun and Garhwál are only acquainted with such localities as shooting and grazing grounds. It follows therefore that the Surveyor has to rely mainly upon his own judgment as to the line of route he is to adopt when going up to the top of ridges and spurs, exceeding 18,000 feet above sea level.

"Accompanying is a statement shewing the amount of work done by the snow party.

"From the two points on the ridge over which the Uttar Dhurra Pass crosses, I obtained a good view of the country to a distance of 12 or 14 miles to the north-west, about 10 miles to the north and a few miles to the north-east. The characteristic features of the whole of this part of the country are precisely the same as those of the northern parts of Ladák. The quantity of snow about it is very small; even at a height of 18,500 feet in many places there is not a vestige to be seen. The spurs and slopes are generally of a soft and undulating character. The only drawbacks to it are its great altitude, the difficulty of moving a survey camp, and the increased contingent expenses that would have to be incurred. It would be better, though not strictly speaking actually necessary, to connect the Níti with the Milam triangulation, but from all I could see, I think the main difficulty in the neighbourhood would be found in the neighbourhood of the Níti valley and I am disposed to look upon such a junction as impracticable."

The area topographically surveyed on the scale of 1 inch = 1 mile, comprises 584 square miles and the country triangulated covers 859 square miles. Considering the very unfavorable weather experienced owing to the monsoon setting in so early and that two of the party were inexperienced hands, this out-turn is I think very creditable to Mr. Ryall and the assistants employed under him.

KUMAUN AND GARHWAL SURVEY.
Tabular Statement of out-turn of work, Season 1873-74.
Details of Triangulation.

NAMES.	No. of stations visited.	No. of triangles completed.	No. of intersected points fixed.	No. of intersected points of previous triangulation refixed.	No. of points whose heights have been determined.	Area triangulated in square miles.	Average altitude above sea level in feet, of stations visited.
E. C. Ryall, Esq.	14	7	72	0	50	460	15,580
Mr. J. Low, ...	24	22	28	18	70	399	8,452
Totals, ...	38	29	100	18	120	859	

Details of Topography.   Scale 1 inch = 1 mile.

NAMES.	Area in square miles.	Average number of plane-table stations per square mile.
Mr. C. H. McA'Fee, ...	84	0·7
„ E. F. Litchfield, ...	228	0·3
„ I. S. Pocock, ...	149	1·1
„ J. F. McCarthy, ...	123	0·3
Total, ...	584	0·6

Extract from the Narrative Report—dated 30th September 1874—of Captain A. W. BAIRD, R.E.,
Officiating Deputy Superintendent 3rd Grade, in charge Tidal and Leveling Party.

(1.) My last annual report informed you of all that had been done in altering the
All instruments &c. ready to be sent off to the Gulf of Kutch. Self Registering Tide Gauges for adaptation to any scale
required, and that all the instruments, material, &c., for carry-
ing out the operations at the Tidal Observatories were ready
for despatch by boat from Bombay.

(2.) A large Puttimar or Buggalow was engaged by the month from the 1st October,
Loading up Puttimar. and this eventually turned out to be a very economical arrangement. Loading was at once commenced, and although I had
relays of coolies, it took 10 days for all the material to be stowed away.

(3.) Meanwhile a small boat had been sent off to Gogo from Bombay, with a detach-
Small Puttimar despatched to Gogo. ment of the men, to march thence to Wadwán and meet me.
Calassies and puttiwallahs had been engaged in Bombay.

(4.) Every thing being ready Mr. Bell, Surveyor attached to the Party, and Mr. Peters
Large Puttimar leaves Bombay. of the Harbour Defence Works (whose services had been temporarily placed at my disposal by the Government of Bombay)
along with 6 Sub-Surveyors and about 24 men embarked in the large Puttimar and sailed on the
13th October for their destination, viz., the site of Okha Tidal Station, opposite the Island of
Beyt, at the mouth of the Gulf of Kutch.

(6.) Having now seen every thing required despatched by boats, and the remaining in-
Remainder of the Party with office stores leaves Bombay for Rajkote. struments carefully stored away in the Harbour Defence Work-
shops, I left Bombay by rail for Wadwán and arrived at Rajkote
on the 24th of October.

(8.) I called on the acting Political Agent at Rajkote and arranged several matters with
Arrangement with Political Agent for assistance from Native States. him regarding the assistance I should require from the Native
State in whose territories the Tidal Observatories and Bench
Marks were to be made. He furnished me with Purwanas, for
use in Kattywar.

(10.) Having been joined by the sowars from His Highness the Gackwar's contingent I
Leave Rajkote for Okha Tidal Station. marched viâ Dwarka to Okha Tidal Station, taking with me the
chronometers and such instruments as I required, and I arrived
at the station on the 21st November.

(11.) Captain Jackson, the Assistant Resident at Dwarka, had kindly come out to settle
The Assistant Resident, Dwarka, visits Okha to arrange for supplies &c. for the camp. matters on the spot with the native officials of Beyt, so that
there might be no delay to the progress of the work : he met
me at Aramra about 4 miles from Okha and the nearest village
on the main land to the station, and accompanied me to the camp.
We found it would be more convenient and economical to get all supplies and even drinking water
by boat from the Island of Beyt immediately opposite the station.

(12.) The Puttimar had arrived safely with Mr. Bell and his detachment all the stores
State of affairs on arrival at station. had been landed which were required for this station, and
work had been commenced on the 5th November, in sinking
the masonry well.

(14.) The well sinking went on steadily, building up one day and then allowing 2 or 3
Progress of the well sinking Bull's dredgers used. days to dry, and excavating inside by Bull's dredgers : 11 feet
9 inches had been completed by the 24th November.

(15.) On the days that work had to be stopped at the well to allow the masonry just
House for the men at the station constructed. built to dry the masons were employed in erecting a house
for the men who were to be left in charge of the station : the
calassies and coolies in bringing stone and mud for this purpose also, and in clearing away the
jungle close to the camp.

(16.) We found that Bull's dredgers acted admirably in soft sand, but when we came
across any hard strata, then the man standing on the opened bucket, caused it to get a better
grip in being lifted up, and so brought up more material ; also this man tamped all round with
his feet close to the wooden frame as each bucket was taken up, thereby not allowing a deep
hole to be excavated in the centre, while the sand remained at its sides : otherwise from the
treacherous nature of the ground, a sudden sinking of the well might have occurred, which
would undoubtedly have ended in a smash. By the 29th November we had got so far down,
that the water inside the well could no longer be kept sufficiently under to allow the man to
go down to work and tamping from the top by a long rod was commenced. By the evening of
the 29th November 17½ feet had been completed, and 25 feet was the total required. Some
rock having been observed cropping up, at low water, a short distance off, I was afraid we
might come across it before the proper depth was reached. I had a long iron bar driven

8½ feet below the bottom of the well, by means of a small pile monkey and was glad to find no rock although the sandy strata below was very hard ; by the night of the 4th December the whole depth of 25 feet was completed.

(17.) During this time I had taken several observations to stars to rate the chrono- **Rating chronometers. Range of Tide roughly determined.** meters : also I had determined roughly the range of the Tide at Okha to be 14·90 feet at Spring Tides ; so as to regulate the scale for working the self registering Tide Gauge ; and, I determined by soundings at low water that at 120 feet out, 19 feet of water was found, as I had previously recorded in the last year's reconnaissance and here the rose at the end of the flexible pipe was to be placed.

(18.) The cylinders having been all cleaned out and painted over, inside and outside, **Cylinders placed in position.** with tar, to keep them from rusting, the upright length of small rigid pipe with its bend was attached to the lower length of the cylinder, and 2 other lengths screwed on above. The gyn, tackle, &c., being all in readiness, these three lengths of cylinder were lowered inside the well, and held in suspension, until 2 more lengths were screwed on, and then 2 more making in all 7 lengths or about 29 feet ; on lowering we found the whole cylinder floating in the water inside the masonry well, and water had to be poured down inside the cylinder to make it sink. On the 7th December the cylinder was finally placed in position.

(19.) The next thing was to lay out the iron pipes : this was a most tedious operation **Iron pipes being laid out from the cylinder.** for the trench had to be of great width on account of the sand falling in constantly at high tide : it must be remembered that in all the operations the amount of plant was limited for we were quite in the jungle and had to use such appliances as were at hand. A wooden frame about 3 feet high and 2 feet wide was inserted in the masonry well for the exit of the iron pipe and stop cock. After keeping all available hands hard at work and the pump going with relays of men, one length of pipe towards the sea was eventually attached on the 10th December—the end of the pipe being carefully plugged up to prevent sand coming in—a thick wall of stone and lime was built all round the stop cock and connected with the masonry well ; also a layer of masonry underneath the first length of iron pipe : but still the water percolated in on all sides, and it seemed perfectly hopeless to keep the stop cock dry and to have access to it. The following day the masonry wall was removed and the length of iron pipe disconnected, and two feet added to the height of the vertical pipe and then the bend with the stop cock fitted on.

(20.) A water tight box 3 feet long and about 1 foot square was made in halves and **Arrangement for keeping stop cock dry and having access to it at all times.** fitted over and under the stop cock, holes having been cut at A and B and carefully caulked up after the box had been fitted over the pipe ; in this way no water could get at the stop cock except over the top of the box. Underneath the first 7 or 8 feet of the pipe leading to the sea a layer of mud and stones of considerable thickness was made and a wall of similar material built all round the stop cock leaving a space about 3 feet square in the centre for standing in, and steps for getting down to it, also mud and sand were thrown down between the iron cylinder and the masonry well right up to the level of the stop cock bend : by the 13th December this was completed, and it was found then that the stop cock was quite dry and access could be had to it at any time however high the tide was.

(21.) Simultaneously with the work at the stop **Laying out remainder of iron pipe.** cock the iron pipes were laid out, considerable difficulty being experienced from the sand tumbling in, and by the 15th December 11 lengths had been fitted.

(22.) At the same time that this was being car- **Observatory put in position and fitted up.** ried out the portable wooden observatory was erected over the cylinder on its piles and cross beams and with a rough masonry platform all round. By the 18th December the observatory was finished and all the fittings placed in it and the aneroid barometer and anemometer set up.

(25.) A temporary Tide Gauge was then set up on a pile a little above low water mark, **Temporary Tide Gauge set up and 3 Bench Marks built.** also three Bench-marks were imbedded in masonry platforms at different distances from the observatory : the top of the platform in each case being about 6 inches under ground. Also a pole was fixed by leveling so as to shew to what height the sea had to rise when it would be safe to open the stop cock.

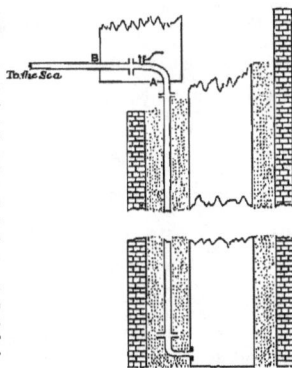

(26.) The self registering Tide Gauge was started on a preliminary trial on the 20th

The S.R.T.G. started on a preliminary trial. December : the float band was altered after one day's work to allow the pencil when near the centre of the barrel to agree with mid tide.

(27.) The cylinder had been pumped dry and the stop cock opened and shut several

Leakage in pipes discovered. times to try and exclude all the air. The temporary Tide Gauge was connected by leveling with the top of the cylinder for comparison of level of water inside and outside : and after a couple of days' trial it was apparent that air was coming in somewhere in the pipes.

(28.) The last three lengths of pipes were taken off and the brass connecting piece at

Iron pipes tested for leakage. the end having been plugged up firmly, the pipes were filled with water, and raised vertically, thus getting a pressure of about an atmosphere and a half, when it was found, that there was a considerable escape between the cast iron flanges and the pipes screwed into them, and also in the brass piece itself water oozed out shewing how badly it had been cast. These three lengths were replaced by others which stood the test, and the brass was hammered where the flaws occurred (as it was imperative to have this part of the system air tight, the other parts being well buried in the sand, or in the water beyond did not require to be so carefully constructed) and the whole relaid again.

(29.) The bed plate of the self registering Tide Gauge was connected by leveling

Every thing ready for final measurement &c. with Bench-marks A, B and C, as to this level of the bed plate all measurements for height of water in the cylinder would be referred ; and on the evening of the 23rd December every thing seemed to be in good order and ready for the final measurements to be taken, clocks to be rated &c. previous to leaving the station.

(30.) About 3 A. M. on the morning of the 24th December the puttiwallah on duty at

Disaster to flexible pipe. the observatory saw a boat which had been sent the previous day to be filled up with stone, drifting down from her anchorage some distance above : he called out lustily to the crew, but they were all asleep : the boat dragged her anchors across the flexible pipe, smashed it in two places, and carried away buoys, anchor, &c., and was brought to near Sainia Island ¼ a mile off. After considerable trouble (its anchor having got fixed among some projecting ledges of rock) the boat was taken back and the anchor and buoy with the chain attached were saved but a good deal of the flexible pipe was quite useless. Some of the piping for the other stations was immediately landed and all the necessary repairs effected by the night of the 24th December.

(31.) Some time before this unfortunate disaster occurred, I had asked the Assistant

Boats warned not to come near the rod buoy. Resident to warn all boatmen at the different Bunders in Okha Mundel not to come within 100 yards of the rod buoy at the Tidal Station. Later on in the season I had printed circulars in Guzerathi issued to all the Durbars for distribution at their different Bunders cautioning all boatmen plying in the Gulf of Kutch not to come near the red buoys at Okha, Nawanár or Hanstal Tidal Stations and the guards at the stations had strict orders to make prisoners of Tindals wilfully infringing these rules : also by your orders I made certain arrangements for protecting the pipe in case any boat should again drag her anchor across the flexible pipe.

(32.) On the 25th and 26th December comparisons were made to compare the level of

Measurement made for connecting position of pencil on S.R.T.G. and distance of water from Bed plate—Rating clocks &c. &c. Temporary Tide Gauge comparison. the sea water outside, as indicated by the temporary Tide Gauge with that of the water in the cylinder : and they were found to agree exactly. The clocks of the self registering Tide Gauge and aneroid barometer were rated many times and the pendulum of each altered as necessary till they appeared to be going very well : the anemometer clock was apparently going in pretty good time.

Measurements were taken at both rising and falling tides to determine the distance of the water in the cylinder from the bed plate which agreed with the pencil being on the central line of the barrel, and from which of course the corresponding depth for the zero line could be deduced. The measurements were made very exactly by means of a tape to the end of which was attached a flat piece of wood about 4 inches square with a thin cake of lead 2 inches square fitted to its centre. At the instant of contact with the water, the position of the pencil was marked on the barrel and the depth from the bed plate recorded to the $\frac{1}{40}$ of an inch : and the distance on either side of the central line of the barrel also taken to the $\frac{1}{40}$ part of an inch. This was repeated about 20 times and the mean value of the set taken as the value for the rising or falling tide as the case happened.

(34.) On the 23rd December I sent off Nursing Dass, Sub-Surveyor, to lay down Bench-

Sub-Surveyor sent off to lay down Bench-marks and Pillars. marks and Pillars, one at about every 10 miles from Okha Tidal Station along the road to Hanstal and thence to Nawanár in Kutch across the Runn. I had ordered him to lay down these Bench-marks also with reference to the nearest G. T. Stations.

(35.) A guard of 4 Sepoys and 1 Naique was supplied from the Battalion of His Highness
the Gaekwar, for the protection of the Station—their duties
Guard, Post runners, Supplies, &c.,   being principally to see that no boat came near the buoy, so far
for the Tidal Station.   as they could prevent it. Three post runners were engaged for
carrying the letters to and from Dwarka (the nearest Post Office) and by this means I could
receive a daily report of the working of the station which the Sub-Surveyors had to fill in from
the printed forms supplied them. The food for the men of the station was to be sent 2 or 3
times a month from Beyt: the Thaundar was responsible for this, and their drinking water
(as the number of men including the guard was now only 9) could be procured from a well
about a mile and half off; coolies being engaged twice a month to fill an iron water tank left
at the station for this purpose.

(36.) Every thing being now apparently in good working order and a supply of stones
filled up in one of the boats, the party embarked on the after-
Embark for Hanstal Tidal Station.   noon of the 27th December for Hanstal.

(37.) I shall now describe the Okha station as left on the 27th December 1873. The observatory is situated on the shore of the Okha Mandal mainland
General Position.   almost exactly opposite the town and island of Beyt, about 300
yards south of the northeastern corner of the land, and which is called "Okha Point" in some
old charts. The flag of the principal temple of Beyt has a bearing of 151° from the observatory;
the pole in the temple on Sainia island bears 7° 30'. The latitude as deduced from G. T. Survey
triangulation charts is 22° 28' 11" N. nearly, and longitude 69° 7' 0" E.

(38.) The observatory is a wooden erection constructed so as to be easily taken to
pieces and fixed on three cross beams fitted on the tops of
The observatory, cylinder, &c.   6 large piles imbedded 8 feet in the sand. A brick masonry
well 4 feet in diameter was sunk to a depth of 5 or 6 feet below low water springs, the
sand excavated at the bottom being very hard and to all appearances in close proximity to rock. Seven lengths of cylinder each about 4 feet 2 inches long, and composed of
wrought iron, with cast iron flanges carefully faced by turning, so as to fit exactly, were
connected together by bolts and nuts so as to be perfectly water tight and lowered inside this
well. The interior diameter of the cylinder was 22 inches—the level of the top-flange being
about 6 feet above high water spring tide, and about 2 feet 6 inches above the floor of the observatory—a board fitted on and screwed to the top of the cylinder, with holes for the float band
to pass through, prevented any thing falling accidentally inside the cylinder.

(39.) Nine inches from the bottom of the iron pipe was taken up
vertically being connected by a small bend and carried up to
Iron pipe from cylinder to low water   within 12 feet 6 inches of the top of the cylinder where there
mark.   is another bend with a stop cock fitted into it. This 2-inch
iron pipe in lengths of about 14 feet with cast iron flanges at each end was then taken out
(having a slight inclination downwards) until it met the natural surface of the sand close to
low water mark, and this pipe was extended till nearly two lengths appeared to be under water
at even the lowest springs, the total length from the cylinder being 175 feet.

(40.) At the end of the rigid iron pipe a brass connecting piece, made as shewn in the
sketch, was fitted, having two outer extremities, to one of which
Brass connecting piece and flexible   a flexible 2-inch suction pipe was fixed and the other closed by
pipe.   a brass disc with a good washer. Two lengths of this suction
pipe were taken out to deep water:
at the end of the outer length
a copper rose of about 15 inches
length 2 inches diameter and having about 150 holes bored in it
was screwed on. This rose was
sustained about 6 feet from the
bottom, being attached to a small
nun-buoy by a chain and shackle
with swivel, the whole being held
in position in deep water at a
place where there is nearly 20
feet of water at low springs by an
anchor. To the top of this small
nun-buoy a chain was attached,
to which was fixed the large buoy floating on the surface with plenty of slack chain to allow
for rise and fall of tide, and this buoy also marks the position of the flexible pipe.

(41.) The observatory is about 12 feet × 9 feet × 9 feet, the cylinder being about
2 feet from the eastern end : the self registering Tide Gauge
Interior of observatory and fittings.   being of course as nearly as possible in the centre of the
building. The aneroid barometer is placed carefully on a shelf on one corner. The ane-

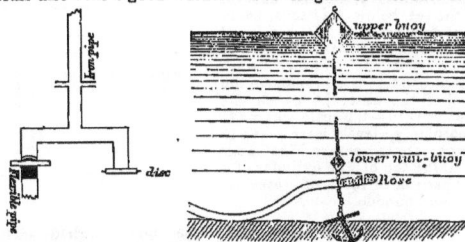

mometer is fixed to a shelf so that the upright pipe passes through the roof close to the ridge at the western end (the Rain Gauge being close to it on the outside). A platform was made to get at the anemometer easily and this served a double purpose, as it was also the framework for a guard to protect the pendulum, and clock of the S. R. T. G., and cloth having been fixed all round it kept any wind from getting to the pendulum. Steps were fixed, convenient for access to the platform. A long box to keep the S. R. T. G. papers on a roller preparatory to putting them on the barrel and which also held diagrams for the other instruments, &c. Also a table made expressly for size to suit the S. R. T. G. sheets being prepared, were placed on one side of the observatory.

(44.) The self registering Tide Gauge was carefully put in its position, so that the
S. R. T. G. in position. band allowed the float to be 3 inches from one side of the cylinder, while it was the same distance itself from the other side. The instrument having been carefully leveled by wedges, the trestle was secured with screws to the floor ; a hole was cut in the floor and a small box let down (properly fitted so as to allow no sand to come in) in order that the counterpoise weight might be able to act for the entire range of the instrument.

The float band was made 35 feet 6 inches long and 33 feet of chain was added to this, and fixed at its other end to the hook under the float, forming a continuous band as it were. The scale of wheels adopted here is ⅓, the barrel being 5 feet long, that scale was the largest that could be used for a 14·90 feet range of tide. The float has a swivel to which the band is attached, and the band also passes through 2 guides fixed to an upright scale on one side, and through another guide fixed to the trestle on the other.

(48.) The temporary Tide Gauge, consisting of a pile firmly imbedded in the sand and

Temporary Tide Gauge.

standing about 8 feet out of the ground, was placed about the level of low water neaps ; to this was attached a box containing a copper float, and a deal rod was attached to it with a pointer about 6¼ feet above the float. The box has a bottom to which is attached a pipe (2 feet long) of small diameter, by means of which the sea has access to the float ; the box itself is about 6 inches square and 6 feet high : the back of it, viz., that side attached to the pile was 12 feet long and has a groove in which the upright rod with the index works (vide sketch) so that by having this upper part numbered from a certain zero the level of the sea below this zero could be at once read off. It was found by careful trial in a bucket of water that the pointer always recorded ·6 feet 2 inches above the level of the water in which the float worked—the scale was made accordingly : levels were taken to connect the temporary Tide Gauge with the top of the cylinder, for comparison of level of water inside and outside.

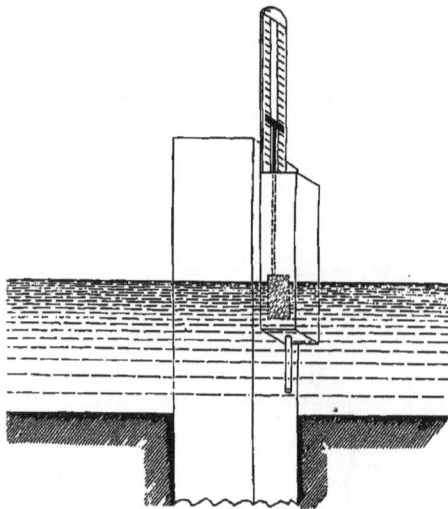

(50.) The Puttimar and other boat weighed anchor on the afternoon of the 27th
Voyage to Hanstal Tidal Station ; December but we had to anchor again off the town of Beyt on
Puttimar stuck on sand bank. account of the tide and remain for the night. On the morning of the 28th we again set sail having a pilot on board the large boat ; after being about half an hour or so under full sail with a stiff breeze, we struck on a sand bank, and heeled over tremendously and then stuck. The tide was falling at the time. On this occasion Mr. Peters' services were invaluable, he at once assumed charge of the vessel and ordered the Nacoda and his men to do what he thought necessary for the safety of the vessel. Heavy spars were lashed vertically to the sides of the Puttimar to prevent it capsizing as the tide fell, and after some considerable delay on the part of the native officials at Beyt,

assistance in the shape of some small boats was sent to us but I must here record that it would have fared very badly with ourselves, the men of the party and the Government stores had not Mr. Peters used prompt measures and taken the command of the vessel out of the hands of the Naccda. A new pilot was obtained from Beyt, and when the boat righted itself in the high tide in the evening we got her out into deep water.

(54.) The ground at Hanstal being black soil, the surface of which was covered by about one inch to one foot of water, at extraordinary high tides, for well, if we could excavate a hole deep enough for the cylinder. This excavation was begun about 30 feet in land from the usual high water line of spring tides, and by the 14th January 16 feet had been finished. After this however it was evident from the sides falling in that we were excavating too perpendicularly, and from the proximity to the water of the creek that a good deal of surface water came in ; on the 23rd I abandoned this site and went in land about 150 feet and commenced the excavation.

Masonry well not required at Hanstal. Excavating hole for the cylinder. miles in land, it was of course unnecessary to sink a masonry

(56.) By making the excavation of considerable diameter and with a pretty gentle slope, in 4 days we had got to the depth required, viz., 25½ feet ; all available hands, coolies, calassies and peons, were kept at this work, and from early morning till dark, because the longer it took there was more chance of the gradual surface drainage carrying down the sides.

(57.) The iron cylinder was lowered into the hole much in the same way as had been done at Okha Tidal Station.

Cylinder placed in position.

(58.) Three Bench-marks, near one of which a pillar was made, were built similarly to those at Okha Tidal Station at different distances from the cylinder : also a house for the men was constructed.

Bench-marks and pillars constructed also house for men.

(59.) The Observatory was next fitted up and placed on its cross beams and piles : steps and side retaining walls having been constructed to have access to the stop cock. Here it was not necessary to contend against the water percolating in to the same extent as at Okha where the foreshore was simply sand. A small box was fitted over the stop cock bend as before and a layer of stone and some cement prevented any great accumulation of water. A temporary Tide Gauge was placed here as at Okha.

Observatory placed in position on its cross beams and piles and pipe being carried out.

(61.) Some time before this one of the reports from Okha Tidal Station brought me information of the entire stoppage of the anemometer clock at that station; some of the wheels having become broken. Finding all the self registering Tide Gauge clocks dirty and that the anemometer clocks wanted generally to be looked at, I found it necessary to get up a first rate watchmaker from Bombay at once ; I kept him hard at work at Hanstal overhauling all the clocks until the station was completed, and then took him on to Okha to repair the damage there.

Watchmaker called up from Bombay.

It was most fortunate I made this arrangement when I did, for he found that the clock of No. 7 Tide Gauge (viz. one of the escapement balance clocks) was quite unfit for work, some of the teeth having been quite worn away : the weight he considered far too heavy. Also all the anemometer clocks had to be carefully cleaned up, for as you will recollect, gold springs had only just been received for them a day or two before I left Bombay and they had been rather hastily put in. I found this Parsee watchmaker a very good workman indeed, and we could not have got on without having all the clocks in good working order.

(62.) As I have already stated I found that there was a great instrumental error in the self registering Tide Gauge, on account of the large amount of back-lash between the wheels attached to the diagram barrel and those of the clock. By a very simple plan I succeeded in quite getting rid of this error and thereby adding very greatly to the value of the performances of the instruments. A small pulley was attached to the trestle by a piece of wood some 6 inches long ; a piece of cat-gut cord fastened by a hook at one end to the clip which held on the paper on the diagram and wound round the barrel, passed over this grooved pulley and had a weight fixed to its other end. In this manner the barrel was always being drawn round, and back-lash was effectually destroyed ; not only that, but this weight acted as a maintaining power, when the clock was being wound up. The weight had to be disconnected, and the cord re-wound round the barrel once a day, and it was so arranged that there was a free fall of quite enough length for 80 hours.

Back-lash weight to overcome the instrumental error in the S.R.T.G.

(68.) Hanstal Tidal Station is situated on the Kattywar side of the Hanstal creek, about ¼ of a mile from its mouth. The foreshore at the station runs nearly east and west, and, at about ¼ of a mile from where the creek joins the gulf, it bends round to a north ' and south direction. The opposite shore is part of the Runn of Kutch and is a mud flat covered with mangrove bushes. The creek at the station is about 2 miles broad. The whole plain between the station at Júria is perfectly flat, without a tree or bush to break the monotony of this Runn, and which has not even a blade of grass growing on it. At extraordinary high tide in the monsoon it is covered with about one foot (in some parts) of sea water. The only thing to mark the site of the observa-

General position.

tory except what has now been made being a Mussulman's "pír" about ¼ of a mile to the west : this pír is a pole stuck into the ground, with a few dirty rags attached to it, and some half dozen stones piled up close to it, to mark the site of some Mussulman's grave. Approximate Latitude of the station 22° 55' 20" N, and Longitude 70° 23' 0" E.

(81.) Four iron tanks and 12 casks were left for the water supply and a contract was
Watertanks, Guard and Post runners. made with the former boatmen to carry water twice a month for the station, taking out at the same time a Bunyá with supplies of food for the men, all from Júria about 25 miles off. A guard of 1 Náik and 3 Sepoys was sent by His Highness the Jam of Nawanagar, and 3 Post runners (old men of the Postal Department) were engaged to carry the letters to and from Júria Post Office. The site of the station had formerly been that of a Postal Chauki when that was the route to Kutch.

(82.) Hanstal Tidal Station being now fairly established, I proceeded with a few of
Detachment of the Party proceeds to Okha and remainder to Nawanár to start work. the men (taking also the watchmaker with me) to Okha Tidal Station to repair the damage to the anemometer clock. I arrived there on the 27th February. The remainder of the party in charge of Sub-Surveyor Nursing Dass and accompanied by Mr. Peters proceeded direct to Nawanár where they arrived on the 24th February.

(85.) The Sub-Surveyor in charge having reported that from the 20th January the
Disappearance of the upper buoy at high water. Breakage of flexible pipe. upper buoy was not seen at high water, arrangements were made by means of a small boat from Beyt to get the anchor, &c., up and see what was the matter. The chain attached to the upper buoy was found wound round and round the anchor, and the flexible pipe had been partially broken at a distance of 40 feet from the brass connecting piece ; and we could not get this part of the pipe in, as it was buried so deeply in the sand under water. All our appliances for effecting repairs, &c., had been sent on to Nawanár and as the neap tides were coming on and the damage to the pipe could not be properly put right, until we took up the last rigid pipe and brass connecting piece, I determined to get some men and the mechanics across from Nawanár and effect the necessary repairs about the 18th March when we would have the spring tides.

(88.) Mr. Peters and his men having arrived from Nawanár on the 18th March (the
Repair to piping effected at Okha Tidal Station and everything left in good working order low tide favouring the work) the last 3 lengths of the iron pipe and brass connecting piece were taken up : but the flexible pipe broke off at 4 feet from the end, and the remainder it was found impossible to save, so deeply was it buried in the sand. The following day the flexible pipe was repaired and strengthened, and a new piece added, making a total of 90 feet : two stout coir ropes were taken along the entire length of the pipe, and secured by coir lashings, the pipe being slack, and ropes taut, also at each end a service of 4 or 5 feet of thin coir line was made, to prevent rubbing, and generally to strengthen these parts. The pipe was re-laid on the 20th March and the upper buoy was done away with ; the chain attached to the anchor was brought in shore, and a strong rope attached to it was secured to the foot of the temporary Tide Gauge, so that the anchor might be raised at any time required. The stop cock was opened and every thing seen to be in good order. Mr. Peters and his men returned to Nawanár while I remained to take some measurements and comparisons at the station. All the clocks having been rated and apparently working very well, and the comparison of the water in the cylinder and temporary Tide Gauge being satisfactory, measurements at rising and falling tides for determining position to correspond with zero of gauge, having been taken, &c., I left by boat for Nawanár Tidal Station which I reached on the 29th March.

(99.) The Station of Nawanár is situated on the western shore of the creek of that
General position. name just at the end of the spit of sand as the creek joins the foreshore of the gulf. Approximate Latitude 22° 44' 20" N. and Longitude 69° 45' 10" E.

(100.) The Observatory is similar to those at Okha and Hanstal and is placed so that
The observatory, cylinder and pipe. its length runs nearly east and west, the anemometer being fixed at the westerly end. The masonry well for the cylinder was sunk to a depth of 23 feet below high water springs, and ordinary high water mark just reached the site of the Observatory. The vertical pipe came up to about 14½ feet from the bottom and then the stopcock bend was fixed and 16 lengths of iron pipe taken out with a gentle decline down to low water spring tides, and the pipe packed up with large stones here and there to prevent settlement. The brass connecting piece was fixed at the end and placed in 3 feet of water at low spring tides, being secured in position by stakes and lashings.

(101.) The flexible pipe was carefully parcelled through its entire length, and two strong
Flexible pipe. longitudinal ropes secured to it, at intervals of 2 feet, and firmly joined to the iron pipe, and when taken out the rose was lowered at about 100 feet from the end of the iron pipe : the buoy sustaining the rose similar to Okha, and the chain for raising up the anchor taken in shore and attached to the temporary Tide Gauge by a stout rope ; this was afterwards attached to one of the hawsers, in connection with the large buoy.

(109.) I left Nawanár Tidal Station with a detachment of the Party on the 26th April
to sail direct for Okha Tidal Station; but at this season of

Okha Tidal Station buoy, anchor and guy hawsers laid down &c. Hawsers at Hanstal.

the year the wind blows almost directly down the gulf, and we had to make for Serráyá Bunder on the Kattywar coast and march thence to Okha. Mr. Peters with the remainder of the men sailed for Mandavie to purchase large coir rope or hawsers; after being nearly wrecked, he reached Mandavie and got the necessary supply of rope and crossed to Okha Tidal Station. The Observatory was inspected, clocks corrected &c., while the heavy anchor and large buoy, side hawsers and piles were being laid down. Mr. Rendell and Mr. Peters then left by boat for Hanstal on 3rd May; passing Nawanár, the hawsers were laid down as at Okha; and they reached Hanstal on 6th May. Here it was found that the hawsers (strong though they were) would not stand the drag of the buoy from the enormous current down the Hanstal creek, so both were put on the same side of the pipe, *viz.*, the side nearest the gulf, as it was considered that boats would not be able to make for the station on the other side.

(110.) All the work having been completed Mr. Peters and the men temporarily engaged left Júria for Wadwán and Bombay on 13th May. I re-

Mr. Peters leaves for Bombay.

ported very favourably on Mr. Peters to Major Merewether as he was most energetic in the performance of his duties and always worked most willingly often at night long after usual working hours and on Sundays when emergencies required it. Mr. Peters had sent all the blocks, pump, &c., lent me from the Harbour Defences, back by steamer to Bombay some time before.

(111.) The stations being now all fairly established and apparently working well, the remainder of the field season was occupied in inspecting them

General work of the Party after the stations had been established.

as required.

(112.) Nursing Dass left Nawanár Tidal Station on the 15th April to complete laying down the chain of Bench-marks from that station round to

All Bench-marks from Okha to Nawanár laid down.

where he had left off on the Kattywar side. The line crosses the Runn of Kutch between Shikárpúr on the Kutch coast, and Mallia on the Kattywar coast. Two Bench-marks were laid down actually in the Runn, on which at the time there was about one foot of water, but he was told by the people at these places that in the months November to February this route is quite dry and carts pass backwards and forwards. The total number of Bench-marks laid down was 38.

(113.) All spare stores having been collected and placed in a large room in one of the towers of the wall at Júria, I moved into Rajkote with the

The Party move into recess quarters at Rajkote.

Party on the 10th June. Mr. Rendell however was still in the field inspecting the station at Okha. He reached Rajkote on the 1st July with the rest of the men.

(114.) I had about this time a great deal of correspondence with the Political Agent in Kutch and the Assistant Political Agent in charge of Hallar,

Political complications regarding Hanstal Tidal Station.

Kattywar, relative to the site of Hanstal Tidal Station, although I avoided doing any thing which might bring about Political complications, yet the fact of the Tidal Observatory being erected at Hanstal seemed to be the occasion for the Durbárs of Kutch and Nawanagar to raise the question of right to the ground on which it was situated. I supplied both the Political officers with a rough sketch of the ground in the immediate vicinity of the station; but the line of demarcation between the two States seems to be very indefinite; and as His Highness the Rao of Kutch is the sovereign of the waters of the gulf, his claim is that all the ground up to high water mark belongs to him; and as this claim if held in its entirety would be tantamount to the whole of the ground, covered by any extraordinary high water during the monsoon, coming under the jurisdiction of His Highness of Kutch, the Durbár of Nawanagar disallow it, and I believe the matter is to be referred to Government for decision.

(115.) About the beginning of May the Sub-Surveyor at Hanstal reported that 2 native vessels came and anchored near the Observatory at Hanstal; the

Boat with armed men from Kutch landed at the Hanstal Tidal Station and gave some trouble.

men who said they belonged to Kutch landed from the boats, most of them being armed; there was some altercation between them and the guard of the station and eventually a spear was taken from one of the Kutch men: after a short time they re-embarked and set sail. It would appear this was the second time something of the kind happened. Shortly after I had received this information, I had copies of letters sent by the Durbár of Kutch to the Political Agent, stating their case, and requesting me to order the guard at Hanstal not to interfere with their men; also copies of letters from the Nawanagar Durbár to the Political Agent in Kattywar, stating that unless he interfered, there was likely to be a fight between the Kutch men and the guard at Hanstal. On receiving these documents I addressed the Political Agent in Kutch requesting him to allow matters to rest as they were until the work at the station was finished, and that as a tentative measure the guard and supplies for the station should be continued from the Nawanagar State.

(116.) Very little work could be done in office during the recess: Mr. Rendell had
Work in Office during the recess. Mr. Rendell takes privilege leave. Inspection of stations during the monsoon. gone on two months' privilege leave from the 3rd July. I had only Sub-Surveyor Nursing Dass to assist me, also I had to visit the Tidal Observatories and inspect the work there. Bad accounts from Nawanár Tidal Station were received about the end of June which made it imperative for me to visit that station as soon as possible. The inspection of the Observatories during the monsoon entailed a good deal of exposure and discomfort, by having to make long marches in the rain. I was actually in the field 38 days between the 7th July and 8th September and had marched nearly 800 miles in that time.

(117.) Fifty-five sets of observations to stars have been made and computed for rating
Star observations for rating chronometers. the chronometers from time to time in the past year. During the monsoon there were very few nights of course in which I could observe. As a rule I managed to rate the clocks previous to leaving for a tour of inspection and immediately on returning. In this way a very exact value of the time could be obtained in rating the observatory clocks, and for final corrections for the diagram of the self registering Tide Gauge sheets.

(169.) Mr. T. H. Rendell, Assistant Surveyor, was transferred from the Kattywar Party
Personnel of the Party. in March last; I have every reason to be satisfied with the way he has performed his duties. I have also to state that from the interest he takes in the work and his mechanical turn he will be particularly useful in this party. Mr. Rendell had two months' privilege leave during the monsoon, and this tied me down very much as I had to take up all the inspection duties and during the most inclement season of the year for travelling.

Nursing Dass, Sub-Surveyor, has been most useful to me in every way; he is sharp, and hardworking, and I quite endorse the character given him by the officer under whom he served previously to joining this Party. I hope you will record his name, for promotion to a higher scale of pay on the first opportunity.

With regard to the Sub-Surveyors at the stations, they have all done their duties remarkably well. Although the work at Nawanár has been almost entirely stopped during the monsoon, yet the Sub-Surveyor in charge there has shown on several occasions a particular aptitude for overcoming any difficulty which presented itself, that Mr. Rendell having reported very favorably on him, I took the opportunity of informing all the Sub-Surveyors at the stations that I should bring the names of those men who proved themselves hardworking and intelligent prominently to your notice at the end of the operations.

(171.) In conclusion I have great pleasure in recording the courteous assistance given
Assistance from Political Officers. me by Captain Jackson the Assistant Resident at Dwarka, during the time Okha Tidal Station was being constructed, and since then, while work has been carried on there.

My acknowledgements are equally due to Captain Goodfellow the acting Political Agent in Kutch for the assistance rendered me at Nawanár. To Colonel W. W. Anderson the Political Agent in Kattywar and the Assistant Political Agent in charge Hallar; I am also greatly indebted for their kind assistance on many occasions: I have to thank the latter officer especially, for more than once, having so strongly represented matters to the Durbár of His Highness the Jam of Nawanagar, that the difficulties arising from the native officials at Júria being careless and dilatory in looking after the supplies for Hanstal Tidal Station, were always overcome, otherwise, there would in all probability have been a cessation of work at that station from the men in charge being actually without food or drinking water.

Extract from the Narrative Report—dated 3rd November 1874—of CAPTAIN W. J. HEAVISIDE, R.E., Deputy Superintendent 3rd Grade, in charge of the Pendulum Operations.

(1.) No report was submitted by me last year. This was partly due to the fact that the party had no recess; and partly because I considered that an account of the operations undertaken for the completion of the Pendulum experiments could more satisfactorily be embodied in one report. I must therefore now go back to the autumn of 1872; when, having previously gone through a course of practice, I commenced my first series of regular pendulum observations.

(2.) This series was taken at Mussoorie in October 1872, just after the break up of the monsoon. The pendulums were swung at the full atmospheric pressure in order that the results might be directly comparable with those obtained there from Captain Basevi's observations in 1866. The results were as follows :—

[SEASON 1878-74.

TABLE OF THE RESULTS.

OBSERVERS.	Number of vibrations in a mean solar day, reduced to an infinitely small arc to a temperature of 72° F. to a vacuum but not to mean sea level.		Means of both Pendulums.
	Pendulum No. 1821.	Pendulum No. 4.	
Captain Basevi, ...	85956·09	86056·77	86006·43
„ Heaviside, ...	85956·16	86056·54	86006·35

(4.) On the 30th of October the party went down to Dehra. From that time till the middle of January, I was engaged in a series of preliminary experiments with the Russian Pendulums of which I had no previous experience.

Separate reports will be submitted, both on the operations with the Russian Pendulums, and also on those with Kater's Pendulum; consequently details of the work done with those pendulums will not be found in this report.

(5.) On the 21st of January 1878, I left Dehra for Kaliána, which is the base station for pendulum experiments in India. Mr. Macdougall had already been sent to Kaliána with the invariable pendulum and apparatus, with instructions to make the necessary preparations there, for a series of observations, both with the invariable pendulums and with the Russian pendulums. After completing this work, he was relieved by Mr. Keelan and returned to Dehra, so that he might march out again to Kaliána in charge of the Russian pendulum apparatus. This change of duties was necessary, in order that Mr. Keelan might be present at Kaliána when I commenced to put together the invariable pendulum apparatus. Mr. Keelan had not previously seen this apparatus, and as he was to accompany me to England as sole assistant, it was requisite that he should have as much instruction in the matter as possible.

(6.) Although the results obtained with the invariable pendulums at Mussoorie, were sufficient to show that the pendulums had undergone no sensible changes in their travels to Thibet and back; yet it was considered advisable to compare my results with Captain Basevi's still further. A short series of observations was therefore taken with these pendulums at Kaliána at a reduced pressure, during the course of the operations with the Russian pendulums. Comparing my results with those taken in 1866 by Captain Basevi I find

For Pendulum.	1866-1879.	Mean difference.
No. 1821	— 0·060 vibrations	
No. 4	+ 0·108 „	+ 0·024 vibrations

(7.) The party left Kaliána on the 10th of March and marched into Muzaffarnagar. Such of the instruments and equipage as I considered it necessary to take with me, were carefully packed in my presence in a railway goods van, which was then locked up and despatched through to Bombay. With the exception of 8 men whom I took to Bombay with me, the native establishment was paid up and dismissed. Mr. Macdougall then returned to Dehra in accordance with your orders, taking with him the instruments and stores I did not require. During the time Mr. Macdougall was with me, he showed himself industrious, willing and most zealous in his duties; but in order to become a valuable assistant he must endeavour to acquire greater accuracy in his work.

(8.) On the 15th of March I reached Bombay. Mr. Keelan who brought down the natives and broke the journey at two places, en route, arrived there on the 19th instant. On the 20th the instruments and stores were moved over to the Colaba Observatory.

(9.) Mr. C. Chambers, the Superintendent, placed at my disposal an out-building in the Colaba Observatory compound, which was well suited for the experiments. The building was 40 feet long, by 30 feet wide, with a solid stone floor, stone walls, and a tiled roof. Inside this again uprights supported the roof and formed an interior space of 24 feet × 14½ ft. This space was enclosed with bamboo matting and within it the pendulums were swung. The objection to the building was its propinquity to the main road of Colaba from which the outer wall of the building was but 8 feet distant. Although the pendulums were swung on isolated pillars, yet it was considered advisable to guard still farther against the vibrations caused by passing vehicles. For this purpose the road was thickly covered for some distance with small bundles of straw laid close together. The construction of the building rendered it necessary to suspend the Shelton clock from a wooden framework which was made for the purpose in Bombay. Owing either to this method of suspension, or to the clock not being on an isolated pillar; the clock, which generally goes very well, had at Colaba, a comparatively irregular rate. The effects of this on the observations, were it is considered, almost entirely eliminated by comparing the clock Shelton at short intervals with the Observatory clock (by Thwaites and Reed) the rate of which was very constant and well known. These comparisons were made twice a day near the commencement, and near the end of each set of pendulum observations.

(10.) I am deeply indebted to Mr. C. Chambers both for the assistance he afforded me in my work at Colaba, and also for his hospitality. I had been in correspondence with him on the subject of the preparations which were required for the experiments, and on my arrival at Colaba I found that the building had been so carefully and efficiently prepared, that it only remained for me to put up the apparatus. Isolated pillars had been built, the observing pit dug, and the roof, doors, windows and interior space covered in with matting, so that the temperature might be kept as equable as possible. A wooden frame had also been prepared for the clock, from a design I had sent. Transit observations were usually taken at the Observatory 3 times a week. But Mr. Chambers kindly arranged to have them taken every night (Sundays excepted) during my pendulum observations. Thus the Observatory clock which was by Thwaites and Reed, and had a very good rate, became a standard with which I could compare my clocks at any time.

(11.) When I had got the vacuum apparatus together and began to pump, a bad leak showed itself. After some time the leak was traced to one of the windows. I therefore took down the cylinder and overhauled it thoroughly. The windows were repacked, and the whole cylinder repainted. This took some time but was a most successful job, as I had no further symptoms of a leak up to the conclusion of the work at Kew.

(12.) After the quiet of Kaliána the noises at Colaba were most distracting. Carriages and people were constantly passing along the road. Occasionally there would be a shout of Ho ! Ram Bak-ash ! Ram Bak-ash ! Ho !! the prelude to a conversation between two natives carried on at a distance perhaps of 200 yards. The ladies of Colaba too, were it seemed to me the most indefatigable musicians, and at first I was sometimes puzzled to determine whether I had compared the clock with a beat of the chronometer or with a note from Semiramide. I was lucky however to arrive at Colaba just at the conclusion of the annual artillery practice, which goes on at a battery just below the Observatory, and which might otherwise have necessitated a change of hours, for swinging the pendulums.

I have since had a good deal of practice in observing amidst noises, and any thing moderate does not annoy me. But I had not realized before, the enormous advantages we Surveyors enjoy in India at our stations, remote from such distracting causes.

(13.) The observations at Bombay were finished on the 18th April, and in accordance with your orders the party was transferred to Lieutenant A. W. Baird, R. E., Assistant Superintendent in charge of the Tidal operations.

At Bombay I engaged a Tindal and 12 Lascars to accompany me as far as Egypt. It was some time before I could find a good Tindal, who was willing to collect the lascars, and trust himself with me. But at length I obtained the services of one, Sheikh Daod. This man and the lascars he brought, turned out treasures. At Bombay they learnt their duties in the Observatory in a few days : their knowledge of ship board, and the assistance they rendered in shipping and unshipping the instruments were most valuable to me ; and they gave me no trouble either in their conduct or with complaints about food &c. They were expensive certainly but well worth the money. I have never before met with natives so intelligent and enterprising as these men were. When the work was finished in Egypt and I was sending them back to Suez, it was with some difficulty that I persuaded them to relinquish a plan they had formed of going to see Cairo.

(14.) Mr. Keelan left Bombay on the 21st of April. I gave him a letter to Lieut. Colonel Goodfellow, R.E. who was in charge of the military works at Aden and he very kindly placed some workmen at Mr. Keelan's disposal, to build the transit pillar and make other preparations necessary for the observations there.

(15.) I did not leave Bombay until the 28th of April. The interval between the 19th and 26th was fully occupied in carefully packing every thing, and in making arrangements for shipping the instruments. The Peninsular and Oriental Company's steamers were very much crowded at that time of the year ; but nevertheless Mr. Parker, the Assistant Agent, kindly gave me a place for the instruments in one of the mail rooms. I may here state that my best thanks are due to the Company's Agents at Bombay, at Aden, at Suez, and at Alexandria ; as also to the officers of the steam ships Deccan, Nubia and Candia who did every thing in their power to assist me in shipping and unshipping the instruments, and in stowing them carefully in safe places. It is chiefly due to them that all the instruments travelled from Bombay to Kew without receiving the slightest damage, and even the Syphon Barometer when compared at

Kew was found to be free from error. Mercurial Barometers are proverbial for getting out of order in travelling. This one was so fortunate as to travel with Captain Basevi into Thibet; to return thence, and to be used by me at all the places at which I observed between Bombay and Kew, where it arrived in good order. A description of it may therefore prove interesting.

(16.) It is a Syphon Barometer of the Gay Lussac principle.

The glass tube is tied down to a strip of wood, on which a paper scale is pasted. The scale is graduated to tenths of inches, and the readings are taken with the assistance of a detached sliding vernier. Three or four small pieces of cork are inserted between the tube and the scale. The strip of wood is screwed down at the two extremities inside half a bamboo, through each end of which a string passes to suspend the barometer by. When travelling, the barometer is inverted; the other half of the bamboo fits on as a cover, and the whole is secured at the ends by two leather caps connected with straps, one of which is long enough to allow the bamboo to be carried over a man's shoulder. This barometer has probably remained in good order so long, because, with the exception of two screws and the mercury, there is nothing metallic about it.

To preserve the knife edges of the pendulums from rust, on board ship, I first oiled them well. I then rubbed off the oil with a piece of silk until the steel was perfectly dry. Tin foil was next pressed down so as to cover completely the steel surfaces, and wooden casings were tied on over this. This method proved perfectly efficacious; but if oil be left on the steel, rust will inevitably form.

(17.) The instruments and baggage were shipped at Bombay on the 26th April on board the S. S. Deccan. On the 28th I sailed, and on the 5th of May I landed at Aden.

Mr. Keelan had secured a store room there which was well adapted for the observations. It was single storied, solidly built with a "pska" floor, and but few windows. It was near steamer point and adjoined the Prince of Wales Hotel.* A transit pillar had been built in a convenient position between this room and the sea. The pendulums were not swung on isolated pillars at Aden. At Aden Mr. Keelan executed a small piece of triangulation to connect the pendulum room with the light ship, the latitude and longitude of which were known. He also took some circum-meridian observations of stars as a further check on the latitude.

(18.) Distilled water is now plentiful in Aden, and the Garrison is not so dependent on the tank water as was formerly the case. During our stay the Brigade Major kindly permitted the establishment of the party to be supplied with water at the Government rate of allowance.

The weather was of rather an unusual type at Aden for May. High winds made the atmosphere pleasantly cool, and there were two or three apologies for showers of rain. The nights were rather cloudy, but otherwise every thing went smoothly, and we left Aden on the 26th of May in the S.S. Nubia.

(19.) We arrived at Suez on the 1st of June. I tried there to hire a steam launch in which to take every thing round to Ismaïlia by the Canal, but I could not obtain one. I therefore landed the instruments and baggage at Suez. Some delay and difficulties occurred in passing the things through the Custom House, but eventually owing to the exertions of our Consul, Mr. West, we obtained the necessary permit. I then hired and loaded a Goods Van, and on the 4th we reached Ismaïlia.

(20.) The observations at Ismaïlia were taken in a room on the ground floor of the Hotel Pagnon, a large double storied building. The pendulums were not swung on isolated pillars, but the floor of the room was laid with encaustic tiles and was very solid. The clock hung from a steel pin firmly driven into the wall; and this method of suspension suited it very well.

For the transit instrument a pillar of stone-work was sunk one and a half feet in the sand in the garden of the Hotel. When the masonry was dry, there were placed on the pillar the 3 large triangular stones which were formerly used for the stand of one of the astronomical circles, and which I had brought with me for this purpose. On the top of these the transit instrument was set up. This extemporised pillar answered its purpose very well.

(21.) The French officers, in charge of the Canal, at Ismaïlia were particularly civil in their offers of assistance. They presented me with plans of the Canal and of the town from which the latitude and longitude of the hotel could be satisfactorily laid off. They also gave me the height of the floor of the pendulum room above the sea level at Suez.

(22.) Ismaïlia is a most remarkable place, and exemplifies very strongly the capacities of the French for producing neatness and beauty under difficulties. The town is situated on the shores of Lake Timsah; a lake about 3 miles long by 2½ wide, which was perfectly dry before the water was let into the Canal, but which now forms an admirable anchorage for passing ships. Ismaïlia is about 1¼ miles distant from the Canal, and except for the waters of the lake, the town is surrounded on all sides by the most utter desert of sand: sand which is constantly shifting, and which is only prevented from invading the town by successive lines of reed

---

* Full detailed descriptions of the positions of the buildings in which the pendulums were swung at Colaba, at Aden, and at Ismaïlia, will be found in the pendulum observation books.

fencing. Yet in the midst of this one finds good roads with avenues of trees : a town of solidly built houses, many of them double storied, and several of them with considerable architectural pretensions. There is a public garden with a pretty kiosk and fountain in the centre, surrounded by beds kept in the neatest order, full of handsome shrubs, and bright with geraniums, zinias and oleanders. Most of the private houses have bits of gardens, and that of M. Lesseps is a most perfect little wilderness. A plentiful supply of water is obtained from the sweet water Canal which surrounds the town, but water alone will not make the desert sand fertile, and the soil of the gardens is black earth which underlies the sand and which has been dredged out of the canal. At one end of the town is a large unoccupied palace built by the Viceroy, and adjoining it are the water-works whence fresh water is pumped to Port Said.

Although the European population might be counted by tens, and is composed almost entirely of Canal officers; yet there are one or two cafés chantant in the town and a bathing establishment by the Lake. The lake is most admirably adapted for bathing. The bottom is all sand, and there is plenty of water a short distance from the shore. Owing to the large amount of evaporation the water is intensely salt, and in consequence wonderfully buoyant.

The weather was remarkably fine during our stay at Ismaïlia. In the middle of the day, the heat out of doors from the glare and radiation was considerable; but within doors it was cool enough; and though one or two of the days were somewhat sultry, yet the heat bore no comparison to that of upper India in June. When we first arrived the atmosphere was wonderfully clear, and the hills near Suez, which were some 60 miles distant did not look more than 15 miles away. Later on we had high winds which filled the air with sand and made it very murky. The nights were of the most glorious description. Even at Mussoorie after the monsoon I have never seen the heavens more brilliant than they were at Ismaïlia, and the milky-way shone like patches of sun-lit clouds.

(23.) On the 25th of June we left Ismaïlia. I took 7 natives of the establishment, on with me to Alexandria to assist in shipping the instruments there. The remainder I sent back to Suez. I had taken the precaution to obtain through Mr. Vivian, Acting Consul General at Alexandria, an export order which enabled me to pass the instruments and baggage through the Custom House there without delay, and on the 26th every thing was shipped on board the S.S. Candia. I then sent back the rest of the natives to Suez, where I had arranged for their passages back to Bombay, with Mr. Sullivan, the Peninsular and Oriental Company's Agent.

(24.) On the 3rd of July we left Alexandria for Southampton. Right glad was I to bid farewell to Egypt. The Egyptians are the most aggravating people to deal with that I ever encountered. At Suez I was obliged to engage a dragoman as interpreter, one Ali, whom I have no reason to suppose was much below the average of his class. I knew he was not to be trusted, and so when I had got a pass from the Custom House at Suez, I went up myself to the Station to arrange for a goods van. I paid for it, and it was to be sent down to the Custom House that evening. When I went over next morning it had not arrived so I sent Ali up to the station for it. He came back with the intelligence "Engine driver not bring waggon les he get 4 shillings." Time was important so I paid. The waggon arrived soon after but with the door locked. Ali was sent for the key, and came back to say "Man not come and open door les he get 6d." When we had nearly finished loading the waggon, an official came and talked with great volubility to Ali, who said he was objecting to the amount we were putting into the waggon. Fortunately he was a little late, the last box was put in and I locked the door and pocketed the key. The same sort of thing went on when we were starting by the train. Surrounded by loafers and beggars with every sort of hideous disease I was stowing the thermometers and barometers safely in the carriage, when Ali came up with some half dozen attendants to say "This man he not label luggage les he get six pence." "This man he weigh luggage and make him 200 under, he want shilling." "This man . . . . ." I thought, fortunately, of the thermometers and said. "Here, take this half crown and settle." But at Ismaïlia when I had got all the instruments safely lodged, I was able to devote a little more attention to Ali, and when on my objecting to the price of some stone he had brought for the transit pillar, he told me "him all come from France by canal boat" I explained to him pretty fully that I could not be called a fool so openly any longer. Ali improved very much after this, though he never could get over his habit of giving a ready answer to every question. But I think the only true thing I ever heard him say was "Every one in Egypt him like money. No do nothing without money." The Egyptians have one good trait. They can and do carry the most wonderful loads. At Ismaïlia we got the air pump and box weighing altogether 374 lbs. on to one man's back, and he managed to carry it in the teeth of a fresh breeze a distance of nearly a quarter of a mile.

(25.) On the 16th of July we landed at Southampton. I had written for a Custom House pass, and for a Furniture Van to meet the Steamer there. On the 17th the instruments were all packed in the Van, and were sent to the Kew Observatory where they arrived and were unpacked on the 18th instant.

(26.) Owing to General Sir E. Sabine's forethought, and kindness I found that the pendulum rooms had been fully prepared for my arrival. The invariable pendulums were swung in the same place in which they had been swung by Mr. Loewy in 1865. The observations with these pendulums were finished on the 25th of August. Sir E. Sabine permitted Mr. G. Whipple, the Senior Assistant of the Observatory, to take transits for me during the time I was swinging the invariable pendulums. This work Mr. Whipple performed to my entire satisfaction. The transits were observed directly by the Shelton clock, the beats of which were plainly audible in the transit room through a tube carried up from the clock. The clock face could be seen from the transit room reflected in a mirror.

(27.) I did not leave Kew until the 13th of July 1874. The interval between August 1873 and this date was spent in taking a complete set of observations with the Russian reversible pendulums for the determination of the length of the simple seconds pendulum at Kew; in reconstructing and swinging the convertible pendulum used by Captain Kater in 1817; and in determining certain factors connected with the invariable pendulums.

(28.) In the original programme drawn up by you for the completion of the pendulum operations it was intended that the invariable pendulums should be swung at Greenwich as well as at Kew. From the known length of the seconds pendulum at Greenwich, as determined by General Sir E. Sabine, a value of the length of the seconds pendulum at the Indian Stations of observations would have been then obtainable. Owing, however, chiefly to the extensive preparations which were being made at Greenwich for the Transit of Venus parties, no space was available in the Observatory for the pendulum experiments, and the Astronomer Royal proposed that the pendulums should be swung not at the point in the Observatory at which Sir E. Sabine has swung his pendulum, but in a building to be erected temporarily for the purpose in the park about 800 yards from the Observatory and pulled down on the completion of the swings. Application was therefore made to the British Government by the India Office for a grant of £200, for this building.

The grant was eventually sanctioned, but in the mean time a change had been made in the programme of operations.

In August Sir E. Sabine suggested that I should undertake a series of observations with Captain Kater's convertible pendulum. You sanctioned this arrangement which by forming Kew into a base Station makes the Indian experiments independent of Greenwich.

(29.) Throughout my stay at Kew, Sir E. Sabine, who took great interest in my work, was constant in his enquiries as to my progress, and in his kind offers of assistance. He placed at my disposal the occasional services of Sergeants Moore and Chadwick of the Royal Artillery whom he employed as writers. These men were both neat and accurate in their work, and were very useful in making out duplicates of the records of my observations and in assisting in the computations. I am also much indebted to Mr. S. Jeffery, the Superintendent of the Kew Observatory for the assistance he afforded me, and my best thanks are due to Messrs. G. Whipple and T. Baker for the numberless little services they so freely rendered me.

(30.) Mr. H. E. T. Keelan, Surveyor 3rd grade joined the party in December 1873. Mr. Keelan was about to take sick leave to Europe, when you offered him this opportunity of accompanying the party to England on duty. Mr. Keelan's services have proved most valuable to me, and although he has occasionally suffered from severe headaches, yet on the whole his health has been better than might have been anticipated. He possesses all the qualifications which an assistant should have and is moreover clever at designing. He made very satisfactory designs and drawings for several things which I required at Kew for Kater's pendulum, and I am indebted to him for many little suggestions in other ways. At Kaliana he was instructed in the methods, of observing coincidences, and of clock comparisons. Throughout the operations he observed some of the intermediate coincidences of the invariable pendulums and took some of the clock comparisons. Towards the close of the work at Kew he practised himself in taking star observations for time with the Transit Instrument; and his average probable error for the mean time of transit of a star for the last four nights of his observations was but ± 0·03 sec. The results of the observations show him to be a very competent observer; and more especially is this the case with the clock comparisons which he took at Kew for the determination of the rate of the Shelton clock from telegraph signals transmitted from the Greenwich Observatory clock to the Richmond Post office. At Aden he executed a triangulation for the determination of the Latitude of the pendulum room, and he took there some circum-meridian observations to stars for the same purpose. Mr. Keelan's work has been more than satisfactory in every respect and I cannot commend him too highly.

(31.) Before I left Kew I handed over to Mr. Jeffery, the Superintendent of the Observatory, who had been deputed by the Royal Society to take charge of them, the invariable pendulums and the whole of the pendulum apparatus. A great part of this apparatus had been constructed at the expense of the Indian Government: but, acting on your suggestion, these portions, including the vacuum apparatus, thermometers and syphon gauges, were presented by the Indian Government to the Royal Society.

After leaving Kew I spent a week in London where I handed over to the Director General of Stores the boxes containing the records of my observations, and the office books and papers for despatch to this country.

The Russian pendulums were shipped under Mr. Keelan's superintendence and were despatched to St. Petersburg, in the same condition in which I had last used them at Kew. I have since heard from M. O. de Struve, to whom they were consigned, that they appeared to have reached Russia in good order. In accordance with a request I made, he has deputed a skilled officer to take a series of observations with the pendulums in the condition in which they arrived, and I trust that the results in India and at Kew will thus become connected with those made in Russia. Such of the few instruments as remained, I transferred to the India Store Department for repairs before being returned to this country. On the 20th of July Mr. Keelan availed himself of the furlough, and I availed myself of the privilege leave which had been granted to us.

I embarked for Bombay by the mail which left Southampton on the 17th of September, and I reached Debra on the 20th of October.

Extract from the Narrative Report—dated 20th November 1874—of J. B. N. HENNESSEY, Esq., Deputy Superintendent 1st Grade, G. T. Survey, In charge Computing Office.

Calculating Branch.

(2.) The following changes have occurred during the year under review. *Computing Branch.* Lieutenant St. G. C. Gore who was posted to this office at the close of the preceding year, to be instructed in the calculations of the Department, having gone through the usual course, and having afterwards done duty in the office, was, on the 1st August, transferred to the Kumaun and Garhwál Party. Mr. W. Todd, Surveyor 2nd Grade, joined on the 1st January 1874 from the same Party and on the same date Mr. J. W. Macdougall was transferred to that Party. Mr. McCarthy, entered as a computer on the 11th June, and having subsequently passed the usual examination, required of candidates for admission to the Junior Department, was appointed an Assistant Surveyor, 4th Grade, on the 11th August. On the 1st February he also was transferred to the Kumaun and Garhwál Party.

Drawing Branch. Mr. Atkinson was absent on two months leave from the 25th August, during which time Mr. H. F. W. Todd officiated for him.

(3.) A large amount of the work performed by the Computing Branch—being, as it is, closely connected with the other Branches of the office—is of such a miscellaneous character that it would be impossible to reduce it within the form of a summary. Such as can be so reduced, is detailed below; but in order to enable you to form a general idea of the progress that has been made I will first briefly capitulate some of the more important subjects that have occupied the time of the office. The printing of Vols. III and IV of the *Account of the Operations &c.* which contain the numerical data connected with the Principal Triangulation of the N.W. Quadrilateral, were, as stated in my last report, then practically in a complete state. They have been put aside in accordance with your directions pending the completion of Vol. II on which you are now engaged, without which they would be to some extent unintelligible. Of this volume about 250 pages have already been passed through the press. No similar reason has existed for retarding the publication of the Principal and Secondary work of the same Quadrilateral (in the form prescribed by yourself) for the use of local officials and others, engaged on survey or other work for which geographical data are requisite. The Quadrilateral is divided into eight series of each of which a synopsis has been or is being prepared, containing the elements of all the principal and secondary points connected with it and accompanied by charts of the triangulation. Of these synopses, Vol. I, or that of the Great Indus Series has been published; Vol. II, or that of the section of the Great Arc between lats. 24° and 30° is now almost ready for the binder; Vol. III, or that of the Karáchí Longitudinal Series, is very nearly equally advanced; those of the Gurhágarh and Jogí-Tíla Meridional Series are complete with the exception of charts, and the Rahun Meridional Series is nearly out of the printer's hands but also needs charts. The two remaining series *i. e.*, the Sutlej and N.W. Himalaya are in a somewhat backward state, only the synopsis of the principal points having been as yet printed; the secondary data of the former are ready for the press, and considerable progress has been made in preparing the data of the latter. The reduction of the secondary triangulation into accordance with the principal triangulation, prior to the preparation of the synopses, necessitated by the final reduction of the N.W. Quadrilateral, has of course entailed much labour on the Computing Branch, as also has the superintendence through the press of the publication of the result. In addition to this considerable progress has been made with the reduction of the next Quadrilateral, *i. e.* the S.E., for which triangles, latitudes, longitudes and azimuths have been computed and the absolute terms of the equations found; also good progress has been made in determining the coefficients of the unknown quantities involved. These calcula-

Calculating Branch.—(Continued).

tions have had to be set aside for the present, as several of the computers are engaged in the reduction of the observations made by Captain Trotter while attached to the Yarkund Mission, in accordance with your wish that every facility should be afforded to that officer, to enable him to complete his report and compile the maps connected with his work as soon as possible. Besides this, Captain Heaviside also has the services of a computer placed at his disposal.

(4.) The details of the ordinary calculations are as follows :—

Angle Books indexed ..	.. .. ..	64 vols.
Deduced Angles examined	.. ..	32 angles
Abstracts of Angles compared ..	.. ..	166 „
Zero and general means computed	.. ..	166 „

Computations in Duplicate.

	Weights computed	192
	Spherical Excesses computed	221
	Simple Quadrilaterals reduced ..	14
Principal Triangulation.	Simple Polygons „ ..	29
	Compound Figures „ ..	14
	Lats., Longs., and Azimuths computed (single deductions)	92
	Traverses computed	6
	Ray Traces „	8
Secondary Triangulation.	Triangles „	1505
	Do. adjusted	632
	Lats., Longs., and Azimuths computed	2258
	Latitudes by Circum-meridian observations ..	121 deductions
Explorations.	Heights by Boiling Point	88 points
	Longitudes by Z. D. .. .. .. about	30 deductions

(5.) The work performed in connection with the Typographic and Photozincographic presses is given under two heads.

For Typographic Office.

Synopsis of the Operations, &c.		Compiled or otherwise prepared.
Letter press	..	26 pages
Principal Triangles	..	13 „
Principal Lats., Longs., Azimuths and Heights	..	29 „
Secondary Triangles	..	136 „
Azimuth Tables	..	64 „
Co-ordinates of Secondary Points ..	..	129 „
„ Peaks (N.W. Frontier) ..	..	6 „

Total 403

For vols. III and IV of the operations &c.

Letter press		45 pages

For other vols. of the operations &c.
Lists, Descriptions and observed angles of

Revised Calcutta Longitudinal Series		104
Great Arc Series, lat. 18° to 24°		66
Jabalpur Meridional Series		10

Total 180

The auxiliary reductions of the figures of the N.W. Quadrilateral have also been compiled for inclusion in Vol. II.

For Photozincographic Office.

Data compiled for projection of Assam Series Chart 55-60 ..		1 sheet

Numerical and other Charts.		Compared or Examined
Engraved proof of N.W. Quadrilateral Reduction ..	..	1 sheet
S.E. Quadrilateral Chart	..	1 „
Assam Series Chart 1855-60	..	1 „
Jodhpúr Series Chart 1872-73	..	1 „
Final Charts Great Indus Series	..	4 „

Total 8

Calculating Branch.—(Continued).

(6.) Observations for time were taken on 10 occasions during the year for the purpose
Instrumental Work. of showing mean time and rating chronometers. Meteorological observations were made in the Dehra Observatory on every day throughout the year, and the daily results were reduced and communicated month by month, as usual, to the Reporter on Meteorology, N. W. Provinces. A table of monthly means is appended to this report. The difference of level between the upper mark of the Dehra Dome Observatory and the B. M. in the wall of the G. T. S. Office was determined by Spirit Leveling; and the large Anemometer, which had for some time been awaiting a suitable place on which to erect it, was put up over the room which surmounts the portico of the office and the clock work with registering barrel placed beneath within the same room.

(7.) I noticed in my last report that on Captain W. J. Heaviside's appointment to the
Pendulum Observations. charge of the Pendulum operations, I was able to afford him assistance in certain matters connected with his work: having more calculations than his own office could perform, he continued to require the aid of the computing office for some time during the year under report. The work executed for him was the computation of the rates of the Russian and English sidereal clocks in connection with his observations at Kaliána; the reduction of 81 sets of observations with the Russian Pendulums at Kaliána and the preparation of an abstract of the same; the bringing up of tables for the reduction of the measurement of length for both pendulums; the recomputation of the Russian clock rates for the Kaliána observations; the copying of 72 sets of observations at Kaliána with the Russian Pendulum No. 2; the computation of the observations with the Russian Pendulum at Moro; the reduction of clock rates for the observations at Dehra, and the reduction of the observations with the Russian Pendulum at the same place; the reduction of the observations at Kaliána made on the occasion of the fourth visit to that station: the bringing up of the abstract of the results; the recomputation of the factor of expansion for the Royal Society's Pendulums and the bringing up of the temperature corrections, &c.

(8.) The preservation of the Principal Stations of this Survey is of course a matter of
Protection of Stations. the utmost importance and entails a good deal of correspondence on this office. Replies to 233 letters on this subject were drafted by Mr. C. Wood under your direction, and 12 original, duplicate and supplementary lists including 76 stations were issued to district officers. Owing to the modern alterations in the boundaries of districts it is often a matter of some difficulty to ascertain what stations are situated in each district and to obtain a complete return from the district officials. Steady progress is however being made, and I am glad to state that since I last reported 53 more districts including 550 stations have been settled, making in all 291 districts of which the lists are now complete. The check lists now include about 2,450 principal stations. A statement was also prepared shewing what district officials had failed to send in Annual Reports of the condition of the stations in their districts, and reminders have been sent to them, the result of which has been in most cases satisfactory.

(9.) A new form for the computation of trigonometrical heights has been devised by
Miscellaneous. which the labour of calculation is considerably reduced and in connection with this form a new table has been added to the Auxiliary Tables. Forms for official and departmental use were supplied to 55 officers, and 446 parcels containing maps and charts were booked and despatched. Twenty-nine officers have been supplied with data, that furnished to Captain Bailey of the Forest Department was more over all reduced to the same terms. Abstracts of observed angles and approximate azimuths were prepared for all the stations of the Biláspur Meridional Series, Southern Section, visited during the season of 1872-73. Lists of pargana, patti, and village names in Kumaun and Garhwál were prepared for submission to the settlement officers for correction of orthography, and 6 candidates for the junior department were examined.

Typographic Branch.

(10.) The work performed by the Printing Office for the past 5 years is concisely stated in the following table.

	1869-70	1870-71	1871-72	1872-73	1873-74
Pages composed,	693	819	1,143	1,420	1,220
Do. printed,	106,231	234,828	241,348	273,157	388,420

Typographic Branch.—(Continued).

The total pages composed last year may be subdivided thus,

For volumes of the G. T. Survey	870
For charts, memos., &c.	224
For Annual Report	126
Total	1,220

Drawing Branch.

(11.) The work executed in the Drawing Office is exhibited in the table which follows this report.

Photozincographic Branch.

(12.) The work performed by this office is shown in the following tabular statement under the heads of Maps, Charts, Diagrams and Forms.

Maps.

Subject	When published	No. of parts	No. of copies printed
Prints of maps published in former years	..	12	750
Kattywar, sheet No. 29	May 1873	1	220
Do. No. 30	" "	1	69
Turkestan Map, sheet No. 2 (2nd edition)	" "	1	464
Do. No. 3 "	" "	1	290
Do. No. 4 "	June "	1	557
Do. No. 1 " addendum . ..	" "	1	253
Index to Mussoorie & Landour Survey ..	" "	1	8
Do. to Triangulation, S. E. Quadrilateral ..	August "	1	34
Guzerat, sheet No. 11	" "	1	123
Kashmir Map (for Major Bates's Gazetteer) ..	September "	1	559
Index to Guzerat Survey..	" "	1	522
Do. to Kattywar	October "	1	681
Forest Map	" "	3	405
Kattywar, sheet No. 18 (N. W. Section) ..	" "	1	61
Index to Kumaun & Garhwál Survey	November "	1	406
" Main Lines of levels (reduced scale) ..	" "	1	412
Trans-Frontier Map No. 9	" "	1	119
Kattywar, sheet No. 18 (S. E. Section) ..	" "	1	55
Turkestan Map, sheet No. 1 (2nd edition *reprint*) ..	" "	1	320
Do. No. 8 (" ") ..	December "	1	333
Kattywar, sheet No. 28	" "	1	132
Do. No. 24	" "	1	132
Do. No. 25	" "	1	25
Do. No. 13 (S. W. Section) ..	" "	1	55
Guzerat, sheet No. 13	" "	1	105
Doonga Gulli Forest Map (reduced)	" "	1	111
Trans-Frontier Map No. 8	January 1874	1	115
Forest Map (Hazara district) W. Section ..	" "	1	58
Do. (") Central Section ..	" "	1	54
Kattywar, sheet No. 10	" "	1	129
Do. No. 20	" "	1	105
Do. No. 21	" "	1	129
Do. No. 11	" "	1	161
Do. No. 22	" "	1	151
Guzerat, sheet No. 12	" "	1	105
Kumaun and Garhwál, sheet No. 25, contoured ..	" "	1	105
Do. " No. 26 " ..	" "	1	105
Forest Map (Hazara district) E. Section ..	" "	1	10
Kumaun & Garhwál, sheet No. 34, contoured ..	February "	1	105
Do. No. 33 " ..	" "	1	106
Forest Map (Khanpur Range of Rakhs &c.,) E. Section ..	" "	1	161
Do. (") Central Section ..	" "	1	6

Photozincographic Branch.—(Continued).

Maps.—(Continued).

Subject	When published	No. of parts	No. of copies printed
Kattywar, sheet No. 13 (N.E. Section)	February 1874	1	55
Index to Preliminary Charts (N.W. Quadrilateral).. ..	March ,,	1	35
Kumaun and Garhwál, sheet No. 84, skeleton	April ,,	1	105
Guzerat, sheet No. 10	,, ,,	1	106
Kumaun & Garhwál, sheet No. 32 skeleton	,, ,,	1	105
	Totals ..	**61**	**9,207**

Besides the foregoing, Blue prints 53 in number were issued.

Charts.

Subject	When published	No. of parts	No. of copies printed
Amua Series No. 1	May 1873	1	66
Do. No. 2	,, ,,	1	68
Assam Longl. Series, season 1855-60 Numerical ..	December ,,	1	65
Brahmaputra Series, season 1872-73 ,, ...	,, ,,	1	65
Gora Series, No. 1 .. ,, ...	,, ,,	1	65
Jodhpur Series, season 1872-73 ,, ..	January 1874	1	65
Biláspur Series ,, ,, (N. Section) Numerical ..	February ,,	1	65
Great Indus Series, Chart No. 1, Final		1	377
Kadappa and Karnúl Minor Triangulation (1871-73) Numerical	March ,,	1	65
Great Indus Series, Chart No. 2. ⎤	,, ,,	1	359
Do. No. 3. ⎬ Final	April ,,	1	375
Do. No. 4. ⎦	,, ,,	1	392
	Totals ..	**12**	**2,027**

Diagrams.

Subject	When published	No. of copies printed
Plates to illustrate Vols. III and IV and other diagrams,	May 1873	710
	June ,,	220
	July ,,	160
	August ,,	160
	October ,,	320
	November ,,	807
	March 1874	1080
	April ,,	100
	Total ..	**3,557**
Professional and Office Forms, ...	1873-74.	28,125

1,400 Maps and 2,702 Charts were issued during the year. The forms are always expended as fast as printed. Contrasting the work performed since 1870-71 we have

Year	Maps	Charts	Diagrams	Forms
1870-71	6,465	839	13,205	10,482
1871-72	10,131	1,375	4,937	13,655
1872-73	6,910	2,206	12,055	12,549
1873-74	9,207	2,027	3,557	28,125

Photozincographic Branch.—(Continued).

An Abstract of the work executed during the past five years stands as follows.

Subject	Number of Prints				
	1869-70	1870-71	1871-72	1872-73	1873-74
Maps, Charts and Diagrams,	12,315	20,509	16,443	21,171	14,791
Forms, ...	13,571	10,482	13,655	12,549	28,125

These tables speak for themselves as to the value of this branch of the office when judged of only by the out-turn of work; but the nature of the work is in many instances such that the convenience of having a small establishment of this kind at hand to execute it is inestimable. The accuracy of the data on the Preliminary Charts and the Charts of Levels alone, which is of the utmost importance, could not be so well assured if this branch were not in direct connection with the drawing and computing branches, without entailing delay and correspondence which would seriously impede the current work not only of the office but frequently of the department itself.

(13.) In conclusion, Mr. W. H. Cole, M.A. has continued to render valuable service in discharging the varied duties that are required of him.

Mr. Wood is as efficient as ever. Mr. Peychers works steadily and to good purpose. Baboo Gunga Pershad continues to be an excellent assistant. Baboo Cally Mohun Ghose has done good service. Baboos Kally Coomar Chatterjee, Gopal Chunder Surcar and Tarapodo Mookerjee are deserving of commendation, and of the new hands Baboos Sham Nath and Shoshee Bhooshan Shome have mostly afforded satisfaction.

Mr. W. Todd has worked with his well known accuracy, care and zeal.

Mr. Ollenbach and Mr. Dyson have both done well.

Mr. O'Connor's zeal and professional ability are commendable.

Mr. Atkinson has conducted his duties as Chief Draftsman with success; his assistants have given satisfaction.

MONTHLY Meteorological results taken from the Register kept at the Office of the Superintendent G. T. Survey of India, Dehra Dún.

YEAR & MONTH	Barometer At 9 A.M. Highest (in.)	At 9 A.M. Lowest (in.)	At 9 A.M. Monthly mean (in.)	At 3 P.M. Highest (in.)	At 3 P.M. Lowest (in.)	At 3 P.M. Monthly mean (in.)	Hygrometer At 9 30 A.M. Temperature of Dew point (°)	At 9 30 A.M. Monthly mean Humidity (°)	At 3 30 P.M. Temperature of Dew point (°)	At 3 30 P.M. Monthly mean Humidity (°)	Thermometer Dry Bulb Max: in Sun's rays (°)	Dry Bulb Min: on grass (°)	Dry Bulb Max: in air (°)	Dry Bulb Min: in air (°)	Dry Bulb Monthly mean in air (°)	Wet Bulb Max: wet (°)	Wet Bulb Min: wet (°)	Wet Bulb Monthly mean wet (°)	Rain No. of days it fell	Rain Fall in inches	Wind Average direction	Cloud At 9 30 A.M.	Cloud At 3 30 P.M.
1873.																							
January	27·854	27·573	27·739	27·779	27·535	27·660	44·7	·698	43·3	·420	83·1	31·0	78·4	35·4	56·7	61·3	32·0	46·8	3	1·08	N.	3	4
February	·912	·514	·740	·835	·434	·653	·477	·611	·456	·276	92·8	39·3	88·1	43·0	62·8	65·0	35·1	51·2	3	0·34	S.	2	2
March	·767	·541	·673	·666	·457	·576	·490	·519	·459	·334	108·1	42·8	91·2	45·8	67·9	67·6	38·2	63·9	4	1·21	W.	3	4
April	·705	·491	·571	·588	·381	·470	·465	·584	·451	·203	109·6	54·6	97·9	57·2	79·1	71·9	41·6	68·2	0	0·00	S. & W.	0	1
May	·712	·388	·555	·643	·263	·470	·478	·445	·566	·362	117·3	57·9	109·1	60·8	79·5	79·1	51·5	63·4	8	2·01	E.	4	4
June	·436	·212	·539	·353	·184	·246	65·7	·461	63·1	·330	116·2	64·9	105·6	63·6	83·2	81·0	55·8	64·1	3	0·60	W.	1	2
July	·462	·259	·349	·346	·203	·281	75·2	·519	75·9	·763	113·8	68·8	103·0	71·0	81·5	82·0	64·8	74·0	26	28·45	S.W.	7	8
August	·556	·408	·478	·476	·331	·396	75·1	·337	75·8	·301	104·1	69·4	100·0	70·8	79·7	81·9	64·0	73·4	20	21·43	N.	6	7
September	·694	·414	·525	·563	·341	·449	71·6	·800	72·6	·753	102·1	62·8	90·5	65·1	77·1	82·0	40·3	69·8	14	10·52	S.	4	5
October	·800	·650	·706	·680	·557	·618	57·0	·619	57·6	·482	99·4	45·2	85·2	49·0	69·3	79·4	40·3	58·3	1	0·00	W.	0	0
November	·931	·743	·849	·834	·643	·762	49·2	·694	49·0	·432	93·0	41·8	78·8	46·1	63·9	67·2	38·6	50·7	0	0·00	E.	1	2
December	·931	·670	·828	·846	·612	·743	·460	·700	·466	·493	84·5	38·1	73·0	41·0	56·6	67·2	32·4	47·9	4	0·74	S.	2	3

NOTE.—The height of the Barometer Cistern above Mean Sea Level at Kurdchi is 2232·41 feet.

Annual Return of work executed in the Drawing Branch of the Office of Superintendent G. T. Survey of India, from 1st May 1873 to 30th April 1874.

DESCRIPTION OF WORK.	Number of sheets or diagrams. Finished	Number of sheets or diagrams. In hand	Scale 1 inch = Miles.	REMARKS.
Compilation.				
Sheets Nos. 2, 3 and 4, Turkestan Map (2nd edition)	4		32	For Photozincography.
Sheet No. 4, Turkestan Map (3rd edition)		1	32	ditto.
Addendum to sheet No. 1, Turkestan Map (2nd edition) ...	1		32	ditto.
Trans-Frontier Maps Nos. 8 and 9	2		16 & 8	ditto.
" Map (containing Rakas Tal and Mánsorawar Lake) ... ... }	1		4	ditto. { Sheet No. 9 for reduction to ⅛ scale.
Map of Kashmir to illustrate Major Bates' Gazetteer of Kashmir ... ... }	1		16	ditto.
Map of Kumaun and Garhwál to illustrate Mr. E.T. Atkinson's Gazetteer of Kumaun and Garhwál ... }		1	4	ditto. Reduction to ⅛ scale.
Sheet No. 6 of Spirit-Levelled Heights		1	2	ditto.
do. " 18 do. do.		1	2	ditto.
do. " 25 do. do.		1	2	ditto.
do. " 26 do. do.	1		2	ditto.
Index Map to Mussoorie and Landour Survey sheets shewing the position of Boundary Pillars ... }	1		2	ditto.
Preliminary Numerical Charts.				
Assam Longitudinal Series, Seasons 1855-60	1		4	ditto.
Jodhpur Meridional Series, " 1872-73	1		4	ditto.
Kadappa and Karnúl Minor Series (Great Arc Revision), Seasons 1871-73 ... }	1		4	ditto.
Mangalore Meridional and Madras Longitudinal Series, Seasons 1871-73 ... ... }	1		4	ditto.
Biláspur Meridional Series (Southern Section) Season 1872-73 ... ... }	1		4	ditto.
Final Charts.				
Great Indus Series	4		4	ditto. Reduction to ⅛ scale
Great Arc "		2	4	ditto. ditto.
Gurhágarh "		2	4	ditto. ditto.
Jogí-Tíla "		1	4	ditto. ditto.
Karáchí "		2	4	ditto. ditto.
Rahún "		2	4	ditto. ditto.
Sutlej "		1	4	ditto. ditto.
Rough Chart of the South-East Quadrilateral	1		20	ditto.
2 Charts of the chains of triangles west of the meridian of Calcutta ... ... }		2		ditto. ditto.
4 Copies of Star Charts		4		ditto.
Miscellaneous.				
Prepared 28 Forms professional and office on Transfer and Drawing paper				For Zincography and Photozincography.
Examined proofs of 81 maps and charts				
Colored 6,862 copies of different maps				
Prepared Diagrams and Descriptions of Bench-Marks for sheet No. 26 of Spirit-Levelled Heights				
Reduced and combined several sheets of levels				
do. several routes				
do. several Russian and other maps for incorporation in Turkestan and Trans-Frontier Maps				
Prepared several tracings for use of Officers				
Examined and reported on 18 fair maps of the Kumaun and Garhwál, Kattywar and Guzerat parties and performed numerous other miscellaneous duties				

Particulars of the transit of Venus across the Sun, December 9, 1874, observed at Mary Villa, Mussoorie, on the Himalaya Mountains, by J. B. N. Hennessey, F.R.A.S., Deputy Superintendent 1st Grade, Great Trigonometrical Survey of India, in charge Computing Office.

PART I.

Naturally sharing in the great interest excited by the transit of Venus, I proposed that I should observe the event with the equatorial of the Royal Society which Captain J. Herschel, R.E. had temporarily placed at my disposal; and the project meeting with your approval and support, I was enabled to provide myself with 4 chronometers, a good alt-azimuth, a barometer, thermometer and other articles of equipment necessary for the undertaking. My especial object in view was to observe the transit from a considerable height, and this condition was easily secured through the circumstance, that in pursuance of my professional duties I was located only some 14 miles from Mussoorie on the Himalaya Mountains; no doubt a station on these mountains would be very liable to an envelope of mist and cloud at the time of year in question, but on the other hand, if really good weather prevailed, I should enjoy the exquisitely clear atmosphere such as I have never experienced save on the Himalayas: add to this, the journey as already stated was merely an ordinary ride, the necessary equipment for my purpose was at hand, and though failure would involve a waste of no inconsiderable preliminary labor, this latter I was willing to incur if need be. Arguing thus, I selected a station some 6½ thousand feet above the sea and proceeded to find my latitude, longitude and height, to observe for time and to rate my chronometers. My numerical results are given in Part II of this Appendix. The remarks now made are restricted chiefly to what I saw with the equatorial.

2. The telescope of the equatorial has a 5-inch object glass of about 5 feet focal length and is driven by an excellent clock; the eye-end of the telescope may be fitted at will with an eye-piece of 55, 85, 125, 200 or 300 power; or with a spectroscope mounting a single simple prism: the polar axis may be shifted for latitude. The equatorial was set up and adjusted in an observatory tent, of which the canvas top was removed during observation.

3. I found from actual trial, that the most suitable eye-piece for both ingress (sun's altitude 2° 24' to 7° 29') and egress (sun's altitude about 26°) was that of 125 power: accordingly this eye-piece alone was employed at the contacts. It was however impossible to adapt the same dark glasses for both the higher and lower altitudes, without sacrificing definition on one of the two occasions; accordingly I selected for ingress two glasses which combined gave a neutral or bluish field, and for egress I changed one of these for a deep red glass so that the field now presented a moderately deep red: the glasses were quite flat and lay against one another in intimate contact giving excellent definition. I may here add, that thanks to Manrakan, Artificer, G. T. Survey, the clock behaved with perfect regularity, nor was there the smallest instrumental disappointment throughout the work. As regards procedure during transit, Mr. W. H. Cole, M.A. with his usual kindness counted seconds audibly from the journeyman chronometer placed before him, while Baboo Cally Mohun Ghose took up a position by my side, pencil in hand, noting down such remarks as the phenomena, viewed through the equatorial, elicited from me. Nor, as we stood informed, were the events to be recorded few in number; at ingress, internal contact, the light between the cusps was suddenly to vary, the cusps were to meet; then should come the "pear drop", the "ligament"; what should be its length, what its breadth in terms of Venus' diameter, what its shape and which of the known descriptions would it resemble; when would it break? Primed on these points, we settled on a programme which included them all, and time after time we went through the necessary rehearsals for perfecting ourselves in our parts. So much for what we had to expect, and now for a few words on the weather.

4. I moved up to my mountain station on the afternoon of the 1st December; the day following I was busy in adjusting my station and adjusting instruments: up to this, the sky had been sufficiently clear; but from the 3rd there set in an alternation of weather, which without running into extremes, kept me in a state of miserable suspense, to say nothing of the additional watching and toil in observing for time. This state of affairs appeared drawing to a climax, when the 8th December arrived and the clouds looked blacker than ever, while the mist, which generally precedes snow-falls here, began to settle down on the internal and still more lofty ranges of hills; about 2 P.M. on this day there were a few drops of rain or sleet, so few that they might almost have been counted, and later on as the sun began to set, the heavy cumuli evolved themselves into strati, which spreading their even canopy over us, left something like decimal 0 of the sky visible; and this at 10 o'clock at night! At 4 next morning (9 December), when again reported on, the sky was without speck or cloud; the air was still, and so clear, so brilliantly clear, that even the most exacting of observers could not have desired more favorable circumstances for viewing the coming transit: in brief, I enjoyed most exquisitely clear weather during my observations, such as occurs not frequently even at Mussoorie. I now proceed to describe the phenomenon of the transit: in doing this I shall have occasion to speak of Venus as she appeared across the sun's limb, when a portion of her limb is seen against the sun

and the other remains against the sky; the former portion I shall call Venus' sun-limb or briefly V_n, the latter Venus' sky-limb or V_k. Again I shall require to mention a ring of light around V_k which I shall call L_k, the corresponding ring around V_n being understood by L_n. Another point is this; any one who has watched, say the sun's limb, especially at a low altitude and with high power, must be aware of the turmoil and ebullition which then appears very like as if the limb was being boiled : I shall denote this kind of turmoil by "boiling."

5. With the telescope well adjusted for focus, I watched for the first external contact;

Ingress. but to no purpose, for I did not see Venus' limb until after it had effected an indentation on the sun's limb; the latter boiled sensibly, yet by no means violently; it appeared jagged and as if with minute spikes projecting inwards, all of which were well defined in the bluish field. Watching V_n I found it also boiling slightly, but in a manner somewhat different to the sun's limb. The appearance was that of boiling vapour coming round, and overlapping V_n, from the face of Venus turned towards the sun; moreover this boiling was not restricted to the edge of V_n but extended 2″ or 3″ beyond, thus forming a kind of boiling annulus in which there were minute sparkling specks dancing and shifting about, appearing and disappearing; the edge V_n was *visible through* the boiling : so much for the portion of Venus seen against the *Sun.*

6. At 8½ minutes before the first internal contact, I happened to look closely into the

Ingress continued. spot where that part of Venus against the *sky* lay, and to my great surprise I found that this portion of her disc was easily visible, because it was edged by a narrow ring of light or L_k ; at first I saw L_k only about 10° or 15° on either side of the point where the chord of Venus' track would cut V_k, or more definitely stated, this light-ring did not reach to the sun's limb ; but within 50″ later I saw the light-ring distinctly round the whole sector of V_k, from edge to edge of the sun's limb. The ring-light was only moderately bright, like diffused light, and at first I estimated the annulus L_k at 3″ in width ; it was probably brightest about the part where the chord above named cut V_k. At 6ᵐ before 1st internal contact, I estimated L_k at 4″ in breadth, at the same time my notes contain the remark "definition excellent". At 3ᵐ 24ˢ before 1st internal contact I remarked "light-ring quite distinct," and 1ᵐ 16ˢ later I stated "light-ring quite bright." Indeed the annulus L_k was so plain, that after recording the time of transit for the *dark* edge V_k, I even made a conjectural record as to the time when the bright edge L_k transited across the sun's limb; of course this estimate was based on *recollection* of the width of L_k and not on any *visible* fact, for as L_k came on the sun's disc the lesser light of the former merged into the latter. On the whole, I am of opinion that L_k was between 2″ and 4″ in width.

7. "And now for the pear drop, the ligament, &c.", I mentally exclaimed as I

Ingress continued. watched the following limb of Venus which had just transited. From what has been stated it will be seen, that as V_k passed onwards from the sun's limb it was immediately followed by the light-ring L_k, so that unless Venus *suddenly shot out backward across this ring of light*, it was plain there could be no "pear drop" and no "ligament." Fully expecting this retrogression, I still watched intently for the event, while Mr. Cole went on deliberately enumerating seconds, amid the complete silence enforced on all others around. But I watched for any such event in vain. Venus glided resolutely onwards, and the streak of *light* she was leaving behind grew wider and still wider, until at last when a belt of light representing 10 or 15 minutes of time lay between her and the sun's limb, I exclaimed, and I believe much to the disappointment of all concerned, "*there is no pear drop and no ligament*." We watched Venus for some ¼ hour after this and then turned to the spectroscope.

8. The substitution of spectroscope for eye-piece cannot be effected in this equa-

The spectroscope. torial without a considerable amount of adjustment. When this had been performed, and we had taken a hasty breakfast, I first placed the slit across the *centre* of Venus' disc and found that it gave a black band all along the length of the bright solar spectrum; *i. e.* Venus' face turned towards us reflected no light. I next placed the slit tangential to Venus' disc; this gave a faint glimmer of narrow light *in place* of the black band; that is, *this glimmer was slightly brighter than the solar spectrum on which it appeared.* I looked intently for any Venus air-lines, but so far as the feeble dispersion of the prism would shew, the lines seen across the glimmering from Venus' edge were identical in all respects with the solar lines. I repeated these experiments as long as time permitted, and then with Maurakan's help reverted to the adjustments and the eye-end and eye-piece employed at ingress. As already stated, it was now necessary to substitute a dark red glass for one of those used at ingress.

9. The field now was red and if anything slightly too dark to show faint lights; the

Egress. definition was intensely sharp. Again, I watched with the utmost care as Venus approached her second internal contact, but *neither pear drop, ligament nor any other connection or shadow appeared between her edge and*

*that of the sun, until at last the two fairly touched.** Of course I again looked for the light-ring and certainly saw it 5^m after this contact when it was far less bright than at ingress : some time later I searched for the light-ring once more, but it was invisible; nor did I again see it, nor yet the disc of Venus against the sky. The remaining external contact needs no remark, excepting that it was seen with considerable exactness.

10. As already stated no *ligament* was visible to me at Mussoorie; it was however seen by yourself at Dehra, and by some other observers at certain of those few stations of observation whence some accounts of the phenomenon observed have been published in the local papers. How far these reports may combine to support one another and lead to the authoritative decisions which may be hereafter pronounced cannot of course now be predicted. For the present it appears to me probable, that height above sea level, inferiority of telescope, insensibility of the eye to faint lights and shadows and other causes, are all likely to conspire together towards producing a *ligament* at the internal contacts; but restricting myself to the first named of these causes, I venture on the following conclusions.

(1.) In view of the light-ring L_R and of the peculiar boiling annulus around V_R which may be called L_R, I have no doubt that L_R was in fact a continuation of the light-ring L_R, which latter beyond all question was plainly visible at ingress and less distinctly but still decidedly seen at egress; and under these circumstances it may be urged, that Venus is surrounded by an atmosphere or envelope, which at the time was made *visible* to the extent of 2″ to under 4″ in width.

(2.) As a matter of fact the pear drop or ligament was visible at a height of 2,200 feet, but at 6,500 feet of height the ligament was invisible; the influence generally of height of station appears undeniable; but the phenomenon still remains to be accounted for definitely. If however an effective envelope or atmosphere of x breadth around Venus be conceded, this atmosphere may be supposed to stop a certain amount of direct light from the sun, producing a slight shade around Venus corresponding to the breadth x; this shade would I conceive be quite invisible when its outer edge is backed by the sun's bright light; but could we contract the sun to a diameter equal to that of Venus plus twice x, and make Venus and the sun concentric, it appears likely that we should see a shaded annulus right round Venus between her limb and that of the sun; further that the annulus may appear darker at low than at higher altitudes, and may become invisible when the observer is raised above a sufficiency of the earth's atmosphere. Should these suggestions prove tenable, the ligament seen would break when the outer edge of the shade, corresponding to x, transited across the sun's limb.

(3.) Solar light shining through Venus' atmosphere (if any) produces no alteration in the lines of the solar spectrum so far as the dispersion of a single simple prism shows. Also Venus' face turned towards us, reflects no light during transit, subject to the same instrumental test.

PART II.

The instruments used were the following :—An Alt-azimuth by Troughton and Simms with an azimuth circle of 8 inches diameter read by 3 verniers, and a complete vertical circle also of 8 inches read by 2 verniers; the circles are divided to every 10′ of arc and the verniers afford readings to 10″, or by estimation to at least 5″: the instrument is well provided with spirit-levels surmounted by scales—the Alt-azimuth was used for fixing the station of observation and for determining time—

A mountain Barometer.

A good Thermometer.

Four Chronometers viz: Dent 2,047 used as a *journeyman* chronometer and packed in wool in a wooden box by itself; Barrauds 885, Dent 2,775 and Arnold and Dent 758, were the three *fixed* chronometers and were placed in the same case within a room, where the temperature had only a moderate diurnal range (probably under 8°); the case was well padded with wool and hemp and the chronometers were never moved between 4th and 10th December.

The Equatorial, has already been sufficiently described in Part I.

The point over which the Equatorial stood is called Venus Station; its co-ordinates are as follows, and were determined by angles from two known points fixed by the Great Trigonometrical Survey of India, viz., Camel's Back and Vincent's Hill Stations.

Venus Station.

Lat. N. 30° 27′ 36″·3; Long. east of Greenwich $\left\{ \begin{matrix} 78° & 3′ & 3^r·2 \\ \text{h.} & \text{m.} & \text{s.} \\ 5 & 12 & 12·2 \end{matrix} \right\}$ Height above sea 6,765 feet.

---

* My notes state successively, that when the two limbs were apart $\frac{1}{4}$, $\frac{1}{5}$, $\frac{1}{8}$, $\frac{1}{12}$ and $\frac{1}{20}$ of Venus' diameter, there was no ligament or other connection.

Time was determined from the zenith distances of a Tauri (east) and a Aquilæ (west) when these stars were nearly on the prime vertical; as a rule 4 pairs of zenith distances were taken to each star, a pair consisting of one observation instrumental face east and another face west, taken in rapid succession; the chronometer time for each observation was obtained from transits over five horizontal wires; the resulting chronometer error by *each* pair was computed. The *journeyman* chronometer was compared with the three fixed chronometers before and after observation; and the errors and rates of the latter thus determined. Proceeding in this manner, and tabulating the *mean* of the results by the three fixed chronometers, it was determined

Astronomical date		Chronometer reading	Fast on local Mean time	Daily rate
		h. m. s.	m. s.	s.
December	4	6 47 18·5	1 31·2	
				+ 6·5
,,	5	6 48 40·6	1 37·7	
				+ 7·5 (1)
,,	6	6 37 19·1	1 45·1	
				+ 6·7
,,	7	(Cloudy)		
,,	8	⎧ 6 42 12·1 ⎫ ⎨ 18 56 17·4 ⎬ ⎩ 23 17 19·4 ⎭	⎧ 1 58·6 ⎫ ⎨ 2 2·2 ⎬ ⎩ 2 3·5 ⎭	
				+ 7·3
,,	9	6 37 52·6	2 5·8	

On the day of transit, the *journeyman* was compared with the three fixed chronometers before and after ingress, and also before and after egress, and by employing the daily rate of + 7·3 and correcting the times of contact determined by the *journeyman* chronometer we obtain,

                                                 Local Mean time

		d. h. m. s.	
1874 1st internal contact occurred, December	8	19 29 19·3	
2nd ,, ,,		23 17 42·9	(2)
2nd external ,,		23 44 59·9	

where the tenths of seconds come into existence through the arithmetical processes involved; the original times were recorded merely to the nearest second, and I have no doubt that the latter degree of rigour was much in excess of what the phenomena were susceptible, so that the procedure adopted for determining time appears amply rigorous.—Speaking roughly, 1″ of Venus' diameter took 26ˢ to transit, and supposing that I could see 0″·1 of the former (which I doubt) each contact should have lasted, visibly, for say 3ˢ. But as regards the estimates of accuracy I actually made *immediately after* the events, I find it recorded that I thought my times might be true within the following limits

               Time of 1st internal contact   ± 3ˢ to 4ˢ
                  ,,   2nd   ,,   ,,   ± 2ˢ   (3)
                  ,,   2nd external   ,,   ± 1ˢ

I am now however of opinion that these estimates (3) should be *increased* by one half. From what has preceded, the Greenwich mean times of contact are

	h. m. s.	
1st internal contact	14 17 7·1	
2nd ,, ,,	18 5 30·7	(4)
2nd external ,,	18 32 47·7	

there is however an incongruity in (4), for in this reduction the Longitude of Venus Station is taken east of Greenwich by 5^h 12^m $12^s\cdot2 = H$, the origin for Indian longitude being adopted at 5^h 20^m $57^s\cdot3$ E., for Madras Observatory; in reality however H refers, not to the *local meridian* necessarily adopted in (2), but to a computed meridian deduced from a concluded meridian of origin adopted for the principal triangulation of the Great Trigonometrical Survey at Kaliánpúr, whereas the times (2) refer to the *local meridian* as already stated. Denoting the value of H corresponding to the local meridian by H_1 we may find (nearly) $H_1 - H = h^s$ thus. Let A_o denote the azimuth of a terrestrial point P as determined by observations to a circumpolar star about its elongation and A_c the corresponding value as brought up by the triangulation from the concluded meridian of origin; also let $A_o - A_c = a''$ and let λ stand for the latitude of P_1 then it can be seen that as a correction to (4)

$$h^s = -\frac{a''}{15} \operatorname{cosec} \lambda$$

now a" is not known at Venus Station, but at Banog station distant 2·9 miles W. N. W, a" = − 14"·54; adopting this value, we find h° = + 1°·9 and the *true* Greenwich mean times of contact become

			h.	m.	s.	
1st internal contact			14	17	9·0	
2nd	„	„	18	5	32·6	
2nd external	„		18	32	49·6	(5)

the results (5) of course supersede (4).

J. B. N. HENNESSEY,

DEHRA DUN,
9th December 1874.

Depy. Superintendent 1st Grade, G. T. Survey,
In charge Computing Office.

Appendix to Notes on Transit of Venus across the Sun.

On 12th December 1874 I received a communication from the Reverend H. D. James M.A. describing briefly what he had seen at his station of observation. In reply I made enquiry on some additional points, to which he replied on 14th instant. Mr. James was located at Chakrata on the Himalaya mountains at a height of 7,300 feet above the sea, in Latitude N. 30° 43' Longitude E. 77° 44'; his station is distinctly visible from Mussoorie on a clear day. The following facts are taken from his letters above mentioned, and appear to deserve being recorded, more particularly from the circumstance that but few observers of the transit are likely to have been placed at considerable heights above the sea.

Mr. James was attended by his son Henry, a young gentleman with plenty of intelligence and a commendable spirit of enquiry. The instrument used was a telescope by Smith and Beck, the property of Mr. James, object glass 3¼ inches and its focal length 4 feet: at ingress, eye-piece 60 power and field a neutral tint; at egress, eye-piece 100 power and field red: for time piece, he used his pocket watch which has a seconds hand; the watch "gained considerably, perhaps a minute in 12 hours".

Under date 9th December 1874, Mr. James states "when she (*i. e.* Venus) was about half "way on (at ingress) the sun, we both noticed a fringe of white light illuminating that rim, of "the planet which was yet on the dark sky. When she went off, we noticed the same fringe of "light, but for a much shorter time and when only about one eighth of her had passed the "sun's disc." His watch times of contact were as follows.

			h.	m.	s.
1st internal contact			7	41	20
2nd	„	„	11	30	15
2nd external	„		11	57	25

After receipt of the preceding I wrote to Mr. James, as already stated. I stated briefly that my view resembled his; that I had seen a ring of light but no "pear drop" or other ligament . at internal contacts. I gave him rough sketches of some of the ligaments described in 1769 and enquired if he had seen any thing like them. I also asked him to describe the fringe of light he had observed, more particularly.

In reply, Mr. James states under date 14th December "when about half her orb had en-"tered (alluding to ingress) my attention was attracted to the other half yet on the dark sky, "to me it was dark, hence I infer that my field was not so light as it ought to have been. "Its outline up to this time quite invisible to me, became now illumined with a fringe of white "light. I then noticed a much fainter thinner edging of light on the outline of the limb "on the sun's disc, which soon ceased to be visible. The fringe external was rather less in "width than $\frac{1}{64}$ of the planet's diameter" * * * "The light somewhat resembled that "which we see so plainly in India lighting up the dark side of the moon 3 or 4 days old, but it "was brighter, not diffusive as that is, its inner edge being clearly marked. It remained visible "as long as there was any appreciable portion of the planet beyond the sun's circumference."

"As the time of the internal contact approached, that half of the planet which was still "entering appeared to lose its semi-circular shape and to become oval. I compared it to the "thinner half of an egg, but since I have examined several eggs and find that my comparison "would represent a distortion greater than I had intended. Just before the contact ceased the "end of the oval seemed as if it were adhering to the sun's edge, and could not get free—render-"ing it difficult to decide when the contact ceased. Another impediment in the way of accurate "timing was that the outline of Venus looked woolly and wave-like from a very annoying "tremor in the air. Hence the notes we entered were "internal contact ceased 7h. 41m. 20s.

"quite clear 7h. 42m. As to the ligament which seemed to knit the two edges together, I am
"disposed to attribute it solely to the billowy motion of the planet's outline, for it had a hairy
"appearance and sun-light could be seen through it."

"In timing the remaining contacts there was no difficulty, for as the sun arose, Venus
"appeared to diminish in size, her outline becoming sharply defined."

"At egress the oval shape did not reappear, but just at the moment of internal contact
"there was a sort of flickering movement, as if the planet's edge had touched, withdrawn and
"touched again. This was at 11h. 30m. 15s. At 11h. 33m. 27s. when nearly one eighth of
"her orb had crossed the border, its outline was for a brief while fringed with an edging of
"light."

"The flickering movement just mentioned, evidently an ocular illusion, induced by the
"eye's weariness from intent gazing, was again noticed at 11h. 57m. 25s. when the external
"contact ceased."

It will be seen that both Mr. James and I observed an edging of light around the dark
limb of Venus and that we agree that it was quite distinct at ingress and less plain at egress.
I saw this edging decidedly as an *annulus* and as stated in Part I, it was continued round the
bright limb. The complete ring thus presented to view was plainly a visible atmosphere or
envelope. Notwithstanding the somewhat conflicting statements, which have appeared since
writing my Part I, as to the phenomena seen at certain stations; and pending the authoritative
decisions which may hereafter be pronounced, it appears to me probable, that height of station,
inferiority of instruments, insensibility of eye to faint lights and shadows, and other causes
are likely to conspire towards producing a ligament (or *pear drop*) at the internal contacts,
provided there is an atmosphere or envelope around the planet to afford a first cause.

J. B. N. H.

ACCOUNT

OF

TRANS-HIMALAYAN EXPLORATIONS

TO ACCOMPANY

THE GENERAL REPORT

ON THE OPERATIONS

OF THE

GREAT TRIGONOMETRICAL SURVEY OF INDIA

DURING

1873-74,

Map

TO ILLUSTRATE

THE REPORT ON

THE TRANS-HIMALAYAN EXPLORATIONS

IN GREAT TIBET

TO THE NORTH OF

THE BRAHMAPUTRA RIVER

MADE DURING

1872.

Scale M Miles=1 Inch or *appar*

BRAHMAPUTRA RIVER

LHASA

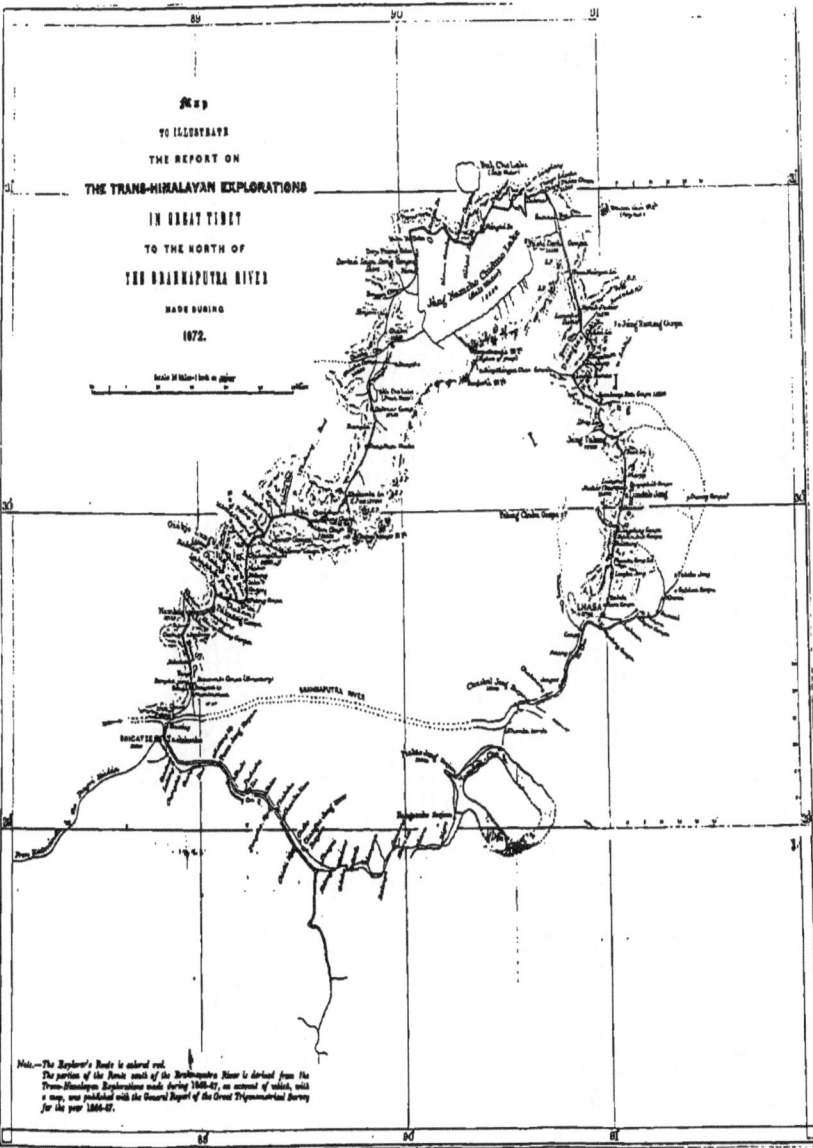

Note.—The Explorer's Route is colored red.
The portion of the Route south of the Brahmaputra River is derived from the
Trans-Himalayan Explorations made during 1865-67, an account of which, with
a map, was published with the General Report of the Great Trigonometrical Survey
for the year 1866-67.

Narrative of an exploration of the Namcho or Tengri Nur Lake in Great Tibet made by a native explorer, during 1872, drawn up by Lieut-Colonel T. G. MONTGOMERIE, R.E., F. R. S., &c., Deputy Superintendent, G. T. Survey of India.

During 1871 a party was organised with a view to exploring some portion of the unknown regions north of the Tibetan watershed of the upper Brahmaputra. The party consisted of a semi-Tibetan, a young man who had been thoroughly trained for the work, with 4 reliable assistants engaged from border districts; one of these latter had been employed on a former exploration in a subordinate capacity and his experience, as far as travelling in such countries was concerned, would have been exceedingly useful, but unfortunately he was unable to get more than a march beyond the frontier because the officials on the other side of the Himalayas were determined to arrest him if he proceeded further, though his ostensive object was trade. This being the case there was nothing for it but to arrange for his return and to substitute another man in his place. This was managed satisfactorily after some delay.

The exploring party then passed from Kumaon into the Tibetan province of Hundes or Gnarikhorsum. At first they got on very well but towards the end of July, when in the neighbourhood of the Mánsarowar lake, their progress was for sometime interrupted by a band of mounted robbers who had made an incursion from the east: they succeeded in evading the robbers but had to take a circuitous route by Púrung, instead of going direct to Shigatze from Mánsarowar as first arranged. The party reached Shigatze on the 24th November and remained there 12 days making inquiries as to the best route to go to the Tengri Núr lake and preparing for the journey. Sheep were the only animals likely to stand the journey, as the roads were too stony for yáks and the country was too cold for donkeys, the explorer consequently purchased 50 sheep and put all the baggage on their backs. The party left Shigatze on the 6th December marching as far as the "Naisáng" village; on the 7th they crossed the great Brahmaputra (or Sangpo) River by means of rafts and encamped at Peting village on the left bank of the river. Peting has about 30 houses. The next day they put up at Chua village. Here the explorer exchanged the silver rupees he had with him for gold which he put into hollow walking sticks prepared for the purpose. On the 11th December they reached Dongdot-lo, a village on the right bank of the Shiang Chu, a tributary of the Brahmaputra; here they found an official from Shigatze who rules over Dongdot-lo and the surrounding villages which are numerous. On the 13th December they reached "Chom", a village of 50 houses with a Buddhist monastery (Gonpa) on its west. This monastery or rather nunnery is occupied by women only, of whom there were about 100. On the 14th they reached "Namling" on the right bank of the Shiang Chu river; here there is a large monastery with about 500 Lámas, all men: the monastery is on a high hill, it is a place of some importance boasting of an iron bridge over the river and commanded by a strongly situated fort which is the residence of the Jongpon, or Governor, with about 500 Tibetan soldiers; Namling itself has about 200 houses surrounded by gardens with a small bazar in the centre. The "Sokpo Giájú" tribe—who bring salt—trade through this bazar which produces all ordinary provisions. The name of Namling is derived from the two Tibetan words " nam " sky and " ling " garden, the monastery being on a high hill with gardens at its foot. On the 17th December the party reached "Kholam" village on the left bank of the Shiang Chu river which was crossed by means of the iron bridge: Kholam has about 50 houses; the land round about is very productive. On the 19th they reached "Gonkiáng" a village of 60 houses with a well built monastery on rising ground. In this monastery there are about 100 Lámas ruled by a Láma of high rank, called Chúringboche, who is very much respected by the people round about.

On the 20th December the party halted at another monastery, called Rabdan Chuling Gonpa, built about 80 years ago; it is the residence of another high Láma called " Shaptung Ringboche " said to be 100 years of age who was both the founder and builder of this monastery. The people of the country say that whilst out hunting he heard a voice which told him to put down his gun and go to a certain spot where he would find unlimited riches buried in the ground, with this he was commanded to build a monastery : he had obeyed the inspiration and had ever since passed his life in religious duties. " Rabdan " means house, "chu" wisdom and "ling" garden. The Láma, when the explorer saw him, was evidently a very old man, his body so small and shrunk that when sitting his knees projected a great deal above his head.

From the time the explorer left Namling on the 14th December it was so cold that the mercury of his thermometer did not rise out of the bulb till after 9 or 10 in the morning. The streams were all hard frozen. The wind moreover blew so hard that their tent was torn by it and they had consequently to make a halt of 5 days in order to repair the damage. On the 26th December they marched on and reached Gunje; the people of this village said white bears called " Tik-dumba" were very common from thence to Namcho lake and committed great havoc amongst their cattle.

On the 27th December he reached Naikor which has about 30 houses and some cultivation; beyond Naikor there was no more cultivation, and the only inhabitants are nomadic, going by the name of Dogpá; they graze sheep, goats and yáks.

On the 28th December the explorer encamped at "Chutang Cháká" where there are some 15 hot springs, whose water was found to be at a temperature of 166° Fahrenheit, boiling water at the same place only rising to 186° Fahrenheit. There were 8 baths supplied by these springs, the baths were put at some distance from the springs so as to allow the water to cool sufficiently for bathing. The water has a smell of sulphur. There were a number of "Dogpá" tents at a short distance from the springs.

From the Brahmaputra river near Shigatze up to these springs the country is called "Shiang Lungba" and that to the north "Lahú-Lungba."

On the 29th December the "Chapting" encamping ground was reached; here there were more "Dogpá" tents; the road was so slippery with ice that one of the men fell and broke a thermometer. On the 30th December they arrived at "Peting Chuja" near which, on the right bank of the Lahú Chu river, there is a large stony place about 120 paces in length from which about a dozen columns of hot water issue, these rise to a height of 40 or 50 feet, and produce so much steam that the sky is quite darkened with it, the noise moreover was so great that they could not hear one another speaking; the water of these jets was found to be 176° Fahrenheit. Similar jets of water were noticed issuing from the middle of the river, shooting up to 40 or 50 feet in height and evidently at much the same temperature as those on land, as they produced clouds of steam, and the river was free from ice for a quarter of a mile below them though everywhere else both above and below it was hard frozen. The Jáwar Gonpa monastery lies about 8 miles to the east of these springs. The explorer went to the monastery which he found had a number of highly ornamented idols, in front of which were arranged a number of petrified stones called Naidhowns, these are in various shapes, such as hands, shells, &c., and are objects of worship as well as the idols. Jáwar is the name the Tibetans have for Suket-Mandi in the Panjáb hills, N. by W. of Simla. This according to a tradition was given in honor of a daughter of a Rája of Suket-Mandi who was supposed to have married "Laban" one of the idols.

On the 31st December the encampment of Sulung Sumdo was reached, here they found some 40 tents. On the 1st January they halted at Sulung which boasts of 50 Dogpá tents. The Dogpás said there were no regular encampments beyond Sulung, the only people about being thieves on the look out for plunder, against whom it would be necessary to be on their guard.

On the 2nd of January the explorer reached, "Naisum Chuja." Chuja or chusa means source of hot water springs. The name is given to the place from the great number of hot springs which there are here on both sides of the Lahú Chu river. The water from these springs is so hot that the river is not frozen for about 3 miles below them though every where else it was frozen over. On the right bank of the river there are two very remarkable hot springs which throw up a jet of water over 60 feet in height; the water in falling again freezes and forms pillars of ice which are nearly up to the full height of the jet. These pillars are about 30 feet in circumference and look like towers with holes at the sides just as if they had been made artificially. The water is thrown up with great violence and noise. The thermometer when put in the water inside the pillars stood at 183° Fahrenheit the boiling point there being only 183°·75.

The party was delayed at Naisum Chuja for 3 days owing to one of the men getting sick; it is said to be a great place of worship or pilgrimage. Owing to cloudy weather the explorer was unable to take any astronomical observations.

On the 6th January they reached Dung Cháká 15,700 feet above sea level where there are more hot springs but not of such high temperature as the last, their water showing only 180° Fahrenheit, while the boiling point was 183°: about 10 miles to the east there is a lofty snowy peak called "Jhomo Gangar" somewhat of the same shape as the Kailás peak near the Mánsarowar; it is a noted object of worship being considered as a female divinity. On the 7th January they encamped at the foot of the Khálamba Lá crossing over on the 8th, the highest part of the pass being 17,200 feet above the sea and water boiling at 180°. The crossing was very difficult owing to a heavy fall of snow which made the descent on the opposite side very dangerous. The only fire that they could make after crossing was from goats' dung with which they managed to warm up a brew of tea. The next day the explorer returned to the pass in order to re-observe the boiling point, not being quite satisfied that the water was properly boiling the first day that they crossed over. He was again troubled with snow and when he got back to camp was half dead with the intense cold, and did not recover till he had drunk a bowl of hot tea. The encamping place is called Dung Nagu Cháká; there were several hot springs round about, the water in them raising the thermometer to 180°, while boiling water only raised it two degrees higher.

On the 10th of January they reached Kiang Lá and on the 11th Dokmar encampment, where the Dogpás generally keep their sheep, goats, &c., during the summer. On the 12th they encamped on a plain and on the 13th reached the "Gháká" camping place from whence they got a view of a very large lake which they found was called by the Tibetans "Jáng Namcho Chidmo" and supposed to be called Tingri Núr in the Tartar language. A camp of several tents was seen to the east at a place called Dungche. As a road was seen to branch off from this camp two of the men were sent in disguise as beggars in order to inquire about the road and as to why a camp was kept there; they found the camp all but deserted the only occupants being an old man and a woman who were seated in one of the tents: the man said the tents belonged to Dogpás who had concealed all their property, women, children, &c., while the men themselves had armed and gone out to meet a band of robbers who they had heard intended to plunder them. As to the road they said it went to "Lhásá" by the "Ninjinthanglá" to Jáng Hiangpa Chan Goupa (monastery) and thence by the Tulung Chubu Gonpa (monastery) to Lhásá.

One mile north of Gháiká the road crosses the Gháiká Chu a large river which coming from the west flows into the "Jáng Namcho Chidmo" lake about 12 miles east of the road. The river though very wide was completely frozen over; in the summer it is said to rise very much.

On the 16th January after crossing the Gháiká Chu river the explorer reached a place called Chákrí which is surrounded by a 10 feet high wall enclosing a space about 200 paces by 200 paces. There were several houses of sundried bricks inside the wall but they were all in ruins; the place was said to have once been the residence of a man of some rank. As a great deal of snow was falling the explorers were very glad to take advantage of the shelter which the ruins afforded. On the 18th they arrived at Simjam where they found about 70 Dogpá tents; as robbers were known to be in the vicinity every tent was guarded by an armed man. The robbers were said to come from a district called Jámaáta De which lies to the north. Jámaáta De is said not to be under Lhásá and the inhabitants consequently plunder the Lhásá districts whenever they are in want, as they often are in consequence of the severity of the climate which kills off their cattle whenever there is an extra heavy fall of snow. Simjam being one of the nearest places to these freebooters has very often been plundered.

The party were detained two days at Simjam owing to heavy snow and did not start again till the 21st of January, when they marched to "Tárá" ~~for the most part along~~ the shores of the great "Namcho" lake which was completely frozen over and seemed to extend to a great distance eastward. The next day they continued their march along the shores of the great lake and reached the monastery called "Dorkiá Lúgu Dong" situated on a small hill overlooking the lake. "Dor" means a rock "lúgu" a sheep, "dong" a face. The monastery looking something like a sheep's head :

A chief Láma lives here with some forty ordinary Lámas. The monastery commands a splendid view of the lake and surrounding snowy mountains which were more especially grand to the southeast.

The lake is a magnificent sheet of water and near Dorkiá it has the advantage of having an island close at hand which sets off the scenery. The island is about a mile long and half a mile in breadth; it has a hill about 400 feet high in the centre which is crowned by a temple of the goddess "Dorje Phámo". The explorer determined to make a complete survey of the lake and he consequently deposited his property in the monastery with 3 of his men, being afraid of robbers, having done this he started off with 3 other of his men; on the 24th January they reached Ringa Do on the margin of the lake, here there is another island, called "Kuhi Ne Dobo" close to this, which is about 1½ miles in length by about 1 mile in breadth.

On the 25th they reached Júdor Gonpa (monastery) here they saw 3 pyramids or cones of earth or sundried mud each about 500 feet in circumference rising to a considerable height. The explorer went under these mounds by an artificial passage and found that one of them was open in the centre. The people say that they were originally all closed and that when a certain very devout Láma, who used to worship under one of these mounds, died he was taken up into heaven through the opening. The Júdor Gonpa has about 50 Lámas. Near the monastery there are a great many fossil stones which are held in veneration, they are called "Naidhowa". The explorer saw a gigantic doorway cut in the rock through which the Lámas say the god "Ninjinthanglá" passes, its height is about 25 feet. Owing to heavy snow the explorer was detained two days at "Júdor".

On the 29th they reached Nángbá Do which is also on the shore of the lake close to some small hills which are considered to be sacred. The next day they halted at "Lángdang"; here they found the "Shukpá" bush very abundant. On a low hill there is a temple of a god called Chogo Lá. On the 30th they got to Dakmar and passing Thuígo Sumna shrine they reached Nai Chu Sumna on the 31st. On their way they crossed the Nai Chu which is a very large stream, being the largest that flows into the lake, it comes from the east. At the time the explorer crossed it was 40 paces in width and completely frozen over.

On the 1st February the explorer reached the Tashí Doche Gonpa, a monastery which is on a low hill near the lake, it has 35 Láma monks. To the southwest of this monastery there are a number of magnificent snowy peaks which are called the "Ninjinthanglá" peaks. The Lámas say the highest peak is a god and that he is surrounded by 360 smaller snowy peaks which act as his servants.

To the east of "Tashí Doche" there is another mass of high peaks called Nuchin Gáá which appeared to the explorer to rise higher above the Namcho lake than the Kailás peak does above the Mánsarowar lake. The whole of these peaks were very imposing as seen from the monastery which also commands a full view of the whole of the lake. Though the water of the lake is so salt as to be unfit for drinking it is nevertheless quite frozen over in November, the lake being about 15,500 feet above the sea; when the explorer saw it the surface looked as if it was made of glass, it is said to remain in that state till May when the ice breaks up with great noise. The lake contains fish, and quantities of small shells are found on the banks. The lake itself is a great resort for pilgrims.

On the 3rd they halted near a small river; on the 4th they reached an open plain at night and were put to great straits owing to a heavy fall of snow. They had left their tent behind at Dorkiá and no shelter being available they had to clear off the snow and lie on the ground without any fire; they thought the cold would have killed them, but they managed to survive the night through; in the morning they found they were well covered with fresh snow. On the 5th they went on to the Gháiká Chu river; it was snowing all the time and they were forced to camp out again without any fuel or covering and passed another very miserable night. On the 6th they saw the sun again and were able to get some fuel and to make themselves tolerably comfortable, but whilst crossing at the side of the lake near a small stream, (the Simjam Chu) one of the men fell through the ice which was covered with snow and would have been drowned had he not got hold of another man who pulled him out again. The man's clothes froze hard directly he got out, and he was only brought round by means of a fire which they at once lighted.

On the 7th February they reached the Dorkiá monastery from which they originally started, having been 15 days in making the circuit of the lake. They halted 3 days at the monastery and started off on the 11th, getting that day as far as " Ringa Do;" on the 13th they reached the Jádor Gonpa before mentioned and on the 14th Nángbá Do. Here the explorer heard there was a lake called Bul Cho about 6 or 7 miles to the north, he accordingly climbed a peak in that direction and saw the lake. He estimated it to be about 6 miles by five. A kind of borax is found by and in the lake, it is called " Bul " and hence the name. This borax is used by the inhabitants of Lhásá and Shigatze as a spice for meat, for tea and for washing clothes, bathing, &c. It is carried away by the traders in great quantities.

On the 15th they reached Lángdang, on the 16th Dakmar, on the 17th the plain of Cháng Pháng Chujá where there are several hot springs in which the thermometer rose to 130°. On the 18th as they were about to start some 60 armed men arrived on horse back and began plundering their property and in spite of their entreaties took away everything except the instruments which they said they did not care to keep in case the authorities should find them on them and ask how they came into their possession. After a great deal of begging the robbers gave them back a piece of cloth each with two sheep and two bags of food, a cooking vessel and a wooden cup to each man; with these they had to be contented, the robbers saying if they troubled them any more they would kill them.

The explorer had intended to make his way from the Namcho lake to the north as far as the city of " Sinning," but after the robbery there was no possibility of doing that and indeed they were so far from habitations that it was a question whether they could exist, and there was nothing for it but to march as quickly as they could to the south in the direction of Lhásá where they were likely to get into inhabited ground soonest. The day after the robbery they halted in order to consult as to the best course to follow. On the 20th February they went as far as the banks of the " Nai Chu " river; here one of the men got sick and they were obliged to remain there all the 21st, their food consisted of one pound of flour and hot water, they had moreover nothing to cover themselves with, the robbers having taken the tent, and were exposed to the snow and wind which blew very hard.

On the 22nd they reached Dam Niárgan Lá. The explorer says that he had got so weak that he took much shorter paces than he had hitherto done. On the 23rd they ascended the Dam Niárgan Lá pass, after crossing they decided to kill one of their two sheep as they had exhausted all their flour; at the same time seeing tents in the neighbourhood all the men went out to beg and after a long round came back with 6 pounds of flour and began to feel more hopeful, on the 25th another man got ill and they were obliged to halt there.

From Dam Niárgan there is said to be a road to Lob Núr and to " Jilling " or " Sinning." From " Dam Niárgan " it is about 10 days journey to Nákchukhá, a place that has a bad reputation as to the number of robbers who prey upon travellers; from thence it is about 45 days' journey to Sokphuil which is quite a barren country infested however by robbers; after passing Sokpohuil the inhabitants are more civilized and are said to be very kind to travellers.

The Lob Núr (? Koknúr) lake is in the Sokpohuil territory, and close to it is the town of Kharká. It is about 15 days' journey from Sokpohuil to " Sinning" city, where a Chinese Amba, a man of considerable authority resides. " Sinning" is described as being very superior to " Lhásá," good horses, sheep, &c., are procurable and the shops are well supplied with silk, woolen articles, carpets, &c.

On the 26th they halted under the Cháná Lá pass, the country up to this point was called " Dam Niárgan." On the 27th they halted at Angchusa where they noticed 6 Dogpá tents. On the 28th they reached " Láchu Sumna" the extremity of the " Bádam " district which begins at Cháná Lá.

The "Urirong" district extends from "Láchu Sumna to "Dhog Lá." On the 29th they reached Siwalungi Ritu (Gonpa) monastery which has some 60 Láma monks. Here the height was observed by boiling point, but owing to the loss of his quick silver, when robbed at Cháng Pháng, the explorer was unable to take Latitude observations he however hoped that on reaching Lhásá he would be able to borrow sufficient money to enable him to refit and to return to this same place on his way north east to China.

On the 1st of March he crossed the Dhok Lá pass encamping on the other side, the district of "Jáng Tálung " extends from the Dhog Lá to the Chak Lá pass. On the 2nd they reached the very large monastery called "Jáng Tálung " which has 2 head Lámas with about a thousand monks. Here they halted during the 3rd in order to rest and examine the monastéry; inside they found a large number of images carved in the walls the whole of these were adorned with gold. The road from Lhásá to Lob Núr (?) and "Jilling " ("Sinning") passes about one mile south of the monastery. The Sinning Kafilas pass by this route with their camels laden with merchandize. On the 4th march he crossed the Chak Lá pass and encamped at its foot on the opposite (south side) near the village of "Lángmo " where they saw the first signs of cultivation that they had met with since the 29th of December. On the 5th they reached "Jhokár Churtan ;" on the 6th Naimár village which has about 20 houses surrounded by a number of smaller clusters of houses. On the 7th they reached the monastery of "Nehlin Dák," on the 8th after crossing the Phembu Gong Lá pass they halted at Lingbu Jong. The Phembu district ceases at the pass of that name. On the 9th of March the party reached Lhásá they were excessively glad to get back to a civilized place again where they would at any rate have no chance of being starved as they were at one time likely to be.

Though the Lhásá people were hospitable enough the explorer found there was no chance of his being able to borrow sufficient money to enable him to march to "Sinning" as he had intended; with the greatest difficulty he managed to borrow 150 Rupees from a trader who was going to Gartok, but he insisted upon the explorer accompanying him and in addition took his aneroid barometer and compass as a pledge for the money, the aneroid which was a large one he apparently took for a magnificent watch and at the end of the journey the explorer's messenger who was sent with money to redeem the instruments had some difficulty in recovering them. Having the command of so little money the explorer decided upon returning to India and after a long and difficult journey reached the Head Quarters of the Great Trigonometrical Survey in safety.

Memorandum by Lieut.-Colonel T. G. Montgomerie, R.E., F.R.S., &c., on the results of an exploration of the "Namcho" or Tengri Núr Lake in Great Tibet made by a Native Explorer.

Amongst other attempts to explore the various countries beyond the borders of British India, I have always borne in mind the necessity to explore the vast regions which lie to the north of the Himalayan range, from E. Longitude 83° to E. Longitude 93°, and I have consequently, from time to time, tried to get more information as to this *terra incognita*; but since the Pundit made his way from Kumaon to Lhásá, I had not till lately succeeded in getting much advance made to the north of his line of explorations, though a good deal was done to the north of the Mánsarowar Lake. One explorer made his way from Rudok on the Pangkong Lake to Thok-Jalung and thence back to the Mánsarowar, passing quite to the east of the great "Kailás" peak. The same explorer subsequently made his way to "Shigatze", but he was unable to penetrate to the north of the main course of the upper Brahmaputra. Though disappointed with this I continued to try and get an explorer to penetrate into those regions, and after many failures I have at last the satisfaction to be able to report that some progress has been made in exploring to the north of Shigatze and Lhásá.

The accompanying narrative gives the details that I was able to gather from the explorer.

As usual the party was troubled at the frontier; but once fairly in Tibetan territory they had no difficulty in making their way down the upper Brahmaputra to Shigatze, at least had no difficulty that would not equally have affected ordinary inhabitants of the country. They found no good opportunity of penetrating to the north till they reached "Shigatze;" there they, as directed, made inquiries about the Tengri Núr Lake. They found that there was a regular route to this lake frequented by traders in borax, salt, &c., and also by pilgrims; they consequently decided to try and make their way there in the character of pilgrims, taking with them a small supply of goods with a view to meeting their wants on the road by barter, the ordinary custom of such pilgrims.

They were told that sheep were the only means of carriage that would answer and they made their arrangements accordingly, purchasing some of the large long-legged sheep with the usual bags for loading. They marched down to the Brahmaputra, crossing that great river by means of rafts; this point was about 11,200 feet above the sea. Ascending the Shiang Chu tributary of the river the party day by day got into still higher ground, until they reached the Khálamba Lá pass, 17,200 feet above the sea, and there crossing over from the basin of the Brahmaputra they descended into the basin of the Tengri Núr Lake, which was found to be about 15,500 feet above the sea.

For 8 days after leaving the Brahmaputra the explorer marched from village to village, passing many Buddhist monasteries and some nunneries with numbers of small villages surrounded by a good deal of cultivation. Naikor was the last village with cultivation; northward they were informed they would find nothing except the camps of "Dogpás", as the nomadic people of that part of the country are called; and they were warned to be on their guard against the white bears which were said to commit havoc amongst the cattle, sheep, &c. The explorer was well acquainted with the brown bear of the Cis-Himalayan districts and he believed this white bear to be a different animal and not the brown bear in its winter coat.

During the great part of his journey to the Namcho Lake the explorer found the streams all hard frozen, and he was consequently much struck by the number of hot springs that he met with and more especially by the great heat of the water coming from them, his thermometer showing it to vary from 130° to 183° Fahrenheit, being generally over 150° and often within a few degrees of the boiling point, being in one case 183° when the boiling point was 183¾°. The water generally had a sulphurous smell and in many cases was ejected with great noise and violence; in one place the force was sufficient to throw the water up from 40 to 60 feet. These springs in some respects seem to resemble the geysers of Iceland; in winter they are very remarkable in consequence of the water when falling being converted into ice which forms a pillar of ice round each jet. The quantity of warm water which escapes from below must however be very considerable, as the streams into which they drain were free from ice for some distance below where the warm water comes in, though everywhere else hard frozen.

The great lake, which at distance was called the Tengri Núr, was found on nearer approach to be called Namcho or Sky-lake (Nam = sky and Cho = lake) from the great altitude at which it is. It proved to be a splendid sheet of water about fifty miles in length by from sixteen to twenty-five miles in breadth. It receives the water of two considerable rivers and several minor streams, but has no exit; the water is decidedly bitter, but owing to intense cold it freezes readily and at the time the explorer saw it was one continuous sheet of ice.

To the south the lake is bounded by a splendid range of snowy peaks, flanked with large glaciers, culminating in the magnificent peak "Jáng Ninjinthanglá" which is probably more than 25,000 feet above the sea. The range was traced for nearly 150 miles, running in a northeasterly direction. To the north of the lake the mountains were not comparatively speaking high, nor were there any high peaks visible farther north as far as the explorer could see from a commanding point which he climbed up to. He only saw a succession of rounded hills with moderately flat-ground in between them. Immediately north he saw a lake of about 6 miles in length which he was told was called Bul Cho from the borax (bul) which is produced there in large quantities, supplying both Lhásá and Shigatze with most of the borax that they require.

The "Namcho" Lake is considered to be a sacred place like the Mánsarowar Lake, and although at such a very great distance from habitations and so high above the sea it boasts of several permanent monasteries and is visited by large numbers of pilgrims. There are several islands in the lake, two of them large enough for monasteries: at the time the explorer was there the Lámas on the islands kept up their communication with the shore by means of the ice, but he did not hear as to what was done in summer. Fish are said to be abundant and modern lake shells were found on the shore as well as fossil shells, which were very numerous and of all sizes; a few of the smaller ones have been examined by Mr. Oldham, the Superintendent of the Geological Survey; he thinks they are not older than cretaceous and are probably, nummulitic "none of them actually agree with the Sind and Panjáb nummulitic "fossils yet described, but they come near them; there is a small Fusus, two specimens at the "upper whorls of a Vicarya or Cerithium with a cast of probably the same species, also a cast "or internal mould of a Tapes." The specimens sent to Mr. Oldham were however too few and too badly preserved to enable him to give a decided opinion about them, I had unfortunately started for England before I knew this, otherwise I should have sent him larger specimens. The first opportunity will be taken to have them more thoroughly examined as also the few modern shells that reached me. The Chief Pundit on his first journey remarked on the stone bones, shells, &c., that he saw in the Lhásá bazar where they are sold in great quantities for medicine, charms, &c. The explorer had also noticed them in other parts, and there is very little doubt but that Tibet will prove to be very rich in fossils and will amply repay the first European that has the luck to penetrate into the country.

The explorer was only able to bring back some of the smaller specimens. In most places the margin of the lake was utterly desolate, but near Lángdang the Shukpá bush was abundant. In another place there was a little vegetation near some hot springs.

The explorer's examination of the lake was unfortunately brought to a sudden close by a band of robbers from Jámañta De the district north of the lake. These robbers stripped the party so completely that they were forced to make their way to Lhásá as fast as they could. They were very nearly starved to death and underwent very great hardships before they got there.

In Lhásá they managed to raise a little money by pawning their instruments, the aneroid which was a large one proving very serviceable, as it was mistaken for a gigantic watch and was valued accordingly.

The proof of the existence of a great snowy range to the north of the Brahmaputra is interesting, the Himalayan system even at that distance, say 160 miles from its base in the plains of India showing no signs of getting lower. The Lámas of the Namcho Lake described the country to the north as being very much the same as that round the lake, and that it was only after advancing some 60 marches farther northeast that there were any signs of a more civilized country. Jámañta De (de means district) immediately north of the lake is not under the Lhásá Government. It must be even more elevated than the country about Namcho, as the inhabitants are said to have great difficulty in keeping cattle, losing numbers every few years owing to heavy and continuous falls of snow. The Jámañta people are a lawless set and always try to make up for any such losses by robbing their neighbours about Namcho, Simjam, &c., and where cattle thrive better. Lob Núr was said to be 2½ to 3 months journey north of Namcho: it was not clear from the explorer's account whether this was the Koko Núr Lake or some other lake more to the west. The route ran north from the east end of the Namcho, leaving at a camping place called Dam Niárgan. From this point Nákchukhá is distant 10 days journey and has a very bad reputation as to robbers. From Nákchukhá it is 1¼ month's journey, to Sokpohuil over a most barren country infested by robbers, but owning no regular inhabitants of any kind. Sokpohuil district is said to be not very far from Lob Núr, near which is the town of Kharká, the residence of a great Láma called Jipchun Ringboche who rules over the Sokpohuil country. Kharká is said to be above 15 days journey from Jilling or Sinning-fu, the large city near the northwestern end of the great wall of China. Jilling was well known to the people about Namcho who admit that it is larger even than Lhásá itself.

The great northern road called the Janglam, which runs far north of the course of the upper Brahmaputra river, passes by the Namcho or Tengri Núr Lake and from thence by Shellifuk Lake to Rudok on the Pangkong Lake east of Leh the capital of Ladák. The route followed by the explorer from Dam Niárgan to Lhásá is the route by which Messrs. Huc and Gabet must have approached that city. The explorer thought he would have been able to make his way along it by the Koko Núr and thence through Sinning-fu to China if he had the necessary funds. Another attempt will if possible be made to do this, as even the slight amount of information gained respecting it is encouraging and it would be a great thing to get a route survey between Lhásá and Sinning-fu, so as to connect our Indian Trans-Himalayan Explorations with a place that has been fixed by the regular survey operations of the French Jesuit Missionaries.

The route survey extends over 320 miles of what has hitherto been veritable *terra incognita*. Latitude observations were taken at places, and heights by observations of the boiling point and of the aneroid at 24 places. The geography of an area of about 12,000 square miles has been elucidated and one northern tributary of the upper Brahmaputra has been thoroughly explored, thus giving us some idea as to how far back the northern watershed of this great river lies.

The Namcho is evidently the lake referred to in old maps as the Tengri Núr. The explorer actually went round it and found that it had no outlet though fed by two large and a number of minor streams.

The length of the explorer's pace has as usual been computed by means of the differences of observed latitude, &c., and was found to be very fairly accordant on different sections.

The difference of longitude between Shigatze and Lhásá as determined by this route survey is nine minutes less than that deduced from the Chief Pundit's survey. The latter was however a much more direct line and the value therefore has been retained. The difference being say 9 miles in 320 miles or about 3 per cent is a satisfactory proof of general accuracy.

The heights by observations of the boiling point were satisfactory, but those by the aneroid show that the index must have shifted very much; for although agreeing closely with an ordinary mercurial barometer up to 7,000 or 8,000 feet above the sea, yet in the neighbourhood of Shigatze (at Peting), which was previously known to be about 11,000 feet above sea, the aneroid observation indicated an altitude of nearly 4,800 feet higher. The aneroid observations on the average give altitudes 4,631 feet higher than those by boiling the thermometer, a most disappointing result, the aneroid being one that was carefully tested under an air pump at Kew when it was found to agree at every inch of pressure from the normal height down to 11-inches.

A similar difference was given by another aneroid that was sent up to the Thok-Jalung gold fields; this was supposed to have arisen from some accidental fault.

Captain Basevi when employed in the elevated ground in the south and northeast of Ladák was supplied with a similar aneroid and noted in his memoranda that the observations taken with it were quite unreliable at great altitudes, as he found that even by gentle tapping on the case the index varied its reading and was always moveable in that way no matter how long he remained at a point.

The only conclusion that can be come to, from the three trials referred to, is that in their present shape aneroid barometers cannot be relied on alone at great elevations until they have actually been tested, and they should always be at any rate supplemented with either occasional observations of an ordinary mercurial barometer or of a boiling thermometer, at any rate until some satisfactory proof of their reliability has been given, the errors apparently not showing when the aneroid was at rest and kept at much the same temperature.

It will be noticed that the explorer actually went along a small portion of the great Brahmaputra river below Shigatze, thus adding to our knowledge of its actual course; no iron suspension bridge was however seen there such as "Turner" supposed to exist near Shigatze. The explorer was much struck with the magnificent glaciers to the south of the Namcho or Tengri Núr Lake and they will no doubt prove to be very extensive, as the man is a good judge of their size being well acquainted with Himalayan glaciers near India.

Altogether the explorer has done very good service, and in this first altogether independent expedition has shown a large amount of skill, observation, and determination. I trust hereafter he will still farther distinguish himself.

Extracts from an Explorer's Narrative of his journey from Pitorágarh in Kumaon viâ Jumla to Tadum and back along the Kali Gandak to British Territory.

After receiving my instructions and the necessary instruments I left Dehra for my home in Kumaun. While there cholera broke out in the village and attacked me and several members of my family, of whom my wife and 3 others died and I was prostrated for 2 months.

On the 1st July I started with my survey from Pitorágarh and on the 3rd day reached Askot. At Askot there resides a man named Puskar Sing Rajwar whose people are frequently passing into Nepál and I went to consult him as to which would be the best place to cross the river Káli, telling him I was a physician on my way to Jumla. I learnt from him that as the rains had set in the ropes by which the river is crossed were put away to keep them from rotting, but that if I went to Ráthi which was higher up the river I might there have a chance of crossing. I accordingly did so and reached Ráthi on the 6th. As there was only a rope by which the river is crossed and men suspend themselves by their hands and feet and bear such loads as are to be carried over on their chests, I had no nerve for it, so had a sling made for myself and was drawn across in it and stopped at Bargáon in the Doa pattí, in Nepál on the 7th. Bargáon has 50 houses and is about the largest sized village in the pattí.

On the 8th I travelled through a tract but little inhabited and along a difficult road and halted for the night without provisions at a deserted sheep fold.

On the 9th after another yet more difficult journey I arrived at Maikholi (2 houses.)

On the 10th I reached Shipti village (30 houses) having crossed the Kotidhar pass 5,793 feet above sea, and the river Tatigúr on the way. Although Shipti is in the Don pattí, on account of its size and importance it is usual to include the villages in its neighbourhood in a pattí which is called after it.

On the 11th I went to Shiri in the Marma pattí. The villages of this pattí are all in the valley of the Chamlia river. Cultivation is extensively carried on in it. The villages are situated where the hills have gentle slopes and the land which is terraced is irrigated by small channels from the Chamlia. Fish which abound in the river, are caught, dried and stored by the villagers in large quantities, for home consumption; they are eaten by all castes. I here intended crossing the river, but found the ropes broken: I went a couple of miles further up and found crossing ropes and passed over. The road for the 2 miles up the river and back to the main road on the opposite side was so difficult that it took me half the day to go over it. Halted at Matiál; formerly a road from Doti to Taglakhar led along the Chamlia through this patti and by a pass across the Marma snowy range. It was given up a long time back owing to a dispute with the Taglakhar people. The snowy range is not more than 14 or 15 miles N. E. of the river.

On the 13th, I marched to Karálá in the Búngnang pattí. This march consists of a difficult ascent to the Machannia-lekh pass; during which no water is to be had, and of a descent. At the summit of the pass the birch and juniper grow, and lower down oak and "ringal" (hill bamboo) and "pangar" (horse chestnut). The lands of the villages in this pattí are well cultivated. I halted at Karálá 5,326 feet above sea level on the 14th owing to rain. On the 15th, I started, crossing and recrossing the Karálágár till it joins the Sangár, a larger river which comes from the snow but which is called Karálágár below the junction. I crossed the Sangár stream by a wooden bridge and continued along the left till I came opposite to Batusherá which is on the right bank of the Karálágár at its junction with the Nabliagár. A road from these parts to Bias goes along the left bank of the Sangár and crosses the snowy range by a high pass.

I procured a pass to Bajangayá from the Thanadar of Batusherá and by midday on the 15th I got to the Kálágár river which joins the Karálágár, and is crossed by the people of the country by ropes, but slings were at hand for those who, like myself, had no nerves for the ordinary way of crossing. I stopped for the night at Bipur on the other side of the river. From Karálá the road lies through villages and cultivated land but no forests.

On the 17th, I crossed the Karha pass, and reached Jakhora village. On the ascent to the pass there are two villages Ranlokh and Kálákáná.

On the 18th, I crossed the Kansia pass and put up for the night at Sain village in the Bajangayá pattí. The road was good, not fit for riding but very fair for walking.

On the onward journey and a little short of a mile from Sain is a temple of masonry on a well cultivated and irrigated spot at the junction of the Saingár and Khatiyarigár both small streams, the former coming from a north-westerly, and the latter from a northerly direction. On the road about ½ a mile further on is Pujári, a small village of 5 or 6 houses inhabited by brahmins, the priests of the temple. Crossing Khatiyarigár and another smaller stream of same name I at midday reached Biasi, a village consisting of 10 or 12 houses to the north of Bhajangayá about ¼ mile. Bhajangayá is an old fort out of repair. Biasi is 5,490 feet above sea level and on a level with Bhajangayá Fort.

The fort was formerly of a circular form and about ¼ of a mile in circumference. It consists of dry stone walls about 10 feet high with two brick and mud 3 storied houses, with sloping roofs, formerly the residence of the Rájá and members of his family, built within the enclosure. There are about 16 houses with mud walls and thatched roofs built on the outside of the walls inhabited by the Rájá's slaves : a small spring to S. and E. of fort about 500 feet below and another to west and a short distance supply drinking water.

Slavery exists here and throughout Nepál all castes being sold into slavery, the father having power to sell his children; but on being sold individuals lose their caste. It is reported however that Jung Bahadur has intentions of suppressing this practice. On the 22nd, I left Bhajangayá and at midday came up to the Bargnjál ghát on the Seti river and about 4½ miles from the former place. The road from Taglakhar to Sil-Garhi and Doti which follows the course of the Seti crosses at this place from the right to the left bank by a rope bridge 180 feet long and about 20 feet above water. The river comes winding from a northerly direction to this place, and from the snowy mountains distant about 3 days march. Between this and the snows is Humla pattí from which hawks, black minas and musk pods are brought for sale to Barámdeo Mandi and Gola Ghát Mandi.

From the ghát my road lay along the left bank for about 2½ miles, and to where the Chanakhola, a river formed by spring water, joins it and then followed up the latter, crossing and recrossing it occasionally. I halted for the night at Majh one of the five villages of Chana pattí, which includes the valley drained by the Chanakhola.

On the 23rd, about midday I left the Chanakhola where it is met by the Jhalaragár, crossed a pass over the Than ridge which was covered with oak and chestnut and entered Bájru pattí and remained at Dogra. Bájru fort, where the Rájá lives is on the summit of a hill about 5 miles from this in a south-easterly direction and on the same side of the Dogragár. It is smaller than Bhajangayá fort being about 500 paces in circumference and contains one house and is surrounded by oak trees ; no cultivation was to be seen about it. There was a good deal of excitement in this place, caused by an order of Jung Bahadur for raising troops. Places which formerly supplied 100 soldiers were now required to give 150 and such as were not formerly required to furnish them were now to raise men according to the revenue paid in by them to the Government. Four hundred men used to be quartered at each of the 3 places Dandalidhura, Sil-Garhi and Dalekh ; there are now 600 men at each place, that is half as many again, and at Sil-Garhi arms are now being manufactured.

On the 24th, I crossed a ridge coming from the Than ridge. Before leaving its summit I came upon a deep round hollow filled with water, about ½ a mile in circumference. The water is blue and is said to contain fish though I did not see any : there is no visible supply of water to the tank. To the east and at the edge of the water is a small temple of masonry, called Thábur Debí. In the month of August at the time of full moon the temple is visited by people of the neighbourhood. The hills about here are covered with oak and rhododendron. About midday, having descended to the Kunragár, passed through the village of Máitoli about 4 miles from the temple and tank, and followed the stream I sighted Kunragarhi on the wooded summit of the ridge to the south of the Kunragár; although called "garhi" there is no fort and all that can be seen are two stone walled, thatched roofed houses where the Rájá resides. The hill is rugged and covered with oak and rhododendron trees and about 1,200 feet above the stream. The so called Rájá is rather a zamíndár who collects the revenue of the Kunra pattí. I stopped for the night at Sudap in the Kunra pattí, the road kept to the left bank of the Kunragár to this place. This pattí has a few villages far removed from each other, there being only one on the road between Máitoli and this. The road was difficult.

On the 25th, I left the Kunragár, which flows eastwards into the Buri Ganga also called Bhaunera about 3 miles and crossed the Pinalekh ridge, the boundary between the Kunra and Jugárá pattís, and came into the village of that name in the latter pattí (25 houses) 5,781 feet above sea level. I left this on the 3rd August, and descended to the River Bhaunera or Buri Ganga about 2½ miles below. This comes from the snowy mountains which are seen to the north-east about 16 miles distant. The river at this time of the year is about 150 feet wide, and 8 or 10 feet deep, with a rapid current. It is crossed at this place by means of a rope, a road following the course of the Bhaunera, goes to Sánpin ghát on the river lower down. To the south of the place where I crossed the river is a high peak on a snowy ridge under which at the height of the ridge is Malka Debí temple, well known and visited by pilgrims from Kumaun and Garhwál as well as from Nepál, during the time of full moon in August. There are approaches to the temple from all sides. From the river I crossed a spur about 1,000 feet high and encountered the Mártorigár a tributary of the Bhaunera a little lower down. This stream though not containing any of the drainage from the snows has deep water and is crossed by wood being thrown across it. About 6½ miles further up the stream is Jili consisting of 10 or 12 houses where I remained for the night. The village which gives its name to the stream consists of 100 houses and is about a mile from the stream on the opposite side at the place where I descended into the valley. On the 4th I followed up the Mártorigár and halted at Rajtoli. There were no villages on the way; Rajtoli consisting of 10 or 12 houses is situated at the junction of two streams which make up the Mártorigár one of them is called the Rajtoligár and the other the Parkhiagár which takes its rise at the Parkhia-lekh hill. On the 15th I followed up the Parkhiagár to its source and crossed the Parkhia-lekh (about 8,095 feet above sea) which is on the boundary between the Bájru zilla on one side and Jumla on the other, and halted for the night at Káláporá village (50 or 60 houses) in the Kunrakhola pattí. On the 6th I followed the Kunrakhola to its junction with the Balarigár about 3 miles from Káláporá about 6,071 feet above sea and crossed the latter, a river which does not take its rise in the snows, but is during the rains too deep, and rapid to be forded. The bridge by which I crossed is wooden and between 40 and 50 feet in length; the depth of the water is about 5 feet. Balarigár below its junction with the Kunrakhola is called by the latter name. The slopes on either side of the stream are cultivated and there are several villages. I kept to the left bank to its junction with the Karnáli river. Here-abouts there are more villages and cultivation on the left bank of the Karnáli than on the right bank. Higher up the river, about 1½ miles above Bánda village I crossed the Karnáli at Jira ghát by a rope bridge about 200 feet in length and 60 feet above water. On the 7th after going north along the river for a short distance I turned up the Khátiarkholagár at its junction with the Karnáli and kept along the stream, crossing and recrossing by small wooden bridges occasionally and halted for the night at a deserted cow shed (Galu-ka-got). About 2½ miles above this a small stream, the Kanwakholagár, coming from a S. E. direction joins the Khátiarkhola, my road lay along the former. There is also a road along the latter which comes from a N. E. direction to this junction, leading to Múngú Bhót. I left the Kanwakhola about 2½ miles above the junction and ascended the hill to the village of Kálákhatá (50 or 60 houses) about 1½ miles above the stream, where I remained for the night, it is 12,484 feet above the sea. On the 9th, I crossed the Kálákhatá ridge—very high (about 14,528 feet)—on which the birch and juniper grow and entering a ravine arrived at Lurkon village on the Sinjakhola or Himawati, a river coming from the snows distant about 13 miles, and entering the Tila river. I halted at Lurkon on the 10th. The Sinjakhola pattí is considered the most productive in these parts. Rice is the only crop, raised by means of irrigation. Ponies are bred in great numbers in this pattí. On the 11th, I crossed the Sinjakhola a little less than a mile above the village of Lurkon by a wooden bridge 2 feet wide, 200 feet in length and 15 or 20 feet above water. The current is very rapid and 7 or 8 feet deep. The road then ascends by a ravine a high ridge, (about 13,000 feet) with birch and juniper growing on its summit, which it crosses. On the 12th, I descended into a ravine which joins the Tila river below Chaughan, and along which the road runs, and arrived at Chaughan (Jumla) situated on the banks of the Tila river and about 8,016 feet above sea level. Chaughan consists of a collection of mud houses forming a street occupied by 5 or 6 bunniahs, 2 or 3 cloth merchants from Doti, 40 or 50 priests of the Chandan Náth Mahadeo temple, a few paces to the east of the street are located the custom house people, 300 sepoys, 3 subhadárs and a captain, Debí Mánsing Basaniath, who is also head man in the Jumla Zillah. To the southwest of the street are the stores of guns, ammunition and provisions within an enclosing wall 600 feet east and west, and 400 feet north and south with a gate to the north, these are also of mud. Chaughan is situated in a plain running north-east and south-west about 3 or 4 miles and about 1½ miles in breadth, surrounded by high mountains about 12,000 feet above the sea. The whole valley is cultivated and there are numbers of villages scattered over it. A road from Taglakhar passes through Chaughan and Dailekh and goes on to Lucknow. Having got a pass and letter of introduction to the Loh Mantang Rájá I left Chaughan (Jumla) on the 18th.

On the 20th I left the Tila river and crossed the ridge to the south by a pass, the Morpáni Lekh, about 12,458 feet above the sea, descended into the Kaikhola valley in the Tibrikot zillah, passed through Bhotia (7 or 8 houses) and halted for the night at a temple between 2 or 3 miles further on and a mile from the Kaikhola river. A road goes from these parts to Lángú Bhot, distant 8 or 10 marches, by the Kaikhola. Next day I crossed the Balangúr Lá pass, lower than the Morpáni Lá, on which oak and rhododendron grow and reached Tibrikot. Tibrikot is situated on the right bank of the river Bheri where it is joined by a small stream from the snows to the north and about 7,226 feet above sea level. To the south of the village about 200 yards, on a hillock about 200 feet high, is a fort (Kot) which encloses a temple and 3 or 4 houses. I was here shown the Civil and Criminal Code of Nepál, which is taken partly from the Shástras and partly from the Indian Code of Civil and Criminal Procedure. It is in the Nepálese language. Having obtained another pass from the Thánadár of this place I left Tibrikot on the 27th.

From Tibrikot I followed the course of the Bheri river and reached Charka on the 4th September having passed some Lámaserais on the road. One of them, called Barphang Gonpa, contains 40 or 50 Lámas. Near another, named Kanigang Gonpa, the river has high perpendicular, rocky banks, and the people have made a tunnel 54 paces in length through the rock. There was originally a crevice and the rock on either side of it was cut away sufficiently to allow of a man with a load to pass through with a squeezing, the height of the tunnel not being sufficient in all parts to admit of his going through standing. Charka is the last village on the river Bheri. On the opposite side of the river is a Gonpa (Lámaserai) to which the first-born male of every family in the village, as is the practice among the Buddhists generally, is dedicated as a Láma. I left Charka on the 5th, and ascended the Digi Lá, about 16,879 feet above sea level, called by Goorkhas Bátali-Pátan, by a gentle incline. On either side of the pass there are snow covered ridges. The pass is broad and there is a cairn on it at the watershed. From Digi Lá I descended to the junction of two streams, one coming from a northerly and the other from a westerly direction, which together take an easterly direction and form the Kingi Chú. On the 7th I reached Kágbeni crossing the Káli Gandak by a wooden bridge. Kágbeni is situated at the junction of a stream coming from Muktináth, with the Káli Gandak, and is about 8,953 feet above sea level. It consists of about 100 houses and is inhabited by Bhots.

From Charka there is also a direct road to Labrang Koja, near Tadum from which after crossing a high snow-covered pass, distant about 20 or 25 miles from Charka, another road branches off to Loh Mantang. Laden sheep, goats and horses are taken over these roads.

From Kágbeni I made a trip to Muktináth, about 11,284 feet above sea, for a day, to see the temple and the country about it. About a hundred feet to east of the temple is a spring with a sulphurous smell which enters a cistern from which the water runs out from 108 spouts, under each of which every devotee passes. The water collecting in a trough below passes out in two streams which flowing to north and south of the temple meet to the west, thus encircling the temple with water. About 6 or 700 feet from the temple, to the south, is a small mound with a little still water at its base, having a sulphurous smell. From a crevice in this mound at the water's edge, rises a flame about a span above the surface. The people of the place told me that the water sometimes increases in quantity sufficiently to flow into the crevice, the flames then disappear for a while and there is a gurgling noise, a report, and the flames burst up and show again. This spot is called Chume Giarsa by the Bhots. To the northwest of the temple, about 1 mile, is a Gonpa with about 30 or 40 resident Lámas. To the east and southeast of Muktináth, about 2 miles, are lofty snowy mountains extending in a northeast and southwest direction from which the stream takes its rise which flows by Muktináth to the north, takes in the temple water and joins the Káli Gandak river at Kágbeni.

On the 9th I returned to Kágbeni, and on the 10th started with my party, following up the river Káli Gandak. About 6 miles from Kágbeni I crossed a small stream coming from Damudarkund, along which the Loh Mantang boundary runs to the east, and from the junction with the Káli Gandak follows up the latter in a northerly direction. 1 here left the river which above this flows through a very confined valley. To the west about 2 miles is a snowy range. There are forests of cedar below the snows : no other trees are to be found. On the 11th I went to Khamba Sambha village. The road which keeps to the hill side, is broad and there is a great deal of traffic on it.

On the 12th, I went to Changrang village crossing the Chungi Lá pass, about 11,000 feet above the sea, on a spur from the snows. Changrang consists of 30 houses and a fort, the winter residence of the Loh Mantang Rájá. A road, chiefly used by pilgrims, from Muktináth by Damudarkund, crosses the Káli Gandak by a ford about 2 miles east of this and joins the other from Kágbeni to Loh Mantang here. It can be ridden over on horse back; the ground over which it passes is not rugged nor high, but there is a scarcity of water and no habitations are met with.

On the 13th after a march of 7½ miles, I reached Loh Mantang. Loh Mantang is situated in the centre of a plain, about 11,905 feet above sea level, between two small streams which meet a little before entering the Káli Gandak, distant about 2 miles : the plain is irrigated by channels. Loh Mantang is enclosed by a wall of white earth and small stones, about 6 feet thick and 14 feet high, forming a square with a side of ¼ mile in length, and having an entrance by means of a gate to the east. In the centre is the Rájá's palace consisting of 4 stories, about 40 feet in height, and the only building to be seen from the outside. In the N.E. corner of the enclosure is a Gonpa containing copper gilt figures and 250 Lámas. There are about 60 other houses, two-storied, and about 14 feet in height, forming streets and lanes. Drinking water is brought in by means of a canal, and this overflowing makes the interior slushy; and since there is always an accumulation of filth the smell is very offensive. Since no census is taken I cannot say how many people there are in the place, but they appeared to be numerous.

Besides the permanent residents there are always numbers of traders from Thibet and Nepál, who either exchange their goods here or take them to dispose of at Lhásá or Nepál. The trade in salt and grain does not extend very far north. Trade is chiefly carried on by " Tháklis " a class of traders of mixed origin, who have the privilege of going to Lhásá and they even go to Calcutta for the purchase of goods. The Rájá, who is a Bhot, collects a revenue from all sources of about 10 or 12000 Rupees a year, out of which he pays about 2 or 3,000 yearly to Nepál from the land revenue, and 10 per cent of the taxes levied on goods brought from across the northern frontier, to the Lhásá Government.

The Rájá was very much averse to my proceeding further, the orders of Jang Bahadur that no one should cross the frontier being very stringent; however I was determined to proceed at all hazards and succeeded at last in procuring a pass.

I may here mention a custom which prevails in this part of Nepál. On a death occurring the head Láma at the Gonpa is consulted as to the disposal of the corpse. On being informed of the day on which the death occurred he consults his writings, and gives orders according to the directions therein contained. The corpse either must be buried as it died, or be cut up and thrown to the birds, or the arms and legs being cut off and thrown out of the town, to north, south, east and west, the body must be buried, or lastly the body must be burnt in a sitting posture.

Leaving Loh Mantang on the 19th, I crossed the pass Photu Lá on the 20th, the boundary between Dehajúng in Lhásá (Thibet) and the Nepál possessions. The pass is about 15,080 feet above the sea. There is a descent of about 250 feet from the pass on to the plain below. I passed thousands of wild horses grazing on the plain ; they were in herds of about 100 each, and are not at all shy. On the 21st I encamped at Chumikgiakdong, a sheepfold on the stream which flows to the west of the plain. Leaving my things at Chumikgiakdong, I went to Labrang Koja an encampment, distant 9 miles. The river is here about 250 feet wide and has a very gentle current. It is crossed by boats made of yak's hides which are sewn at the ends and are attached to sticks at the sides; they are kept dry and thus retain their shapes. After 2 or 3 crossings they are drawn on shore to dry. They are propelled by 2 or 4 oars and 2 or 3 men can cross in each. Next morning, the 23rd, I started for Loh Mantang, and crossed the Cháchú Sángpo 2 miles above its junction with the Brahmaputra. This stream is about 3 feet in depth and 60 feet wide, and comes from a snowy ridge about 14 or 16 miles north of Mantang; I forded it and going ¾ mile further on arrived at Tadum.

Tadum consists of 12 houses and a Lámaserai (Gonpa) situated at the foot of spurs coming from the snows to the north. The former are occupied by men whose duty it is to forward property or letters for the Lhásá Government, or such as they may receive orders to forward. For this purpose they have ponies, yaks, goats and sheep, and their beat lies 2 or 3 marches either way. They are not remunerated directly for their trouble, but escape taxes, the head man of each station, " Tarjum ", only receiving a small percentage on the taxes. The " Gonpa " only contains 10 or 12 Lámas. The day following my arrival the head man, " Gopa ", sent for me and questioned me as to the object of my travels. I told him I was a physician on my way to Lhásá and shewed him my passes. He however refused to allow me to proceed as it would be at the peril of his own life. I was then locked up for the night. Next morning I made an ineffectual attempt to see the Gopa and my messenger returned with a sowár who had orders to see me across the frontier. On the second day after my arrival I began, with great reluctance and under threats of personal violence, my return journey and reached Loh Mantang on the 28th.

I reached Kágbeni on the 1st of October and on the 2nd started south following the course of the Káli Gandak. The road first keeps along the bank of the river for about 7½ miles and then crosses by a wooden bridge 55 feet long and 10 feet above water, depth of water 4 feet, and goes to the village of Marmáli (100 houses) about 3½ miles further on where I remained for the night.

On the 3rd, following the right bank of the river, I passed through the village of Tukja, consisting of about 100 houses, at which there is a custom house and having crossed the river by a wooden bridge about 70 feet long, I recrossed the river to Lidi village where I remained for the night. On advancing from the first crossing of the river about 2 miles, I came opposite a large village situated on the right bank of the river, called Thak, consisting of about 150 houses. Lidi is a small village of 4 or 5 houses ; the inhabitants of which are traders and do little in the way of cultivation. On the 4th about ½ a mile from Lidi, I passed another village of the same name, consisting of about 25 houses, and at midday reached Ghás Bhansár where there is a custom house. I stopped at Dan Bansár which also owns a custom house.

On the 5th no villages were met with during the march and the road passed through jungle the whole distance, crossing several small streams running into the Káli Gandak. I passed the night in the jungle.

On the morning of the 6th I crossed the river about 1 mile below the last halting place. 2½ miles further down on the right bank is the Ráni Powa Dharmsála (rest house), above which on the hill side and to the west is a large village. A further walk of 1½ miles brought me to the Rangár river, which comes from a westerly direction from the snows and joins the Káli Gandak. I crossed it at the junction by an iron suspension bridge, constructed at the expense of the Ráni who built the rest house. The bridge is about 175 feet long, about 15 or 16 feet above the water. The bridge consists of two thick chains to which the roadway of planks is suspended by iron rods, but as these are of equal length the roadway has the same curve as the chains. Nearly 2 miles further, on the same side of the Káli Gandak, is Beni bazar, a village of about 200 houses. There is another village with shops, on the opposite side of the Káli Gandak, called by the same name. There is communication between the two villages by a rope bridge ; and a road not fit for horses goes to Pokhra. To the west of the village on the hill side is a copper mine which is worked, and the copper is either sold and taken to Pokhra, or it is converted into vessels in the village, or coined.

On the 7th I crossed the river Maidi by an iron bridge similar to the one over the Rangár, and marched to the village of Báklúng situated in the Báklúng Pattí. It consists of 50 or 60 houses and 15 or 16 shops. There are copper mines on the hill sides. A captain is stationed here to look after the coining of pice at this place and at Beni and the revenues from all sources.

On the 8th I crossed the river Káli Gandak ¼ mile to the east of this by a boat, the current being so gentle as to admit of it without risk. Tho river is about 250 feet wide : the water at this time of the year is not clear and fills the channel. I remained the night at the Rájá's residence at Panglang which is 1 mile from the river. I halted on the 9th and on the 10th started, and arrived at Kusamchaor bazar at the junction of the Moti Naddi with the Káli Gandak. This village which gives its name to the Pattí to the north of the Moti and east of the Káli Gandak, consists of about 100 houses scattered over a plain about 2 miles long and about ¾ mile broad. There are copper mines along the hills on the opposite side, but none on this side. Moti Naddi rises in the snows to the northeast and flows in a southwesterly direction, carrying into the Káli Gandak about ⅓ the quantity of water the latter contains above the junction. It is crossed 1½ miles above the junction by an iron suspension bridge 135 feet long and about 12 or 14 feet above the water which is about 7 or 8 feet deep, similar to those over the Rangár and Maidi. A road to Pokhra fit to ride over starts along the left bank of the Moti from the bridge : horses have to ford the river.

On the 11th I passed through a large village, Dámar, well cultivated, containing about 100 houses, on the left bank.

On the 12th I went to Púrthi Ghát on the river's edge about 2,036 feet above sea level. Púrthi Ghát contains about 50 houses and 15 shops and is in the Gúlmi Pattí. To the west of this about 2 miles on the hill side are copper mines which are being worked in 50 places, and it is said there is abundance of the ore along the hills to the right of the Káli Gandak between Báklúng and this. I remained at Púrthi Ghát 14 days with the intention of spending the winter there and then making another start for the north to carry out the orders I received, but changed my mind and determined on going to Dehra, in order to submit what I had succeeded in doing, as my time would thus be employed and I should besides avoid the risk of losing my notes in case of discovery, to which suspicion on the part of the authorities might lead. I left Púrthi Ghát on the 26th and reached Lúnthigáon that night. Next day I passed Aslewá Phedi or Aslewá Tár, a village consisting of 25 houses, in the Gúlmi Pattí, situated on a plain and about ¼ mile from the Káli Gandak, crossed the Rúdar at Badiár Ghát, where the river is about 125 feet wide and 5 or 6 feet deep, and staid for the night at Riri bazar, about 1,305 feet above sea level, at the junction of the Riri Khola with the Káli Gandak. Riri bazar contains 50 shops kept by Niwars, a mint where pice are coined, and a custom house. The pice, called Gorakhpuri pice, are forwarded from this for circulation in the Gorakhpur district, where they are current amongst the people though not received at the Government Treasuries. The only copper coin current in Nepál is a mixture of iron and copper made at Katmándu, 48 Katmándu pice go to the Nepál "Mohur" and 2 Mohurs and 2 annas of the Indian coinage go to the Indian Rupee. Two great roads cross here, one coming from Sil-Garhi Dailekh and Salena and going

to Pokhra and Katmándu, and the other from Muktináth and Loh Mantang in the north to
Gorakhpur in the south; there are postal arrangements along these high roads, the runners
being Brahmins who have this work made over to them in consideration of their caste, no
other calls for work being made on them. There are stations along the roads at the distance
of 3 kos or 6 British miles.

On the 20th I halted at Tánsen, which is about 4,668 feet above sea level, and gives its
name to the Pattí. At Tánsen there is a fort, a gun foundry and manufactory of small arms,
40 or 50 shops and numbers of huts in which the sepoys quartered here live. The fort is a
square building about ¼ mile in circumference, the walls are about 12 feet high and made of
brick and mortar with an entrance to the north. Inside are two-storied houses of brick and
mortar which are used as the Magazine, Court-house and Treasury, and to the west is the
residence of General Badri Naraing, Governor of the district, with an exit from the fort by a
small door to the west, through which the members of the household go to the temple, about
30 feet from the fort. Formerly 1,100 men used to be stationed here, but now there are
1,600, who are drilled daily by 2 discharged subhadárs of the Indian Native Army : there are
no barracks or lines for the men and they are accommodated in huts. Guns as well as small
arms are manufactured in a small brick and mortar building to the south of the fort. To
the southwest is the parade ground. During winter the place is deserted, the general and
troops going to Batoli, distant 15 miles, the other inhabitants also moving to warmer quarters.

On the 14th November I came to Pilhua village, which gives its name to the Pattí
and the next night to Ratamati village in the Rámpúr Pattí. The valley here opens out
for some distance to the west, and there are numbers of villages of average size on either
side of the river ; on the hill sides are forests of pipal, sál, bar and other tropical forest trees.
On the 15th I followed the course of the Káli Gandak on the right bank, and 2¼ miles from
Ratamati came upon the roads from Batoli and Deoniagarh which join here, cross the Káli
Gandak at Kilri Ghát, and go onward to Katmándu, joining the road from Pokhra to Katmándu
at Chorkatiatar near Gorkha Darwar, from which another branches off and following up the
Buria Gandak communicates by Nubri with Thibet. I remained for the night at Thalitár.
On the 16th, still keeping to the right bank, I arrived at Kúmalgáon or Ghumari, consisting
of 25 houses inhabited entirely by Kúmhárs, who besides cultivating the land make baked earthen
pots which they dispose of in the surrounding villages. On the 17th I remained for the night
at Tárigáon which is distant from the river about 1,000 feet on the slope and about 6 or 700 feet
above it. On the 18th I reached Naoakot by a gradual ascent of nearly a mile along the hill
side. From Naoakot the road goes to Arkhali village, distant about ¾ mile, containing about
15 houses, and thence to Bishartar village (36 houses) where I remained for the night. The
Káli Gandak is about 1 mile distant, and about 7 miles lower down is joined by the united waters
of the Tirsuli Gandak and Buria Gandak rivers. The junction is called Deb Ghát and is held
in veneration by the Hindoos, a temple being built there. Below the junction, the river is called
the Naraini and has a southeasterly direction. On the 19th, I remained the night at the village
of Múkundpúr. None of the villages I passed through on the march had any cultivation in their
neighbourhood, but were merely summer residences of the people who during the winter months
take all their belongings to the plains to the south, where they have their rice fields. My next
halting place was Kunjoli. To the west of Kunjoli about 6 miles is Nawalpúr where there is a
Thánah with a captain and 25 sepoys whose duty it is to look after the timber floated down the
Gandak or Naraini. On the 21st I went to Lináwar village, containing 100 houses, distant
10½ miles, where I remained for the night. On the 22nd I intended crossing the river at
Kúlhúá Ghát 6½ miles lower down, but finding no boatmen I remained at Kúlhúá village for the
night and crossed the next morning.

I remained for the night at the junction of the Naraini and a small stream called the
Panchperna and Saonmukhi where there is a brick and mortar temple and rest house (Dharmsála) and 4 or 5 huts belonging to the customs officials, I crossed the river by boat next
morning the 24th. The river at the place of crossing is about 800 feet, at the ferry on the
right are some huts to which the captain and 25 sepoys employed in the floating timber
business come during winter. I went on to Gidhagáon distant about 9½ miles in a south-
westerly direction. About 3 miles from this in the same direction I came upon Bhojágáon,
a frontier village of Nepál, where there is a custom house and passes are shown and luggage
examined. A little beyond Bhojágáon I crossed the boundary, and though disappointed at my
want of success in Thibet, I felt thankful that I had been able to return to British territory with
such information as I had got together.

GENERAL REPORT

ON THE OPERATIONS

OF THE

GREAT TRIGONOMETRICAL SURVEY OF INDIA,

DURING

1874-75,

Prepared for submission to the Government of India.

BY

COLONEL J. T. WALKER, R.E., F.R.S., &C.,

SUPERINTENDENT OF THE SURVEY.

Dehra Dun:

PRINTED AT THE OFFICE OF THE SUPERINTENDENT G. T. SURVEY.
M. J. O'CONNOR.

1876.

THE OPERATIONS OF THE
GREAT TRIGONOMETRICAL SURVEY OF INDIA
IN 1874-75.

The following is a summary of the several operations of the present year, given in the order in which they will be found described in this report.

(2.) The operations carried on during the year under review have produced the following out-turn of work;—of Principal Triangulation, with the great theodolites of the Survey, 89 triangles, covering and area of 6,416 square miles, and disposed in chains which, if united, would extend over a direct length of 297 miles, and in connection with which 2 astronomical azimuths of verification have been measured;—of Secondary Triangulation, with smaller theodolites, an area of 4,049 square miles has been closely covered with points for the topographical surveys, and an area of about 6,000 square miles has been operated in *pari passu* with the principal triangulation;—of Topographical Surveying, an area of 2,176 square miles has been completed in the Himalayas, on the scale of one inch to the mile, and areas of 2,141 square miles, on the two-inch scale, and 1,208 square miles on the four-inch scale, in the course of which 2,026 linear miles of boundary and check lines have been traversed;—and of Geographical Explorations, much valuable work has been completed, on the Northern Frontier of Afghanistan, and on the lines from Ládákh to Lhása, and Lhása to Assam.

(3.) The principal triangulation has been executed with the great theodolites, whose azimuthal circles have a diameter of 24 inches, and are read by 5 equidistant microscopes. The average theoretical probable error of the angles, and the average geometrical error, of the triangles—the amount by which the sum of the three observed angles of each triangle differs from 180° + the spheroidal excess—are shown in the table given in the margin. The number of parties employed on the principal triangulation—which was originally fixed at six, but had by last year been reduced to four—has this year been reduced to three, the party employed on the Brahma-

Section.	Probable Errors of Observed Angles.		Geometrical Errors of Triangles.		Nature of country operated in.
	Number.	Amount.	Number.	Amount.	
I.	106	±0″·17	42	0″·55	Plains.
II.	56	·25	19	·48	Hills.
V.	84	·16	28	·47	,,
Averages,...	...	±0″·18	...	0·51	

putra Meridional Series having been transferred, on the completion of that chain of triangles, to undertake secondary triangulation in Burmah.

(4.) The financial administration of the Department during the present year has been exceedingly difficult and embarrassing. A large increase of expenditure had been occasioned by the introduction of the system of consolidated salaries, which was effected in 1874, under the anticipation that the increase might be met by 'savings in other quarters'; these savings have turned out to be illusive, and a further increase of expenditure has been incurred by the resumption of operations in Burmah, where almost every description of work is very much more expensive than it is in India proper. The orders and instructions for giving effect to the above measures were followed very speedily by orders for large reductions of expenditure; the latter could not be immediately carried out without keeping a large portion of the establishment of officers and surveyors unemployed; they are now to be gradually carried out within the next three years, by the stoppage of promotions, and a reduction of numbers as vacancies occur by death, retirement, or transfer to other Departments.

(5.) I now proceed, as usual, to report on and give an abstract of the operations of the several Survey Parties and Offices. Further details will be found in the Extracts from the Narrative Reports of the Executive Officers given in the first appendix; and a full account of the Trans-Himalayan Explorations will be met with in the second appendix.

NO. I.—TRIGONOMETRICAL.

THE RAMNAD LONGITUDINAL SERIES; PARALLEL 9¼°.

(6.) The operations for the revision of the portion of the Great Arc which

PERSONNEL.

Major B. R. Branfill, Dy. Supdt. 2nd Grade.
Mr. G. Belcham, Surveyor 4th Grade.
„ C. D. Potter, Assistant Surveyor 1st Grade.
Mr. E. W. Laseron, Asst. Surveyor 2nd Grade.

lies to the south of Bangalore having been completed, as stated in my last Report, the Madras party was deputed to commence the Rámnád Longitudinal Series, which is to trend east-wards from the Great Arc on the parallel of 9¼°, and had been approximately laid out during the previous year.

(7.) Several stations had to be built and the rays between them to be cleared, before the final observations could be commenced; the series had also to be extended along the coast to the Island of Rámesweram, with a view to the proposed connection of the Survey of India with that of Ceylon. Major Branfill himself took in hand the completion of the stations and rays of the first figure, and sent his assistants to build the stations and clear the rays further in advance. He commenced the final observations on the 29th December and completed six stations by the 20th January, when, finding that he was likely to overtake the station-building and ray-clearing operations—which would have brought his own work to a stand still—he left his assistant Mr. Belcham to continue the observations and proceeded in person to direct and accelerate the operations in advance. It was fortunate that he did so, for the belts of dense palmyra forest, intermixed with groves of cocoanut trees, made the selection of stations very difficult indeed. To carry a zigzag traverse in the vicinity of each ray through the forest was possible, but to clear the straight lines between the stations, down to the ground level, as usual, was found to be impracticable; thus to raise the stations to a sufficient elevation to overlook all intermediate obstacles was the only thing to be done, although the palms grew to a considerable height, and the ground was generally flat. By availing himself of sand hillocks, and constructing an ingenious portable braced stand for the theodolite, and lofty scaffolds for the signals, Major Branfill succeeded in overcoming all obstacles, so that by the end of the first week in March the work of station building and line clearing—to the extent of cutting down or lopping the branches of some of the most obnoxious palms—was complete, as far as Rámnád. The observations proceeded without interruption and were brought to a close by the 1st May.

(8.) Major Branfill's next care was to extend the approximate series from Rámnád to Rámesweram, with a view to the Ceylon connection. After examining the country, he decided, on account of the increasing density of the palm forest and the rapid narrowing of the land, to utilize the islets of the coral reef which lies parallel to the mainland at the distance of 4 or 5 miles; he thus extended the series by a succession of quadrilaterals as far as the land's end. Next season the remaining portion of the triangulation to connect the Survey of India with that of Ceylon—a sketch map of which is given in my last annual report—will, it is to be hoped, be completed; the work however cannot be begun before the end of the month of January, when the violent winds of the north-east monsoon moderate, and open boats—the only craft this Department can afford to entertain—may ply between the islands in the Straits, to supply the signal and observing parties with water and food.

(9.) The out-turn of field work consists of 27 principal stations fixed by 42 triangles, forming 9 polygonal figures (6 quadrilaterals and 3 hexagons) which cover an area of 791 square miles, entirely in the plains, and extend for a direct distance of 90 miles from west to east. A set of star observations for azimuth was also taken, and 35 secondary points were fixed. I have every reason to be satisfied with the vigorous manner in which Major Branfill has carried on his operations, and with his judicious efforts to reduce their cost, by modifying the structure of the stations of observation, so as to utilize the advantages afforded by the timber of the palmyra trees, as a set off against the serious difficulties presented by the superabundance of these trees, on the ground over which he was operating.

(10.) For some years past Major Branfill has been making a collection of the common place-names met with in Southern India, with their traditional root-meanings and local applications. A list of these will be found in the Appendix to this Report. Similar lists, collected from other parts of India, would doubtless be of much value to the ethnologist and philologer, as well as to the topographer, throwing some light on the language and history of the inhabitants, and even on the physical geography of the country.

NO. II—TRIGONOMETRICAL.

THE OPERATIONS IN THE ASSAM VALLEY.

(11.) Lieutenant Harman relieved Mr. W. Beverley of the charge of this

PERSONNEL.

Lieutenant H. T. Harman, R.E., Officiating Asst. Supdt. 2nd Grade.
Mr. W. O'Sullivan, Sur. 4th Grade.
„ J. O. Hughes, Asst. Surveyor 3rd Grade.

party at Shillong, in October 1874, under instructions that he would be required to join the Survey Detachment accompanying the Field Force which was to be sent into the Daphla Hills in December. Thus it was a matter of great importance that he should take the field at the earliest date that it would be safe to do so, and mark out work for his European assistants and Native establishment to perform, during his absence with the military expedition. Starting from his Head Quarters at Shillong on the 3rd November, he was able to devote upwards of a month to the preliminary operations of the triangulation in the country between the Civil Stations of Jorhát and Dibrugarh, and to frame instructions regarding the work which was to be carried on in his absence.

(12.) On the 12th December he reached Borpathár, the second encampment of the Field Force, and reported himself to Major Godwin-Austen, of the Topographical Survey Department, who had been selected for the charge of the Survey Party which was attached to the expedition. He accompanied the Feld Force, as Assistant to Major Austen, until the 7th January, when he was deputed to make a reconnoissance of the Ranga Valley and the hill ranges to the east of the tracts occupied by the Force. Starting from the vicinity of North Lakhimpur, he marched for some distance along the course of the Páns river, taking the most direct and best line to the Daphla villages in the Ranga Valley, which line, though crossing the outer hill ranges, is more open and easily traversed than the route along the Ranga river. Even here however no roads or well trodden foot paths were found, the country was overgrown with dense forest and jungle, and the progress made in each day's march was very small. It was known that no food would be obtainable en route, and very little at the Daphla villages when they were reached; supplies of food had therefore to be carried with the party, by coolies, and their daily consumption rapidly decreased the general stock provided for all. Thus Lieutenant Harman was obliged to content himself with a guard of only 12 sepoys; and after reaching the Daphla villages he found that even these men were more than he could feed, and that he would either have to return at once with them, re infectá, or to dismiss them and trust himself entirely to the people of the country. He chose the latter alternative, and succeeded in making good friends of the simple mountaineers; and, after completing his survey of their country, he eventually persuaded them to take him back to Lakhimpur by the Ranga Valley route, though at first they stoutly objected to doing so. They represented the track as very difficult, a mere hunting track, not passable for any man with a load, and certainly not for Assamese coolies, whom they appear to regard with great contempt. Lieutenant Harman found that their accounts of the difficulties of the route were not much exaggerated, as there were places over which even his dog had to be carried; but latterly it appeared that the chief objections on the part of the Daphlas to taking him by this route were caused by apprehensions that they might thereby incur the enmity of their more powerful neighbours, the Abors, and be punished by them for so doing.

(13.) Lieutenant Harman worked right well, and showed much patience and tact in his transactions with the semi-barbarous inhabitants of a country which no European had ever before entered. He underwent much roughing and exposure, and incurred many risks, but these have been repaid by the success which has crowned his exertions. He has drawn up a very interesting account of his own operations and of the country and people, which will be published by the Surveyor General as an appendix to the Daphla Military Expedition Survey Report, by Major Godwin-Austen.

(14.) Lieutenant Harman had expected that his services with the Expedition would not be required for a longer period than six weeks. But it was not until the month of March, after an absence of nearly three months, that he was able to rejoin his own party and resume the trigonometrical operations. He then found that the amount of progress which had been made during his absence was not as great as he had anticipated; several lines had still to be cleared before the observations of the angles could be commenced. He laboured very vigorously to push the work forward, but found the difficulties too great to be surmounted in the short time remaining before the setting in of the rains and the consequent termination of the field season. In many places the forest was very heavy and dense; and worse than all were the occasional patches of jheel-canes "terribly armed with crooked thorns on every surface," through which the native line-cutters, with their wooden sandals and naked legs, could scarely creep without suffering severely, and it was found impossible to clear the lines more rapidly than at a rate of little more than 100 yards in a day. Thus the rains had commenced before Lieutenant Harman was able to begin final observations at the stations between which the lines were clear; and very soon the country was flooded to such an extent as to become impassable. Lieutenant Harman had therefore no alternative but to quit the field and return with his party to his head quarters, at Shillong; he completed only two triangles, after expending an amount of labour and exertion on his work, which would have sufficed for a long line of triangulation in almost any other part of India; much of what was done will however be of future value, and tend to expedite the operations of the next field season.

NO. III.—TRIGONOMETRICAL.

THE SECONDARY TRIANGULATION IN BURMAH.

(16.) In May 1874, I received an intimation from the Secretary to the

PERSONNEL.

W. Beverley, Esq., Offg. Assistant
Superintendent 1st Grade.
Mr. J. W. Mitchell, Surveyor 4th
Grade.
Mr. D. J. Collins, Asst. Surveyor 4th
Grade.

Government of India, in the Department of Revenue Agriculture and Commerce, that the want of proper topographical maps had necessitated the suspension of the Geological Survey in Burmah, that isolated town surveys were being carried out; that Marine Surveys of the coast were shortly to be commenced; and that the government wished me to take early steps for the vigorous prosecution of the triangulation in Burmah.

(17.) Accordingly the party which had recently completed the Brahmaputra Series, as reported last year, was re-organized and transferred to Burma— under the charge of Mr. W. Beverley,—with instructions to carry chains of secondary triangles, from the nearest principal sides of the Eastern Frontier Series, in order to fix all large towns, prominent and permanent objects, peaks, &c., for Topographical and Geological Surveys, and the light-houses, &c., along the coast, for the Marine Survey.

(18.) The establishment was formed into two detachments; one was immediately under Mr. Beverley himself; the other was under his senior assistant Mr. Mitchell, who was now transferred from the Eastern Frontier Series, in connection with which, he had, during the previous season, laid out the design of a secondary triangulation to Pegu and Rangoon. This he was now to finish, while Mr. Beverley worked in continuation, in the country to the south of Rangoon.

(19.) Before commencing his own work, Mr. Beverley examined Mr. Mitchell's selections and found that they required to be modified to some extent. He then reconnoitered the country to the south, and laid out a triangulation down to the coast line near the mouth of the Rangoon river. He took observations to fix the positions of Elephant Point Column and Eastern Grove Light, and various points in the town of Rangoon for the Seaport Towns Survey. He then commenced the observations at the stations, north of Rangoon, connecting his stations to the south with the Eastern Frontier Series, but was unable to observe because of the unfavorable condition of the atmosphere. Two more attempts were made subsequently, on the commencement of the rainy season, but both without success; and the same result attended the resumption of the triangulation along the coast towards China Bakir Light.

(20.) Mr. Mitchell spent much time in reconnoitering the ground and laying out the triangulation to the north of Rangoon, and he took observations from seven stations; but owing to very bad weather, frequent attacks of illness, and other causes, he failed to carry out his share of the operations, and thus Mr. Beverley's work still remains unconnected with the principal triangulation, and consequently does not give any but roughly approximate results. It is expected however that the requisite connection will be made early next season, when the atmosphere will probably be clear and favorable for the observations.

NO. IV.—TRIGONOMETRICAL.

THE EASTERN FRONTIER SERIES, BURMAH.

(21.) In previous years the triangulation of this series had been brought

PERSONNEL.

W. C. Rossenrode, Esq., Deputy
Superintendent 3rd Grade.
Mr. H. Beverley, Surv. 1st Grade.
„ J. C. Clancey, Assistant Survey-
or 3rd Grade.

down from Prome to the northern portion of the Shoay-Gheen Districts, the terminal side spanning the Sittang Valley at a distance of about 30 miles above the town which gives its name to the District. During the present year the series has been extended in a south-easterly direction, to within 40 miles of the town of Moulmein, the stations on the eastern flank resting on the hill ranges which separate the British territories from the Shan States tributary to Siam, while those on the west flank are near the coast of the Gulf of Martaban. Stations have also been selected in advance, through the Province of Tennaserim, to a short distance below the town of Amherst.

(22.) In Section V of my last Report I have given a very full account of the great difficulties which are met with in conducting the operations of this Survey in Burmah, in consequence of the dense forest and growth of tropical vegetation which is usually met with everywhere, the sparse population, the reluctance of the Burmese to work for hire, and the practice in which they indulge of firing the grass jungles during the field season, and thus obscuring the atmosphere to an extent which renders all observations to distant points impossible. I need not repeat what has been said on this subject, but allusion to it is necessary, because similar difficulties have attended the operations of the present field season. Moreover some of the stations had to be placed on obligatory peaks of the hill ranges, so far away from the nearest human habitations, and so thickly fringed with forest, that no one was known to have ever reached them; the surveyors had to pioneer themselves with their compasses, and to cut their way onwards through the jungle, scaling great rocks and precipices, without any guide to lead them.

(23.) The out-turn of work comprises a quadrilateral, a double polygon and part of a hexagon, covering an area of about 3,150 square miles and advancing the series a direct distance of about 100 miles. Numerous secondary points were fixed both within and external to the principal triangulation. The preliminary operations for future triangulation were carried over a distance of about 100 miles, and have reached the parallel of Kálégouk Island, on which a station-site has been selected. The principal towns wherein points have been fixed are Shoay-Gheen, Pegu, Sittang and Bhiling; a secondary triangulation has been commenced towards the new Civil Station of Paphoon. The out-turn of work would be considered very good in any part of India, under far more favorable conditions for its achievement; under the actual circumstances of the operations it is all the more creditable to Mr. Rossenrode, and to Mr. H. Beverley, by whom the preliminary operations were conducted.

NO. V.—TRIGONOMETRICAL.

THE JODHPUR SERIES; MERIDIAN 72½°.

(24.) Captain Rogers returned from furlough and relieved Captain Hill of the charge of the party on the 20th November 1874.

PERSONNEL.
Captain M. W. Rogers, R.E., Officiating Deputy Superintendent 3rd Grade.
Mr. W. C. Price, Surveyor 4th Grade.
" O. P. Torrens, Assistant Surveyor 3rd Grade.
Mr. P. P. Prunty, Assistant Surveyor 4th Grade.

(25.) The triangulation was extended northwards, through the Deserts of Jaisalmir and Bikanir. These tracts are apparently so called because, though inhabited by a comparatively large population during the rainy season and the early portion of the cold weather—when there is still a supply of water in the tanks—they are deserted in the hot season, when the tanks are all dry, and drinkable water is in many parts only to be obtained by being sent for to great distances. The water in the wells is usually brackish and unfit for human consumption; thus water for the survey camps had to be brought from distances averaging 10 to 20 miles, throughout the greater portion of the season.

(26.) The out-turn of work has been very good and creditable to Captain Rogers and his assistants. The principal triangulation was advanced 104 miles along the meridian by a series of polygonal figures, consisting of a pentagon, two hexagons and one double polygon, which cover an area of 2472 square miles. An astronomical azimuth of verification was measured at one of the principal stations. The preliminary operations, for the selection of the sites of stations in advance, were carried over a distance of 64 miles, towards the Sutlej Series. The positions of the towns of Bikanir and Pugal, and other points, were fixed by secondary chains of triangles.

NO. VI.—TOPOGRAPHICAL.

THE SURVEY OF KATTYWAR.

(27.) The operations of this topographical survey have been carried on under the executive charge of Captain Pullan, owing to the continued absence of Captain Trotter on duties connected with the Geographical Explorations in Eastern Turkestan and other regions beyond the British Frontier. The year has been uneventful in the history of the survey, but good progress has been made, both in the field work and the mapping.

PERSONNEL.

Captain A. Pullan, S.C., Offg. Deputy Superintendent 3rd Grade.
J. McGill, Esq., Offg. Assistant Superintendent 1st Grade.
Mr. F. Bell, Surveyor 3rd Grade.
„ N. C. Gwynne, Sur. 4th Grade.
„ W. A. Fielding, Assistant Surveyor 2nd Grade.
Mr. W. Oldham, Asst. Surveyor 3rd Grade.
„ G. T. Hall, Ditto   3rd „
„ H. Corkery, Ditto   4th „
Visaji Ragonath and 11 Native Surveyors and Apprentices.

(28.) The out-turn of final topographical work, on the scale of 2 inches to the mile, by this party embraces an area of 1749 square miles, comprising parts of Prants Hállár and Machhu Kánthá in Kattywar and a portion of the southern sea-board of Cutch. The area is less than what was covered last year, but this is satisfactorily accounted for by Captain Pullan, in his report. The triangulation executed in advance for the operations of next year covers an area of 2,200 miles, 200 of which are intended for the Survey of the Cutch Coast. In addition to the above, 1,117 linear miles of traversing were executed in order to demarcate the boundaries of Native States, and to check the details of the plane table survey.

(29.) In my Report for 1872-73, para. 47, I stated that when the operations of this survey should reach the shores of the Gulf of Cutch, every effort would be made to connect them with the survey of that Gulf which was made by Lieutenant Taylor, I.N. This has now been done, and the agreement between the two surveys is reported by Captain Pullan to be very satisfactory.

(30.) As regards the mapping, four new sheets, Nos. 32, 33, 34 and 35, have been drawn in such a manner as to be suited either for reproduction on the full scale of 2 inches to the mile, or for reduction by photography to the 1-inch scale.

NO. VII.—TOPOGRAPHICAL.

THE SURVEY OF GUZERAT.

(31.) During the present year Major Haig has been carrying on the system of operation which has been very fully described in Section VIII of my report for last year, whereby all surveys of British lands, which had been previously made in detail for fiscal purposes, by the Bombay Revenue Surveyors, are combined together, supplemented by topography wherever necessary, and mapped on the scale of 4 inches = 1 mile,—while the remaining portions of the British Districts, and the whole of the Native States, are surveyed and mapped on the 2-inch scale, as in Kattywar.

PERSONNEL.

Major C. T. Haig, R.E., Deputy Superintendent 2nd Grade.
Lieut. J. E. Gibbs, R.E., Assistant Superintendent 2nd Grade.
Mr. J. Peyton, Surveyor 1st Grade.
„ A. D'Souza,   „   1st „
„ A. D. L. Christie, „   4th „
„ C. H. McAFee,   „   4th „
„ E. J. Connor, Asst. Sur. 1st „
„ J. Hickie,   „   2nd „
„ G. D. Cusson,   „   2nd „
„ G. Hall,   „   3rd „
„ S. Norman,   „   4th „
„ C. Norman,   „   4th „
Gopal Vishnu and 11 Native Surveyors and Apprentices.

REVENUE SURVEYORS.

Mr. T. A. LeMesurier.
7 Native Surveyors.

(32.) An area of 1,375 square miles has been topographically surveyed, of which 983 square miles was on the scale of 4 inches to a mile and 392 square miles on the 2-inch scale. Thus the out-turn of work, as measured by the area completed, is almost exactly double what it was last year, when the operations were of a tentative nature, and the best method of utilizing the Revenue

Survey details had still to be ascertained, by careful trial and investigation.

(33.) In the Dang Forests an area of about 550 square miles was triangulated. A small area in Sheet 79 was also completed with data points, by traversing, and a further area of about 300 square miles of British territory previously triangulated was prepared for survey on the 4-inch scale, by effecting the necessary connection between the fiscal details of the Revenue Survey and the stations, of the triangulation by means of traversing.

(34.) The country topographically surveyed includes portions of the Dholka, Viramgám and Dhandhuka talukas of the Ahmedabad Collectorate and of the Limri, Lakhtar, Wadhwán and Cambay States, all which have now been completely surveyed, and appertain to Sheets 81 and 82 of the general maps; also portions of the Ankleswar taluka of the Broach Collectorate and of the Olpád taluka of the Surat Collectorate, appertaining to Sheet 14.

(35.) The mapping has progressed very satisfactorily. Major Haig has introduced a valuable printed form, called the "Section Register", in which all the different stages through which each map has to pass are tabulated, so that it progresses regularly, and passes from one class of draftsman to another, according as the stages are divided among the different classes.

(36.) An interesting report by Lieutenant Gibbs of the country in the Dangs, in continuation of the one which was published in my report for last year, will be found at page 36—n of the Appendix.

(37.) The Surveyor General has expressed very decided opinions against the desirability of making any use whatever of the Bombay Revenue Survey details; he has represented to the Government that, in his opinion, the Guzerat maps, on the 4-inch scale, in which full use is made of those details, are not as essential for the requirements of the country as maps on half that scale, obtained from more speedily executed surveys, made without reference to the Revenue Survey work; and he has particularly advocated the early procuring of materials for the completion of the sheets of the Indian Atlas, which are engraved on a scale of somewhat less than ½-inch to the mile. A Committee of Survey and Engineer Officers was therefore appointed by the Government of India to report on the subject. The Committee were not able to agree upon any report; no definite conclusion was arrived at with reference to the utilization of the work of Bombay Revenue Surveys for topographical purposes; and irreconcileable differences of opinion existed regarding the relative cost and utility of surveys on the 4-inch and the 2-inch scales. Under the circumstances the Government had adopted a medium course, and directed that the 2-inch scale is to be employed in future, but that the Revenue Survey maps are to be utilized in the operations.

NO. VIII.—TOPOGRAPHICAL.

THE SURVEYS IN DEHRA DÚN AND THE SIWALIKS.

(38.) These surveys are being made conjointly by a portion of the Kumaun and Garhwál Party under Captain Thuillier, and by the survey branch of the Forest Department which has been lately created and placed under Captain Bailey—with a view to executing special surveys for the requirements of forestry—and, while under formation, has been temporarily affiliated to this Survey.

Personnel of the portion of the Kumaun and Garhwál Survey Party employed in the Dún.

Captain H. R. Thuillier, R.E., Offg. Deputy Superintendent 1st Grade.
Lt. St. G. C. Gore, R.E., Offg. Asst. Superintendent 2nd Grade.
Mr. C. J. Nouville, Surveyor 2nd Grade.
Mr. J. Low, Surveyor 3rd Grade.
 „ L. J. Pocock, Surv. 4th Grade.
 „ H. Todd, Asst. Sur. 1st Grade.
 „ T. Kinney, „
 „ E. F. Wrixon, „ 2nd Grade.
11 Native Surveyors.

(39.) The survey of the non-forest tracts of the Dehra Dún District, by Captain Thuillier and his party, has made good progress during the year, and Captain Thuillier hopes to be able to complete it, as well as the survey of Jaunsár Báwar, in the next field season.

(12)

(40.) The field operations were commenced early in October and continued to the end of April. 225 square miles of country were topographically surveyed on the scale of 4-inches to the mile in the Dún. The whole of Jaunsár Báwar was covered with a net-work of triangles, comprising an area of 470 square miles; 398 linear miles of boundary traverses were executed, and 63 miles of check lines were run over the topographical work of the surveyors.

(41.) The country surveyed presents ground of very varied descriptions, from the flat cultivated lands in the vicinity of the River Asan—a tributary of the Jumna, and the main drainage channel of the Western Dún—to the crest of the Mussooree range, which rises to a height of 5,000 feet above the level of the Dún. The low spurs and broken tracts about the foot of the hills gave an infinity of trouble, both in delineating the features of the ground, and in chaining the boundary traverses; in the latter operation very heavy corrections were required for the reduction of hypothenusal to horizontal values.

(42.) Captain Thuillier reports favorably of the progress of his Native Surveyors, who are said to be improving in the art of delineating ground with the plane table; their traversing work was all reduced in the field and found to stand the usual tests in a satisfactory manner. As the survey advances and the Native Surveyors become better trained, the introduction of this cheap agency may be expected to have a very appreciable effect in expediting the completion and reducing the cost of the work.

(43.) The Index Map of the Dehra Dún and Siwalik Survey, which is attached to this report, shows very clearly the extent of work completed and remaining for execution by Captain Thuillier's party. The uncoloured portions of the map represent the forest tracts which have been or are being surveyed by Captain Bailey.

(44.) Captain Bailey's Annual Report has already been submitted to Government through his own Department, together with my review of his operations. It is here therefore unnecessary for me to say more than that the out-turn of topography is about 288 square miles, which has been done on the same scale as the non-forest tracts by Captain Thuillier; the amount of the boundary and interior traversing was 326 miles. The ground operated over was very broken and difficult, more particularly in the interior of the Siwalik Hills, the intricacy and ruggedness of which are probably unsurpassed by hill ranges of the same altitudes in any part of the world.

(45.) The out-turn of topography executed by these two parties may be considered small, as compared with that of other topographical parties working on the standard scale of 1-inch to the mile, in Native States and in Districts where minute delineation of the features of the ground is not required; or even with that of Revenue Survey parties, working on the same scale and with much attention to detail, but in flat and open country, which requires little or no topographical delineation. In Captain Thuillier's operations the average monthly out-turn of topographical area, during the field season, by a party of plane table surveyors, consisting of 1 European and 2 Natives, was 10 square miles; in Captain Bailey's with two more natives in each party, it was 7¾ square miles; in both cases the native surveyors were new hands under training, but the Europeans in the former were, as a rule, older surveyors and better skilled than in the latter. I am satisfied that there was no want of exertion and painstaking in the execution of the operations, and that a larger out-turn could only have been secured by a sacrifice of fidelity and exactness, in the delineation of the ground.

(46). The conjoint survey will form a map in 42 sheets; of these 18 have been completed and deposited in this office, and 15 have been reproduced to full scale and published by photo-zincography.

NO. IX.—TOPOGRAPHICAL.

HIMALAYAN SURVEYS IN KUMAUN AND GARHWAL.

(47.) During the rainy season of 1874, a detachment from Captain Thuillier's Party, under Mr. Ryall, was located at Almora, the nearest point to the scene of the future field operations at which the recess quarters of the party could be established. Before the rains were well over, Mr. Ryall and his assistants had to take the field, in order that they might reach the lofty ground they had to survey, and make the most of the short interval during which the snow line is at its highest and the atmosphere is bright and clear; this occurs between the cessation of the autumnal rains and the setting in of winter weather.

PERSONNEL.

E. O. Ryall, Esq. Officiating Assistant Superintendent 1st Grade.
Mr. C. H. McAFee, Assistant Surveyor 1st Grade.
Mr. E. F. Litchfield, Assistant Surveyor 3rd Grade.
Mr. I. S. Pocock, Assistant Surveyor 4th Grade.
Mr. J. F. McCarthy, Assistant Surveyor 4th Grade.

(48.) Mr. Ryall conducted a series of triangles through a stupendous gorge overhung by the lofty mountains of Chirkhana and Husaling; an undertaking which, he says, required all his skill and nerve. He also supervised the operations of his assistants who were employed in plane tabling on the scale of one inch to the mile. The difficulties this little detachment had to contend with in the lofty region in which they were employed, and which were successfully overcome, are fully detailed in the Appendix and they reflect credit on all concerned. Captain Thuillier draws particular attention to Mr. I. Pocock's work in the upper part of the Mána Valley, where the average height of the ground surveyed was over 21,000 feet and the maximum height reached was 22,040 feet above sea level.

(49.) The area topographically surveyed comprises 2,176 square miles, and the portion of country triangulated in advance covers 800 square miles. There now remains only about 1,200 square miles in the Mulla Jower, Dharma and Báyáns Valleys to survey, which will complete the unfinished portion of Garhwál. But as the operations in these desolate regions—to which supplies of food and fuel have to be transported from great distances—are necessarily of a somewhat costly nature, their completion has been postponed for the present, and it will not be undertaken until the expenditure can be met by savings in other quarters.

NO. X.

SPIRIT LEVELING OPERATIONS IN THE MADRAS PRESIDENCY.

(50.) Captain McCullagh, on his return from furlough, succeeded to the charge of these operations, vice Lieutenant Harman who had been transferred to Assam. He commenced work at the S.W. end of the Bangalore Base, the height of which had been provisionally ascertained by triangulation which rests on a determination of the mean sea-level at Madras, by Colonel De Haviland. He then carried a line of levels, vía Túmkúr, Sira, Hiriyur Tallak and Rámpur, to to Honur H.S. and into Bellary, from which station the work was continued, vía Alúr, Adoni, and Máduwáram to Raichore Railway station, where it was closed on the 3rd April 1875. The operations were carried on in a very satisfactory manner, and the aggregate length of the lines completed is 297 miles.

PERSONNEL.

Captain J. R. McCullagh, R.E., Officiating Assistant Superintendent 1st Grade.
Mr. A. H. Bryson, Assistant Surveyor 3rd Grade.
Two native recorders.

(51.) At Bellary a junction was effected with the line of levels which had been carried from there to the Port of Karwar—on the western coast—by Lieutenant Harman, in the preceding field season. Captain McCullagh's height of the point of junction is 4·5 feet greater than Lieutenant Harman's; but the discrepancy is believed to be in great measure due to inaccuracies in the determinations of the datum points of the respective lines, both of which are provisional only; final results will not be obtained until the mean sea-level has been exactly determined at Karwar, and probably at Madras also; the difference of level between Madras and Bangalore also needs to be more exactly determined than at present.

NO. XI.—TIDAL OBSERVATIONS.

DETERMINATIONS OF MEAN SEA-LEVEL IN THE GULF OF CUTCH.

(52.) The primary object of these operations is to determine the existing

PERSONNEL.

Captain Baird, R.E., Offg. Deputy Superintendent 3rd Grade.
Mr. T. Rendell, Asst. Sur. 1st Grade.
Narsing Dass, and other Sub-Surveyors.

relations between the level of the land and the sea at certain points on the coasts of the Gulf of Cutch, as a first step towards investigating the question whether progressive changes are taking place in the level of the land at the head of the gulf, as has long been supposed to be the case. It is under contemplation to repeat the operations a few years hence, at the same points, with a view to ascertaining the relations which will then obtain between the land and sea; a comparison between the results of the two series of determinations will show whether any sensible variation of level has occurred in the interim.

(53.) The operations were commenced in 1873; their annual progress, and the several instruments employed, have been very fully described in my reports for 1872-73, and 1873-74. I may here however repeat that the tidal stations are three in number, and are situated respectively at Hanstal Point, near the head of the gulf; at Nawanár Point, half way up on the northern coast; and at Okhá Point, on the southern coast and near the entrance to the gulf. At each station a self-registering tide gauge was set up, and it was a part of the programme of the operations that the relative levels of the three stations should be determined by running lines of very carefully executed spirit levels between them. No harbour walls or piers being available, at either place, for the tide gauges to be erected on—over deep water—it was found necessary to set up the instruments on shore, at the nearest points to deep water, and to connect them with the sea by a system of piping, of which the land portion was rigid and the sea portion flexible. The flexible piping terminated in a 'rose', which was suspended from a buoy in deep water, while the rigid piping was conducted to the bottom of an iron cylinder, which was sunk vertically—its lower end being closed by an iron plate—into a masonry well over which the tide gauge was erected. The sea water passed freely through the piping into the cylinder when the tide was rising, and back again when the tide fell, the level of the water in the cylinder being always identical with that of the sea at the same moment, when there was no air in the piping; by means of a stop-cock which was attached to the highest bend of the piping, any air, which might have accumulated internally—as occasionally happened—could be readily expelled whenever the level of the sea rose above that of the stop-cock, which occurred twice daily. The float of the tide gauge rested on the surface of the water in the cylinder, and its rise and fall was duly registered on the barrel of the gauge. Each station was furnished with self-registering instruments for recording the direction and velocity of the wind and the barometric pressure. A native surveyor with a few assistants was placed in charge, and located in a hut in the immediate vicinity of the station. Periodical inspections were made by Captain Baird, and by his assistant Mr. Rendell, and on these occasions the clock errors were determined, the cylinders and pipes cleared of any silt which had been deposited in them, and the instruments thoroughly overhauled.

(54.) Much time was necessarily occupied in the construction of the stations and in getting the instruments into good working order. The regular tidal registrations were commenced, at Okhá in December 1873, at Hanstal in March 1874, and at Nawanár in April 1874. It was hoped that they might be carried on continuously for at least a year, if not longer, at each station, a shorter period being inadequate to furnish the requisite data for an investigation of each of the principal tidal constituents. Considerable anxiety was however felt as to what might happen during the season of the monsoons, when heavy gales are prevalent; but every precaution was taken to strengthen the wooden observatories in which the instruments were set up, and to anticipate and provide for all possible contingencies.

(55.) The monsoon of 1874 set in with great severity and lasted long; but the observatories all stood firm, and the tide gauges and the other self-register-ing intruments remained in good working order, at all the stations, throughout the season. Unfortunately however at Nawanár the entire configuration of the fore-shore became altered, and an extensive sand spit was formed, below the low water level, on the line of piping, which became completely buried. This occurred in the month of July, and necessitated the suspension of the registra-tions at Nawanár, until such time as the piping could be extracted and again put into communication with deep water. It was expected that the original confi-guration of the fore-shore would probably be restored by natural causes, when the wind veered round to its usual direction, which would occur soon after the commencement of the cold weather months; but this expectation was disappoint-ed, and, as the cold season wore on, it became only too certain that the piping which lay beyond the low water line would never be recovered. A supply of new piping was therefore obtained from Bombay and attached by Mr. Rendell to the land portion of the original pipe, and by the commencement of the month of March 1875, after a break of nine months duration, the tide gauge was once more in free communication with the sea, and there appeared to be every probability that it would so remain, at least until the setting in of the next monsoon.

(56.) But the station of Nawanár appears to have been fated to be a trouble and a vexation. Within a fortnight after Mr. Rendell had re-started the tide gauge, he returned, from an inspection of Hanstal station, to see how mat-ters were progressing, and found that during his absence considerable changes had again taken place; the fore-shore had been rapidly shallowing, and the new piping was being fast covered with a deposit of silt and mud, which had nearly reached up to the level of the rose at its outer extremity. He cut it away at once, and substituted several lengths of iron piping, which were held in sus-pension above the surface of the shore, by being attached—at a level a little below that of the lowest spring tides—to stakes driven vertically into the ground for the purpose. Mr. Rendell remained on the spot for the next two months, taking steps to prevent the rose from being reached by the constantly rising mud and silt; he thus succeeded in getting satisfactory and continuous registrations for the whole of the time, and he checked them by a series of hourly readings taken *pari passu* on a graduated staff, which had been set up in the sea, in deep water, in order to afford a means of verifying the indications of the self-register-ing gauge.

(57.) At Okhá station all went on most satisfactorily throughout the monsoon of 1874 and the following field season; there were very few breaks of continuity in the registrations, and they were very short and of no importance. At Hanstal the breaks were more numerous and longer; here the water was very muddy, and not pure and clear as at Okhá; consequently there was a tendency for a sediment of mud to be deposited in the cylinder of the gauge and in the piping; this sediment had to be cleared out occasionally and then the registra-tions were necessarily interrupted; but the breaks in the curves are of no ma-terial importance, and they can be filled in by hand from the outlines of the collateral curves, without any risk of significant error.

(58.) The most trying and difficult portion of the operations was the carrying out of the periodical inspections during the monsoon of 1874. This had proved to be so arduous, and to entail so much exertion and exposure on the officer on whom the duty devolved, that I felt I should not be justified in requesting Captain Baird to carry on the operations through the monsoon of 1875. I therefore directed him to continue the registrations up to within a few days of the commencement of the monsoon, and then to dismantle all the stations, and remove the instruments. These instructions were duly carried out in the month of May.

(59.) Thus the periods during which the tidal heights have been continuously registered at the three stations, are 16½ months at Okhá, 14 months at Hanstal, 2 months at Nawanár in 1874 and 2 months more in 1875. Simultaneous registrations of the direction and velocity of the wind, and of the barometric pressure, were made by the anemograph and the barograph, which were set up at each station.

(60.) The long break in the registrations at Nawanár is to be regretted. But as the station lies nearly midway up the gulf, it is probable that the values of the difference between the mean level for the periods of actual observation and the mean level for the entire year, which are given by the registrations at Okhá and Hanstal, may be safely applied to the results at Nawanár, to obtain the mean level for the year there. Captain Baird has already done this, and obtained very accordant and promising results.

(61.) During the field season of 1874-75, the work of inspecting the observatories, rating the clocks, and maintaining every thing in satisfactory working order, devolved chiefly on Mr. Rendell. Captain Baird was principally employed in conducting spirit leveling operations, for determining the relative levels of the datum points of the three tidal stations, and of the stone bench-marks which had been laid down, a year previously, along the lines to be leveled over. The length of the main lines connecting the three tidal stations was 275 miles, which was leveled over independently by Captain Baird and Narsing Dass, in accordance with the rigorous system of operation which has been followed for several years past in this Department; 29 miles of branch lines were also executed, in order to connect the stations of the Kattywar triangulation with the tidal stations.

(62.) In working between Nawanár and Hanstal, Captain Baird had to make a considerable detour round the head of the gulf, crossing the Runn between Shikarpúr and Malliá. Several bench-marks were fixed on the Runn, and they will be important points of reference when the operations are repeated some years hence. The existing surface level of the Runn has been obtained at a number of points, for Captain Baird took the precaution of having all the pins on which the leveling staves were set up, driven downwards until their heads were exactly flush with the surface of the ground.

(63.) At the close of the field season, the instruments were taken down and the observatories were dismantled. At each station the vertical iron cylinder, in which the float of the gauge had acted, was left in statu quo, together with a length of about 50 feet of the iron piping extending sea-wards from the cylinder. The cylinder was filled with clean dry sand, and closed above with a thick planking, after which a massive pile of stones was raised over the ground around it to serve the double object of a protection, and an indication of the position for future reference. The three bench-marks in the immediate vicinity of the cylinder, with each of which the datum of the gauge had been connected, were similarly covered over. Finally the several cairns were placed under the protection of the local officials; and it is to be hoped that the cylinders and bench-marks will be readily discovered whenever the second series of operations are commenced, and that they will be found to have remained undisturbed meanwhile.

(64.) Thus the first series of operations, to determine whether the relations of land and sea are constant or changing, is now an accomplished fact. Great credit is due to Captain Baird for the manner in which he has conducted the task entrusted to him. The difficulties he had to contend with, in obtaining exact registrations continuously for such long periods, were very serious and formidable; all the stations were situated at points on the coast line which were very far from the nearest habited localities; and the inspections during the season of monsoons, which work was done entirely by himself, necessitated constant travelling during the most inclement time of the year, and entailed an amount of risk and exposure which would tell on a constitution of iron.

(65.) The final reduction of the registrations at each station has been commenced, but it will still take some time to complete. The following preliminary results have however been obtained from the combined tidal and leveling operations—*viz.*, that the mean sea-level is higher, by 7 inches, at the head of the gulf, and by 4 inches, midway up, than it is at the mouth of the gulf.

(66.) During the present year the tidal observations which were taken at the Port of Tuticorin, in the year 1871-72,—with a self-registering tide gauge, similar in all respects to those employed by Captain Baird—have been reduced by the harmonic method, by Mr. Roberts of the Nautical Almanac Office, who has long been employed in reducing tidal observations for the British Association, and whose good services, in aiding Captain Baird in the preparation of his Notes on the Harmonic Analysis of tidal observations, I have already acknowledged in my report for 1872-73. Mathematical expressions have been deduced for each of the several tidal constituents, by means of which the height of the tide, at any moment, may be computed with great exactitude.

NO. XII.—GEODETIC.

ELECTRO-TELEGRAPHIC DETERMINATIONS OF LONGITUDE.

(67.) In consequence of Captain Herschel's absence from this country, on leave to Europe, and of the services of Captain Campbell having been placed at the disposal of Colonel Tennant for an entire year—to assist in the operations connected with the observations of the Transit of Venus at Roorkee—the differential determinations of longitude by the electro-telegraphic method, which were commenced in 1872-73, have been suspended, and the two assistant surveyors and small native establishments employed on them were transferred temporarily to the parties under Major Branfill and Captain McCullagh.

(68.) Captain Campbell's services were replaced at my disposal at the end of April, when the field season of 1874-75 was so nearly ended that it would not have been practicable to resume the electro-telegraphic operations. Captain Campbell came up from Roorkee to Mussooree to frame with me a programme of operations for the following field season, to be undertaken by himself and Captain Heaviside, whose services would be shortly available, for the purpose.

(69.) The first part of the programme was to endeavour, during the approaching season of recess, to ascertain the cause of the imperfect performances of one of the Transit Instruments, while employed in the operations on the line Madras-Bangalore-Mangalore, and to dispense with the induction coils—involving troublesome batteries and frictional electricity—which had hitherto been a constantly recurring source of failure and disappointment in the manipulation of the electric chronographs; *vide* paras 79 and 85 of my report for 1872-73. Both these duties have now been successfully accomplished, as will be seen on reference to Captain Campbell's report in the Appendix. The reduction of a portion of the previous observations—which remained in hand when the party had to be broken up, and has been held in abeyance ever since—has now been completed by Captain Campbell; the final results from the whole of the observations have been found to differ by only ·03 of a second of time, from the preliminary results by a portion of them which have been already published.

NO. XIII.—GEOGRAPHICAL.

YARKAND MISSION. TRANS-HIMALAYAN EXPLORATIONS.

(70.) In my report for last year I stated that, on the return of Sir Douglas Forsyth's Mission to Eastern Turkestan, Captain Trotter—who had been attached to the Mission on my recommendation, in order to utilize any opportunities which might occur for prosecuting geographical investigations—had returned to the Head Quarters of this Survey, and was supervising the reduction of his astronomical observations and the compilation of a map of the country, which were being done for him in this Office.

(71.) The map and his Narrative of the Geographical Operations, with full details of the results, have already been submitted to the Government, and are published in the Official "Report of a Mission to Yárkand in 1873, under the command of Sir T. D. Forsyth, K.C.S.I., C.B.", which was printed at the Foreign Department Press in 1875. It is now therefore only necessary for me to give a brief capitulation of the geographical acquisitions which were the fruits of the labours of himself, and of the Pandits and other natives especially trained for Himalayan Explorations, who were sent to assist him.

1st. The positions of Káshghar, Yárkand, Tashkurghán and Kila Panjah (on the River Oxus, in Wákhán) have been very exactly determined, by astronomical observations; they have been used as the basis of the mapping, and the positions of all other places have been laid down differentially from them.

2nd. The routes from Káshghar to the Chadirkul Lake, on the north, to the Belowti Pass, on the north-east, and to Marálbáshi, on the east, have been surveyed, the two first by Captain Trotter and the third by Captain Biddulph. The one to the Chadirkul Lake had been previously surveyed by Russian Officers, and it serves as the first connecting link between the British and the Russian Surveys in Central Asia.

3rd. The routes from Káshghar to the south-west, to Badakshán and Kabul, viá Tashkurghán and the Pámir Lands, have been surveyed up to Kila Panjah and to points in Wákhán and near the sources of the River Oxus, some of which had been previously fixed in 1837 by Lieutenant Wood of the Indian Navy, and others by the Native Explorer who is known as the Mirza.

4th. The course of the Panjah Branch of the River Oxus has been surveyed from Wákhán through Shighnán, and down to Kila Wámar and Pigish in Roshán, whereby a considerable portion of the remarkable bend in the river, along the northern border of Badakshán, of which nothing was known previously, has now been clearly defined.

5th. The routes from Yárkand to Khotan, and from Khotan to Kiria and the Sorghák gold fields, on the road to China, and from Kiria southwards, across the Kuen Luen range and the Thibet plateau to the vicinity of Gartokh and Rudokh, have been surveyed.

6th. Various routes between Ladákh and Eastern Turkestan over the Karakoram and the Kuen Luen ranges have been surveyed, some for the first time, though of others we were already in possession of maps of varying degrees of accuracy, which had been constructed by Messrs. Johnson, Hayward and Shaw.

(72.) All these, and more particularly the surveys of the routes over the Pámir Lands and of the course of the Oxus, are very valuable additions to the geography of Eastern Turkestan; and they are especially gratifying to myself as having been obtained, almost entirely, through the instrumentality of an Officer of this Department who was attached to the Yárkand Mission on my recommendation, in order to make the most of the opportunities which would be afforded for surveying these interesting, but hitherto badly mapped, regions.

(73.) On the completion of his map and report, Captain Trotter was about to proceed to Europe, when the Havildar who had been deputed to make a survey of the unknown portions of the course of the River Oxus, and the Pandit who had been deputed to survey the direct road from Ladákh to Lhása and then to make further explorations, returned to Head Quarters, almost simultaneously, though from such opposite directions. Each of them brought with him numerous journals and records of astronomical observations and route surveys, from which maps had to be constructed and the information extracted and put into a suitable form for publication, as has been done by Major, now Lieut. Colonel, Montgomerie in his reports of the Trans-Himalayan Explorations. Believing that this work could not be performed by any one better than by Captain Trotter, I asked him to postpone his return to Europe, and to undertake it; and he cordially assented to my proposal, though he was thereby disappointed of the gratification of an early return to Europe, which he had been looking forward to. It is to him therefore that I am indebted for the "Report on the Trans-Himalayan Explorations during 1873-74-75", which accompanies this report, and of which I now proceed to give a brief epitome.

(74.) Starting from Kabul, the Havildar struck at once to the north, instead of taking the usual circuitous route to the west, by the Bámian pass. He crossed the Hindú Kúsh range by the Sarolang pass, and, descending to Khinjan, took the direct route by Nárin and Ishkamish to Faizabad in Badakshán, the greater portion of which had never before been surveyed. Thence he proceeded *via* Rusták to Koláb, crossing the Oxus at Samti. His instructions were to follow the course of the Oxus upwards, as closely as possible; but he found that this would have led him away from the main lines of communication and rendered him open to suspicion, and that to advance at all into this *terra incognita*, it would be necessary for him to preserve his assumed character of a travelling merchant, and to keep to the most frequented roads. He proceeded in a north-easterly direction, *via* Khawáling and Ságri-dasht, to Kila Khumb (the capital of Darwáz) where he again struck the river - here called the Panjah—at the northernmost point of its course through the mountains, between its rise in the Pámir plateau, and its downward plunge into the plains of Koláb and Badakshán. From Kila Khumb the Havildar advanced for a distance of about 50 miles in a south-easterly direction, along the right bank of the river, making a detour to Kila Wanj *en route*; and finally be reached Yazghúlám, the frontier village of the principality of Darwáz. Most unfortunately he was turned back at this point, under orders from the Khan of Darwáz, who happened at the time to be at enmity with the Khan of Shighnán. Thus his exploration of the river was stopped at a distance of about one long day's journey from Pigish, the lowest point reached by Captain Trotter's native surveyor from the opposite direction. Being ignorant of what this man had already done, and most anxious to complete his survey of the bend of the river, the Havildar eventually returned to Faizabad, and went on to Ishkashim, the well known village on the river, at the eastern end of the bend; he then followed the river downwards, but was again stopped and turned back, this time by the Khan of Shighnán. There is therefore a gap, probably of about 20 miles, between the work of the Havildar from the west, and that of Captain Trotter's agent from the east, which is to be much regretted; but on the other hand it is a matter of congratulation that so large a portion of the course of the Oxus, which was unknown when that river was adopted as the Northern Boundary of Afghanistán, by the British and the Russian Governments, has now become clearly defined.

(75.) Compelled to return from Yazghúlám to Koláb, the Havildar, instead of directly retracing his steps to Faizabad, struck westwards, through regions, on the north bank of the Oxus, of the geography of which very little was known. His route determines the position of the important town of Kabádián, and proves that the Surkháb River—which rises in the Alai plateau to the south of Khokand, and passes through the principality of Karátigin—joins the Oxus, not near Koláb, as has long been supposed, but at a point about 80 miles lower down. His route survey was carried southwards from Kabádián,—crossing the Oxus at the Iwachik ferry—down to the well known town of Khulm, and thence eastwards, *via* Kunduz and Talikhán, back to Faizabad.

(76.) While the Havildar's observations were being worked out and mapped in this Office, information was received of the Russian expedition to Hissár, in the summer of 1875. As yet no full accounts or maps, which may have been published by the members of the expedition, have reached this country; but from the "Glance at the Results" by Herr. P. Lerch, which is translated from the *Russische Revue*, and published with notes by Colonel Yule in the Geographical Magazine for November 1875, it appears that Koláb and Kabádián are two of the points which were visited and fixed by the Russian Officers. Thus a second connecting link has been obtained between the British and the Russian surveys in Central Asia.*

(77.) A Mullah, who had been recently trained by the Havildar, was deputed to explore the course of the Kunar River, from its junction with the Kabul River near Jalálabad, to Chitrál, and then on to its source in the Hindú Kúsh range. This man ascended the river as far as Asmár, where he found any further direct advance impossible at the time, because the people of Asmár were at war with the neighbouring Káffir tribes. He therefore made his way over the range of hills on the left bank of the river to Janbatai, a place on the Havildar's route in 1870 from the Punjab to Badakshán, which route the Mullah followed as far as Chitrál. Thence he struck into new ground, ascending the course of the river, *vid* Mastuj, up to the Baroghil pass; and after crossing the pass he worked up to Sarhadd Wákhán, the position of which had been fixed by Captain Trotter. His work was very carefully executed, and it has shown that the positions for Dir and Chitrál, which were determined by the Havildar, require to be altered by a few miles. It gives the entire course of the Kunar river with the exception of a length of about 25 miles through the Káffir hills immediately above Asmár.

(78.) Pandit Nain Singh—the Pandit *par excellence* of Major Montgomerie's Trans-Himalayan Explorations, whose name it is no longer necessary to suppress as he has recently retired from active employment—was one of the explorers who were attached to Sir Douglas Forsyth's Mission, with a view to being sent into the countries lying either to the north or the south of the Gobi Desert, should an opportunity present itself. As this was not found to be feasible, he was sent, on his return from Yárkand to Leh, on an exploration to Lhása, by a route lying considerably to the north of the one which he had previously taken, and which is described in my report for 1866-67. His instructions were to return to India from Lhása, *vid* China, if possible, otherwise by some hitherto unexplored route through the Bhotan Hills.

(79.) He left Leh in July 1874, and succeeded in crossing the Thibetan frontier, in the disguise of a Láma, or Buddhist priest. Passing about 15 miles to the north of Rudokh, he travelled nearly due east for a distance of more than 800 miles, over a new line of country, separated from the valley of the Tsanpo— or Great River of Thibet—by an almost continuous range of snow mountains, which trends eastwards from the Alang Gángri peaks, in longitude 81°, up to the Ninjin Thangla peaks, south of the great Tengri Nur Lake, in longitude 90½°. His road lay, throughout, over an extensive table land ranging in height from 13,900 to nearly 16,000 feet above the sea level, a region containing a few gold

---

* While those pages were being passed through the press I received a copy of the table of "the Latitude, Longitude and Altitude of certain points in Hissár by M. Schwarts, a member of the Scientific Expedition of 1875 to that country", which is published in the Russian Turkestan Gazette No. 49 dated $\frac{9}{21}$ December 1875. The positions it gives for Koláb and Kabádián are very fairly accordant with those deduced from the Havildar's work as will be seen from the following values.

| By M. Schwarts | | | By the Havildar | |
Latitude.	Longitude.		Latitude.	Longitude.
37 54 32	69 46 24	Koláb,	37 50	69 48
37 34 28	68 12 15	Kabádián,	37 22	68 11

The longitudes are referred to the meridian of Greenwich.

fields, and numerous lakes and streams, and almost covered with rich pastures; the inhabitants are bands of nomads, who dwell in tents and regulate their movements by the supply of grass and water available for their flocks and herds. The Pandit struck the Tengri Nur Lake at its north-west corner, and travelled along the northern coast of the lake—a distance of nearly 50 miles—to the opposite corner, whence he turned southwards to Lhása.

(80.) He had spent three months at Lhása on the occasion of his first visit, without being discovered to be a British employé. On the present occasion, one of the first men he met was a Muhammadan merchant whose acquaintance he had made at Leh. Fearing that he might be betrayed, he hurried away at once, without waiting for the arrival of a caravan from Leh which was bringing him ample funds for further explorations. It was thus necessary for him to abandon all idea of working his way back through Western China, as his remaining funds would barely suffice to carry him back at once to India.

(81.) The most direct route for him to take was happily one which lay considerably to the east of any that had been previously explored. He followed the Tsanpo (or Brahmaputra) River for a distance of 30 miles, in a portion of its course through Thibet about 50 miles lower down than the lowest which had been reached by previous explorers, and his observations have enabled the course of the river to be laid down approximately for a further distance of about 100 miles, so that the part which still remains unknown is now materially reduced. He crossed the Bhotan Hills by the route from Chetang vid Tawang into Assam, which lies nearly north and south on the meridian of 92°. And finally he brought his work to a close at the town of Odálguri in British territory, and, going down the Brahmaputra river by steamer, reached Calcutta on the 11th March 1875. His astronomical and boiling point observations were very numerous and satisfactory, and his work has been excellent throughout.

(82.) Thus a rich harvest of geographical results—now published in detail for the first time—has been obtained from the labours of the Pandit, the Havildar, and the Mullah; and happily it has been acquired without loss of life or serious misadventure, such as have too frequently been met with in these arduous and hazardous explorations.

NO. XIV.—THE COMPUTING OFFICE.

EXAMINATION, FINAL REDUCTION AND PUBLICATION OF THE OBSERVATIONS.

(83.) Mr. Hennessey—who has for so many years been in charge of this Office, and to whom its present state of efficiency is so greatly due—has been absent on furlough to Europe since the 1st January 1875. The honours have been recently conferred on him of being elected a Fellow of the Royal Society of London, and an M.A., *Honoris causâ*, of the University of Cambridge. During his absence the charge of the Office has devolved on Mr. Cole, by whom its varied and responsible duties have been carried on to my entire satisfaction.

PERSONNEL.

J. B. N. Hennessey, Esq., F.R.S., M.A., &c., Deputy Supdt. 1st Grade.
W. H. Cole, Esq., M.A., F.R.A.S., Offg. Dy. Superintendent 3rd Grade.

Computing Branch.
Mr. W. Todd, Surveyor 2nd Grade.
„ C. Wood, „ 3rd „
„ H. W. Peychers, Surveyor 4th Grade.
Mr. J. Keating, Assistant Surveyor 4th Grade.
Mr. J. Kennedy, Assistant Surveyor 4th Grade.
Baboo Gunga Pershad Computer.
„ Cally Mohun Ghose, „
„ Kally Coomar Chatterjee and 11 other Computers.

Printing Branch.
Mr. M. J. O'Connor, Printer.
19 Compositors and 3 Pressmen.

Photozincographic Branch.
Mr. C. G. Ollenbach, Zincographer.
„ C. Dyson, Photographer.
2 Apprentices, 1 Map Keeper and 3 Pressmen.

Drawing Branch.
Mr. G. W. E. Atkinson, Surveyor 3rd Grade.
5 Draftsmen, 4 Asst. Draftsmen, and 12 Apprentices and map Colorists.

(84.) The Office has been employed in its usual duties of carefully examining and reducing the observations, and publishing the ultimate results of such portions as have been finally treated, and preliminary results of the portions which await the completion of further triangulations before they can be finally disposed of. The 3rd and 4th Volumes of the "*Account of the Operations, &c.*", have been completed and are now in the hands of the binders. They contain full details of the principal triangulation which is contained in the Sectional Figure known as the North-West Quadrilateral, the limits of which are,—on the east, the middle Indian meridian, 78°,—on the south, the western half of the line from Calcutta to Kurrachee,—on the west, the British Frontier line from Kurrachee to Peshâwar,—and on the north, the western half of the Himalayan Range. Of the Synoptical Volumes—which give the results of the principal and secondary triangulation for each series included within these limits, in a condensed form, for the use of geographers and surveyors—three had been published by the date of my last report; in the present year two more, viz., No. 4, the Gurhágarh Meridional Series, and No. 5, the Rahún Meridional Series, have been published: No. 6, containing both the Jogí-Tílá Meridional and the Sutlej River Series, has been completed and is now in the hands of the binders; and No. 7, containing the North-West Himalaya Series and the Kashmir Triangulation has been got ready for the press.

(85.) Another Sectional Figure of the principal triangulation is known as the South-East Quadrilateral; its limits are,—on the north, the eastern half of the line from Calcutta to Kurrachee,—on the west, the central meridian of 78°,—on the south, the eastern half of the line from Vizagapatam to Bombay,—and on the east, the coast line from Calcutta to Vizagapatam. This section I had fixed on to be taken up, for final reduction, on the completion of the North-West Quadrilateral; and it has now been disposed of in a most satisfactory manner, under the supervision of Mr. Cole, to whose interesting report on the subject (in the first appendix), I must invite attention. The third Figure, known as the North-East Quadrilateral, comprises the whole of the country between the one now completed and the eastern half of the Himalayan range (up to the meridian of 89°); its reduction is now in hand.

(86.) Though Volumes III and IV of the *Account of the Operations, &c.*, are now in the book-binders' hands and might be shortly issued to the public, I propose to postpone their publication until the completion of Volume II, which should be issued simultaneously with them. That volume is intended to give an historical account of the triangulation, and descriptions of the methods of procedure and of the instruments which have been employed; to set forth the mathematical formulæ which have been adopted for the several calculations, and to give full details of the final steps in the reduction of the North-West Quadrilateral, when the several chains of triangles are regarded, no longer as separate series, but as a single triangulation, which has to be made consistent *inter se*, and with the four base-lines at its corners. A considerable portion of the volume has been completed and passed through the press, but the part appertaining to the North-West Quadrilateral is still in hand. The preparation of the volume has necessarily fallen in great measure on myself, and it has frequently had to be laid aside, when other matters of more immediate interest required my attention. Of these one of the most important has been the final reduction of the Pendulum Observations, and the preparation of the results for publication. Happening from my long personal as well as official acquaintance with the late Captain Basevi, to be more familiar than any one else with the work he had done, and with his ideas regarding the reduction of his observations, I felt it incumbent on me to set aside Volume II—which is on subjects that are familiar to several of the Officers of this Department, who might complete it in case of mishap to myself—and take up the volume which is to be devoted to the pendulum operations.

(87.) A great mass of experimental observations which Captain Basevi had made—for the determination of the reduction of the given vibration-numbers of the pendulums at the actual temperatures and atmospheric pressures under which the swings were observed, to the corresponding vibration-numbers in a standard temperature and in a vacuum—were still awaiting investigation and discussion at the time of his death; and until this work was completed the final reduction of the observations at the several pendulum stations could not be performed. I took it in hand about the time of Captain Heaviside's return from England, after completing the swings at the stations in the original programme of operations which Captain Basevi did not live to visit. It proved to be a very formidable task; for, excellent as were the experimental observations and great the care which had been bestowed on them, they presented many perplexing anomalies for examination, and these had to be patiently investigated *seriatim*, before any final decision, as to the inferences to be drawn from them, could be formed. All these investigations have now been completed, and the whole of the observations at the several stations visited by Captain Basevi and by Captain Heaviside have been reduced accordingly. A descriptive account of the general operations from first to last, of the several investigations just mentioned, and of the methods adopted in reducing the observations, and full details of the observations themselves—with the results obtained after the reductions—have now been completed and printed for publication; they fill 379 closely printed quarto pages, which will probably form part of Volume V of the *Account of the Operations &c.*, of this Survey.

(88.) It is intended to devote the remainder of the volume to papers by Captains Herschel and Heaviside. Captain Herschel is engaged in investigating the reduction of the pendulum vibration-numbers, from the values deduced for the respective levels of the several stations, to the corresponding values at the sea-level. In previous operations of this nature the reduction to sea-level, which is a question of attraction, has never occupied much time or been of much importance, owing to the fact of the stations having been usually situated at places near and very slightly above the sea. Here on the contrary the selection has, in some cases, been made expressly for the purpose of experiment in the direction of attraction. The stations on the table land of Southern India, and on the skirts of the Himalayas, and more particularly the station of Moré, at an altitude of 15,400 feet in the interior of the Himalayas, are of this kind; and a considerable majority of the stations, on the meridional axis of the Indian continent, are situated at elevations of upwards of 500 feet. There are also several stations which are either at or very little above the sea-level; for one of the objects of the operations was to investigate the relations of sub-oceanic to sub-continental attraction.

Captain J. Herschel, R.E., F.R.S. &c., Deputy Superintendent 2nd Grade.
Captain W. J. Heaviside, R.E., Deputy Superintendent 3rd Grade.

(89.) But enquiries of this nature are far from easy. The calculation of the attraction of a mass of known simple form is often troublesome; but where the mass is a mountainous district, it is absolutely necessary to make a variety of assumptions, of a more or less precarious character, on the legitimacy of which the result must depend. The principal of these has reference to the configuration of the surface. The effective attraction is separable into two parts of which the chief requires an accurate knowledge of the contours immediately round the station; while the other, depending on the curvature of the earth, does not become sensible for some distance, and then continually increases in importance—or more correctly, would do so, but for the general tendency of increased area to present a lower average height,—so that it is hardly too much to say that the effect of distant continents must not be entirely overlooked. Thus a knowledge is required in detail of the masses standing on given areas, and Captain Herschel has necessarily devoted much time to their estimation. The mean height of about 500 half degree squares have thus been obtained for Northern India, Kashmir, Turkestan and Thibet, by a close study of the best available maps. It is probable that the area to be dealt with will have to be extended so as to include a great part of the Indian continent, should it appear worth the labour. Under the circumstances, there is still much work to be done, before the results of the pendulum operations can be satisfactorily elucidated and prepared for publication.

(90.) On his return from England, Captain Heaviside was employed in this Office, for nearly a year, in completing the reduction of his own observations with the Royal Society's pendulums and in supervising the printing of them and of the greater portion of Captain Basevi's observations. He also completed the reduction of his observations with the Russian pendulums—which had been sent to India to be swung at some of the Royal Society's pendulum stations, with a view to establishing a connection between the operations in India and in Russia— and with Kater's convertible pendulum, which had originally been employed in determining the relations between the length of the seconds' pendulum, and the British Standard Yard, and was re-employed by Captain Heaviside for the conversion of the differential results by the Royal Society's pendulums into absolute values. Full accounts of these operations, and details of the observations and reductions, have been printed in readiness for publication, either in Volume V or in a supplemental volume; they occupy 181 pages of closely printed quarto. The results have been provisionally reduced to the sea-level, but corrections may have to be applied to this portion of the reductions, after the completion of Captain Herschel's investigations. The result of the determination of the present relations of Kater's convertible pendulum to the Standard Yard, which is now being made in the Ordnance Survey Office, Southampton, by Colonel Andrew Clarke, R.E., C.B., is also awaited, to complete the subject, before publication.

(91.) I have every reason to be much obliged to Captain Heaviside for the assistance which he has rendered to myself, and the pains he has taken in completing his own share of the pendulum work. He is now employed with Captain Campbell in the determination of electro-telegraphic longitudes in the Madras and Bombay Presidencies.

NO. XV.—CARTOGRAPHY.

(92.) The preparation of a 3rd Edition of the Map of "Turkestan, and the Countries between the British and the Russian Dominions in Asia," was commenced last year. Each of the four sheets comprising the map had been entirely redrawn, on the same scale as that of the two first editions, viz. 1 inch = 32 miles, and a large amount of valuable and newly acquired information of Khiva and the regions on the eastern borders of the Caspian Sea—obtained directly from the Topographical branch of the Russian War Office—and of the Northern Frontier of Persia, from British sources, had been inserted. But the completion of the map was postponed until the results of Captain Trotter's surveys, in connection with Sir Douglas Forsyth's Mission, and of the explorations of the Pandit, the Havildar and the Mullah—which I have described in the Geographical Section of this Report—could be introduced into the map. It was then finished and published.

(93.) A new map of Northern Afghánistán, and the Countries to the north of the Trans Indus Frontier—on twice the scale of the Turkestan Map— has been prepared under Captain Trotter's supervision, to indicate the results of the explorations of the Havildar and the Mullah; it is appended to this report. It is exceedingly interesting, its larger scale permitting of much detail being shown which had to be omitted from the Turkestan Map. Two maps, compiled from the Pandit's surveys of the routes from Ladákh to Lhása and thence to Assam, also accompany this report, and contain much new and valuable geography.

(94.) Of other work done in this office I may specify the preparation of Captain Trotter's Preliminary Map of Eastern Turkestan, which has been published with Sir Douglas Forsyth's Report; the completion of the Gazetteer Maps of Kumaun and Garhwál, of 23 Final Charts of the triangulation, in illustration of the Synoptical Volumes, and of 5 Preliminary Charts of triangulation which as yet has not been finally reduced; and the revision of the Map of Routes in Northern India. A tabular statement of the work is given at the end of the first appendix.

(95.) It now only remains for me to acknowledge the valuable services which have been rendered by my Personal Assistant, Mr. H. Duhan, who has relieved me of a considerable amount of official routine work, that would otherwise have taken up much of my time. Mr. L. H. Clarke, has rendered good service by the careful and punctual performance of his duties in the corresponding office and as general store-keeper; and he also acted for three months as Personal Assistant, during Mr. Duhan's absence on leave.

(96.) An abstract of the out-turn of work executed by each of the Survey Parties, whose operations can be exhibited in a tabular form, is given on the following page.

J. T. WALKER, COLONEL, R.E.,

Supdt. Great Trigonometrical Survey.

DEHRA DUN;
Dated 3rd March 1876.

Post-script. 27th March 1876.

Circumstances, which I am not at present in a position to explain, have disappointed me in the expectation of being able to append Captain Trotter's account of the Trans-Himalayan Explorations, during 1873-74-75, to this Report. An account will I trust be published hereafter, and at no very distant date.

J. T. W.

Abstract of the out-turn of work executed by the Great Trigonometrical Survey Parties, during the Official year 1874-75.

	1	2	3	4	5	6	7	8	9	
DESCRIPTION OF DETAILS.	Banmid Longitudinal Series 24-inch Theodolite.	Assam Valley Triangulation 12-inch Theodolite.	Eastern Frontier Series 24-inch Theodolite.	Burmah Secondary Triangulation 12-inch Theodolite.	Jodhpur Meridional Series 24-inch Theodolite.	Kaidywar Topographical Survey.	Guzerat Topographical Survey.	Dehra Dún Topographical Survey.	Kumaun and Garhwál Survey.	TOTAL.
Number of Principal Stations, newly fixed, ...	27	...	13	...	28	...	...	...	...	68
Number of Principal Triangles, completed, ...	42	...	19	...	28	...	...	...	...	89
Area of Principal Triangulation, in square miles,	791	...	3,153	...	2,472	...	...	...	...	6,416
Lengths of Principal Series, in miles, ...	93	...	100	...	104	...	...	...	...	297
Average Triangular Error, in seconds, ...	0·55	...	0·48	...	0·47	...	...	...	...	...
Average Probable Errors of Angles, in seconds, ±	0·17	...	0·25	...	0·16	...	...	...	...	...
Astronomical Azimuths of verification, ...	1	...	...	...	1	...	...	...	...	2
Number of Secondary Stations whose positions and heights have been fixed, ...	34	...	24	5	12	185?	24	98?	26?	356?
Number of Secondary Stations whose positions only have been fixed, ...	1	...	...	14	...	...	3	...	...	18
Number of Secondary Triangles of which all 3 angles have been observed, ...	10	...	24	11	22	211	85	119	28	455
Length of Secondary Series, in miles, ...	...	...	...	28	55	...	...	...	...	83
Area of Secondary and Minor Triangulation, in square miles, ...	1,096	...	2,240	2,000	681	2,200	559	490	800	10,075
Number of Points fixed by intersection, but not visited, ...	36	30	40	41	14	668?	92	596	56	1,570?
Length of boundary lines and check lines traversed, in miles, ...	...	...	...	...	...	1,117	448	461	...	2,026
Area topographically surveyed on scale of 1 inch = 1 mile, in square miles, ...	...	...	...	...	...	...	...	...	2,176	2,176
„ topographically surveyed on scale of 2 inches = 1 mile, in square miles, ...	...	...	...	...	...	1,749	392	...	...	2,141
„ topographically surveyed on scale of 4 inches = 1 mile, in square miles, ...	...	...	...	...	...	...	983	225	...	1,208
Number of Revenue Survey Stations and boundary junction pillars, fixed by triangulation, ...	...	...	...	...	1	...	...	22	...	23
Do. of Principal Stations selected in advance, ...	20	...	10	...	7	...	...	...	...	37
Lengths of Approximate Series, Principal, in miles, ...	59	...	100	...	64	...	...	...	...	223
Do. of Approximate Series, Secondary, in miles, ...	...	38	...	94	55	...	...	...	...	187
Number of Towers constructed, ...	5	...	1	...	...	...	...	...	...	6
Do. of Pillars and Platforms constructed for Principal Stations, ...	19	...	13	...	17	...	...	...	...	49
Do. of Pillars constructed for Secondary Stations, ...	...	6	3	7	26	...	...	...	...	42
Do. of miles of Rays cleared, ...	118	106	...	29	15	...	...	...	...	268
Do. do. Path-way made, ...	2½	...	190	5?	1	...	...	...	...	198½?
Do. Hill-tops cleared of forest and jungle, ...	...	...	28	7	...	...	...	5	...	41
Do. Principal Stations whose elements were computed, ...	27	...	10	...	42	...	...	...	...	79
Do. Secondary and Traverse Stations... whose elements were computed, ...	35	...	50	71	101	...	...	6,871	...	7,128
Do. Preliminary Charts of Triangulation, ...	1	...	1	...	1	...	...	...	...	3
Do. Topographical Maps completed, ...	...	...	...	...	...	16	14	7	13	50
Do. Principal Stations placed under official protection, ...	35	...	...	...	17	...	...	...	...	52
Do. Stations protected and closed, ...	12	...	...	...	24	...	...	...	...	36
Do. Points fixed by traverse, ...	...	...	...	...	...	?	1,133	6,005	...	7,138?
Do. Aneroid Determinations of Height,...	...	...	...	...	...	...	...	236	148	384
Do. Azimuths computed, ...	1	...	...	...	3	...	...	...	...	4

APPENDIX.

EXTRACTS FROM THE NARRATIVE REPORTS

OF THE

EXECUTIVE OFFICERS IN CHARGE

OF THE

SURVEY PARTIES AND OPERATIONS.

PLAN of a G. T. SURVEY STATION with OBSERVATORY and SIGNAL PLATFORMS shewing
BRACED STAND for the GREAT THEODOLITE, designed by MAJOR B. R. BRANFILL, Depy. Supdt.
G. T. Survey, for the RAMNAD LONGITUDINAL and MADRAS COAST SERIES (S. Section).

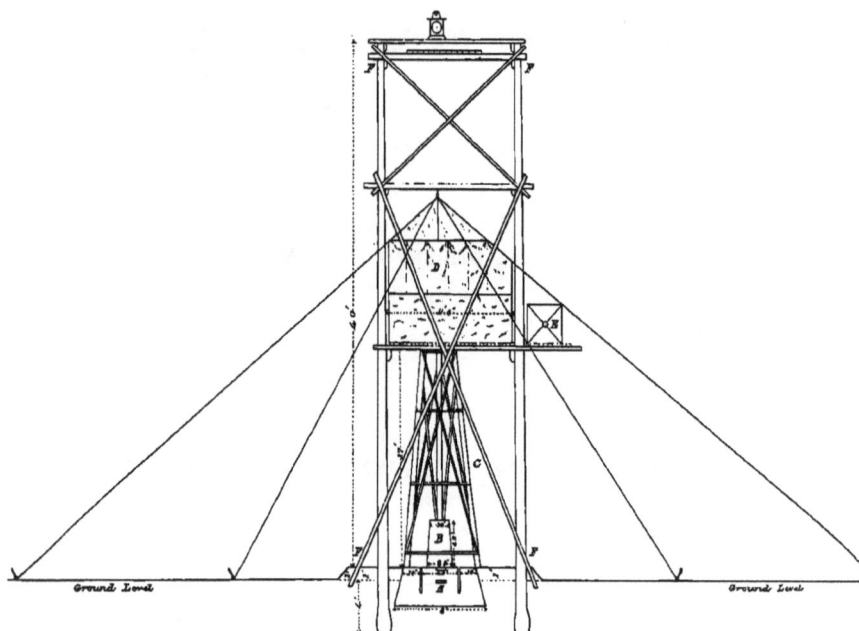

REFERENCE.

A Masonry pillar and annulus, section and plan.

B Closing pillar in section.

C Wooden braced stand, elevation.

c'c' Masonry-support for ditto, in plan.

D Observatory tent, ⎫
E Theodolite box, ⎬ in elevation and plan.
FF Palmyra platform, ⎭

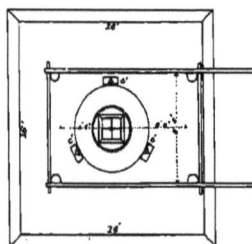

Scale 1 inch = 8 feet.

Photozincographed at the Office of the Superintendent, Great Trigonometrical Survey, Dehra Dún, November 1875.

G. BYRON, PHOTO.   C. G. OLLENBACH, ZINCO.

Extract from the Narrative Report—dated 30th September 1875—of MAJOR B. R. BRANFILL, Deputy Superintendent 2nd Grade, in charge Madras Party.

(2.) The party took the field at Bangalore on the 9th of November, reached Trichinopoly on the 6th of December, Madura on the 12th and the scene of operations on the 20th of the same.

(3.) The Rámnád Longitudinal Series had been approximately laid out the previous season

The Season's work to be done. as stated in my last Annual Report (para. 15). There remained to build most of the stations and clear the rays between them, to select a few of the station sites which had not been precisely determined on, to observe the final angles, and to close and deliver the stations. Besides this the Series had to be extended along the coast to Rámeswerem with a view to the Ceylon connection.

(4.) I myself took in hand the completion of the stations and rays of the first figure, a quad-

Disposition of Party. rilateral. I sent Mr. Belcham to complete the next figure in advance, also a quadrilateral, and the other two Assistants to build the stations and clear the rays further in advance; one on the northern flank and centre, and the other on the southern flank along the coast.

(5.) I commenced observing on the 29th December at the stations of Kulayanallúr and

Final observations after three weeks entrusted to Mr. Belcham. Kovilpatti, forming a side on the east flank of the Great Arc (Lat. 9°) and completed final observations at the six stations forming the first two figures (quadrilaterals) by the 20th January, when I was joined by Mr. Belcham, whom I had recalled to take up the observations, a more mechanical process requiring only the skill and care which I felt sure Mr. Belcham possessed and would use.

I was impelled chiefly to take this step in consequence of the great probability of the observing overtaking the approximate series (which eventually it actually did) and because I felt that the most important duty in such difficult country (wooded plains) is the laying out the series in advance to the best advantage, and directing the "Approximate Series" operations generally. I remained instructing and assisting Mr. Belcham for a week, when after seeing him through the observations at two stations I felt confident that I might leave him to pursue the duty successfully.

(6.) I then proceeded to inspect Mr. Potter's work on the north flank and centre, and, after

The Executive Officer in charge proceeds to the front. selecting a station in advance and tracing and clearing the ray to it, visited Mr. Laseron, and gave him a little practical and personal instruction in the art of ray tracing, &c. I next proceeded to build the stations and clear the rays on the south flank, leaving Mr. Laseron to combine his efforts with Mr. Potter in pushing on the building and ray-clearing of the centre and north flank, where the most masonry work was required to be done.

(7.) The stations of the north flank and centre of the Series were hollow masonry pillars

Stations of the north flank and centre, hollow masonry pillars with timber scaffolds. 15 to 25 feet in height, banked up with earth and gravel as high as practicable to prevent vibration, with a timber scaffolding to support the observatory, run up to a much greater height for the signal.

(8.) The south flank lay along the series of sand hillocks and ridges that skirt the coast

Temporary stations of timber provided on the south flank. enveloped for the most part in dense palm forest. The shifting hillocks of drift-sand were not suitable for permanent principal stations, but by their means, temporarily occupied by stations composed of wooden piles, all the permanent buildings on the coast which could be observed, were fixed, and the series rendered a double one throughout. A large mark-stone was buried deeply in the sand, and should the sand hillocks remain, may be found for many years to come. I propose having a pile of (coral) stones placed over each such station more permanently to mark the site in case the sand does shift.

(9.) By the end of the first week in March the Approximate

Completion of Approximate Series. Series on the south flank and centre was complete as far as Rámnád.

(10.) The south coast of Rámnád, from the lands-end (Toni Turei="boat ferry") opposite

Difficulty of the palm forest. Pámban, for 50 miles to the westward, is fringed with a belt of dense palmyra forest, intermixed with groves of cocoanut trees, through which it was very difficult indeed to carry on the series, but there was no alternative thereto. To traverse or "trace" each ray through the forest was possible, but to "clear" it quite impracticable; to overlook it was the only thing to be done, although the palms grow to a height of 60 feet and the ground is generally quite flat. At a distance of a mile or so inland from the sea shore there is a ridge or series of hillocks, rising from 10 to 50 feet above their base, formed probably by the constant action of the sea breezes blowing the dry surface sand of the beach inland, and depositing it in the palm forest where it is sheltered from farther action of the wind. After selecting and erecting high flags on the most promising of these sand hillocks for stations, the line between them had to be traversed and the height of the intervening hillocks and of the palms carefully noted. The latter has to be done by climbing the highest palms and examining the height of the forest in the direction of the ray. About midway the most prominent palm in or near the line is sought for and marked with a flag, whence the flags of the two station sites at the ends of the line can be seen ; a sextant here may be used to measure the angle contained by the rays to the station flags, which, with the traversed (perambulated) distances gives the approximate position of the true ray, and one is able to judge by examining the top of the forest whether the ray is likely to prove practicable or not, and where most clearing is necessary. Having found the direction of the ray, (and if it still seems practicable) a trial line has to be carried, from one or both ends, over the palm tops, the leaves of which have to be cut off leaving a clear gap of 10 or 12 feet in the forest. If the trial line proves all right it has to be widened some scores of trees have to be cut down and their price, (from one to four shillings each), settled and paid to the owners.

(11.) As the sand hillocks do not attain the height of the palms, within 15 or 20 feet probably, the eye and signals have still to be raised, and for this purpose
Means for raising eye of observer and signals. I prepared a portable braced stand of wood 17 feet in height, or else in its place set up palmyra logs steadied by piles of sand, and found they both answered well, and thus the eye of the observer was raised more than 20 feet above the top of the sand hillocks. A much greater height was necessary for the signal, and this was obtained by means of lofty scaffolds, for which as regards length, the palmyra is well suited. The longest, straightest and most convenient trees cut down on the line were selected and split up into halves for the four uprights, and into quarters and eighths for the beams, braces, ties, &c. The stalks of the palmyra leaves furnish the rope by which the scaffold is put together and made fast. Such a scaffold takes two or three days to erect under ordinary circumstances and costs about Rupees 30 (thirty).

(12.) In one instance I met with a great disappointment and the loss of several days. The lofty gopuram, or entrance-tower, of the Tirupulláni Temple, (a sacred
The brahmans refuse permission to occupy as a station the Tirupulláni temple tower. Vishnu fane,) offered a tempting site for a station, eighty (80) feet above the ground, by which five rays to adjacent stations over the palm forest were well commanded. I visited the place and was allowed to mount and observe with a small theodolite from the summit of the tower without demur, and was informed that I might use it as a station, engaging to do no damage that I would not make good. When however I came subsequently to prepare the station, and had been allowed free access a second time, and had taken the necessary measurements, for the platform, &c., the brahmans and others attached to the temple, and a large portion of the inhabitants of the village that profits by the temple funds, turned out to the number of some hundreds, and surrounded my tents in a state of much excitement, protesting against my again entering the tower, unless I was prepared to pay many thousands of rupees for its purification, whilst some of them demanded money for the pollution that had already occurred through my presence. I tried for sometime to conciliate them but without effect : they refused me farther access, locked the door, and kept a watch to prevent by force any attempt on my part to effect an entrance, which of course I did not make, though it was with much reluctance that I felt obliged to abandon so advantageous a site. I afterwards learnt that on the day of my first visit a subscription was made and a sum of one or two rupees collected to enable the priests to perform certain purification ceremonies on account of my visit. On hearing this I sent word to the temple manager that I was ready to pay a rent equal to the amount of any such expiatory sacrifices as they deemed absolutely necessary, for as long as we occupied the tower, but they refused. They added that they had already caused the unhallowed government telegraph wire to be removed from passing too near their holy building to a distance of some hundreds of yards, and that they could not let me use their tower at any price. No anger or ill will was displayed on either side, but I was not prepared for such persistent obstructiveness, considering I had already established a station on the unfinished gopuram at Uttara Koshamangei, a celebrated Shiva temple only a few miles distant, without any difficulty. The gopuram, or entrance-tower, of any Indian temple is perhaps of less use, from a religious point of view, than the ordinary tower of an old English Church ; and in this instance, as is common in Hindu temples, the tower being the sole resort of monkeys and bats, and seldom or never cleaned, was in a most filthy state, and so disgustingly loathsome as to be almost unendurable to any

one passing through it. That my presence should be thought a greater pollution to the temple than that of these unclean beasts and birds, reveals a state of mind that is somewhat remarkable. I lost no time in searching for another point, but the delay caused by the abandonment of this cost me about a week in the busiest time of the season.

(13.) My next care was to extend the series to Rámeswaram with a view to the Ceylon connec-
Eastern extension for the Ceylon connection by an island series. tion. After a careful examination of the country to the south-east of Rámnád, I found that the increasing density of the palm forest and the rapid narrowing of the land, obliged me to attempt to utilize the islets of the coral reef which lies parallel to the shore of the main land at the distance of 4 or 5 miles. I accordingly threw out a quadrilateral to the southward based on the last, (south-easternmost) side of the triangulation which lay convenient for the purpose, and found no great diffi-culty in extending the series by a succession of quadrilaterals as far as the lands-end.

(14.) The islands are scarcely above the sea at high water of spring tides, and are composed
The islets of the coral reef. of coral and sand and devoid of fresh water or anything to live upon, although they are covered with a coarse grass, weeds and some bushes and trees, the last planted by the fishermen who resort there from the main land: several of them were densely covered with high tangled bushes that caused much trouble to clear a ray through. Labor, material, food and water have to be transported thither by boat, and as constant communication by open boats or canoes must be maintained, there are only about three months, February, March and April, between the monsoons, during which this work can be carried on. The last four stations built and observed at, are of good permanent masonry, as also are two of those in advance, on the island of Rámeswaram, observed to but not yet observed at. High scaffolds were required at all of the island stations, and in building these only one accident occurred throughout, which I think very fortunate, considering that we were all of us inexperienced in this kind of work, and that our materials and implements were of the most unwieldy and roughest description. An ordinary palmyra freshly cut down weighs about 1¼ tons, and each half tree over forty (40) feet in length, probably ¾ a ton, to raise which we had a working party of from 12 to 20 common coolies and 3 or 4 klassies. A few stout bamboos for sheers, props, &c., a pair of metal blocks with a stout cotton rope and plenty of "Coir" (cocoanut fibre) rope were all our implements, but they proved sufficient for the purpose.

(15.) The one accident alluded to, occurred by a faulty beam, injured in the felling of the
Accident. tree, having been inadvertently used on the top of the scaffolding to support the signal platform. On noticing this I ordered its removal, but it gave way in the process, and two klassies were precipitated to the ground from a height of about thirty (30) feet; one of them was hurt a good deal, and is scarcely well yet.

(16.) I completed these stations and cleared all the rays by the middle of April, when I
Conclusion of the island Approximate Series. found it necessary to desist, as it was useless to prepare the remain-ing stations in advance, some of which must be temporary stations, (being unavoidably on hillocks of drift-sand), unless the final observations could be carried beyond them to two or more perma-nent stations still farther in advance, and this was quite out of the question. I therefore contented myself with visiting the Islands of Kachi, and Neduvan (or "Delft") and ascertaining that there was no great difficulty in any of the rays in advance, as far as the completion of our share of the series.

(17.) Mr. Belcham meanwhile pushed on the final observations with vigour and success
Progress of the final observations. without interruption, except for one or two days when he overtook the building parties. On reaching Rámnád S. on the 18th March I joined him for the Azimuth observations, and after two days and nights instructions and assistance, found him quite able to complete the work alone, which he did after I left him without any mishap. I am glad to say he continued to work steadily, and made good and uninterrupted progress, until he brought the work to a close by the 1st May, when I ordered him to desist, and to return to quarters, as the entire party was much exhausted, and a large portion of it sick or ailing, officers included.

(20.) Mr. Belcham has done a good season's work having conducted the final observations
Mr. G. Belcham. with the 24-inch theodolite very creditably to himself, this being his first season, and quite to my satisfaction. The conduct of the observing and signal parties for the island series required much forethought and good arrangement; but he was equal to the occa-

sion, and no mishap or failure occurred to hinder the work throughout.

(21.) Mr. Potter has worked willingly and well as usual, taking an interest in his work. He has built 7 masonry pillar stations, and traced and cleared 19 miles of rays. He suffered severely in health towards the end of the season.

Mr. C. D. Potter.

(22.) Mr. Laseron commenced the season's work under the disadvantage of not having had any previous practical experience of ray tracing and clearing in a flat and wooded country, and he found much difficulty in making the "trial lines," laid off from his ray trace observations, come out right, even after repeated trials, and in this way he lost considerable time. He appears however to have worked hard and willingly, and will I do not doubt master the difficulty with a little more practice. He has built 3 high signal scaffolds, traced and cleared 64 miles of rays, and built, partially or entirely, 6 masonry stations. He also built closing pillars at, and delivered over charge of, 12 principal stations.

Mr. E. W. Laseron.

(24.) The country is as flat as possible, although there is a slight slope down towards the sea of a few feet per mile. Inland the country is generally deep black (cotton) soil, which is immediately succeeded near the coast by deep sand. The black soil is extremely rotten, becoming impassable in wet weather and nothing but yawning cracks when dry. The former inland, is much wooded and intersected by tanks, and a net work of bunds, dykes, and supply channels for collecting water, and it is everywhere cultivated with high growing corn crops, so that the view in all directions is obstructed or confined to a limit of a mile or so even when the observer's eye is raised above the corn which grows up to ten feet in height. Moreover every tank bed (and tanks abound, witness Indian Atlas Sheet No. 80), is overgrown with a dense thicket of thorns of a kind of hard and matted "Bábul" (mimosa Arabica) that is exceedingly tedious to clear a ray through.

General features of the country, soil, &c.

Except for the occasional sand hillocks, the vicinity of the coast offers no advantage over the inland tract, in as much as it is overgrown with palm forest, thorn jungle and cocoanut groves.

(25.) Compared with previous seasons' triangulation, with hill stations, the signals and observations were very wild, as was to have been expected. Excepting the first few, nearly all the rays were unavoidably very low, grazing within 10 or 15 feet of the ground, and a few much closer still.

Bad signals and grazing rays.

(26.) We have eleven rays more or less clear over the land giving a mean factor of positive refraction $= + 0.023$ of the contained arc. Thirty-six rays graze more or less badly over the land, giving a mean factor of negative refraction $= - 0.111$: the largest of these is $- 0.289$, and there are several others about one fourth of the contained arc.

Factor of Refraction, inland largely negative: over sea positive, but small.

Of sixteen rays over the sea, some clear and some grazing, only one gives negative refraction, $(-0.087,)$ the rest are all positive, and generally between $+ 0.020$ and $+ 0.040$, the mean being $+ 0.032$ of the contained arc, or about half that of an ordinary series of hill stations.

(28.) Besides the plan of the Island Series for the Ceylon connection, one hexagon of the Madras Coast Series to the north of Rámnád was laid out, and three of the stations built by Messrs. Potter and Laseron, and the former has also reconnoitred the country with a view to another hexagon in advance, but nearly all the rays require regular tracing and clearing.

Extension of the Madras Coast Series.

(29.) It is much to be regretted that the remaining portion of the Island Series for the Ceylon connection cannot be begun before the end of January when the violent wind of the North-East monsoon moderates, and permits open boats, the only craft our funds admit of, to ply between the islands of Palks Straits to the east of the Pámban channel and Adam's bridge, and keep the signal and observing parties furnished with water and supplies.

Plan of work for the ensuing season.

I therefore propose employing the strength of the party on the approximate series (Madras Coast) to the north of Rámnád under my own immediate supervision, selecting and building the stations, tracing and clearing the rays between them until enough of the series has been laid out to occupy the observing party until it is time to take up the Island Series, so that as little time as possible may be lost in traversing the interval between the advanced part of the Madras Coast Series, and the uncompleted part of the Ceylon connection.

(30.) I am happy to state that I believe a considerable reduction may be effected by the adoption of only low masonry pillars and platforms, no larger than absolutely **Reduction of cost.** necessary for the sake of permanence, in place of the usual high towers. I commenced the Rámnád Longitudinal Series by building **high masonry pillars with timber** scaffoldings. Ten of these pillars, with a mean height of 21 feet have cost at the rate of Rs. 175 each and the cost of the observatory **Comparative cost of masonry pillars and timber scaffold stations.** platform was Rs. 40 making a total of Rs. 215 per station, exclusive of supervision.

(32.) Latterly I have constructed log or pile stations for the sand hills, and low masonry piers for the ordinary soil, with lofty scaffolds for the signals. I find the average cost of eleven observatory signal· scaffolds with a mean height of 27 ft. to be only Rs. 30 per station, and I estimate the cost of low masonry platform stations to be about Rs. 20 each, making a total of Rs. 50 per station, showing a saving of Rs. 165 per station. I enclose a plan and elevation of such a station as I have found best adapted for this series and most economical, shewing the portable braced stand with observatory and signal platforms.

(33.) I may notice moreover that the 17 ft. stand has proved more steady in a wind than the **Stability of 17 ft. braced stand.** 20 ft. pierced masonry pillars previously used.

(34.) One disadvantage of the lofty signal scaffolds is the difficulty of plumbing the signal **Disadvantage of lofty signal scaffolds.** apparatus in a wind, particularly in a high wind. This may be obviated by using heavier plummets supported by fine brass wire, and by protecting the plumb line by a long strip of cloth or matting spread on the windward side.

(38.) Mr. Bond, Assistant Surveyor of No. 2 Extra Party, was placed under my orders for temporary employment in the vicinity of "Bangalore," so as to be **Mr. J. Bond, No. 2 Extra Party, temporarily attached for special employment near Bangalore.** ready to join Captain Campbell, R.E., at any time during the season on short notice, in case that officer (who was employed at Roorkee in the observations of the Transit of Venus,) should become available for Latitude observations on the Madras Meridional Series, or **Ordered to execute some minor triangulation in Mysore.** other work. I accordingly directed him to execute some minor triangulation in Mysore which was much needed by the fiscal and other surveys, to make a more extended connection of the G. T. Survey principal triangulation with that of Colonel Lambton, and to fill up a gap left in the net work of triangulation of the latter, on the north flank of the Bangalore Longitudinal and between the Great Arc and Mangalore Meridional Series, lying to the south of the "Chitaldroog" district of Mysore.

(39.) He left Bangalore on the 24th November with a party of 12 Klassies most of whom were quite new to the work, and starting from the side Rámadevara-botta **Takes the field and lays out the Series.** —Dodur-manga. H.S. of the Great Arc (in Lat: 18° 30′) he proceeded westwards, and in about seven weeks laid out a series of thirteen triangles reaching as far as Shimoga S., about 108 miles in length, and covering an area of 1,096 square miles. Two of these stations are previous G.T.S. points, besides the three initial and terminal stations above named, and four of them are identical with old stations of Colonel Lambton's Survey at which the ☉ mark was found.

(40.) He then commenced to retrace his steps observing the angles, but was very shortly prostrated by sickness and obliged to return to Bangalore for medi-**The observations stopped by sickness for seven weeks.** cal treatment. The season was a very unhealthy one generally throughout that part of Mysore and the men of the party suffered considerably from fever, &c., as well as Mr. Bond.

The delay from this cause was more than a month. As soon as permitted by the doctor, Mr. Bond again took the field and the observing was resumed on the 28th of March after an interval of seven weeks during the best season for the observations, and continued till the end of May when he had completed 10 triangles in all.

(41.) But he now discovered that one of the rays of his approximate series which he had accept-ed without due examination, on the credit of Colonel Lambton's Chart **Approximate Series impracticable.** of the triangulation in which this ray is shown (and therefore might well have been supposed practicable) was obstructed, and the observ-ing was therefore brought to an end.

Revised.

Bad weather prevents completion of the Series.

An alternative station was selected but the cloudy weather of the S.W. monsoon had set in, and no farther observations could be obtained. After waiting for three weeks more in the hope of completing the series, I ordered Mr. Bond to return to Bangalore where he arrived on the 24th June, leaving the three triangles connecting his work with its proper base, incomplete. I trust however that he may be able to complete this work shortly before the ensuing field season.

(42.) Mr. Bond appears to have worked energetically and to have done his best. His men were many of them new to the work and insufficiently trained, and he was much delayed for want of good and timely signals, as well as by sickness.

List of the proper names of the stations and points fixed, &c., given.

(43.) I beg to append to this Report an alphabetical list of the proper names of the stations and land marks fixed during the season, together with those of the surrounding villages and some of the neighbouring towns, that will appear on the records of this party. The vernacular (Tamil) form of each place-name was obtained on the spot, as well as its etymology or root-meaning.

I do not suppose that all I have given in the list is correct, but it may be accepted as the current local tradition and usage, and as a near approximation to the approved method of transliteration.

Root-meanings of the place-names presumed to be of use and interest.

(44.) I apprehend that such information, if faithfully and carefully collected, may prove of much general interest, and of special use towards removing from the face of the English maps and charts of India, the great diversity of rendering and erroneous spelling that have hitherto disfigured them, and I propose to give annually such a list as I have now drawn up of the common and particular place-names met with during the field season.

Proper Names of Places and Common Village Names met with on the S. E. Coast of India, chiefly in the Madura District of Madras (Tamil Country).

Agraháram	From S., a village, street, or quarter of a town, set apart for brahmans.
Alankulam	Vil. pr. n. (?) = "*Banyan tank*" fr. álei, the banyan, and kulam, a pond or tank.
Alattúr	Alei, the banyan (tree), and úru, a village or town.
Ammá	Mother, "*mamma*", Lady. Amman-Kovil = "*Lady chapel*", a temple or place of worship devoted to one of the female deities or demons.
Anakattu	Eng. "*anicut*"; fr. Tel. addamu, between, across, and kattu (to bind) a bund, dam, embankment; also T. anei, a dam, dyke, &c.
Anappan	Pr. n. A Canarese caste or tribe found in Madura.
Ancipár Tívu	Anei = elephant, párei = rock; and tívu = island (Madura coast) = "*Elephant-rock Island*".
Annapúnaikon-patti	Contr. for annapúva-náyakkan, a man's pr. n., and patti, a fold, or small village.
Appanúr	Vil. pr. n. (?) fr. appu, a stake or large peg, a wedge; or fr. appan = father, and úru = town, or large village.
Appá Tívu	"*Abbot's Island*". Appa = " papa", a term of respect. This island is also called "Shéra mudili" (loc. corr. for *Maulavi*) the name of a Muhammadan saint, whose tomb or shrine is much venerated.
Aramanei	"*King's house*", a palace; fr. arasan, a king, and manei, a house, dwelling.
Areikulam	Written *árei*, an edible water-plant, (marsilea quadrifolia), but stated to mean "*six tanks*", as if fr. T. áru, six, and kulam, a tank, reservoir.
Armugam Kottei	"*Six faced (one's) fort*"; áru = six, and mukham; fr. S., the face; a name of Kartikeiya, the War-god, Subramanya.
Aru	A river. Com. use same as for six; in comp. árr, pronounced. átt: see below.
Asuran	Fr. S., a demon.

Athodei	"*River course*"; fr. áru q. v., and odei, a course (fr. otu=run, drivo).
Attánkarei	"*River bank*" or "*River side*"; fr. áru q. v., and karei, a bank, shore.
Atúr	A common village name in S. I., possibly for 'álattúr', q. v.
Aykkudi	"*Shepherd's abode*"; fr. áyan, a shepherd, pastor; and kudi, a habitation, dwelling.

B is not a letter of the Tamil Alphabet, but p is sounded like it sometimes, as after m and n, and, with v, is used instead of it in foreign words, and also for p'h, and b'h.

Chadayan	(?) Pr. n. of a caste or tribe in S. I., erroneous for kadeiyan.
Chakkili Modu	"*Currier's mound*"; fr. chakkiliyan, a currier; and medu, a hillock.
Chakrákottei	From chakrá, S., the discus, Vishnu's weapon (a quoit) and kottei, a fort.
Chattram	Vulg. use for chattiram, a native rest-house. Hind.=chhattar.
Chávadi	The Anglo-Indian "*choultry*" of old writers, a native rest-house for travellers.
Cheri	An assemblage, a hamlet, a small village; allied to C. keri, a street, row, cf. H. khorá, Ar. and H. karya, a hamlet or small village.
Chinni appa Dargah	(?) "*Papa Chini's Dargah*" (Muhammadan shrine), a pr. n.
Chippi-kulam	"*Shell tank.*"; fr. T. chippi, a little shell.
*Daghopa and Dahgop	S., fr. deh, the body, and gup, to hide; a Buddhist altar, vimána or shrine (see foot note).
Dalaváy-puram	Dalaváy, the minister, or commander-in-chief, in S. I., and puram, a town.
Devipattanam	"*Devi's town*" S., Devi=goddess, a name of Párvati, Shivá's consort, and pattanam, a town, a seaport (?).
Dhanu-kodi	"*Bow's point*"; fr. S. dhanus, a bow, and kodi, a point. The extreme S.E. point of Rámesweram Island, a sacred bathing place.

In vulgar colloquial use y is commonly prefixed to e initial.

Endal or Yenthal	A small tank; a com. affix to names of small villages in Madura.
Eri	A large street of water, lake, a big tank.
Etteyápuram	Pr. n., a town and zemindári (estate) of the Ettappan (a Náyakkan) family of Tinnevelly.

G only represented in Tamil by k which is pronounced as k when initial, or double, but like g when medial.

Gandha máua-parvatam	Pr. n. of the highest point of Rámesweram Island. S., parvata=a hill.
Giri	S. A mountain in S. I.; com. applied to a hill named in Hindu mythology or history.
Gopala pattanam	"*Cowherd's town* (or port)"; fr. S. gopál, a cowherd, and pattanam or pattinam, q. v.
Idam-bádal	Perhaps fr. idam, loft, as there is a "*Valam* (=right)-bádal*" across the fen close by. Idam also means a place. If for Ithambádal="*Sweet songs*".
Ideiyan	A man of the herdsman caste, or tribe; (?) fr. idei=middle= middle-born, i. e., from Iswaru's breast.
Ilampunam	Corrupt. for llama-nattam. Nattam is the village-site, or building ground.
Iswara	S. The deity, Supreme God, Lord. In S. I. used for Shivá. "Issuran-koil"="*Shivá's Temple*".
Kachi Tívu	"*Shingle Island*"; fr. Kachchi, a broken shell or sherd; this island is formed of broken coral.

---

* NOTE.—Pagoda (formerly pronounced pá-god) may be derived from this by metathesis pa-go-da= (da-go-pa, Dr. Sargent). It may be from Pey-gudo Tel. (=Tam. Pey-kovil)="*Demon's, or devil's temple,*" or house.

Kadaládi	" *Sea bather* "; fr. kadal, the sea, and adi, a player, bather; (fr. a local tradition).
Kadaleiyúr	Corrupt, fr. kadasi=last, final; ellei, a boundary, limit; and úru.
Kádamangalam	Perhaps fr. kadu, a jungle, and mangalam=prosperity, fortune. A flourishing village.
Kadavu-Santei, or Kathavu-Chanthei	" *door, or gateway fair* "; fr. kathavu, a door.
Kadeiyákkulam	" *End tank* "; fr. kadei=end, (market). The root-meaning is last (born)=low caste. The Kadayar are below the Kallar.
Kadeiyár (kulam)	" *Kadeiyan's (tank)* "; a caste or tribe of fishermen (mostly Christians now) about Rámesweram.
Kádu	A barren place, jungle; an untilled or un-irrigated field.
Kal, Kallu	A stone, rock.
Kál	The leg; a quarter, (cf. H. páon, and páo) a stake, stem, prop, pole, shaft, &c.
Kalak kudi	Fr. kalam, a threshing floor, barn. Open field (see Kalari).
Kalari	Barren or brackish ground, a threshing floor=" *arena* ".
Kaliman gundu	" *Clay-mound* ", kaliman, clay, and kundu, a lump, boulder, heap.
Kallan	One of an indigenous tribe, addicted to thieving. Plur. kallar, the " colleries" of Orme's history and others.
Kammei, for Kanmáy	Com. use in Madura for an irrigation tank or reservoir, a common village name.
Kamma-patti	" *Tank fold* "; fr. kanmáy, a tank for irrigation, and patti, q. v.
Kammaya-naiken-patti	Pr. n. =" *Kammaya Naik's fold* ". Patti, a cattle fold, hence, a small village.
Kánjarangudi	Pr. n. (?) fr. kanjiram=" Strychnos nux vomica", and kudi, a habitation, dwelling.
Kappal-madei	An anchorage; fr. kappal a vessel, a ship, and madei (?) allied to madu, a pool, a place in the sea deep enough to anchor in.
Káppiliyan	One of a Canarese agricultural caste or tribe in Madura, with com. agnomen " Gaundan" (T. *kavandan*).
Karei	A border, shore, bank. Common affix to village names.
Karisal-puli	Karisal=black soil, blackness, or any thing black, and puli= tiger.
Karshá-Kulam	Vulg. (?) for Karisara, for karisal, q. v., and kulam, a tank.
Kasavangundu	(?) for kusavan, or vulg. koshavan, a potter, and gundu, a boulder, rock :=" *Potter's mount* ".
Katari (or kithari)-Amman Tívu	Kithari, corrupt. for Catharine=" *Lady Catharine's Isle* ", so called from an old R. C. Shrine there.
Kidáthirukei	Kidá (?) short for Tadáthagei, n. of Minákshi; tiru, holy, and kei, the hand.
Kilakarei	" *East-shore* ", v. sup.; about the largest seaport town between Tuticorin and Pámban.
Kíla-kidáram	" *East Kidáram* " (?) kidáram=a bowl, copper boiler, &c.
Kíle	In comp. =eastern; fr. kílo, below, because the country falls to the eastward.
Kodi-kánal	" *Creeper wood* "=" *Rattan (cane) forest.* " The first English settlement on the Palney hills.
Kodi-modu	" *Flag-mount* "; fr. kodi, a flag, streamer, a creeper, &c., and modu, a mound.
Kodumudi	" *Flag (staff) point* "; fr. kodi, a flag, v. sup., and mudi, a crown, crest, topknot.
Kokkádi	(?) " *Cranes play* "; fr. kokku, a crane, and ádi=player.
Komba-úthi	" *Horn blast* " or " *Horn blower* "; fr. kombu, a horn, and úthu, blowing.
Koneri	" *King's lake* "; fr. kon=king, and eri, a lake, a large sheet of water.
Kottan Kulam	The old name of this place is Kunthi-nagaram, once a place of pilgrimage.
Kottei	A fort. Com. affix to pr. names of fortified villages.
Kovil or Koil	A (Hindu) temple or place of worship (?) fr. ko=king, pastor, and il, a house.

Kovil Kulam	"*Temple-pond*"="*Church-lake*."
Kovil-patti	"*Church-fold*"; fr. kóvil, a temple, and patti, a cattle fold, a small village.
Kúdal-i	A junction. Com. term for the confluence of rivers.
Kudi	A house, dwelling.
Kudisei	A small dwelling=huts, cottages.
Kudi-irupu or Kudiyiruppu	A dwelling, residence; com. n. for a small hamlet in S. I., especially near the coast.
Kudirei-katti-mundal	"*Horse-bound-point*", local name for the Periapattanam headland; fr. kuthirei, a horse, and kattu, to bind. It is said a horse sacrifice was made here.
Kulam	A pond, tank, reservoir of water; usually for irrigation.
Kulaya-nallúr	Pr. kula-Sekhara-n.="*Race head-ornament*"; fr. the n. of an early Pándyan king; and nallaúru="*good-town*"="*fair-ville*".
Kumára-kurichi	Fr. a pr. n. of Subramanya, Kumáran=son (of Shivá), and kurichi =a settlement, village.
Kundu-kál	(?) "*Squatting point*"; kunthu=setting (on), kál, the leg, (?) going on tiptoe. The W.S.W. point of Rámeswaram Island, fr. a legend about Hanumán.
Kunru	Pronounced kundru (and in Mal. kunnu), a hill, a small hill, a round stone, a boulder rock.
Kurichi or Kurichchi	A settlement. Com. n. for a small village or hamlet in S. I. properly on a hill, for kundrachi (?).
Kurtálam	(Vulg. "*Courtallum*")=(?) "*Stunted Banyans*" (? fr. kuttru, ? dwarf) and álei, the banyan.
Kurusadi	"*Cross-foot*"; an island nr. Pámban; so called fr. a R. C. Shrine, (kurukke=a cross) and adi, the foot.
Kuruvi-nattam	Fr. kuruvi, a bird, a small bird, and nattam, a village site, a village.
Kuttam	A tank, a large pond.
Kúttam	A collection, assemblage, a crowded group, cluster, &c.; applied to a collection of huts, a hamlet.
Kuttei	A small tank.
Kúvar-kuttam or Kúvat-kuttam	(?) "*Noise-tank*"; fr. kúval=cooing, a crowing noise, and (?) kuttam, q. v., applied to a little village of a few inhabitants.
Latchmi	Fr. S. Lakshmi, pr. n. of Vishnu's consort, or Sakti, goddess of wealth, fortune.
Letchmi-puram	"*Lakshmi's town*".
Lingam	The sacred phallic emblem, symbol of Shivá under which he is worshipped by Saivas.
Madam	Fr. S. and H., math, a school or college for brahmans, a cloister, monastery.
Madura	Town and district or collectorate : derivn. doubtful; perhaps more prly. spelt Madhura (Nelson).
Malei	A hill, mountain, com. use; hence Malabar for Malei-war, and Maleiyálam, the Malabar language.
Malei	Rain. Hence Malenádu, the Maluád or rainy district of Mysore.
Maleipatti	"*Hill-fold*"; very com. n. for vil. at foot of, or near a hill.
Malesworapuram	Pr. n. (?)="*Hill-gods-town*".
Man	Earth, soil.
Manal	Sand.
Manapád (?)	"*Sand-hill*"; pr. n. of a headland on the Tinnevelly coast between Trichendúr and Cape Comorin.
Manaar	Vulg. use for Mannár=a town, settlement, fixed abode, fr. mannu to be fixed, lasting, to remain; or (?) fr. manuár=enemies, foes.
Mandalam	Fr. S., a region, circle, district, (cf. L. mundus, the world) "Coromandel" (?) for cholamandal, cf. tondamandalam, also= a small temple or shrine.
Mandala-mánikam	Pr. n.="*Region of gems*", or rubies. Mánikkam (fr. S. mani, a gem), a precious stone, gem, a ruby.

Mandapam	A covered court or hall, built with pillars, a rectangular open-sided hall, before or near a temple.
Manditop	Pr. n.; fr. mandi=a monkey, and toppu, a grove, a "tope".
Mangalam	Matrimony, praise, delight; com. affix to pr. ns. of wealthy villages of brahmans, rich in rice fields=a flourishing village.
Mannáli	Pr. n. of an island, perhaps fr. its being composed of manal=sand.
Mantri	A chief counsellor, prime minister; a com. prefix.
Marakkayar-pattanam	" Skippers' town (or port)"; fr. marakkalam, a ship, (mara, wood, and kalam, a vessel), marakkaya=ship-owner.
Máriyúr	Once a large seaport town on the Gulf of Manár.
Maravan, pl. Maravar	Pr. n. of a tribe of the inhabitants of Madura, of lawless and predatory habits.
Máyákulam	" Everlasting-pond"; fr. máy-á, that vanishes not, and kulam, a pond, tank.
Medu (see Metu)	A height, &c., comly. pronounced more as if written modu, moedu, or möru; e. g., Nagari Mor, a hill near Madras.
Mela-kal-úruni	Pr. n.=" upper (i.e. western)—kal-úruni", (perhaps stone tank); fr. úruni, a common village tank.
Mela-madei	" Upper (i.e. west)—sluice "; fr. madei, a small water-sluice for irrigation, &c. The land first watered being nearest to the sluice is called Mel-madei, and the lowest or last watered land is called Kíl-madei.
Mele	In comp. mel=up, upon, (upper), hence western, west; because the country rises to the west.
Melmánthei	" West mánthei " (?) for manthei, mandei or mantei=a herd, flock, (?) assembly.
Metu or Medu	A height, hillock, rising ground, com. use for a swell of high land.
Mínáchi, also in T. Mínátchi	For S. Mínákshi=" Fish-eyed"; a name of Párvati, consort of Shivá=káli.
Mínaugudi	(?) " Fish-village".
Mottúruni	Pr. n.; fr. mottei, bald headed, bare, (?) from being en an open bare plain, devoid of trees, &c.
Mudaliyár or Mudali	A title of respect, in com. use in Madras, applied to a Tamil caste.
Mudukulattúr	" Old-tank-town "; fr. muthu, ancient, kulam, a tank, and úru, a town.
Múkkeiyúr	Pr. n.=" Cape-town" or " Bill town"; fr. múkku, the nose, bill, beak; (?) so named fr. being near a headland.
Mulli Tívu	" Conch (shell)—Island "; fr. mulli, a shankh, or conch shell, once abundant here.
Mundel or Munthal	A headland, cape, point, loc. use for munei, a headland, promontory.
Murugei-talei	Fr. murugei, coarse coral rock, and (?) talei, the head: a common affix, cf. leatherhead, gateshead, &c.
Musal Tívu	" Hare-Island"; fr. musal or muyal, a hare. Hares are still found on Hare-Island at Tuticorin.
Muttupottei	" Pearl-town "; fr. muttu, a pearl (cf. H. moti), and pottei, a (market) town, a village with shops, a bazaar.
Muttúruni	" Muttu's úruni" (i.e. tank). Muttu, perhaps the name of the man who had the tank made. A common proper name fr. muttu, a pearl.
Nádu	A district, country, as opposed to town. In Madura comly. applied to Kalla tracts, (see kallan). The opposite of Kádu jungle.
Naduvupatti	" Middle-fold"; fr. nadu, middle, and patti, a fold or small village.
Naiken	Short for Náyakkan, a title borne by men of Telugu (or Telinga) race, a chief, leader.
Nája-mundel	Pr. n. (?) and mundel (q. v.) a headland.
Nallatanni Tívu	" Sweetwater island "; fr. nalla, good, and tanní, water (properly tanníru=cool water).

Nallúr	" Good-ville " ; fr. nalla, good, fair, and úru, a town.
Naripeiyúr	(?) " Fox-bag-ville "; fr. ' nari, a fox, pei (or pai), a bag, and úru, a town or village.
Nattam	The village site, ground reserved for building on. Com. village name in S. I.
Náyakkan	Fr. S. náya, a leader=náya, guiding. In S. I. a title of warlike Telingas, (the " Poligars")=chief, leader; allied to náyar, the honoured Sudras of Malabar.
Neduvan Tívu	On old maps " Nedöen", locly. pronounced Nedum=" Long island".
Negapatam	Vulg. for Nága-pattanam. Nága, snake, " dragon", and pattanam, a town, (?) a seaport town.
Nellúr	" Rice town", fr. nel, raw rice, "paddy", and úru, a town.
Nerinji-nattam	" Thistleham" or " thornville " ; fr. nerunjil (vulg. " nerinchi "), a weed bearing a thorny seed: (tribulus terrestris).
Nerinji-patti	" Thistlefold." See above.
Nochchúruni	Fr. nochchi, a medicinal tree (vitex negundo), and úruni = a tank or well.

In Tamil w is vulgarly prefixed in pronouncing words beginning with o.

Oppilán	Pr. n.=(?) " the incomparable "; fr. oppu=likeness, comparison, and illádavan=one destitute of,="he who is without". (?)
Ottangudi	(?) " Builders' village " ; fr. ottan, a well digger, or builder (a caste), and kudi, a dwelling.
Ottapidáram or Otta-pandáram	Fr. a man's name, and a corruption. of " (Alagiya)-pándiya-puram", the ancient name.

P. in Tamil is pronounced like b sometimes, as after m and n, and stands for the labials (Surd and Sonant alike) p, p'h, b, and b'h.

Pád	Tel. a hill, (?) corruption of H. pahár, a hill.
Pádi	A village or town, (in comp.bádi) a row; com. affix to vil. pr. n. (?) a bar (in the sea).
Pádu	A place, situation, location, besides many other meanings.
Pákkam	Com. affix to vil. names near Madras ; (?) allied to pakkam T., a side, vicinity, or (?) to bágam, a division, share.
Palaya	Old. Cf. Gr. palaios, old.
Páleiyam	A place or district under feudal tenure (a fief), a cantonment, military suburb, a village.
Pálkulam	" Milk-tank " ; fr. pál, milk, (cf. C. nál, and Gr. gala, milk).
Pallam	A ditch, hole, pit, ravine, water course, hollow, &c.
Pallan, pl. Pallar	A very low caste of labourers in S.I.
Palli	A hamlet, also a small town, a village : a fane, mosque, &c.
Palli-vásal	Com. use on the S. coast for a mosque, place of worship; fr. palli, a place of assemblage, and vásal, a door or gateway.
Palliamunei	Derivation. uncertain : n. of an island said to be named from the mainland of which it perhaps once formed a part.
Pámban	Fr. S. pámbu, a snake. Pr. n. of the town on Rámesweram Island, at the channel, dividing it from the mainland.
Pámbár	" Snake-river". A small river of the Madura country.
Paneiyúr	" Palmyra-ville"; from panei, the Palmyra palm, and úru, a town.
Paneiyeri-Enthal	" Palmyra-climbers' tank " ; fr. panei, v. sup. eru, climb, and enthal, a tank.
Pápánkulam	" Brahmans' tank". Brahmans are called pápa, and pápán, for · párpan (? = " Seer") in S.I.
Pápanásham	Fr. S. = " Sin-extinction", a sacred bathing place near the lowest cataracts of the Támraparnei river.
Pár	(?) for párei, a rock, crag : a common affix to pr. n. of villages, &c.
Parambu	High ground, a stony mound, gravelly waste, a ridge.
Parapana-valasei	(?) " Brahmans' retreat"; see pápán, valasei, Tel. a retreat.
Párei	A rock, com. use.
Pareicheri	" (Vulg. Parcherry)"="Pariah's hamlet", or quarters; fr. pareiyan, an out-caste, drummer, and cheri, a hamlet, place.

Parutti	Cotton, the cotton shrub.
Párvati	Pr. n. daughter of Himálayah, and consort or Sakti of Shivá; also called Durgá, Devi, Bhaváni, Káli, &c., at Cape Comorin ("kanniyá-kumári—the virgin maid") where there is a famous old temple in her honour; she is also called Bhagavati.
Pattanam	Fr. S., a town, a city, a large town.
Patti	A cattle-fold, herdmen's village, a small village (=c. hatti).
Pattinam *	A town by the sea or on a river. A seaport town, (a port).
Peisás-mundel	Fr. S. pisácha="*Demon-cape*". The northernmost point of Rámesweram Island.
Peria Kulam	"*Great tank*"; fr. periya, great, and kulam a tank.
Periapattanam	"*Great town*". This is said to have been an exceedingly large city some centuries ago.
Periúr and Perúr	"*Grand-ville*".
Perumál	"*Great one*"; fr. periyu, great, and ál, a person. A common name for Vishnu in S. I.
Pettei	A suburb, a town or village with shops, a market town, usually contiguous to a fort.
Pey-kovil	"*Devil's temple*". The Shánár (or Sánáns) and other low tribes worship a demon for god, i.e. a malignant deity.
Pillei	A child, son, a title assumed by some of the higher Tamil castes (cf. L. filius; fr. fil, &c.).
Ponthampuli	Pr. n. (?) fr. pontu, a hole, cave, and puli=tamarind (tree).
Pothikulam	"*Baggage-pond*"; fr. pothi="*full of sacks*", or packs. A tank where they unpack and rest, &c.
Poy-chal-lá-meyir-ayan-kovil	Pr. n. "*The lieless truthful (i.e. most true) lord's temple*".
Pú	A flower; also pushpam or pudpam from the S.
Pudu or puthiya	New, com. use. Pudúr="*new town*"; Pudu-kottei="*new fort*", (vulg. "*Poodoo-Cottah*").
Pudu-madam	"*New College*"; fr. the previous, and madam, a school or college for brahmans.
Pul	Grass.
Púlánkál	"*Púlám-branch*"; fr. púlám, a plant (the twigs of which are used for a toothbrush), and kál=a leg, properly limb-branch.
Puli	A tiger.
Puli	A tamarind (tree) sourness.
Pulieri	"*Tamarind-lake*"; fr. puliya (-maram) the tamarind (-tree), and eri, q. v.
Pulli	A spot, point.
Púmurichán	"*Flower-broken*"; from pú, a flower, (which the coral much resembles), and murichán=plucked or bruised. Name of a channel through the coral reef.
Puram	Fr. S. pur, purá and púr, a town, city, a considerable town with brahman inhabitants; waram, or veram is vulgarly used for this word, as in "Conjeveram", for Kánchipuram; "Mauliveram" for Mahá-bali-puram, near Madras.
Puram	T. a side, the outside: comly. applied to an outlying village, a suburb, com. T. affix to v. and pr. n. This word is said to have no connection with the previous "puram".
Putti Tívu	(?) "*Hummock Island*". Putti and pottei, are applied locally to shoals, reefs and sandbanks in the sea, cf. pottei, a mound or hillock, local usage.
Púvarasanshallitívu	"*Portia (-tree)-Shingle Island*", puvarasu-maram=the tulip tree.
Púvanáyakkanpatti	"*Púva Naik's fold*", (pronounced more like Boghanaiken-p.), a man's pr. n., and patti, a fold = a small village.
Baghunáthapuram	Pr. n. "*Raghunáth's town*".

NOTE.—In Northern India "Pattan" is frequent, on the rivers of the Panjáb, as Pák-pattan, Hari-ka-pattan, &c., and it is said to mean *a ferry* there (cf. H. patni, a ferry man); also on the "Jumna" and "Ganges"; e.g. Indrapat (F), Patna; also it is exceedingly common on both coasts of Southern India;—"*Seringapatam*" (Sri-ranga-pattanam) is on the river "*Cawery*" (Káveri).

Rájákapáliam — Vulg. for Rájákal-páleiyam. Rájákal (plural of Rájá) = kings, and páleiyam, q. v., = "*Kings'ton*".

Rámaswámi-madam — "*Rámaswámi's College*", on the S. coast of Madura founded by a former zemindár.

Rámesweram — Fr. S., Rámá, iswara=God, and puram (=? "*The town of Ráma's lord*").

Rámnád — Pr. n. of the zemindári estate and the town com. called by the natives Rámá-nátha-puram (*Lord Ráma's Town*) for which it stands.

Reddi — One of a Telinga (or Telugu) agricultural tribe or caste, of which there are some colonies in Tinnevelly and Madura.

S. in Tamil stands also for ch, j, jh, and sh, and the Sanskrit ksh, and is pronounced and transliterated variously.

Sambutti-yendal — Pr. n. Endal or yenthal, a small tank, com. in Madura.

Santei — (Vulg. shandy) a fair. The com. weekly village market of S. I.

Sáyalakudi — (?) "*Belle-house*" com. pr. n. of vils; fr. cháyal, beauty, and kudi, a dwelling.

Se- sen- sev-, &c. or Che- chen-, &c. — A. com. prefix meaning red. See following.

Senchadainátthapuram — "*Red-shocked lord's-town*"; fr. sen, red, chadai, matted hair, nátha, lord and puram, town.

Sengalanarodei — "*Red-water-course*"; fr. chongal (sen-kal, red-stone) neru, water and odei, a course (fr. odu=run).

Serveikárau — The title of the Ahambádiyan, tribe of Madura Tamils., hereditary servants or clansmen of the Sethupatis (Zemindárs of Rámnád).

Sethupati — "*Lord-of-the-causeway*" ; title of the Prince of the Maravars, Zemindár of Rámnád; fr. chedu, a causeway = Adam's bridge, and the ancient causeway of Rámesweram.

Sevalpatti — "*Red-fold*"; fr. sivappu, red, and patti, a fold, village.

Shalli-Tivu — "*Shingle-island*"; fr. challi, broken pieces of stone, brick, shell, &c.

Shomanúr — Pr. n. perh. derived fr. Shapana, or Sámana, a Jaina sect in S. I.

Shera-mudali or muthali — Pr. n. for maulavi, a Muhammadan worthy, saint, or sage named Shera.

Shevelmedu — "*Red-mound*"; fr. sivappu, red, and medu, a mound, high ground.

Shivá or Sivá — The 3rd deity of the Hindu triad; Saivas regard him as creator, destroyer and regenerator, and worship him in the form of the linga, his type or emblem.

Sonciporiyán-Kottei — "*Grandee's-spring-fort*"; fr. shonci, a (water) spring, poriyán = great one and kottei, a fort.

Sri — A name of Lakshmi, the consort or Sakti of Vishnu, goddess of prosperity, fortune.

Sundaramudeiyán — "*Beautiful-Udeiyán*"; fr. sundaram = beautiful and udeiyán, a title of the kallan tribe.

Suplápuram — Corrupt for Subramanya-puram = "*Town of subra-manya*" the Hindu Mars, god of war, son of Shivá.

Súrangudi — Pr. n. of a chief (súran = a hero; fr. S. suria, the sun), and kudi, a dwelling.

Taleimanár — (?) "*Head of Manaar*"; fr. talei, the head. The Ceylon end of Adam's bridge.

Taleiyáli — N. of an island; fr. talei, the head.

Támraparni — "*Copper-coloured*"; fr. S. támra, copper and varna, colour.

Tangamma-puram — "*Golden-lady-town*" (?).

Taui-chanthei — (1) "*Only-fair*"; (?) santei = a fair, market, (vulg. shandy). Old name Tani-cheyum.

Tanui-turei (? toni-turei, q. v.) — "*Water-ford*"; fr. tannir, water (prop. cool water), and turei, a ghát, ford, shore, &c.

Taravei — (?-vu.) A salt-marsh-swamp. com. use near the Madura coast.

Tareigudi — (?) "*Landham*", or (?) "*flat-house*"; fr. tarei, the ground, earth, a place, and kudi, q. v. (? a level place, flat).

Tattanadi — "*Parrot-river*"; fr. tattei, the green parrot, and nadi, a river.

Tedal or Tidal	High ground, a dry place in a river or marsh, a heap, swell of rising ground ; tidar, titei and tittu all mean very much the same.
Tekkei	Vulg. for terku (ten) south, southern, in oppn. to vada, north, northern.
Tenkadá	For ten–kadal="*south-sea*", a place on the south coast of Rámeswaram.
Tenkási	"*South Kási*", or Benares.
Teppukulam	"*Raft-tank*"; fr. teppam, a raft on which the idol is floated about.
Teri or Theri	Local name for the drifting sand hillocks or red sand wastes of Tinnevelly and Madura.
Thalaváypuram	"*Field marshal's town*"; fr. Talaváy=Dalaváy, title of the commander-in-chief, or minister of a South Indian Native Government.
Tidar	(Tedal, q. v.) a mound, dry bank in a marsh or river, &c.
Tinnevelly	Vulg. Eng. for com. Nat. pron. Tirnaveli, wh. is for Tiru-nel-veli= "*Sacred-rice-hedge*". The town stands in the midst of rice fields.
Tiru	Blessed, holy, sacred ; a name of Lakshmi=good fortune.
Tiruchúr	(Vulg. "*Trichoor*") (?) corruption of "Tiru-Shivá-per-úrú" = "*Holy Shivá's great town*".
Tirumálugandán Kottei	(?) "*Shivá-server's fort*"; fr. Tirumál, Holy one, and ukandán, obeyed.
Tirupatúr	(Vulg. "*Tripatoor*") for Tiru-pati (vulg. "*Tripetty*")=sacred-lord, and úru.
Tiruppuláni	Pr. n.; fr. tiru, holy, pul, grass, and áni ((?)=wearing) fr. the legend of Rámá having once slept here on the sacred (sacrificial) grass.
Tívu	An island (on Coromandel Coast *dívi*, on Malabar Coast *tiv.* and *dív.*) fr. S. dwípa=two waters.
Tíyanúr	Fr. tíyan= low-born, base.
Toniturei	"*Boat-ferry*", "ship-ford"; fr. toni, a boat, and turei, landing-place, ford, road=ghát.
Tulkapatti	"*Turks-fold*". Tulukkan or Tulukkar, as Muhammadans are called in S. I.
Turei	A landing place, the ford of a river, the haven of a sea.
Tuticorin	Corrupt. for Túttukudi, q. v.
Tutti-nattam	Fr. tutti, a plant ("*Sida Mauritana*") and nattam a village.
Tutti	A trifle, insignificant.
Túttukudi	The native name of "*Tuticorin*", said to mean "*scattered-habitation*"="*winnow village*".

U final is so softly sounded in Tamil as to be nearly mute.

Umuriampádu	"*(Sea)-weed-shore*", (?) from the accumulations of sea-weed so common about here.
Uppár	"*salt river*"; fr. uppu, salt, and áru, a river.
Uppu-tanni-tivu	"*salt-water-island*", in oppn. to "Nalla-tanni-tívu" (q.v.) an adjacent island where good water (to drink) is found.
Uru or Ur	A village, town, country ; com. appd. to large villages of Canarese or Telugu people in Madura.
Uruni	A tank or well. The common village tank, accessible to all in the place.
Uth	Com. affix. (for urru, prond. úttru) a spring, fountain.
Uttan or Vuttan	V. pr. n. (?).
Uttarakoshamangei	Pr. n., more fully, "Tiru-uttara-shri-koshamangei", a famous but decaying Shivá temple near Rámnád, about which there is a long legend.

V is used sometimes for b and w in writing foreign words in Tamil.

Vada	In comp.=north. By the English called Wada and Bada, e.g. Vada-karei, Wada-k. and Bada-k. "*North-bank*", *North-shore*.

Valam-bádal	(?) Perh. "Right (hand)-bádal", in oppn. to Idam-bádal, a vil. to left of the marsh close by.
Valasei	Tel.="*Removal*"=flight from home for fear of an army in the field, == " *a retreat*", com. n. of a village so occupied, Vulg. "Walsa".
Valei Tívu	(?) " *Sword-fish-island*" ; fr. vál-mín=the sword-fish.
Válinokkam	Pr. n. of a headland S. coast of Madura.
Váram or-Voram	Vulg. colloq. form of puram a town, also waram and weram.
Vásal	A doorway, entrance, gate ; pallivásal, a mosque loc. use.
Vayal	An open plain, a field, C. bailu. The vulg. "bile," "byle", vail, and boyal, &c. of Eng. maps.
Veli	A hedge, ward, wall ; com. affix to village names, as " Tirnaveli" see " *Tinnevelly*".
Medu Vellakára	" *White-man's-mound*" ; fr. velli, whiteness.
Velleiyammanpuram	" *White-goddess-town*" ; fr. vellei, white, ammál, goddess, and puram, a town.
Vembár	" *Margosa river*" ; fr. vembu, the margosa or " *Nim*" tree, and áru=river.
Veppam-kulam	" *Margosa tank*" ; fr. veppu, the margosa or " *Nim*" tree, and kulam, a pond or tank.
Vettilei-mandapam	"*Betel mandapam*", written Verrilei (rr prond. = tt) on the mainland opposite to Pámban.
Vijayápati	" *Vijayá's lord*", (i. e. Shivá) Vijayá=" Victorious", a n. of Párvati : hence Eng. "*Beejapore*" (for Vijayápur) and "*Viziana-gram*" (for Vijayámaunagaram).
Viláttikulam	(?) Vilátti, occas. form of vilá=the wood-apple (Feronia Elephantum), and kulam, a tank.
Vilvamarattupatti	" *Bel tree village*" ; fr. Vilva-maram (in comp. marattu)=the sacred Bel tree (cratava religiosa).

W is not a Tamil letter, but it is vulgarly pronounced before o initial and u sometimes.

In Tamil y is vulgarly inserted or pronounced before a and e initial.

Yánei or anei	An Elephant.
Yelavelankál	(?) " *tender thorn branch*" ; fr. yel == tender, velam == thorn (tree) ("*Acacia arabica*") and kál, the leg, a prop, branch, &c.
Yenádi	Pr. n. = (?) "why-first"?
Yendal	A very small tank, or reservoir com. affix to pr. n. of villages in Madura.
Yervádi or Ervádi	Pr. n. ; (?) fr. eru a buffalo, and vádi an enclosure, yard.
Yettiyal	Pr. n. (?) for yetti-vayal ; fr. Etti = a bitter and poisonous tree ("*Strychnos nux vomica*") and vayal, a plain, field, &c.

ABBREVIATIONS.

C = "Canarese"; Gr. = Greek; H. = Hindustani; L.=Latin; M.= Malayálam; S. = Sanskrit; T. = Tamil; Tel. = Telugu; R.C. = Roman Catholic; S. I.=South India; N., E., S., W. = North, East, South, West; == means equivalent to; com. = commonly; fr. = from or derived from; n. == name; pr. = properly; t. = town; v. = village; besides others in more common use.

Extract from the Narrative Report—dated 23rd August 1875—of Lieut. H. J. HARMAN, R.E.,
Assistant Superintendent 2nd Grade, in charge Assam Valley Triangulation.

(1.) I arrived at Shillong from Bangalore on October 4th 1874 and took over charge of the Party from W. G. Beverley Esq., on October 6th 1874.

(2.) The Party left "Gauháti", by march to "Jorhát", on November 5th 1874, in charge of Messrs. W. J. O'Sullivan and J. O. Hughes. With a few men I took passage in a steamer to "Kamlábári" near "Jorhát" and made arrangements for fixing the Treasury building in "Jorhát" from the stations "Bor Bhiti" and "Phakwa Dol", by running ray traces from these points into "Jorhát".—The final rays were each 6 miles in length and were opened out by Messrs. O'Sullivan and Hughes.

(3.) Meanwhile I visited the stations of the side of continuation and the stations "Bor Ghop" and "Gohaingáon" which were selected last season : and on the sands of the river laid out a triangulation to give data for cutting the ray "Bor Ghop" to "Gohaingáon" and to the Revenue Survey Pillar on the banks of the "Dikhu". This done I selected the position for the station of "Melankur" and obtained the bearing that the right flank ray from "Gohaingáon" should have so as to skirt the forest which borders the old "Dhy Ali". I could not get to the position of the "Dimú" Station, but got near enough to warrant the ray being cut through at once as a final ray. This line was successfully carried by Mr. O'Sullivan, and he suitably placed the "Dimú" Station at nearly 6 miles from "Gohaingáon". I returned to "Sibságar" on December 2nd and as I was under orders to join the Military Expedition (which had already left "Naraínpúr," for the "Daphla" Hills) I visited the parties at "Jorhát" and reported myself to Major Godwin Austen (in charge of the "Daphla Expedition" Survey Party) at "Borpathár" (campNo. 2) on the 12th December.

(4.) The force had but a short distance to march, and I did not anticipate being with it more than 6 weeks, but it so happened that I did not get back to my Party until March 3rd, on which day I reached "Disangmuk". Now I had directed that as soon as the rays to "Jorhát" were clear, the party should move on at once to "Sibságar" and work solely in advancing the approximate series, because I intended to return by "Jorhát", build the station there and take the observations for fixing it : this plan was frustrated, and the angles must be observed on the march up next season.

(5.) During my absence Mr. O'Sullivan was in command of the party, with instructions to observe to any new peaks not already fixed by Mr. Beverley, but an opportunity did not offer. The rays to the Revenue Survey Pillar on the "Dikhu" were cut. A length for the side "Bor Ali" to "Bor Ghop" obtained, but a mistake crept in, and the ray "Bor Ghop"—"Gauriságar" in consequence fell out a good deal ; this ray was 5½ miles in length and had very heavy forest on it. The ray "Bor Ghop"—"Gohaingáon", 7 miles in length, passed entirely over grass country, except in the middle of the ray where it traversed a belt of trees bordering the "Darika" river. The rays on to "Melankur" station from "Bor Ghop" and Gohaingáon were carried up to the left bank of the "Brahmaputra", and the right flank ray from "Gohaingáon" to "Dimú" carried as before stated in para. 2.

(6.) On March 4th I crossed the river and cut the two rays on to "Melankur" till they met ; the ray from "Gohaingáon" fell on the spot indicated on the chart, but the line from "Bor Ghop" was considerably out ; the final ray to "Bor Ghop" was cut and the station of "Melankur" built by Mr. O'Sullivan (a post station requires 3 days to erect if the materials are near at hand). I ran a ray trace between the "Melankur" and "Dimú" stations, the cutting of the narrow gap took 15 men four full working days, but the final ray took 20 men 20 days, Mr. Hughes cutting the heavy forest extending from the "Brahmaputra" to the "Bolemár" river, a distance of 1 mile, while my detachment cut from the "Dimú" side to the "Bolemár". On this ray fell 2 miles of jheel, a formidable obstacle, traversed by elephants with very great difficulty. On March 15th I visited Mr. Hughes, who was then carrying a right flank ray from "Dimú" to "Tengápánia" ; this line was for the first 1¼ miles clear, being across a jheel, then came a huge cane forest for ¾ of a mile up to a jheel full of trees of extreme hardness, and the men were working up to their waists in water ; I found Mr. Hughes far from well, he had written to say that he feared he would not be able to stay out the season, and some cases of sickness were showing in his detachment, so I removed this party to the banks of the river and Mr. Hughes cut the forest portion of the "Melankur"—"Dimú" ray as above mentioned.

(7.) I had not been able to visit "Tengápánia" before I left for the "Daphla" Hills, nor had Mr. O'Sullivan the opportunity subsequently, and from a misconception of my letter of instructions, in which I wished the rays to "Melankur" to be completed before advancing, this ray was undertaken without a reconnoissance having been made, and it landed us in trouble ; finding so much labor had already been expended on the line I did not like to desert it as in 3 miles more it would cross the old Assamese raised road, the "Dhy Ali ;" so on March 17th my party shifted to the head of the ray ;

the two following days I was on the line and we worked very hard, but accomplished 220 yards only ; the jheel cane was terribly armed with crooked thorns on every surface, I have seen no cane like it elsewhere : the natives with their wooden sandals and naked legs could barely creep through the fallen stuff, and they suffered severely.   On March 20th I left my party on the ray, and with a few men went to reconnoitre " Tengápánia" : the tract of country between the " Dimú" river and " Tengápánia" is intersected by the " Bolemár" river, several streams, and the old " Dhy Ali"; and has not been surveyed by the Revenue Survey, so to find where the ray would emerge on the " Dhy Ali" I ran a traverse from " Lasua Mírigaon"; this done we dragged a boat through the forest and I went down the " Bolemár" and decided to carry the line on.

(8.)   I then selected the stations of " Kherkutia" and " Sísa" and gave off the ray " Melankur"— " Kherkutia", which Mr. O'Sullivan carried, building the station close to the spot selected.   I measured a base on the sands of the river and laid out a plan for triangulating this side, which work Mr. Hughes executed and I also measured another long base at " Lasua" to connect on with this work and to find the sides " Kherkutia" to " Sísa".   Mr. Hughes now took up the ray " Kherkutia" to " Dimú", of which I had already cut a part from the " Dimú" side, leaving 2½ miles of forest and cane to be cut by Mr. Hughes from the river side.

(9.)   On April 1st I returned to " Disangmuk" and reported to you my intention of at once taking up observations on the 4 triangles now ready ; but reports came in, that the " Tengápánia" ray was still in cane, though better progress was being made.   The spring rain set in violently, and I got news that an elephant had been lost in the jungles about " Dibrugarh" for five days ; so taking some men I went up to " Dibrugarh" ; the river rose rapidly and I was able to take my boat everywhere and so selected the 7 stations necessary to carry the series on to " Dibrugarh" Church tower, and see the country well.

(10.)   On April 11th I returned to " Disangmuk", and found that my Jemadar, 2 elephants and men from the " Tengápánia" ray, had not returned as ordered ; they had not been heard of for 7 days and as it had been raining heavily since April 1st, and all the rivers were up and the country flooded, I went the next-day in search of them ; we had rather a rough time of it, but on April 17th were all safely back at " Disangmuk".   On my journey I visited Mr. Hughes' ray " Kherkutia"—" Dimú" and found it had gone a mile and was in heavy forest and cane.   On April 22nd Mr. O'Sullivan crossed the river from " Sísa" to aid Mr. Hughes in pushing on this line.   On April 25th the ray suddenly got flooded from the overflow of the " Bolemár", and a few days afterwards as the water was still up, I directed that the work should cease for the season.

(11.)   The forenoon of April 21st I left " Disangmuk " to observe the 4 triangles ready, and so much water was then out that it took us till nightfall to get over 5 miles of the path to " Sibságar."   As expected I could not encamp within a mile of any of the stations " Gohaingaon", " Bor Ali " or " Bor Ghop".   I had put off taking observations till so late because from December to March they cannot be speedily done, and I thought it most important I should examine the country ahead, and get all the stations selected this season up to " Dibrugarh", if possible.   I was delayed at " Gauriságar " on account of the branch of a tree on the ray to " Bor Ghop " cutting the heliotrope and giving a grazing ray ; and also at " Bor Ghop" on account of the heliotrope at " Gohaingaon" not being visible at the time of minimum refraction ; it was difficult to remedy these defects, as all the lines wore under water, so after having visited 4 stations and obtained the elements of the side " Gauriságar" to " Gohaingaon", from which the Topographical Survey were taking their triangulation into the Nágá Hills, I closed work on May 10th and dropped down the river " Brahmaputra " in my boats to " Gauháti", reaching that place on May 16th, the same day that Messrs. O'Sullivan and Hughes arrived by steamer from " Disangmuk", the steamer having been greatly delayed.

(13.)   Mr. O'Sullivan managed the party satisfactorily while I was in the " Daphla Hills".   The amount of final ray opened was 49 miles of which 6 miles were in forest, 30 over Chapori jungle, and 3 of village cutting ; he selected the " Dimú" station and built excellent post stations at 3 places.

(14.)   Mr. Hughes opened out 20 miles of final ray of which 7 miles were in heavy forest, 7 miles of light work and 2 of village clearing : built good post stations at " Bor Ghop" and " Dimú ": built the high platform for shewing a heliotrope above " Phakwa Dol", and observed the angles for measuring the side " Melankur"—" Kherkutia " and for correcting the trial ray " Jorhát" to " Phakwa Dol".

Mr. Hughes has not worked this season in the manner I wished and had shown him ; on most of his rays the work expended has not been at all judiciously applied and the labor has been excessive.

(15.)   A man mounted on an elephant can rarely see over the surrounding grass, or whatever it is; so I tried to introduce the plan of aligning the main flags by the parts of the flags which overtop the grass, and not by the lower half of the flags which is the usual custom.

A tiny gap is carried as straight as can be done with small hand flags placed at very short inter-vals, and at every half mile a man ascends a small portable bamboo frame so as to overlook the grass and plant a tall flag in the alignment with the back tall flags: this method obviously requires the least grass cutting possible: I have tried the method and with success; but this season, owing to Messrs. O'Sullivan and Hughes being sick and unable personally to superintend the cutting it has not been employed: again, in carrying a trial ray through forest it is plain that large trees should be avoided by shifting the line a foot or two parallel to itself, but for the same reason this has not been done; so that with exception of the ray "Melankur."—"Dimú" all the rays have been cut through as final rays, which is in great measure the cause of the small progress made, especially as the stations and the heliotropes are placed above the line of grass and the only obstacles are the trees. Before leaving "Gauháti" the establishment were put through a course of trying frames of cut bamboos, and any 12 men could construct and erect a stiff frame 50 feet high in 40 minutes, of course 50 feet is never necessary, 20 to 25 feet suffices in almost every case.

(16.) The district worked in this season (excepting "Gohaingaon" near "Sibságar") has only a small "Miri" village here and there; no local labor worth mentioning was available or procured: next season the "Miri" villages will be fewer in number; when nearer "Dibrugarh" the Commissioner will make special arrangements for us. There are no roads, only one or two paths were found of use; the main communications are the river and the rays cut; for the former, boats larger than small dug-outs are very scarce and men not easily found to work them, and a ray cut through forest is almost impassable for elephants. Provisions have to be entirely supplied to the parties at work from depôts where they are collected, so that to maintain local labor and move it on the work is rather a task. The leeches in April and the swarms of mosquitos about the middle of April were great plagues.

(17.) Of the ray "Kherkutia."—"Dimú" 1 mile remains uncut and of the ray "Dimú."—"Tongápánia" 1¼ miles: when this work is done, there will be little cutting on the left bank of the "Brahmaputra", the whole of the remaining lines into "Dibrugarh" are over Chapori jungle, chaurs, and the river.

(18.) We came across several old Assamese embankments and "Alis" (roads) on our lines this year, all covered with tree forest, they are not shown on the maps. While travelling in my boat up one of the jáns (small deep streams) north of the "Dihing" river in search of a suitable site for a station I came upon the trijunction of 3 old "Alis" in the thickest tree forest, but whither they led the "Miris" who accompanied me could not say. Near the "Tongápánia" station is the junction of the "Dhy Ali" and the "Motiárigarh" (old embankment), and the angle is curiously enclosed with a great circular road.

(19.) The out-turn of area this season is insignificant, but I hope, Sir, you will take into consideration the many retarding influences we had to contend with.

Extract from the Narrative Report—dated 22nd September 1875—of W. C. ROSSENRODE, ESQ., Deputy Superintendent 3rd Grade, in charge Eastern Frontier Series.

(3.) Owing to the difficulty of obtaining carriage and the country being still under water, I sent on the baggage and some provisions in charge of the tindel on the 7th November 1874, to Jungjungia, which was to be my first station of observation.

(4.) I left Moulmein on the 19th November, accompanied by Mr. Beverley, in boats, reached Sittang on the 30th November, hired boats at once, and joined my camp at Jungjungia H.S. on the 1st December.

(5.) On the afternoon of the 1st December the men who had gone to Suplitong H.S. with the signal party, returned with the intelligence that they could not find the path to ascend the hill, nor could they induce the villagers to accompany and guide them. The guide took them to the foot of the hill and would go no further, for fear of losing himself in the dense grass and tree jungle. I manned a fresh party with axes, billhooks and sickles and ordered them to cut their way and get up to the station as quickly as they possibly could, without waiting or trying to obtain aid from the inhabitants. To wait for assistance was hopeless. Suplitong H.S. is so situated that for 20 to 25 miles in every direction there are no villages.

The party I sent cut their way up and reached the station on the 6th day after leaving camp, and directed their signals the day after clearing the jungle on the summit.

(7.) The observations at Jungjungia H.S. were concluded without further interruption on the 11th December, Kuladong, The-ye-khu, Myayabengkyo, Kaneindong, and Keokpondong Hill Stations were then visited in succession. From Keokpondong H. S. I had to march to Kambungun Tower Station. The route lay through the extensive Pegu plain covered with reed and grass jungle: this during the rains is an immense swamp and it was still wet. Even in the middle of January some portions were impracticable for elephants. The march was circuitous and difficult and occupied 7 days, the direct distance from station to station being only 26 miles.

(8.) On completing the observations at Kambungun Tower Station on the 25th January 1875, I marched the next day and arrived at Chaiteo H.S. on the 1st February. A description of it is necessary, this hill being held in great sanctity by the Burmans and all the other tribes in the Province.

(9.) Chaiteo H.S. is 3600 feet above sea level. Stupendous projecting rocks, surmounted with masses of rock, rivet the attention of the traveller on his attaining the summit of this mountain, and he is lost in thought and speculation at the wonderful phenomenon which presents itself. The priests assert that superhuman agency alone has accomplished the miraculous lifting of these huge masses of rock in successive tiers, and that the gods who executed the work, reside beneath them. Each of the above rocks is crowned with a pagoda dedicated to Gaudama the Budhist Deity, and the Burmans, Shans, Karens, and other tribes, make pilgrimages from all parts of the Province to the shrines (pagodas) constructed on this sacred mountain.

(10.) The Principal pagoda, named Chaiteo, is constructed on a rock overhanging the south-western face of the hill ; directly below it is a yawning precipice several hundred feet in depth. The pagoda as it stands on the rock overhanging the precipice gives one the impression on seeing it from a distance that it is poised in mid air. On approaching it however the rock, an immense one, it is seen, has firm hold of the hill side and projects like a rhinoceros horn over the precipice. On this projecting portion the pagoda has been constructed. This is the principal and most sacred pagoda in which are deposited the bones and a tooth of Gaudama. There is nothing artistic in the edifice itself, the nerve and courage of the artificers commend themselves to the admiration of all visitors who are able to appreciate these qualities. The pagoda is roughly constructed, its defects however are hidden by the covering of gold leaf over a thick coating of some black looking adhesive substance which is prepared by the Burmans and used for this purpose to obtain a smooth surface. This substance consolidates and adheres most tenaciously to the structure and the gold leaf put over it is so tenaciously grasped by it that when dry it becomes a solid mass difficult to remove.

There are several other pagodas which have their history, and the pilgrims visit each in succession daily during the dry months from December to May. A grand festival is held annually, during March and April. The day of the full moon in March was this year the grandest day of the festival. Prior to the commencement of this carnival, sheds and booths spring up in all directions all over the hill, constructed by one or more members of each community, for the accommodation of themselves and their families. Traders have their stalls well stocked with every requisite and fabulous prices are realised by them, the demand increasing as the days run on towards the termination of this festive season. To obtain a blessing, it is necessary to worship at each pagoda and each pilgrim must at all times use a lighted candle during worship, the consumption of candles is therefore enormous. They sell at 4, 6, 8, 10 and 12 annas each, the former prices are obtainable during the first month, and the latter during the succeeding month. After the expiry of the two months, the festival concludes and the pilgrims retire to their respective homes. Near the principal pagoda is a fissure in the rock, about 4 inches in width, 7 feet long, and 15 feet deep, into this offerings are cast, consisting of silver and copper coins, gold leaf, (beaten gold) rubies and other stones of lesser value. This fissure is the treasury box of the Budhist Deity Gaudama. On the pilgrims retiring, after making their offerings, men with long thin rods with bird lime attached to the ends, endeavour to secure for themselves the coins and other valuables cast into it, whatever adheres to the rod is brought up and appropriated. Cloths of cotton and silk are also offered, should the cloth be of great length it is wrapped round the pagoda, the smaller pieces do duty as flags, streamers and banners. Cocoanuts and plantains and food are the usual offerings to the priests and monks.

(11.) A well 20 cubits deep has been sunk near one of the pagodas, this feat was accomplished by a single man working daily for 6 years through the rocky strata ; he was rewarded for his patience and perseverance by hitting upon a spring which provides a plentiful supply of water, and the well has never been known to be dry.

(13.) After completing the observations at Chaiteo H.S. I had to visit Toungoundong H.S. The routes to it were very circuitous and would have occupied me 9 and 10 days to reach the station. I ascertained that an old road through the hills was still partially in use which would save me 5 stages. I had this path, for it was nothing more, cleared, widened, and the overhanging branches removed, and although the marching was difficult and tedious and occupied 8, 10 and 12 hours daily, I saved 5 days by adopting it.

(17.) Suplitong H.S. was dreaded by every man in the native establishment. They had heard how Mr. Beverley had fared there the previous season ; how the men with the signal lamps and heliotropes had been detained in a howling wilderness, in the early part of the season, until re-inforced by me ;

how the men I had sent out their way up to the station; how members of this party had returned sick and disabled, and suffered from fever for 2 months, one having died a raving maniac from fever contracted there; how Mr. Clancey who had cut the road, nearly succumbed from fever and how all his men, public and private had been prostrated and sent to Hospital, one having died there. His servants and Interpreter had deserted, and another Interpreter I had sent him had taken his discharge. The exaggerated accounts given by the men who had been there, of the dangers and difficulties to be encountered on the journey to Suplitong made such an impression on the minds of the men of my camp, that they dreaded the idea of going there. Disheartened and desponding they commenced the march. They were well fed and cared for. The preparatory arrangements had been well made for going and returning, the healthiest time was chosen after the jungle had been fired, and the difficulties and dangers, which were so appalling became less and less as the camp proceeded onwards. The summit was attained, the theodolite put up and the observations were completed the third day and we descended the hill returning by the same road and encamping at the same spots.

(19.) From Suplitong I proceeded to Thulu H.S. which I reached on the 10th of March making 12 consecutive stages. Owing to smoke and haze, the observations were not completed until the 21st I then visited Chaideo H.S. where I was detained 7 days from bad weather.

(20.) From Ohaideo I visited Kyunkabun Station situated near the mouth of the Bheling river, here I was detained 8 days. The ray from this to Kalamatong H.S. was 32′miles in length and passed over a large expanse of water, the signals were at first unfit for observing; when the weather cleared up I succeeded in getting good signals and completed the observations. This was a most uncomfortable station to encamp at. Standing as it did close on the bank of the Bheling river, near its mouth, in dense tangled jungle difficult to cut and difficult to penetrate. The spot selected for the station was the highest available. A circular clearance of a hundred yards was made for the encampment. The elephants horses and the sick under the Native Doctor were located in a village 4 miles away.

(21.) I arrived at Kyunkabun Station on the 4th April during the spring equinox. Two days after the sun was partially eclipsed. The spring tides on this occasion were unusually high. The first washed over the encampment and submerged it, the platform was the only dry spot, upon which all the baggage, provisions, and other valuables were placed. As soon as the tide receded, a strong scaffold 15 feet high was erected for the baggage, and the tents were pitched upon raised scaffoldings 4 feet in height. It was most fortunate that no storms occurred during my stay at this station, for had one broken upon us and raised the water, as storms generally do, to a great height, we should one and all have perished, for there was not the remotest chance of escape encompassed as we were by tangled and impenetrable jungle, by the river and by two creeks, which would have proved formidable barriers.

(24.) There is a bar at the mouth of the river and the bore here is more formidable than any I have witnessed in other tidal rivers.

(25.) From Kyunkabun I proceeded to Kathbatong H.S. the centre of the next hexagon; owing to the smoke and haze with which the atmosphere was impregnated, observations proceeded rather slowly. The monsoon set in on the 21st April, with storms and rain, its usual accompaniments. The heavy down pour ushered in fine observing weather and I completed my observations and pushed on to Kalamatong which I reached in four days. Notwithstanding daily showers of rain, I hurried on not to lose the fine weather following rain, but on arriving at Kalamatong I found myself enveloped in cloud and mist. The rains had set in from the first shower which fell on the 21st April, every day was wet and the clouds and mist delayed me greatly. I took advantage of every break in the weather and completed my observations on the 13th day after my arrival.

(26.) There had been no rain from November to the 20th April, and I naturally expected a long break of a fortnight or three weeks duration between the first showers, and the regular setting in of the monsoon, which bout of good observing weather, would, I had hoped, enable me to complete the Kathbatong hexagon. In this however I was disappointed I could not visit the two remaining stations of this hexagon owing to the daily rain and the country becoming gradually submerged and Kalamatong which was the highest mountain for miles around, being generally capped with clouds; no signals from it to Mizantong with which it is connected, could be obtained. I had no other alternative but to close work and return to recess quarters.

(27.) In a densely wooded country, sparsely inhabited, without roads, the time occupied in marching alone is considerable, 85 days were this field season spent in travelling. The routes from station to station are circuitous, the tortuous course of the hill streams being generally adopted to save time and expense in cutting new and direct roads. Labor is the great drawback in Burma. It cannot be obtained, the inhabitants, as a rule, are unwilling and disinclined to work. The laboring classes all over India readily present themselves, when work offers, to add to their comforts, by earning as much as they are able. The Burmans are too lazy to do so, and throughout the Province, they themselves engage the Madras and Chittagong coolies to plough their lands and reap their fields.

(31.) During this season the positions of the following towns have been determined, Shoaygheen, Sittang, Chaito, Bhiling, Thatone, Moulmein, Amherst and the Great Pagoda in Pegu. I find that the observations taken at Thelakitong in season 1869-70 to Pegu Pagoda were incorrect, some other Pagoda was taken and an erroneous position was therefore assigned to it. The observations taken at Sanwinguntong during season 1869-70 were correct. This season the Pegu Pagoda was observed from five Principal and one Secondary station. Many Pagodas have been fixed and the positions of a great many more will be determined during the ensuing season when the two remaining stations of the Kathbatong figure and some of the stations of the Makbo Pentagon are visited. To secure as much secondary work as I possibly could, I engaged a Native Recorder, and was thus able to detach Mr. Clancey.

(32.) There was less sickness this season than the previous one, the average number of sick was 8 in my camp and 4 in Mr. Beverley's. There were 5 casualties. Three men were sent home, their recovery in this climate being hopeless, owing to continued debility and emaciation from fever.

(33.) Mr. Henry Beverley, Surveyor 1st Grade, has been engaged the whole season on approximate work. He commenced work by selecting the stations of Toungoundong and Thulu. He then proceeded to Sittang and constructed the pillar at Kámbúngún in the plains, surrounding it with a wooden platform 16 feet square and 18 feet high. He then constructed the wooden scaffolding over Chaideo rock, 26 feet high. Every description of work takes time to accomplish in this Province, and the construction of the above pillar and two wooden scaffoldings, detained Mr. Beverley from 18th December to 20th January. Had Colonel Brown, the Commissioner of Tenasserim, not interested himself, by personally addressing the Extra Assistant Commissioner (a Burman), Mr. Beverley would have been delayed much longer than he was.

(35.) On completing the above, he resumed approximate operations, and selected two simple figures, a Hexagon and a Pentagon, and closed work at Sendong H.S., after having fixed most of the stations of a compound figure in advance. Owing to the setting in of the rains this latter figure could not be completed. Some of the sides of the compound figure are long owing to Mr. Beverley's having no choice of ground, the isolated, inaccessible lime-stone hills rugged, jagged and fantastically shaped, in the valleys of the Attaran and Wiang rivers, being hopelessly unsuitable.

(36.) I had directed Mr. Beverley to observe all Pagodas, which were visible at each station that he visited, and to use his best endeavours to determine the position of the Pegu Pagoda. He was successful in seeing it from Thulu and Shoay-yongbia Hill Stations. He selected and constructed a station at Amherst which was finally fixed by his observations there and at Toungzun, and my angles at Kalamatong H.S. Mr. Beverley also contributed some secondaries, while carrying on approximate operations, and many other Pagodas, which he has observed in advance of the final work, will be fixed during the ensuing season when I visit the Principal Stations.

(37.) The lime-stone ranges of hills on the eastern flank of the Series are mostly precipitous and inaccessible and Mr. Beverley had great difficulty in fixing suitable stations. He had to abandon Zway-ga-beng and other hills more favorably situated, because the 24-inch Theodolite could not be carried up. With all his picking and choosing, he was compelled to adopt two of these difficult hills of lime-stone formation Mizantong H.S. and Makbo H.S., which with the aid of ladders and ramps, he managed to ascend. As this Party has, during its progress, encountered difficulties of every description, and every variety of ground, these two hills need not cause anxiety.

(38.) Mr. Beverley has accomplished a very satisfactory season's work. He lost the most favorable time of the year from the 13th December to 20th January in preparing the pillar and scaffolding at Kámbúngún and Chaideo stations; notwithstanding this loss, he with his usual zeal and energy advanced the approximate triangulation 100 miles of direct distance in a trying and difficult country with commendable cheerfulness and alacrity.

(41.) Mr. Clancey has worked well and satisfactorily. He takes much interest in his duties, and is assiduous to please. He has learned the Burmese language which will be very useful to him.

Extract from the Narrative Report—dated 13th September 1875—of W. G. BEVERLEY, ESQ;,
Officiating Assistant Superintendent 2nd Grade, in charge of the Burmah Party.

(2.) The Party was constituted under Departmental Order No. 44 of 6th August 1874, the
establishment being transferred from the late Brahmaputra Series. Its object is to carry chains of
secondary triangles from principal sides of the Eastern Frontier Series, in order to fix all the large towns,
prominent and permanent objects, peaks, &c., in the province of British Burmah, for detail and
Geological Surveys, and the light-houses &c. along the coast, for the Marine Survey.

(3.) A part of the establishment and heavy baggage left Calcutta for Rangoon with Mr.
Collins on the 1st November; and the remainder with me on the 7th. Mr. Mitchell was transferred
from the Eastern Frontier Series, and joined the Party at Rangoon. Work was commenced before the
end of the month.

(4.) During the preceding season, Mr. Mitchell had in connection with the Eastern Frontier
Series reconnoitred the country, and laid out an approximate triangulation from the principal side
Keokpongdong H.S. to Kaneindong H.S. down to Rangoon, so as to fix that town, as well as Pegu.
I considered it advisable, on commencing work, to examine Mr. Mitchell's selections and found it
necessary to modify his plan to some extent, to save time in clearing rays and hill tops.

(5.) On my return from examining the country to the north, I took up the triangulation
southwards to the coast, selecting stations after a careful reconnoissance of the ground. Most of these
stations are fixed on old Pagodas, by which there was a great saving of time as regards ray cutting,
and of expense in building stations. The approximate work of selecting stations, and the final work of
observation, were carried on together as far as practicable. The triangulation was carried down to
the mouth of the Rangoon river.

(6.) Mr. Collins had been left to clear the rays at the hill station of Ayodong; and as he had
now nearly completed his work, I returned to take up the final observations from the stations north of
Rangoon, as the atmosphere which hitherto had been pretty clear was gradually getting hazier, I went
up as far as Taongnio H.S., but as Yomá H.S. in advance had not been cleared nor occupied by the
signalmen, I was unable to complete my observations there. The angle at Cháglibá H.S., between
Ayodong and Taongnio stations, could not be observed, as the signalmen had been compelled to abandon
the latter station on 4th March, from the only spring there having ceased to run, and there being
no water known to exist within 10 or 12 miles.

(7.) The triangulation from Taongnio and Chágibá to the coast is incomplete; as the very dense
haze, which prevailed from the beginning of March, prevented the requisite observations being taken at
Ayodong, Chágibá, and Shántoji, as shown by dotted lines in the chart accompanying. Two attempts
were made after the rains set in to obtain observations, but without success.

(8.) The triangulation along the coast towards China Bakir light-house, was resumed in the
middle of March; but from the nature of the ground the progress made was slow. Work was closed on
the 24th of April, when the southwest monsoon set in with severe storms, and very heavy and continuous rain. In fact, the country had been gradually getting under water along the large streams, from
the rising of the Irrawaddy river since the middle of March, when the snow at the sources begins melt-
ing. The cutters were frequently up to their waists in water, and suffered great inconveniences from the
absence of drinkable water under a burning sun.

(9.) Mr. Mitchell at the commencement of the field season, opened the ray Chanakpho H.S.
to Insingpaiá Station, and partially cleared the hills of Ayodong and Taongnio, taking some observations at the latter station. He took up the clearing of the ray Chanakpho to Ayodong, which was
ultimately abandoned: he also took some final observations at Insingpaiá.

(10.) As there were no means of reaching Yomá Station directly from Taongnio, but by a
circuitous route which would occupy nearly a fortnight, Mr. Mitchell was deputed to clear the summits
of Kamlútong and Yomá, selected by him the previous year, to build the stations there, and commence final observations from the side Káneindong H. S. to Keokpongdong H. S., closing on the
stations of Taongnio and Chágibá to be visited by me. This was partly in conformity with the plan
laid down by himself, and which, from my examination of the country, appeared to be feasible. Mr.
Mitchell, however, after a second examination of the country, and after visiting 3 or 4 points where he
took rough observations, found numerous difficulties in so carrying the triangulation, and was obliged
to resort to the side Kámbúngún T.S. to Júngjúngiá H.S. from which he thought he could get over
the country more rapidly.

(11.) Mr. Mitchell took observations from seven stations; but owing to very bad weather and
frequent attacks of illness, he was unable to carry his final observations up to the point where they

would have been connected with the work executed by myself. He endeavoured, at risk of health and much inconvenience, to complete his work by remaining out until the middle of June, when field work was impossible from the incessant rain.

(13.) Mr. Collins was employed in clearing the stations of Cháglíbí, Engtago and Ayodong, and building masonry pillars on them. The forest at the latter station was extremely dense, and the rays from it to Jnsingpaiá and Shánteji were cleared over three broad wooded ranges. Upwards of a month was occupied at Ayodong alone. The delay was chiefly due to the difficulty of procuring labor, Burmese coolies could not be obtained after the middle of December, and the immigrants entertained were almost useless. Several of these latter deserted shortly after obtaining an advance of pay; while those from the immigration office contained a large percentage of Brahmins, who systematically abstained from any and every kind of work on the pretence of illness.

(14.) When the rays at Ayodong were all cleared, Mr. Collins took some final observations there, and also at Kaiúngále Station with the 8-inch theodolite, and then proceeded and built a masonry pillar at Shánteji, but could not get observations, on account of the haze which had now become unusually thick. He joined me on the coast at the end of March, and was employed in carrying rays, &c.

(15.) Mr. Collins has throughout the season shown a great deal of zeal and energy, is a good and careful observer, and is rapidly becoming an efficient surveyor.

(16.) Two Burman interpreters and writers were entertained for this Party. One of these with Mr. Mitchell, died from fever in the field. The other was of very great service to me.

(17.) The men of the Native Establishment have worked well and cheerfully although in a new country and ignorant of the language and customs, and have given satisfaction. They are trained men selected from the Establishment of the late Brahmaputra Party, and sent to Burmah on higher rates of pay, but still much less than the pay given in this Province, and in some instances less than that given to the same class of men in the Eastern Frontier Party. In spite of the inducements of less work and very high wages offered in the Public Works Department, they have remained faithful to their agreements. The elephant keepers alone have been as usual with that class of men a cause of trouble and annoyance, and anxiety for the health and safety of the animals in their charge.

(18.) The triangulation has been carried over a variety of ground. The hilly portion is low and densely wooded, and the difficulties peculiar to this tract have been fully pointed out by Mr. Rossenrode, and noticed by yourself in your last year's Report to Government. These difficulties were to a certain extent greater to our Establishment which was quite new to the Province. The country along the coast is an equally difficult one for triangulation. It is low, and cut up with numerous tidal creeks and rivers. There are few or no paths through the low thick tamarisk and thorn jungle; and no drinkable water except at the villages which are small and far apart. The work on the coast can only be done by boats and coolies, both to be entertained at Rangoon, as they can rarely be got in the villages, and then only at exorbitant rates. Elephants cannot be used on account of the scarcity of fodder, and small supply of water procurable. The ground too, after inundation at every high tide, is extremely dangerous for laden animals.

(19.) The out-turn of work for the past year, would have been more satisfactory if there had been no break in the triangulation; and as the members of the Party are now better acquainted with the peculiarities of the country and people, a greater out-turn may be confidently expected in the ensuing field season, under favorable circumstances. The chief causes of delay in Burmah are the difficulty of procuring labor, and in moving with rapidity from one place to another; but the greatest is the haze arising from the burning of jungle and rice straw. On the coast, there is less haze to contend with, as there is very little jungle that can be burnt for clearings. Very little rain falls during the dry season: between the 7th of November and 23rd of April, there were only two slight showers.

(20.) There was much sickness in the camps at the commencement of the season; and both Messrs. Mitchell and Collins, and nearly every man of the Establishment, have suffered from malarious fever. In fact, there was always a large percentage of sick throughout. Three deaths occurred.

Extract from the Narrative Report—dated 16th August 1875—of Captain M. W. ROGERS, R.E.,
Officiating Deputy Superintendent 3rd Grade, in charge Jodhpur Series.

(2.) I returned from furlough on the 28th October, and on the 20th November relieved Lieutenant Hill, R.E., of the charge of the Party which he had held during my absence.

(3.) All arrangements for the field season had been made by Lieutenant Hill and he had sent
off the assistants before my arrival. I had engaged the carriers for the Great Theodolite whilst at
Ahmedabad and there was therefore no delay in taking the field which was done on the 23rd November.

(4.) I marched viâ Jodhpur to Nok H.S. in Jaisalmir, where observations were commenced on
the 17th December; from thence the observations were carried on continuously through the heart of
the great Jaisalmir and Bikanir desert as far as Marot in Baháwalpur and were closed at Bhulan H.S.
on the 21st of March.

(5.) The following is a general statement of the season's work. Observations were taken at 25
principal stations forming a pentagon, two hexagons, and one double polygon, fixing 23 new principal
stations, embracing an area of 2472 square miles, and extending the series 104 miles along the meridian.
An azimuth was observed at Mugrálá H.S. to two circumpolar stars. The Approximate Series was
extended 64 miles to its junction with the Sutlej Series. The positions and heights of Bikanir and
Pugal were fixed by minor triangulation, the area of which, exterior to the series, was 681 square
miles.

(6.) Some explanation is needed as to the dearth of secondary and intersected points; this is
due to the nature of the country, in which there are neither natural nor artificial objects of interest.
   The total intersected points on the principal series were 8, of these 7 were intersected from the
four last stations of the series, leaving a tract of about 90 miles by 30, in which there was only one
point which could be intersected.

(7.) Mr. Price was in charge of the Approximate Series and extended it through the desert to
Mr. Price. the Sutlej Series. Bearing in mind the great difficulties of the
country, I consider the amount of work he has done and the well
proportioned good figures which he has been able to obtain, reflect great credit on his zeal, intelligence
and hard work.

(8.) Mr. Torrens laid out and observed a minor series to Bikanir by which that city was fixed
Mr. Torrens. in height; he closed on to a side of the series emanating from the
Gurhágarh, with very satisfactory agreement in results. He also
fixed the position of Pugal by a short series and the Revenue Survey trijunction at the junction of the
Bikanir, Jaisalmir and Baháwalpur boundaries. He also closed 17 stations in Bikanir and Jaisalmir.
   He observed with a 10-inch theodolite and his average triangular error was 1″·7. He has worked
well and cheerfully and I am much pleased with the quality and quantity of his work.

(9.) Mr. Prunty joined the party from Head Quarters during last recess, and accompanied me
Mr. Prunty. during this season as observatory recorder. He is painstaking, willing and neat, and has now acquired the accuracy which was all he
needed to make him a very good recorder. He has learnt the use of the theodolite and perfected himself
in departmental routine and I am very well satisfied with him.

(12.) The country through which the series passed this season, is a sandy desert; the sand hills
in Jaisalmir are from 50 to 150 feet in height and are distributed in such a confused manner over the
country as to make it a work of great difficulty to select stations or to obtain any but very short sides.
Towards the north, in Baháwalpur, they diminish in height and become merely mounds ·of drifting
sand, interspersed with open spaces of hard clay which are perfectly level like the beds of immense dry
tanks.

(13.) The sand hills of Jaisalmir and Bikanir are covered with high coarse grass, which grows
in large tufts, and with shrubs, of which the most common and largest is the Phog, a leafless shrub,
from 5 to 8 feet in height with green twigs and pleasant smelling flower.

(14.) In the Jaisalmir desert there is a good deal of cultivation mostly " bájri". Most of the
numerous small valleys formed by the sand hills are ploughed and sown, although miles from any
village, and I believe that the grain produced is very good.

(15.) The villages are few and far apart; attached to each are numerous " dhánis ", that is two or
three huts erected in the desert, wherever there is either a well of brackish water or a small excavation

in the hard soil (which crops out at intervals) in which water collects during the rains. These 'dhánis' are inhabited during the rains and cold weather, when the desert is comparatively populous, but are deserted in the hot weather, when the inhabitants return to their villages.

(16.) In the portion of Bikanir, through which the series passed, there is hardly any cultivation. The occupation of the inhabitants is almost entirely pastoral, and they have large herds of cattle, sheep, goats and camels. From Pugal in Lat. 28½° to the valley of the Sutlej, with the exception of the villages lying on what was the bed of the old Hurkara river—about 40 miles south of the Sutlej— there are no villages and only a few wells of brackish water; this tract is the most desolate I have yet met with, and the inhabitants desert it in the hot weather, taking their camels into Sindh; this custom deprived me of my supply of water camels and obliged me to return earlier than I otherwise should have done.

(17.) In the cold weather, up to the end of December, this portion of the country is alive with flocks and herds which got water from innumerable "tobas" or small tanks excavated in the hard clay, which are as I have already mentioned abundant in Baháwalpur and N.W. Bikanir, and I apprehend no difficulty whatever in taking the series in November through the portion remaining from which I had to retreat this season.

(18.) All the villages have large numbers of camels which roam in the desert and return every few days to the wells to drink, when such as are wanted are caught.

(19.) Nearly all the country I worked through belonged to three influential Thákurs, Bikampur and Birsilpur in Jaisalmir and the Rao of Pugal in Bikanir, which last belongs to one of the oldest Bhatti Rájput families and is reported to have held Pugal for more than 1,000 years.

The villages in which they live are larger, but quite as wretched in appearance as any I met with, the only distinction being that the Thákurs live in a sort of a half house, half fort built of mud and stones.

(20.) The cold was very great at times, the minimum thermometer twice registered 16°; this was very trying to the men who however enjoyed good health as a rule. My experience of the desert is that it is very healthy for people who are well fed and have good water to drink.

(21.) The city of Bikanir to which a minor series was taken this season to fix its height, is a

Bikanir.

fine city built on a slightly elevated spot in the desert where the ground is hard and stony and intersected by ravines. It has a wall 3½ miles in circuit, wholly built of stone and in good repair, it has 8 gates and three sally-ports; the wall is from 15 to 30 feet high and it has a ditch on three sides about 15 feet deep. There are many highly carved houses in the city and two imposing looking Jain temples. Water is plentiful from many very fine wells. The chief productions are sugar-candy and blankets, both of which are of a very superior kind. The population is about 35,000.

(22.) The fort of Bikanir which contains the Maharajah's palace is about 300 yards N.E. of the city. The palace rises above the battlements and gives it an imposing appearance : it is 1,100 yards in circumference and has two gates, numerous bastions and a ditch all round.

(23.) The Governments of Marwar, Jaisalmir, Bikanir and Baháwalpur sent officials and men to accompany the camps, in their respective States, and rendered every assistance in their power, and very greatly was their assistance needed, for without it the work could not have been carried on for a day as the water for the camps, had to be brought on an average, 10 to 20 miles on camels.

My best thanks are due to the Political Agents Colonel Minchin, Major Walter and Captain Burton.

Extract from the Narrative Report—dated 8th September 1875—of Captain A. PULLAN, S.C., Officiating Deputy Superintendent 3rd Grade, in charge Kattywar Survey Party.

PERSONNEL.	*Head Sub-Surveyor.*	
	Mr. Visaji Ragunath.	

Captain A. Pullan, S. C.,
John McGill, Esq., Asst. Supdt.

Surveyors and Asst. Surveyors.

Mr. J. Peyton.
  „ F. Bell.
  „ N. C. Gwynne.
  „ Wyatt.
  „ W. A. Fielding.
  „ W. Oldham.
  „ G. T. Hall.
  „ H. Corkery.

Sub-Surveyors.

Govindji Mahalay.
Narsu Dinkar.
Krishna Govind.
Shridhar Succaram.
Vishnu Moreshwar.
Bholaji Bhoseker.
Nilkant Vital.
Keshu Vital.
Tukaram Chowdry.
Ganesh Rámchandra.
Vishnu Bulwant.

The out-turn of field work for the season 1874-75 was not so large as in the two preceding seasons. A considerable portion of the country under review, lying as it does along the borders of the Gulf of Cutch, was very difficult and tedious to survey, not only on account of the treacherous mud banks and almost impassable mangrove swamps, but also from the variable winds and sudden changes of tide among the creeks which throw constant hindrance in the way of the surveyors.

An area of 1877 square miles inclusive of overlaps, or 1749 square miles within graticule, was topographically surveyed, consisting of parts of Pránts Hállár and Machhu Kánthá in Kattywar and a portion of the southern seaboard of Cutch, which was surveyed in order to render the Sheets of Kattywar more complete and to delineate more clearly the head of the Gulf of Cutch. 2200 square miles were trigonometrically surveyed, 200 for the survey of the Cutch coast during the same season, and 2000 in advance preparatory to ensuing topographical operations, and 1117 linear miles of traverse were carried over the area of country topographically surveyed, demarcating the boundaries of States and checking the details of the Plane Table Survey.

It must be borne in mind that the out-turn of work for the two preceding seasons was exceptionally large owing to the wide area of flat ' Rann' it included, and such an out-turn can hardly be expected in future. I may here state that the agreement between our survey of the head of the Gulf and the coast line given by the Marine Survey of Lieutenant Taylor, I. N., is decidedly satisfactory, taking into consideration the difference of scale and mode of delineating ground.

At Rájkot, hearing from Mr. Bell, who was triangulating the seaboard of Cutch, that the nature of the ground on Sathsaida Bet rendered a stone or masonry pillar unadvisable, I devised a pillar composed of piles of hard teak seven feet long, four feet below the surface and three above, arranged in a circular form, the mark-stone being imbedded in the mud beaten hard all round with small pebbles and straw to bind it, and the cylinder being then filled up with shingle from the beach mixed with mud. This pillar is calculated to stand the wash of the monsoon waters better than a masonry pillar, which would offer unyielding resistance and tilt over from its own weight, whereas in the case of the pillars now erected the force of the water is dissipated, and I think they will all be found next season, *in statu quo.*

On arrival at Jámnagar or Nawánagar, the capital of the territories of H. H. the Jám, I found that the border of the Gulf, studded as it is with numerous small islands, intersected by tidal creeks, offered a very difficult piece of work for the Plane Tabler, not only on account of the heavy mud and quicksand, but also from the fact that the work had to be done by boat principally, and the surveyor would have to study carefully the state of the tide and the direction of the wind. This work I took up myself and completed all the northern and difficult portion of the board by the time that it became necessary to cross over to Cutch and examine the Plane Table work on that coast and also about Hanstal Creek. I therefore started on the 26th February for Hanstal *viâ* Juria.

On arriving at Hanstal, I found Mr. Hall getting on very well and surveying the swamps with correctness and facility. I passed on, after examining Mr. Hall's Plane Table, to the opposite coast of Cutch and spent four days in a careful examination of Govindji Mahalay's Plane Table which I found correct and neatly executed. I then returned to Juria and marched along the coast to Balachori in order to judge for myself of the general character of the coast line and swamps ; the journey was a fatiguing and dangerous one and I was very nearly swamped in a quicksand from which I was with difficulty extricated by my khlassies.

I marched from Molila on the 6th April *en route* for Gogo. The heat was at this time intense, far greater than I had hitherto experienced in Kattywar, and the hot season threatened to be exceptionally severe, I therefore reluctantly gave up the plan of completing Sheet 45 which would have kept the Plane Table parties out until near the end of May, and sent orders to the surveyors and sub-surveyors to the effect that when they had completed the boards they were working they were to march and join me at Gogo and from that port make arrangements for return to recess quarters.

After receiving all the Plane Tables and comparing their borders before taking them to Poona, I started from Gogo on the 12th May and opened office at Poona on the 17th May 1875.

Mr. McGill left Wadhwán on the 21st November 1874 to take up and complete the triangulation

J. McGill, Esq. Asst. Supdt. of Sheet 10a of Kattywar which had been left unfinished by Mr. Wyatt. After completing this work Mr. McGill marched *viâ* Malia and the borders of the Kann and examined the southern Plane Tables of Sheet 31. Mr. McGill proceeded thence *viâ* Rájkot to Gondal where he commenced the triangulation of Sheets 36 and 37—these Sheets were completed on the 6th April and Mr. McGill marched to Gogo at my request and thence proceeded to Poona.

Mr. McGill worked with the same zeal and ability which has characterized him for many years. His interesting memorandum on Sheet 10a is appended to my report.

Mr. Bell left recess quarters in advance of the rest of the party as I required him to furnish

Mr. F. Bell, Surveyor 3rd Grade. some few extra points on the seaboard of Cutch. Proceeding by boat to the port of Mandir, Mr. Bell commenced work on the 15th November at Charakla H. S., and worked very hard and well; having completed his triangulation he joined my camp on the 21st December and we conjointly computed and projected the points on the Plane Tables and made them over to the Plane Table Surveyors. Mr. Bell then proceeded to take up the triangulation of Sheet 38 which he completed by the end of March. His out-turn of work was 800 square miles, and I have every reason to be satisfied with the number and position of the intersected points.

Mr. Gwynne, after completing Fair Sheets 33—35 of Kattywar, took up his first Plane Table

Mr. N. C. Gwynne, Surveyor 4th Grade. on the 15th January 1875. Mr. Gwynne worked throughout the season with the willingness and energy which distinguish him, turning out 125 square miles of very difficult and hilly country in admirable style besides instructing Mr. H. Corkery, Assistant Surveyor and Sub-Surveyor Vishnu Bulwant. Mr. Gwynne's steady application in the drawing office during recess is worthy of particular notice.

Mr. Fielding started from Wadhwán on the 24th November for Sheet 31. He was accompanied

Mr. W. A. Fielding, Asst. Surveyor 2nd Grade. by Messrs. W. Oldham and H. Corkery, Assistant Surveyors, Sub-Surveyors Nilkant Vital and Ganesh Rámchandra and Traverse Surveyor Tukaram Chowdry. The whole of the Plane Table parties and Traverse party I placed under the orders and general superintendence of Mr. Fielding of whose intelligence and carefulness I had formed a high opinion and I was well satisfied with the result. Mr. Fielding having completed Sheet 31 marched southwards and took up R. Plane Table, S.W. Section of sheet 43. Mr. Fielding's out-turn of work was 154 square miles, very creditable when it is taken into consideration that in Sheet 31 he had to superintend the work of 2 European and 3 Native Assistants besides doing some Plane Table surveying himself.

Mr. Oldham worked well throughout the season, first under Mr. Fielding's superintendence in

Mr. W. Oldham, Asst. Surveyor 3rd Grade. Sheet 31 and afterwards on Sheets 43 and 45 under my own eye. I found Mr. Oldham's work very carefully done on every occasion that I examined it. He requires further practice in neat drawing and printing, and when these are acquired satisfactorily, he will be a valuable Plane Table Surveyor. His out-turn of work 200 square miles for this, his first season, is most creditable to him.

Mr. Hall worked very well throughout the season both on the borders of the Gulf of Cutch

Mr. G. Hall, Asst. Surveyor 3rd Grade. and also in hilly ground in Sheet 44. His out-turn of work was 180 square miles, and I have every reason to be satisfied with its quality.

Mr. Corkery was employed throughout the season in topographical work; his out-turn was 144

Mr. H. Corkery, Asst. Surveyor 4th Grade. square miles, and both Plane Tables in execution and delineation of hilly country are very creditable to a young hand and show a marked improvement.

Mr. Visaji Ragunath was employed during the major part of the season in projecting Plane
Mr. Visaji Ragunath, Head Sub-Sur-   Tables, computing Lats., Longs. of intersected points, and in general
veyor.   miscellaneous work; at the beginning of April, I sent him to run a
Check Traverse across the Cutch portion of Sheet 31. This work he satisfactorily completed.

Govindji Mahalay executed the Plane Table survey of 171 square miles of country in his usual
careful and artistic style. He has also been very useful as a draughtsman during the recess season.
Narsu Dinkar was employed in running boundary traverses and check lines during the whole season.
He executed in a satisfactory manner 323 linear miles of traverse, and is a useful and hardworking
assistant. Krishna Govind was employed during the season as recorder to Mr. Bell. Shridhar Succaram
executed 167 square miles of Plane Table survey slowly but accurately.

Vishnu Moreshwar worked very steadily throughout the field season. His out-turn was 196 square
miles, and there was some improvement this season in his delineation of hilly ground. Bholaji Bhosekar
was employed throughout the season in boundary traversing and running check lines; he completed
273 linear miles of traverse. In consequence of information received from you respecting the amount
to be expended on the Native Establishment of this party, I was obliged to reduce two parties, one Plane
Table and one Traverse party; Bholaji Bhosekar being the least useful of the Traverse Surveyors was
therefore discharged. Nilkant Vital executed 164 square miles of topography with accuracy and some
improvement in his style of drawing. Keshu Vital executed 146 square miles of topography; there is
much room for improvement in his style of sketching ground. He is a good computer. Ganesh Rámchandra executed 170 square miles of topography in a very creditable way for so young a hand.
Vishnu Bulwant is very useful in the drawing office and promises in time to be a really good draughtsman.

The principal towns contained in the country now under consideration are; 1st, Jámnagar or
Principal Towns, &c.   Nawánagar, the capital of the territories of the Jám of Nawánagar
                                  which district comprises, roughly speaking, with the exception of a
few small detached holdings, Sheets 42, 43, 44, 45 and the eastern halves of 52 and 53. The town which
is on the banks of the little river Nágmati is clean and well built with good streets. The population according to the last census amounts to 34,744 souls. The Jám, a Jhareja Rájput, is gentlemanly and pleasant
and from either liking or policy affects the society of Europeans, treating all who visit his territories
with much courtesy and hospitality.

The other towns of note in the Jám's territories are Hariana, Dhunwao and Balamba. The last
named town is supplied with good water by means of a canal four miles long which carries the sweet
waters of the Aji up to the town; tradition has it that a rich Brahmin of Balamba was enamoured of
the daughter of a Brahmin of Latipur; but as Balamba was notorious for its bad brackish water, the
girl's father refused his consent until his daughter was sure of good water to drink in her new home.
The suitor thereupon set to work and had the canal cut which now exists thereby winning his bride.
A dam is now in course of construction near the village of Madhapur on the Aji which will, when completed, render the canal always full of sweet fresh water.

The town of Malia, on the banks of the Machhu was 50 years ago a very strong place; it is the
only place of importance in Sheet 31 : the inhabitants are principally "Miani" Mahomedans, but the
Rája is a Jhareja Rájput of the Cutch family.

Near Jámnagar is a little pleasure house and temple called Rozi Mata, a favorite summer resort
of the Jám's, situated on a small island or rather isthmus which juts out into the lagoons and swamps
of the Gulf; the fresh breezes from the sea render Rozi a pleasant place of sojourn during the hot
months; the island is covered with long grass and tangled thicket giving cover to herds of "Nylghai"
or " Roz" which roam at will unmolested, the island as its name implies being their favorite haunt. Near
the small village of Balacheri there is a bungalow on the shore of the Gulf built by the Jám and occupied
during the hot months by the political officers; at a short distance from the bungalow is the village of
Sachana, the inhabitants of which drive a thriving trade in fish of various kinds, and send a regular
supply to the British Station of Rájkot.

The Machhu river flowing into the Rann of Cutch at Malia and losing itself in the salt sand and
Rivers.   mud of the Gulf, is the principal drainage line in the country survey-
                                  ed this season. The others are the Nágmati which rises in the hilly
country 30 miles south of Jámnagar, the Aji the head of which only enters these sheets where it de-
bouches 3 miles north of Hanstal tidal station into the Hanstal Creek, the Nani and Moti Phuljar, the
Und and the Mauwar.

Sheet 31 calls for no further particular description as what I said in my Narrative Report for season 1873-74 of Sheet 32 will apply equally to the country in Sheet 31.

General appearance of the country.

Sheets 42 and 43 are flat and well cultivated up to the very edge of the mangrove swamps which are a leading feature of the country and which spread along the Gulf in a broad belt from Hanstal and even higher than that, southward over all the coast surveyed last season, near the town of Jámnagar all the islands and spits of thick rich mud are covered with tangled mangrove jungle in some places rising to an altitude of 40 feet but generally averaging from 8 to 10 feet in height. At high tide a little fleet of boats puts out from Bari Bunder carrying the wood cutters to their work in the lagoons, the white sails gleam on all sides among the masses of rich green foliage and the labourers cut and stack mangrove till a returning tide bears them homeward; the stock of firewood thus obtained is a godsend to Jámnagar as the supply of wood round the city is scanty, a large quantity is also laid in by the Bombay bound craft that put in at the little port of Bari.

The country in Sheet 44 is undulating, crossed here and there by low ridges—a stony and sterile land poorly cultivated; there are few villages of any size in Sheet 44 except on its eastern border where the country is somewhat less stony and the soil richer and better cultivated.

Throughout the low ranges which cross Sheets 43 and 44 are numerous stone quarries, where a coarse white sandstone is excavated; this stone though porous and friable when first brought to the surface, hardens greatly by exposure to rain and sun and becomes a useful building stone.

Quarries.

To meet the wishes of the Political Agent, I propose next season to triangulate Sheets 46, 47 and 48 in advance, and to survey topographically Sheets 36, 37 and 38 and the portion of Sheet 45 which still remains unfinished—the small portion of coast near Diu of which Sheet 41 consists, I shall also, I think, be able to complete as the triangulation has been done and nothing remains but the boundary traverses and topographical detail Survey.

TABULAR STATEMENT OF OUT-TURN OF WORK IN KATTYWAR DURING THE FIELD SEASON 1874-75.

Triangulation.

No.	Observers' Names	Instruments used	Area triangulated in square miles.	No. of Points Heights fixed.	No. of Points Position fixed.	No. of stations visited.	Triangles, & Angles Observed.			Triangles, 2 Angles Observed.		Remarks.
							No. of triangles.	Mean triangular Error.	Discrepancy per mile.	No. of triangles.	Average discrepancy per mile.	
1	John McGill, Esq., ...	Cooke and Son's 7-Inch	1400	253	595	80	135	10·2	Feet 0·8	950	Feet 1·3	
2	Mr. F. Bell, ...	Troughton and Simms' 6-Inch	800	69	206	55	76	9·3	0·5	438	0·8	
		Totals, ...	2200	322	801	135	211	Mean 9·8	Mean 0·7	1378	Mean 1·1	

Topography.

No.	Plane-Tablers.	Area surveyed Scale 2 inches = 1 mile.	Average No. of plane table stations per square mile.	Remarks.
1	Captain A. Pullen, s.c. ...	30	5·8	
2	Mr. N. C. Gwynne, ...	125	7·3	
3	" W. A. Fielding, ...	154	8·9	
4	" W. Oldham, ...	200	12·8	
5	" G. T. Hall, ...	180	5·5	
6	" H. Corkery, ...	144	12·5	
	Native Surveyors.			
7	Govindji Mahadoy, ...	171	6·0	
8	Shridhar Succaram, ...	167	9·0	
9	Vishnu Moreshwar, ...	198	12·7	
10	Keshu Vishi, ...	146	10·0	
11	Nilkant Vishi, ...	164	12·6	
12	Ganesh Rāmchandra, ...	170	12·4	
13	Vishnu Balvant, ...	90	7·5	
	Total number of square miles surveyed inclusive of overlap ...	1877	...	

Traverses.

No.	Names.	No. of Linear Miles Traversed.		Average error per 1000 links.	Remarks.
		Taluka Boundary.	Check Line.		
1	Mr. Vimji Ragunath,	...	21·33		
2	Naren Dinkar,	160·30	162·66	0·69	
3	Bholaji Bhosekar,	179·94	93·33	0·54	
4	Tukaram Chowdry,	148·78	355·26	0·79	
	Totals, ...	489·02	632·92	Mean 0·67	

GREAT TRIGONOMETRICAL SURVEY OF INDIA.

· INDEX CHART OF THE KATTYWAR TOPOGRAPHICAL SURVEY.

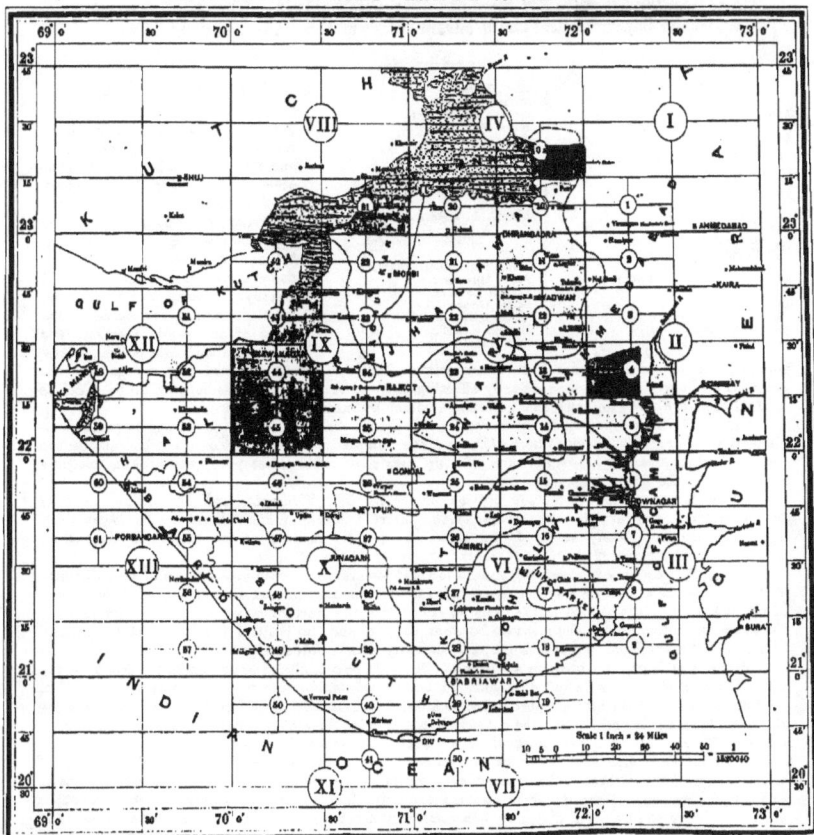

Extract from the Narrative Report—dated 15th October 1875—of Major C. T. HAIG, R.E., Deputy Superintendent 2nd Grade, in charge of the Guzerat Survey Party.

PERSONNEL.

Major C. T. Haig, R.E.
Lieutenant J. E. Gibbs, R.E.
Mr. J. Peyton.
" A. D'Souza.
" A. D. L. Christie.
" C. H. McAFee.
" E. J. Connor.
" J. Hickie.
" G. D. Ousson.
" G. Hall.
" S. Norman.
" O. Norman.

Native Surveyors.

Gopal Vishnu.
Luximon Gorpuray.
Ganesh Narayen.
Ganesh Bapuji 1st.

Racji Narayen.
Mukand Dinkar.
Ganesh Bapuji 2nd.
Bhow Govind.
Govind Gopal.
Bulwant Rajaram.
Monaji Aboo.

Revenue Survey.

Mr. T. A. LeMesurier.

Native Surveyors.

Keshowram Ravishankor.
Jugal Mansukram.
Dowlat Lalbhai.
Gopal Ganesh.
Kubor Purbhudass.
Parbhu Kisor.
Trimbaklal Govardhan.

(3.) During the season an area of 1375 square miles was topographed: of this 983 square miles was on the scale of 4 inches to a mile and 392 square miles on the 2-inch scale. In the Dang Forests an area of about 550 square miles was triangulated, but this will have to be supplemented with further triangulation and traversing to furnish a sufficiency of data points for the final Survey. A small area in sheet 79, which remained incomplete at the close of the previous season, was completed with data points, by traversing; and an area of about 300 square miles of British territory previously triangulated was prepared for Survey on the 4-inch scale, by effecting the necessary connections between the fiscal details of the Revenue Survey and our triangulation stations by means of traversing.

(4.) The area topographically surveyed comprises the whole of sheets 81 and 82 (which completes the topography of Degree Sheet III), and the completion of sheet 14 of which one quarter was surveyed in the previous season; it thus fills up two gaps which last year presented an unsightly appearance on the Index map.

(5.) Sheets 81 and 82 include portion of the Dholka, Viramgám, and Dhandhuka talukas of the Ahmedabad Collectorate and portions of the Limri, Lakhtar, Wadhwán and Cambay states which have now been completely surveyed and sheet 14 includes portion of the Ankleswar taluka of the Broach Collectorate and of the Olpád* taluka of the Surat Collectorate.

(6.) The country in sheets 81 and 82 is very flat and the north-east portion of 81 and south-west portion of 82 are very woody. These sheets include the mouth and about 33 miles of the course of the Sábarmati river and about the same length of the Bhádhar, Bhogáwo and Rodh rivers, and also the water connection during the monsoon between the Nal and the Gulf of Cambay which I mentioned in para. 16 of my last year's report as probably existing. It is now established that during the monsoon the Peninsula of Kattywar becomes an island. Sheet 81 also includes a portion of the Nal lake, the greater portion of which is included in sheet 80, and was mentioned in my last year's report. When I wrote that report I thought the portion left in sheet 81 was so small that I spoke of sheet 80 containing the whole lake, but it appears that the extents of the lake in November varies very considerably from its extent in March. Many square miles which are dry in March and become the haunts of wild boar and wolves, are in November several feet under water. I would remark generally that the drainage of Guzerat is, from the flatness of the country, very capricious; some of the rivers lose themselves in marsh or in sand, resolving themselves into streams again further on, in their passage to the sea; others change their course in a perplexing way, and none of them have a sufficiently rapid fall to carry off at once any extraordinary rain fall, and so every year the towns on their banks and the bridges are in danger. The Sábarmati, which has lately overflowed its banks and done such damage to the city of Ahmedabad and to many villages on its banks—for the second time within the last few years—is also remarkable for the capricious way in which it alters its course. I have the Revenue Survey map of a village (Rinjha) dated 1856 on which an alteration in the fiscal details was made in 1867 owing to a change in the course of the Sábarmati, the left bank shifting ¾ and the right ¼ of a mile, the new left bank being $\frac{3}{16}$ of a mile to the right of the old right bank, and our Survey this year shews a still further divergence from the old course. To give another instance, it will be found in the correspondence of the Bombay Party that in 1855 a stage erected at a place called Sikutar Mátha for taking tidal observations, was washed clean away by the force of the current, the site of that stage is now half a mile inland and is only flooded at spring tides.

(7.) Sheets 81 and 82 are crossed by the Ahmedabad and Gogo road, but it scarcely deserves mention as in nearly the whole of its extent across these sheets it is out of repair, and in some places

* In last year's report para. 22, I gave three different ways in which this town is spelt, Olpád is now a fourth, but is that recently adopted and established by the Government of Bombay in the official list of names.

totally obliterated. Dhandhuka the chief town of one of the talukas of the Ahmedabad Collectorate is on this road and is about halfway between Ahmedabad and Gogo. It is in sheet 82. Dholka another taluka town and next to Ahmedabad the most important in the Collectorate, is in sheet 81. On account of the importance of Dholka I had all the principal thoroughfares traversed with a prismatic compass and chain so that the town could if necessary be mapped on a larger scale than that of 4 inches to a mile; but on this scale it is a most imposing feature in the map, being nearly 6 inches from north to south and 3 inches from east to west. The Thákur's towns of Koth and Gángad are also in this sheet, and Dholera (well known in connection with cotton) is in sheet 82. Sheet 81 contains a large area of Talukdari land interspersed with the Khálsa (I explained the meaning of these terms in para. 20 of my last year's report) but in sheet 82 the two classes of tenure are more separate, and I was therefore enabled to survey an area of 392 square miles of Talukdari land in that sheet on the 2-inch scale.

(8.) The country in sheet 14 is flat, and fairly wooded with babool and palm trees, though along the coast there is a considerable expanse of sand and mud which, on account of the number of intersecting creeks and nalas, required as much labour in surveying as cultivated land and even more, because of the difficulty of moving over the ground. The Kim and Sena rivers cross Sheet 14 from east to west. They are neither of much importance, not being navigable for large craft, but the Kim is the larger of the two; both have considerable estuaries, increasing the expanse of mud. The villages in this sheet are much more closely packed than in sheets 81 and 82 : in the portion surveyed this season these are none of any great importance though all are fairly populous. Perhaps Eláo in the Anklesar taluka and Bagwa and Kursad in the Olpád taluka are the most so.

(9.) Leaving Poona on the 11th November we commenced work in sheet 81 on the 21st. Having a sufficiency of ground triangulated in advance for two years, I gave Plane Tables to both Mr. Christie and Mr. Connor who had previously always worked with a theodolite. The two Messrs. Norman and three Native Surveyors having but recently joined the Department in September and October, had also to learn the use of the Plane Table. I could not commence the instruction of all these pupils at once, and therefore I employed those who had to wait, in my Office, where there was always plenty of miscellaneous work to be done in connection with the mapping.

(10.) One new feature in the administration of my Party was the formation of a permanent Drawing Office. I found this absolutely necessary, because my mapping power had been most severely overtaxed by the great amount of mapping thrown upon it by the adoption of the 4-inch scale and I therefore kept Mr. Peyton and six Native Surveyors at my Head Quarter Camp and I supplemented this force at the beginning of the season by those hands who were waiting to be taught Plane Tabling. The Revenue Survey Surveyors were employed solely in plotting the traverses on the Plane Table Sections, as they came in, as checks to test their accuracy, and in transferring on to them the fiscal details from Revenue Survey village maps.

(11.) On leaving Ahmedabad I apportioned off the work to the different Surveyors, and took my Head Quarter Camp to a central position in their midst from which I could run out and see them each at work : I was disappointed at the rate at which the Survey of sheet 81 progressed, some of the talukdari villages interlaced with the Khálsa gave a great deal of trouble from the fiscal demarcations being obliterated, and from the patches of cultivation along the margins of the marshy connection between the Nal and the Bhádbar river not conforming to the field partition shewn on the village maps. All these patches were surveyed, but at the cost of a great deal of time. On the completion of sheets 81 and 82 we moved into sheet 14, which was completed by 15th May, and I myself opened Office in Poona on 20th April.

(12.) During the early portion of the season, that is till the end of January, Lieutenant Gibbs was engaged in Plane Tabling, and he completed two Plane Tables in sheet 81 on the 4-inch scale, comprising 36 square miles. After this I sent him to examine the Plane Table containing the town of Dholka and then to continue the triangulation of the Dangs, which he commenced in the previous season.

Lieutenant Gibbs, R.E.

(16.) He succeeded in fixing a great number of points, but found it impossible to fix any down in the ravines, on account of their being so tortuous and precipitous; it will therefore be necessary to supplement his operations with traverses running along the ravines, in order to give data points to the Plane Tablers who will be obliged to work either on the tops of the hills, or the bottoms of the valleys, and sketch in the precipices, and when in a ravine they would never be able to see the stations on the heights.

(17.) Lieutenant Gibbs had a very difficult task, as may easily be imagined from the fact that the whole of the country in the Dangs is mountainous and wooded and intersected with precipitous, tortuous ravines, and that his stations vary in height capriciously between 1500 and 5000 feet.

(18.) I kept Mr. Peyton during the whole field season at my Head Quarter Camp as the head
of the Drawing Office, the strength and duties of which I have
mentioned in para. 10.

Mr. Peyton.

(19,) Mr. D'Souza supervised all the Native Surveyors' Plane Tabling on the 4-inch scale, and
instructed as well as supervised Messrs. Christie, S. Norman and C.
Norman (partly instructed also by Mr. McAFee) and Gopal Vishnu,
Govind Gopal, and Bulwant Rajaram, so that he was actively employed the whole season, as he altogether
examined 41 Plane Tables on the 4-inch scale, and 1 Plane Table on the 2-inch scale, comprising an area
of 736 square miles.

Mr. D'Souza.

(20.) Mr. Christie was employed the whole season in Plane Tabling on the 4-inch scale, and considering that it was his first season at that work, his out-turn is very
creditable, both as to quantity and quality. Mr. Christie is also
very observant of the country he surveys, and has given me a report describing fully each Plane Table
that he completed.

Mr. Christie.

(21.) Mr. McAFee joined me on the 31st December and I kept him at the Head Quarter Office
till the 5th February, when I gave him a Plane Table in sheet 81 on
the 4-inch scale, and sent Mr. C. Norman with him for instruction.
After starting Mr. C. Norman he was employed for the remainder of the season on the topography on
the 2-inch scale in sheet 82, and had working under him Ganesh Bapuji 1st and Raoji Narayen; he is
a very careful and accurate worker.

Mr. McAFee.

(22.) Mr. Connor, though he had learnt how to use a Plane Table before in the Kattywar Party,
had never learnt how to utilize the Revenue Survey materials, Mr.
D'Souza therefore gave him a helping hand at first, and then he soon
went on with his Plane Table independently, but owing to his eyes failing him, not being strong enough
to stand the continual glare, I had to find other work for him at my Head Quarters, in projecting the
Plane Tables and other miscellaneous duties.

Mr. Connor.

(23.) Mr. Hickie was employed the whole season through in Plane Tabling, first in sheet 81
where he completed 3 Plane Tables on the 4-inch scale, then a Plane
Table in sheet 82 on the 2-inch scale, and then 2 Plane Tables in
sheet 14 on the 4-inch scale. He is a careful and accurate worker.

Mr. Hickie.

(24.) Mr. Cusson was also employed the whole season in Plane Tabling, first in sheet 81 where
he completed 3 Plane Tables, one of which included the large town
of Dholka, which he surveyed very accurately and mapped very
neatly. He then completed a Plane Table in sheet 82 on the 2-inch scale, and then 2 Plane Tables in
sheet 14 on the 4-inch scale. He is a very neat draftsman.

Mr. Cusson.

(25.) Mr. Hall after completing one Plane Table in sheet 81 on the 4-inch scale was transferred
to the Kattywar Party.

Mr. Hall.

(26.) Mr. S. Norman was only appointed to the Department on 1st September, so he had every
thing to learn. He rapidly acquired a knowledge of Plane Tabling,
and during the season completed an out-turn of 94 square miles on
the 4-inch scale very accurately and neatly.

Mr. S. Norman.

(27.) Mr. C. Norman only joined the Department on the 12th October, so like his brother had
every thing to learn. His out-turn was only 59 square miles on the
4-inch scale, but he was employed in my Office projecting Plane
Tables and on other miscellaneous work until the 8th February. He too promises well for duties both
in the field and in office.

Mr. C. Norman.

(28). Mr. D'Souza reports well of all the Native Surveyors working under him. Gopal Vishnu who
had hitherto been employed as a Traverse Surveyor, has turned out a
very fair Plane Tabler. The two new hands Govind Gopal and Bulwant Rajaram both promise well.

Native Surveyors.

(29.) The Native Surveyors of the Revenue Survey Party were divided between two duties.
Mr. T. A. Le Mesurier, the Assistant Superintendent, in charge with
8 Native Surveyors were employed traversing in sheets 31, 32, connect-
ing the village boundary trijunctions and village sites of the British territory with the triangulation,
while 4 Native Surveyors were employed in my Office transferring the fiscal details from the Revenue
Survey village maps to our Plane Tables as they came in.

Revenue Survey.

(30.) It will perhaps be noticed that in my last year's report I only mentioned the Revenue
Survey Party as consisting of 5 Native Surveyors, whereas in this report there are 7. Each season I
have to consider the proportion of Native Surveyors to underlings that I require, and the Superintendent of the Guzerat Revenue Survey supplies me either with more Native Surveyors and less funds to

pay for underlings, or *vice versâ;* the total salaries of both being limited to Rupees 500 a month. During the past season I only required very little more ground to be prepared in advance of the topography, but that the drawing power was insufficient to meet my requirements. I therefore drew on the Superintendent Revenue Survey for 2 more Native Surveyors for employment in my Office.

(34.) I beg to inform you that, when we take the field at the end of this month, I expect that

Mapping.
with the exception of part of the inking in of the fields on 4 sections, the whole of the *drawing* of the sections on the 4-inch scale will be completed, but there will remain a quantity of printing work on several sections, which will be carried on by the permanent Drawing Office that I shall take into the field. The drawing of the sections on the 2-inch scale has also been commenced, but will have to be finished in the field. I expect to have all the sections now in hand completed before we return to recess quarters.

(35.) I am happy to inform you that there is a marked improvement in the mapping of this recess over that of last year. Last year we worked under great disadvantages, but we learnt several lessons, which have been turned to account this year, and now the hands are classified into (1) free hand draftsmen, (2) second class draftsmen and (3) mechanical draftsmen, and the printers are also divided into (1) hand printers, (2) and (3) 1st and 2nd class type printers. To each section, before it is begun, is stitched a printed form called "Section Register" in which all the different stages through which the map has to pass are tabulated, and against each there is a space for the signature of the draftsman or examiner, who passes it through the particular stage, so that each map progresses regularly, and passes from one class of draftsman to another, according as the stages are divided among the different classes. This method could not be arrived at at once, and the want of it last year was the cause of many errors, which have taken up a great deal of time in correcting.

Computations.
(36.) All computations have been completed.

Extracts from Notes on the portion of the Dangs visited by Lieutenant J. E. Gibbs, R.E., in February—May 1875.

(1.) The country in which I have been working this season comprises portions of the Dang Forest, together with some Gaekwar territory, part of the Pimpalner taluka of Khandesh and part of the Báglán taluka of Násik.

(2.) I must preface my remarks with a few words concerning the notes that were published in the General Report for 1873-74. They were in some cases merely records of the impressions with which I was struck at the time, and which I was content to leave as such till I should verify or correct them this year, having no idea that they would go farther than the office table. I shall now have occasion to correct some of my statements of last year.

(3.) The whole of the hills forming the Dangs may be looked upon as the first step of the trap

Aspect of the country.
formation leading to the Deccan table land. The second step is at the Gháts bordering the east of the Dangs. The lower step is deeply cut into, as with a graver, by the water courses of the torrents of the rainy season. At the foot of the upper step the valleys rise to nearly the original level of the ground; thus in a direct distance of about 40 miles the water courses have a fall of about 1500 feet. The 'trend' of the lower step, and its valleys are clothed with forest. The upper step is fringed along its western edge by high peaks. The strata are perfectly horizontal and the peaks consist of vertical columns of basalt. Where these are equal in height they give the appearance of a tower, but where of unequal height and arranged like the half of a set of organ pipes, they give at a distance the illusion of *tilting,* which I noted last year, and which I again noticed on leaving the Dangs this year. On the upper step the aspect is quite different. From one of my stations on the peaks of the fringe, which there ran roughly north and south, to the north-east lay a flat plain dotted with low conical hills, bare of trees, to the east and south-east were high hills with flat tops, or peaks, but only clothed below with forest. To the west lay the Dangs, a monotonous expanse of forest. Looking down there scarcely appeared to be any hills, the valleys being too steep-sided and winding to show. Generally speaking the aspect of the country is wild and inhospitable, but occasionally picturesque gorges, and dells may be met with, though always of a wild character.

(4.) In the course of my work I visited the hill forts of Rupgarh, Songarh, and Sáler belong-

Hill Forts.
ing to H. H. the Gaekwar.

Rupgarh Fort was taken from the Bhíls by one of the Gaekwars, but has long since been abandoned, and is in ruins. It lies in a very silent position on the frontier, and at one time was useful for keeping the Bhíls in check. Last year I made a note of a perennial spring supplying a tank in the fort. Dissatisfied at the time with the information I received that the tank was supplied by a spring, I examined the place, and thought over the matter this year. The level this year in March was within an inch or two the same as in May last year. The tank is at the highest part of the fort, which stands on a mass of rock high above any thing else within miles, so that it could not be a spring of descent. The water is cold, and there is neither motion in it, nor overflow, as would be caused by a spring from a great depth. A syphon could not exist through rocks of so jointed a kind as trap. The only explanation therefore that I can give for the presence of this constant supply is that, as in the case at the ponds made on the South Downs of England, the daily sea breezes laden with vapour reach Rupgarh almost without obstruction, and there, being checked and meeting with the cold surface of the water already there, they are deprived of their vapour, which condenses to collect in the tank.

Songarh Fort is on the hill to the west of the once walled town of Songarh. It was originally seized from the Bhíls, some families of whom still hold Jaghírs in connection with it. It has a garrison of 25 men, and there are 35 guns in it, which are rusty and honey combed. The only portion of the defences at all kept in repair is the entrance at the northern end. From the top of the hill two high walls run down splaying out, and are connected at the bottom by a very high wall in which is a gateway. In the lower part of the enclosed space are the ruins of what must have been a fine palace with several stories. Songarh is the Head Quarters of the Pargana.

Sáler Fort stands on an immense mass of basaltic rock on the top of the upper step. This mass of rock is very steeply precipitous on the southern side, where it is slightly concave, the horns of the crescent flanking the town. The security of the fort lies in its natural inaccessibility. The ascent is by a zigzag rock-cut staircase up the southern cliff, completely in view from the ridge above, as far as the simple but ingenious system of gate-defences that bar access to a narrow ledge along and half-way up the western face. From the northern end of this ledge is another rock-cut staircase leading to the second set of defences that are just below the level of the spring of the 'roof'. The most active of goats could not ascend by any but the regular path. On the top are cattle and goats that have been carried up when young, a good supply of water in tanks at the foot of the roof-slope (which is about 200 feet high), and rock-cut casemates for the garrison.

(5.) I think that the evil reports about the Dangs are exaggerated. Whether this year and the
last have been exceptionally healthy or not I do not know, but judging
Climate and Health. from them I think that with a little care there need be very little
danger of sickness between the end of February and the middle or end of May. I believe that during that period there is little or nothing to fear in the air. Without doubt the water is unfit to drink, not only because in many places it is mixed with the rank products of rotting vegetation, but that it is still impregnated with the malaria of the cold season. The sovereign cure for this I believe lies in distilling all water for drinking or cooking purposes. Hindús, who drink water in large quantities, and who will not touch distilled water because stills were unknown to their forefathers, suffer considerably, and I had several very serious cases of remittent fever among the Hindús of my party. The rest all enjoyed very good health.

(6.) Last year the statistics I collected about 14 villages that I visited in forest tracts, showed
that the percentage of children was 36·55 and this year the statistics
Inhabitants. of 26 villages gives as the percentage 37·96. On comparison with
the Census Report of the Bombay Presidency, I find that the proportion is a little over that for the whole Presidency taken together, and therefore my conclusion last year that the population here was rapidly decreasing may be erroneous, still I believe I was not very wrong, and think that, considering the few old people one sees, the percentage of children is small.

The hillmen generally are very superstitious and their worship being dictated by fear, stones erected to Wághdeo (the tiger god) and Nágdeo (the snake god) are very common.

As I worked more in the heart of the Forest this year than last, I naturally saw more Bhíls. They are however disappearing from the country. The Bhíl chiefs are 14 in number, 5 being styled Rájá, and the rest Naik.

I visited a manufactory of Káth, the Parsee Overseer showing me every thing. The process was just the same as I described last year. I was amused, if not shocked, by the nonchalance of primitive innocence with which several young women, habillées peutêtre, mais non vêtues, stood around. Some were absolutely less clad than the men. The dirtiness of the people is rivalled by the dirtiness of the process.

At one village *vidi mirabile monstrum* in the form of a young woman built by nature to be a left-handed amazon. Her right breast was supplying the wants of her baby, but it is fortunate she had not twins.

(7.) While working in and along the boundary of Gaekwar territory, I was surprised to see the wretched state of the trees, especially teak. One might reckon **The Forest.** on the core of any teak tree over a foot in diameter being rotten, and the trees were all misshapen. I was agreeably struck by the contrast on working into the Dang States. The superiority in size, symmetry and healthy growth of the trees under the Forest Department over those in the uncared for Gaekwar districts, catches even the untrained eye at once, and speaks volumes in praise of the care and efforts of the Department. The trees are tall, thick and straight, and solid throughout, and the old trees that are felled are replaced by healthy saplings. In some dells the trees were particularly fine with tall straight trunks, not branching till they had attained a great height.

(9.) Last year in my notes the trees &c., mentioned were put down irrespective of order, I have **Botany.** therefore repeated their names in the following list of species I have identified. The native names are those given me by the hillmen, who seem to have names for all trees and plants. Besides the following I noticed several that I hope next year to be able to identify.

Capparideæ—Capparis pedunculosa, a small shrub with recurved thorns and umbels of small white flowers having long gynophors.

Malvaceæ—Hibiscus Rosa Sinensis (Jasodi), the shoe flower in Sáler gardens.

Bombax—Malabaricum (Sáonwar), red silk cotton tree, described last year.—Dang Valleys.

Sterculiaceæ—Sterculia urens (Khandol) described last year.—Dang Valleys.

Tiliaceæ—Grewia abutilifolia (Dhamon), a small tree with 3-nerved leaves and cymes of small yellow flowers, having petals much smaller than sepals; drupes small yellow said to be edible; wood hard and strong.—2000 feet.

Rutaceæ.—Ægle Marmelos (Bil) with 3-foliolate leaves (emblematic of the Hindú Trinity), and large globose fruit having a woody rind and many seeds in a sweet aromatic orange pulp, valuable in dysentery.—1500 feet.

Anacardiaceæ.—Mangifera Indica (Am), the common mango, near village sites.

Celastrineæ.—Celastrus paniculata (Kárkángun), a scandent shrub with pendulous panicles of tiny greenish flowers; the seeds yield lamp-oil.—Dang Valleys.

Rhamneæ.—Zizyphus rugosa (Turan), a small tree with recurved prickles; fleshy white fruit with crustaceous stone, having a mawkish taste, and being much eaten by the inhabitants.—Common even over 3000 feet (See Hooker's Flora of India).

Rhamnus Wightii (Ragatrura), a small shrub with shortly acuminate fascicled leaves; panicles starting opposite to one of the lowest leaves of a tuft; berries, ⅜ size of a pea, superior, 4-seeded, red-orange; calyx persistent—evidently rare as I only saw one specimen, and few of the villagers knew its name.

Leguminosæ—Erythrina Indica (Pangara), a tree armed with black prickles; leaves 3-foliolate; racemes of bright scarlet flowers in March. Wood used for sword sheaths (Bird-wood).—Dang Valleys. Erythrina suberosa (also called Pangara), very similar to the above but with cork like bark.—Dang Valleys.

Butea frondosa (Palas Kankara), known to Europeans as the Dák, a shrub with 3-foliolate, leaves leaflets large, used as plates or drinking cups; tomentose racemes of large silky orange-red flowers in February and March; legumes downy, one seeded.—Everywhere.

Pongamia glabra (Kurunj), a tree with 5—7-foliolate leaves with large glabrous leaflets; axillary racemes of shortly pedicelled pink and white papilionaceous flowers.—Dang Valleys.

Dalbergia latifolia (the Sisu of the Bombay Presidency), the black-wood tree.—1500 feet.

Dalbergia ougeinensis (Tanaj), a large tree with 3-foliolate leaves, leaflets large, reddish when young; racemes of small pink flowers; wood tough, strong, and heavy.—Up to 1500 feet.

Cassia fistula (Báwa), a small tree with pinnate leaves having 5 pairs of leaflets; pendulous racemes of bright yellow flowers; pods long, cylindrical, divided by spurious traverse plates into one-seeded cells; seeds hard, shiny, collected by red beetles.—Everywhere.

Tamarindus Indica (Amli or Chinch), near village sites.

Bauhinia Racemosa (Aapta), a small tree or shrub; leaves used when dry for making 'biris' or native cigarettes; terminal racemes of small white flowers.—Common everywhere.

Acacia Catechu (Khair) mentioned last year.—Common everywhere.

Albizzia Lebbek (Siris), a large tree with black bark, and dark heart-wood somewhat like black-wood; leaves abruptly bipinnate; pinnæ 2—6 pairs; leaflets 10—15 pairs, very oblique; raceme axillary, long peduncled with many close 10—15 flowered heads.—Up to 1500 feet.

Cicer Arietinum (Chana), gram cultivated about Songarh.

Phaseolus Mungo (Urid) cultivated in small patches in the Dangs.

Combretaceæ.—Anogeissus Latifolius (Dáora), a tree with white bark and wood, and light green elliptical leaves; it yields a very fine strong white gum.—In valleys and up to 1500 feet.

Terminalia Chebula (Herdi), leaves large, oblong and downy when young; petioles short with pair of glands at apex; panicles of purple oval drupes having a bloom; drupes (myrobolans) valuable for their tannin.—2500 feet.

Terminalia Arjuna (Mota Sádra), a large tree with smooth bark and dark heart-wood.—Up to 1500 feet.

Myrtaceæ.—Sizygium Jambolanum (Jámbul), a tree with light colored bark and opposite, entire shining leaves; 3-forked panicles of small white flowers with calyptrate corolla; good timber and edible fruit.—Near village sites.

Sizygium Salicifolium (Jámbul), a shrub with willow-shaped leaves; lax panicles of small white flowers.—In beds of rivers.

Careya arborea (Kumbi), a tree with large entire membraneous leaves, much eaten by a small white caterpillar; leaves after flowers; flowers with 2—3 hundred long white stamens; style long, honey at base; fruit the size of a small apple, edible.—2000 feet.

Cucurbitaceæ.—Cucumis trigonus with oval fruit, yellow striped with green, very bitter; climbing or creeping about shrubs.—2000 feet.

Loranthaceæ.—Loranthus bicolor (Bhandgol), a very common parasite especially on the Aapta; flowers long, slender, scarlet and green; leaves opposite, entire; also accrescent round inferior ovary.—Everywhere.

Rubiaceæ.—Nauclea cordifolia (Hedu), a large tree with roundish downy stipulate leaves, and round heads of flowers.—Valleys.

Gardenia dumetorum (Gúl), a small spinous tree with opposite, simple entire leaves having interpetiolar stipules; flowers sessile, axillary, solitary, white fading to yellow; fruit round.—Everywhere.

Gardenia lucida? (Tondrum), very similar to the above but with large flowers; flowers full of honey; stigma large, brown and sticky.—Everywhere.

Compositæ.—Blumea holoserica, a small downy herb with deeply serrate leaves, and yellow flower-heads in elongated panicles. So common all over disused clearings, that at first I thought it must be cultivated.

Oleaceæ.—Jasminum Sambac (Bhat Mogra), a shrub with fragrant, double white flowers.—In Sáler Gardens.

Sapotaceæ.—Bassia latifolia. (Mahwa), mentioned last year. There appear to be 2 varieties, the one with red and the other with green leaves.—Both in great numbers above the Gháts near Pimpalner, and also common in the Dangs.

Ebenaceæ.—Diospyros exsculpta (Temburni), a small tree with large leaves downy beneath; fruit edible with rather pleasant flavour.—1500 feet.

Apocynaceæ.—Carissa Carandas, a spinous shrub with shining coriaceous leaves, and fragrant white flowers; purple berry with sweet acid pulp; flowers in March.—Common everywhere.

Wrightia tinctoria (Kála Kura), a small tree or shrub with white wood, and lax panicles of fragrant white flowers appearing in April; style very short and anthers low down the tube.—Common everywhere.

Holarrhena antidysenterica (Doli Kurli), a shrub very similar to the above, but with wider leaves, and puberulous flowers having partially coherent anthers which form a pyramid above the limb of the corolla.—Common everywhere.

Asclepiadaceæ.—Calotropis Gigantea (Madár), a shrub abounding in milky juice, opposite leaves and interpetiolar umbels of purple flowers.—Common on all clearings.

Bignoniaceæ.—Bignonia Quadrilocularis (Waras), a very handsome tree when in full bloom with its large bunches of crimped white flowers.—Valleys and up to 1500 feet.

Cordiaceæ.—Cordia Myxa (Bhokar), a small tree with simple alternate leaves, panicles of white flowers, and edible berries with glutinous pulp.—1500 feet.

Verbenaceæ.—Tectona Grandis (Sagwan), the teak tree.—Valleys and up to 1500 feet.

Gmelina arborea (Sheoni), with opposite entire leaves, velvetty beneath; inflorescence a raceme; drupes yellow, superior, calyx persistent; fruit much eaten by wild animals.—1500 feet.

Vitex Nirgundi or Bicolor (Nirgundi), a shrub with opposite β or 5-foliolate leave and panicles of small bluish purple flowers.—Common in valleys and above the Gháts.

Euphorbiaceæ.—Phyllanthus Emblica (Aonla), a small tree with axillary clusters of flowers ; drupe fleshy, edible.—Valleys.

Urticaceæ.—Ficus benghalensis (Waror Bar), the Banyan tree.—Common everywhere.

Ficus religiosa (Pipal), with cordate, narrowly acuminate leaves.—Everywhere.

Ficus pseudotjiela (Pipri), a tall handsome tree with long petioled, oblong-ovate, shining leaves.—Common.

Ficus cordifolia (Páer), a tree with leaves somewhat like those of the Pipal, and clusters of small seasile round fruit.—Common.

Ficus glomerata (Umbar), a crooked tree covered with figs, purple when ripe, and always full of worms or flies.—Common especially by streams.

Artocarpaceæ.—Artocarpus integrifolia (Panas), the Jack tree, with shining dark green coriaceous leaves and huge fruit with shagreen exterior.—Western borders of Dangs.

Orchidaceæ.—I saw several specimens on trees, but none in flowers.

Amaryllidaceæ.—Crinum parvum (Karwand), stem about 9 inches high, about 3 white flowers in umbel; the bulbs were generally so fixed in the crevices of rocks that they could not be taken out whole; flowers in May.—Common on Dang hills and on the Gháts.

Palmaceæ.—Borassus flabelliformis (Tári), tapped for its saccharine juice, drunk under the name of tári or toddy.—Common in the western Dangs and again at the foot of the upper Gháts.

Phœnix Sylvestris (Kajur), the common wild date palm; fruit yellow when ripe.— Western Dangs.

Gramineæ.—Eleusine coracana (Nágli or Násni), cultivated for food and export, being given to Banjáras in exchange for salt.

Oryza sativa (Chokha), common rice, occasionally raised in small quantities for food.

Holcus spicatus (Bájri), cultivated for food.

Bambusa vulgaris (Wolu), growing to 60 feet high in thick clumps.—Western Dangs·

Bambusa stricta (Bás), a small straight species of Bamboo with long thin branches.— Western Dangs.

There is of course a great sameness in the lithology of the district, the greater part of the rocks varying from black to grey crystalline basalts, diorites, and the like.

Geology.

On the tops of several of the hills of the 'lower step' I met with rocks full of acicular white crystals. I saw very few large crystal masses. There are no alluvial deposits, and the rocks of the river beds are polished and rounded by the attrition of the gritty particles carried down by the monsoon torrents.

INDEX CHART OF THE GUZERAT TOPOGRAPHICAL SURVEY

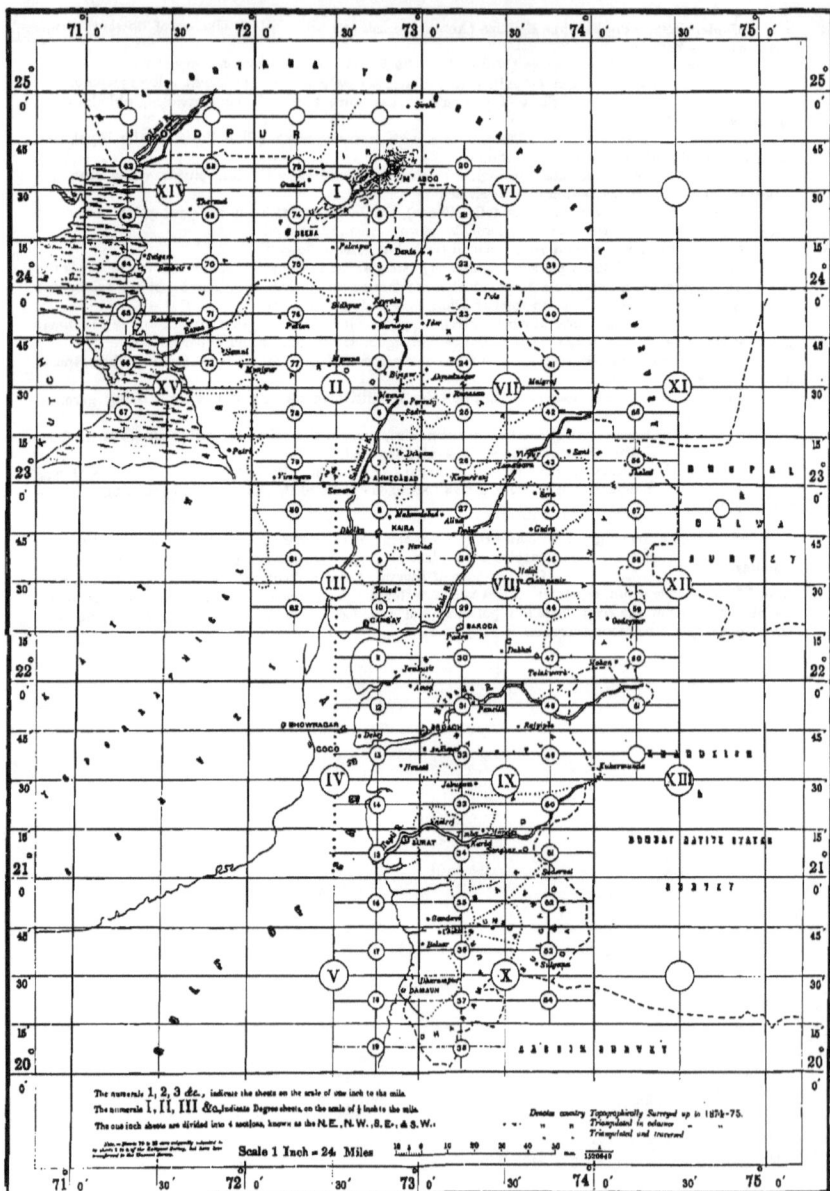

The numerals 1, 2, 3 &c., indicate the sheets on the scale of one inch to the mile.

The numerals I, II, III &c., indicate Degree sheets, on the scale of $\frac{1}{4}$ inch to the mile.

The one inch sheets are divided into 4 sections, known as the N.E., N.W., S.E., & S.W.

Denotes country Topographically Surveyed up to 1874-75.

" " Triangulated in advance
" " Triangulated and traversed

Scale 1 Inch = 24 Miles

TABULAR STATEMENT OF WORK IN GUZERAT, DURING THE FIELD SEASON 1874-75.

Triangulation.

Observer's Name.	Instrument used.	Area triangulated ed sq. miles.	No. of Stations visited.	3 Angles observed. Triangles.	Triangular error.	Error per mile.	No. of Heights.	Discrepancy in Height.	2 Angles observed. Triangles.	Error per mile.	No. of Points.	No. of Heights.	Remarks.
Lieut. J. E. Gibbs, ... (Recorder Bulwant Atmaram.)	Troughton & Simms' 10-inch	147* / 41†	27	85	4·6″	17½ in.	24	0·95 ft.	138	4·1½ in.	93	64	*Primary Triangulation. †Secondary Triangulation. ‡Mean diff. of 15 common sides. ||Mean diff. of 40 common sides. §Mean diff. of 21 common heights.

Plane Tabling.

No.	Name.	Plate Tabling in Square Miles. 4-inch scale.	2-inch scale.	Stations per sq. mile.	Remarks.
1	Lieut. J. E. Gibbs,	87·3	......	6·6	*Employed the whole time in supervising native mukrus and in teaching new hands.
2	Mr. D'Souza*	124·4	......	13·3	
3	„ Christie,	12·5	140·0	6·4	†Joined 31st December, was also employed in supervising natives and in teaching Mr. C. Norman.
4	„ McAfeet	18·3	......	22·8	
5	„ E. J. Connor,	94·6	70·1	10·7	‡Transferred to Kaitznur Party 9th January.
6	„ J. Hickie,	85·4	57·8	7·8	
7	„ G. D. Cusson,	18·9	......	16·7	
8	„ G. Hall‡	99·7	......	18·3	
9	„ S. Norman,	59·8	......	11·5	
10	„ C. Norman,				
	Native Surveyors.				
1	Gopal Vishnu,	87·7	......	12·5	
2	Bapji Narayen,	99·7	98·5	9·6	
3	Bhow Govind,	58·8	23·8	9·8	
4	Luximon Gorpurray,	54·8	......	16·9	
5	Mahad Dinkar,	52·1	51·8	11·0	
6	Ganesh Bapji 1st,	57·8	......	11·1	
7	Govind Gopal,	89·0	......	15·5	
8	Bulwant Rajaram,			14·5	
	Total, ...	1067·6 or 1468 sq. miles	400·4	average 10·7	Total No. of Plane Table Stations 15,636. Including overlaps.

Traversing.

No.	Names.	Triangles.	Error per mile.	No. of Points.	No. of Heights.	Linear Distance in miles.	Remarks.
1	Mr. E. J. Connor,					3·649	A sufficiency of traverses has not been computed as yet for obtaining a fair average for the errors.
2	Ganesh Bapji 2nd,					129·298	
	Revenue Surveys.						
1	Jugul Manakram,					169·555	
2	Gopal Ganesh,					117·110	
3	Trimbaklal Goverdhan,					27·984	
	Total, ...					447·584	
	Number of points fixed, ...					1138	

Permanent Drawing Office.

No.	Name.	Employment.
1	Mr. J. Peyton,	Head Draftsman.
2	Ganesh Narayen,	Draftsman left sick on 27th Decr.
3	Monaji Abou,	Head printing.
4	Luximon Gorpurray,	Printing from 29th January.
5	Mukund Dinkar,	„ „ 16th February.
	Revenue Survey.	
1	Kenhowram Ravishankar,	Plotting Traverses and Revenue
2	Kuber Parbhudass,	Survey fiscal details on Plane
3	Dowlat Lubhai,	Tablet.
4	Parbhu Kisor,	

Extract from the Narrative Report—dated 15th November 1875—of Captain H. R. THUILLIER, R.E., Officiating Deputy Superintendent 1st Grade, in charge of the Kumaun and Garhwal and the Dehra Dun Survey Parties.

In the spring of 1874, the Establishment of the Kumaun and Garhwál Party was broken up into two detachments; one was sent under Mr. E. C. Ryall to resume the Survey of the higher ranges in Kumaun and Garhwál, the operations of which will be described hereafter, the other detachment, as per margin, under my own superintendence, was employed during the field season 1874-75 in carrying on the Survey of Dehra Dún which was commenced in the previous year.

PERSONNEL.

Captain H. R. Thuillier, R.E.
Lieutenant St. G. C. Gore, R.E., Asst. Supdt.

Surveyors and Asst. Surveyors.

Mr. C. J. Neuville.
„ J. Low.
„ L. J. Pocock.
„ H. Todd.
„ T. Kinney.
„ E. P. Wrixon.

Native Surveyors.

11 Native Surveyors.

(2.) The field operations commenced early in October. Lieutenant Gore, was entrusted with the supervision of the village boundary traverses: Messrs. Low, Todd and Kinney, each with two Native Surveyors, were deputed to take up the topography of the Western Dún commencing at the Jumna. Mr. L. Pocock was directed to complete the triangulation of the Eastern Dún and subsequently to proceed to Jaunsár Báwar for the same purpose; and Mr. Wrixon to carry main traverses in the Eastern Dún for fixing trijunction pillars for checks on the boundary traverses.

(3.) During the season, 225 square miles of country have been topographically surveyed on the scale of 4 inches to the mile; the triangulation of the Dún has been completed and the whole of Jaunsár Báwar covered with a net-work of triangles, comprising a total area of 470 square miles. 70 linear miles of main theodolite traverses, 328 miles of boundary traverses and 63 miles of check survey lines were run.

Out-turn of work.

(4.) The whole of the topography has been done most carefully and the measurements have been very searching. 63 linear miles of check survey were executed across the detail work of the Native Plane Tablers to test its correctness, and the hill sketching was examined *in sitû* during the progress of the work. The results of these tests were very satisfactory and proved the work to be minutely accurate.

Topography.

(5.) The area topographically surveyed is smaller than I had expected to have completed, but several causes tended to this result. The Native Surveyors with only two exceptions were raw hands and had to be taught Plane Tabling, for their work during the previous season (which was their first season of surveying) had been restricted to traversing. Their progress too when trained proved far slower than I had anticipated, so that the brunt of the work fell on the European Assistants. This in a great measure however was due to the intricacy of the ground, and the large amount of detail met with throughout the ground over which the topography was carried. The tabular statement will show this by the amount of chaining and the large proportion of plane table stations which were found requisite for filling in the interior details. For the first 3 months of the field season also, the luxuriant vegetation for which the Dún is proverbial and the high *bhábur* grass which covers a large proportion of the low-lands, proved a great obstacle to the progress of the Plane Tablers. This grass is generally burnt in the month of February and until that time the surveyor is much delayed by having to cut lines for his chain measurements. The field season also was shorter than I might have made it, but this I was compelled to cut short owing to the large amount of mapping which had to be undertaken during the recess, this having been greatly augmented by the large area brought in by the Kumaun and Garhwál detachment during the same season. Under these circumstances and bearing in mind that it was our first season of working on the 4-inch scale, I trust this out-turn will be considered satisfactory.

(6.) The whole of the traversing required for the completion of the Survey of the Dún was finished. All precautions, as described in my last report, were taken to insure accuracy of results. The main theodolite traverses were in all cases run between trigonometrical stations, but in consequence of the ground being more rugged and broken than that met with in the previous season, the ratio of error is somewhat larger, though still satisfactory.

Traverses.

(7.) The boundary traverses were all completed and comprise 121 villages and estates. These traverses are in all cases well tied in by check points furnished either trigonometrically or by the main theodolite traverses. They were executed by the Native Surveyors with the plane table and circular protractor, and were all reduced in the field and found to stand the usual tests in a satisfactory manner. The ground was more or less bad throughout for chaining, especially about the low-lands at the foot of the hills, a large portion of

Boundary traverses and their errors.

the work having to be carried over broken ground and ravines with steep declivities, the measurements of which required very heavy corrections for reduction to the horizontal level. The boundaries also were very intricate, the average distance between each station in 5726 stations being only 4·58 chains. Notwithstanding these trials, the errors are very fairly small.

(8.) The country surveyed during the season comprises ground of every variety, from the flat cultivated lands in the vicinity of the Asan, a tributary of the Jumna and the main drainage channel of the Western Dún, to the crest of the Mussooree range which rises to a height of over 7000 feet above sea level. The low spurs and broken ground about the foot of the hills gave an infinity of labour and trouble in surveying, being for the most part covered with thick Sál forest and cut up by deep precipitous ravines and 'raus' with beds of boulders lower down; these raus spread out leaving broad undulating plateaux between them which are for the most part well cultivated, except in places where shingle crops out.

Remarks on the country.

(10.) Numerous heights, in addition to those obtained trigonometrically, have been fixed by Aneroid barometers throughout the season's work.

Aneroid heights.

(11.) The amount of triangulation and traversing in advance of the portion topographically surveyed, covers in the Dún an area of 125 square miles, this being the extent of the Zamíndárí lands which remains to be surveyed by this party. In addition to this, the whole of Jaunsár Báwar, comprising an area of about 360 square miles, is ready for the topography to be commenced. The survey of this portion of the district which is composed entirely of hills and mountains, is to be done on the scale of 2 inches to the mile and will admit, I am afraid, of little are no traversing.

Triangulation and Traversing in advance of the detail survey.

(12.) I now proceed to report separately on each officer's work, the details of which are tabulated on page 45—a.

(13.) Lieutenant Gore took the field on the 7th October and was employed until 22nd November in superintending the village boundary traverses in the neighborhood of Rájpur and Dehra. On relieving him of this duty I entrusted him with the topography of sections 13, 14 and 24 bordering the Jumna. Having completed these sections, he took up sections 38, 39 and 49 in the beginning of February. About the middle of March, I sent Lieutenant Gore's party to complete all the low village lands lying among the forest of the Eastern Dún, in the vicinity of the Song and Suswa; this being the most favorable time of the year for surveying this ground, on account of the *bhábur* grass being all cleared and its freedom from the malaria of the neighbouring marshes. Much of this land is covered with rank vegetation nourished by the amount of water furnished by these streams and their numerous tributaries. The greatest obstacles to the survey being the cane brakes which were inaccessible to man or elephant. Lieutenant Gore with the help of the Native Surveyors completed the work allotted to him by the 20th April. Lieutenant Gore having been transferred to the topographical branch of the department, I have much pleasure in recording the valuable assistance I have invariably received from him since he has been under my orders, during which time he has conducted his duties with ability and energy to my entire satisfaction, and I consider him in every way qualified for independent charge of survey operations.

Lieutenant Gore, R.E.

(14.) Mr. Neuville was employed the whole season in my office in the miscellaneous current work of which there was a large amount.

Mr. Neuville.

(15.) Mr. Low was employed all the season in Plane Tabling. He commenced on section 7 in the Khádir lands of the Jumna, where he experienced much delay from the high grass which covers all that portion. In January he took up the north and east portions of section 27 which was most intricate and difficult ground, cut up by deep ravines and low hills covered with forest. He then completed the hilly portion of section 37, and leaving his two Native Surveyors to fill in the low ground, he commenced section 46, which consists entirely of hills and runs up to the Mussooree and Landour settlement. By the end of the season he completed this section and section 57 which also consists entirely of hills. I was well satisfied with Mr. Low's diligence and the accuracy of his work.

Mr. Low.

(16.) Mr. Pocock was employed from the middle of October till the beginning of April on triangulation. He first completed the remaining portion of the Eastern Dún covering an area of 110 square miles, and on 22nd January started for Jaunsár Báwar, the triangulation of which he successfully completed by the end of March. This portion of his work embraces an area of 360 square miles, which is well covered with points. I have every reason to be well satisfied with Mr. Pocock's exertions and the results of his work.

Mr. L. Pocock.

(17.) Mr. Todd was employed on topography throughout the season. He commenced work on 19th October with two Native Surveyors and during the season completed sections 9, 15, 26 and half of 56. Of these sections the ground in 15 and 26 was most intricate and difficult. The delineations of the features have been very artistically and faithfully rendered and the varied character of the ground has been shewn with excellent effect, but the labour involved in surveying such a large amount of detail was great and very tedious. The work of the Native Surveyors was rigorously examined. Section 56 consists entirely of hills, the ground being very precipitous and difficult to move about in. This portion of the work was also done with Mr. Todd's usual care and accuracy and the quality of his work is highly creditable to him. Mr. Todd closed work on the 30th April.

Mr. H. Todd.

(18.) Mr. Kinney commenced field work on 17th October and was engaged in Plane Tabling during the entire season. He was first entrusted with sections 3 and 8 in the low ground of the valley of the Asan, and was provided with two Native Surveyors whom he had to train. He completed these sections by the 20th January, when I transferred his Native Surveyors and sent him to take up the topography of the hills in sections 25, 35 & 36. The ground in the two former of those sections is high with bold open features rising to a height of about 7000 feet and was easy to sketch, but in the central and lower portions of 36, the hills are much broken up into small confused masses, covered for the most part with forest and intersected by narrow and intricate ravines, resulting in an unusual amount of detail in the smaller natural features. A portion of this section which I had hoped to have had completed had to be left for the next field season. Mr. Kinney has worked hard and well, his sketching and delineation of ground is remarkably good and characteristic.

Mr. Kinney.

(19.) Mr. Wrixon was employed in minor triangulation in the rough ground between the Dehra and Rájpur road and the Song Nadi. He subsequently took up the traverse of the road from Dehra to Hardwár and then carried a line up the right bank of the Ganges from Hardwár to Tapoban. I regret I am unable to report favorably of Mr. Wrixon's work or conduct.

Mr. Wrixon.

(20.) The topography done by the Native Surveyors, considering that it was their first season in Plane Tabling, was very fair and found to be minutely accurate, but they are very indifferent draftsmen. In this however they are improving, and will I have no doubt next season turn out more artistic work. I have been well satisfied with the diligence of all the Native Surveyors with two exceptions, one of whom was discharged and the pay of the second reduced.

Native Surveyors.

(21.) The party was employed during the recess on computations and mapping. All the computations connected with the previous season's triangulation and traversing were completed. The mapping includes the preparation of 7 Sheets of the Dehra Dún Survey on the scale of 4 inches to the mile which have been completed and sent to the Head Quarter's Office for publication.

Recess of 1875.

(22.) The detail survey of the remaining portion of the Zamíndárí lands in the Dún will be resumed and completed. The topography of Jaunsár Báwar, on the scale of 2 inches to the mile, will also be taken up by a portion of the party at the commencement of the field season, and I trust to be able to complete the survey of this portion of the district also during the ensuing season.

Programme for field season 1875-76.

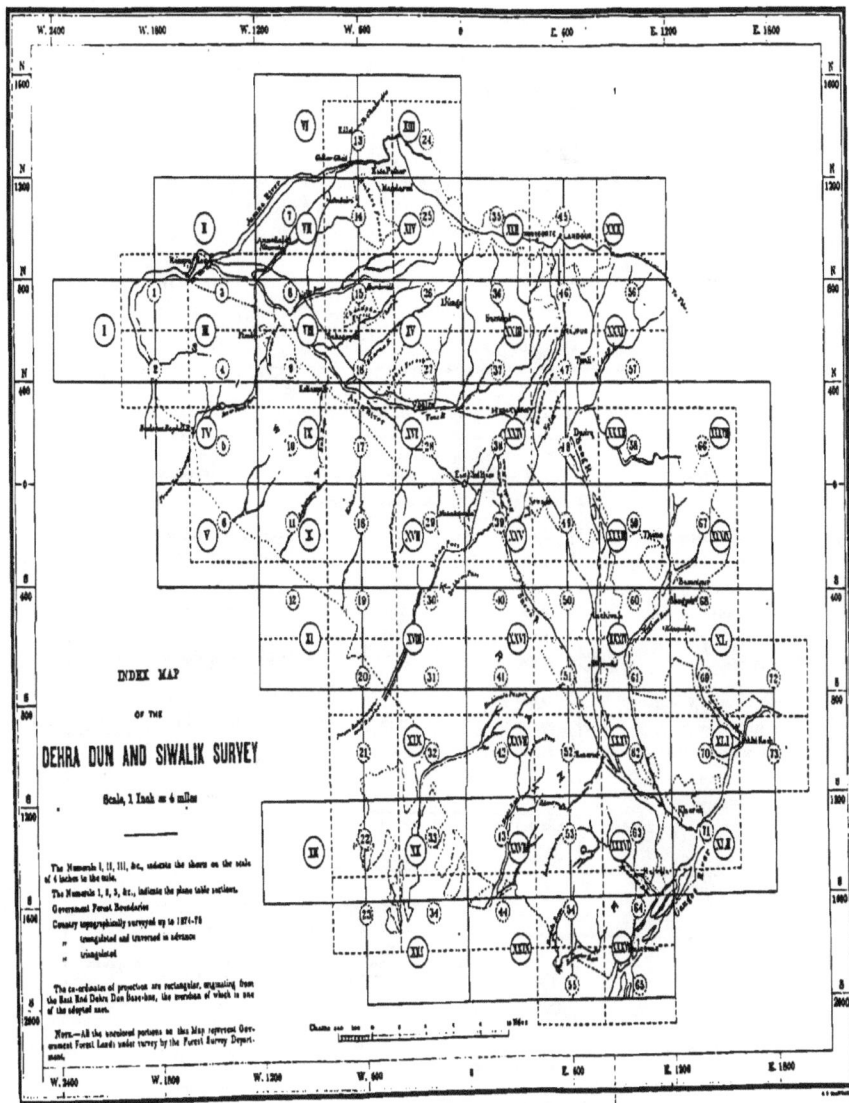

GREAT TRIGONOMETRICAL SURVEY OF INDIA

INDEX MAP

OF THE

DEHRA DUN AND SIWALIK SURVEY

Scale, 1 Inch = 4 miles

The Numerals I, II, III, &c., indicate the sheets on the scale of 4 inches to the mile.
The Numerals 1, 2, 3, &c., indicate the plane table sections.
Government Forest Boundaries
Country topographically surveyed up to 1874-75
    ,,   triangulated and traversed in advance
    ,,   triangulated

The co-ordinates of projection are rectangular, originating from the East End Dehra Dun base-line, the meridian of which is one of the adopted axes.

Note.—All the uncoloured portions on this Map represent Government Forest Lands under survey by the Forest Survey Department.

DEHRA DUN SURVEY.

Tabular statement of out-turn of work.   Season 1874-75.

Details of Triangulation.

Observer's Name.	Instrument used.	Area triangulated in square miles.	No. of stations visited.	No. of points fixed by intersection but not visited.	No. of stations whose positions and heights have been fixed.	No. of stations whose positions only have been fixed.	No. of hill tops cleared of forest.	Average number of trigonometrical points per square mile.	Average area in square miles to each trigonometrical height.	No. of triangles of which all three angles have been observed.	Mean triangular error.	No. of triangles of which only two angles have been observed.	No. of boundary pillars fixed.
Mr. L. Pocock, ...	Inch. 12	470	75	557	191	441	5	1·4	2·4	112	11″	1064	7
„ E. Wrixon, ...	7	*20	23	89	...	63	...	...	...	7	40	108	15
Totals, ...	...	490	98	596	191	503	5	...	...	119	...	1167	22

* Approximate.

Details of Topography.   Scale 4 inches = 1 mile.

Names.	Area in acres.	No. of acres per Plane Table Station.	Linear Miles. Chain measurements.	Linear Miles. Check lines.	Remarks.
Lieut. St. G. Gore, R.E., ...	36,825	3·8	627·3	17·7	Level and broken ground.
and 4 Native Surveyors, ...	5,992	10·5	...	...	Hills.
Mr. J. Low, ...	15,404	2·3	329·0	} 19·3	Comparatively level ground.
and 2 Native Surveyors, ...	6,630	3·3	115·8		Ravines and low hills covered with [forest.
	8,178	25·7	6·3	...	Hills.
Mr. H. Todd, ...	24,379	1·9	578·1	9·9	Very intricate ground consisting of ravines and low hills mostly covered with forest.
and 2 Native Surveyors, ...	4,600	19·4	...	...	Hills.
Mr. T. Kinney, ...	22,620	7·0	233·6	15·7	Partly level and partly ravines and [low hills.
and 2 Native Surveyors up to 20th January, ...	15,760	22·1	...	...	Hills.
Mr. E. Wrixon, ...	3,369	11·2	40·4	...	Flat and tolerably open ground.
Totals, ...	1,43,757 or 224·6 sq. miles.	...	1932·4	62·6	

Details of Traversing.

Names.	Linear miles of traverse.	Number of stations.	Average distance in chains between stations.	Average error per 1000 links.	Average angular error.	Remarks.
Mr. E. Wrixon, ... (Theodolite traverses)	70	271	20·67	1·00	11″	
Native Surveyors, ... (Plane Table and protractor traverses)	328	5726	4·58	2·90	...	
Totals, ...	398	5997	...	...	...	

KUMAUN AND GARHWAL SURVEY.

(23.) My last report treated the operations of this party up to the beginning of July 1874, when it returned to recess quarters at Almora, which place was selected on account of its being close to the ground of field operations—a matter of much importance on account of the limited period in which survey operations could be carried on in the higher snowy ranges. Experience has proved that the best time for operations in these high altitudes is immediately after the rainy season, when the snow line is at its highest and the atmosphere bright and clear.

(24.) The party, which consisted of the members as per margin, had but a short rest at Almora and made an early start for the field while the rains were still in progress. This involved much discomfort on the march and some risk of malarious fever, but was necessary in order to secure every day of the short time available for surveying.

E. C. Ryall, Esq. Asst. Supdt.

Assistant Surveyors.

Mr. O. H. McAFee.
„ E. F. Litchfield.
„ I. S. Pocock.
„ J. F. McCarthy.

(25.) Mr. Ryall has submitted the following report of the operations under his charge.

"Active operations were commenced on all sides by the 13th September.

"It was my original intention to conduct a series of triangles along the Tibetan frontier with a view of laying down peaks, &c., in the Sutlej Valley. I abandoned this project when I learnt that the undertaking would press too heavily on your estimate of expenses. I proceeded instead therefore to inspect the topographical work finished during the previous summer and the ground where the Plane Tabling was about to be done. After completing my inspection tour, I proceeded to continue the Milam triangulation. The total length of the Milam triangulation is 48 miles, of which 32 was finished during previous and 16 during the season under review. The greater portion of this work was very trying; it required all the skill and nerve I possessed to pierce to stupendous gorge overhung by the lofty snowy mountains of Chirkhana and Hasaling with a series of triangles. The steepness of the gorge may be conceived when it is understood that the direct horizontal distance from Hasaling snowy peak to the Gori river is rather less than 1¾ miles and that it towers 14,000 feet above it. In this triangulation Mr. McAFee assisted me by observing at three of the base stations.

"The extent of triangulation finished by me covers an area of 200 square miles, comprising five stations visited of an average height of 13,300 feet above sea level.

"As far as regards altitude and physical formation, the two districts of Kumaun and Garhwál may be divided into five belts or zones. I shall describe these in succession beginning with No. 1 from the north.

Description of country.

No. 1 Zone. The average width of this belt is about 15 miles. In length it extends from the Mánu Valley in the west to that of Byáns, bordering on the Nepal frontier, in the east. It comprises within it, besides the two above mentioned valleys, those of Níti, Milam, Rálam and Dharma. The average height of the basins of these valleys is about 14,000 feet above sea level, the higher basin (15,500) being that of Mánu and the lowest (12,500) that of Byáns. The average altitude above sea level of the main and minor ranges within this belt is about 20,000 feet. The ground though lofty, is for the most part undulating. Access to the tops of most of the spurs or ranges is not difficult, though very trying in consequence of the great tenuity of the air. With the exception of the main ranges which divide the above mentioned six valleys, the whole formation of this zone is of slate of almost every conceivable color and in various stages of decay.

The ranges that are excepted, are entirely composed of granite, that is so far as I could judge, for I could not perceive any or the slightest order of stratification among them. Fuel can be seldom had over 12,500 feet; grass never over 13,500.

No. 2 Zone. This belt consists of ranges of extremely precipitous and rugged lofty mountain barriers running parallel to and south of Zone No. 1. Its average width may be put down at 10 miles, its maximum is about 17. The whole of these ranges are stupendously lofty, the mean height of the peaks on them being about 22,000 feet, and the formation throughout is of granite, except in some few places where it is of gneiss. The drainage from the comparatively undulating and open valleys of Mánu, Níti, Milam, Rálam, Dharma and Byáns lying in Zone No. 1, breaks through these enormous barriers, and the six gorges so formed average in mid-height about 4 miles in breadth. The widest, the gorge of the Níti or Dhauli river, towards Joshimath, being about 6 miles. The narrowest is that of Milam being about 3 miles. The tops of these gorges are overhung, as a matter of course, by almost sheer precipices, capped by towering needle-like peaks. The easiest of them, where the triangulation has been carried through, were converted into stations, ascent to most of which was not accomplished without imminent risk of life. The widest portion *viz.*, 17 miles of this belt consists entirely of a wild and uninhabited valley called the Rishiganga, at the head of which is the Nanda Devi mountain 25,669 feet high. This valley is extremely precipitous and broken; the ground beyond the first 7 or 8 miles consisting of bare rocks, snow-beds and glaciers, with no signs of vegetation. The hills fall abruptly down to the river which dashes like a torrent between perpendicular walls of rock, which form its banks.

"No. 3 Zone consists of from 6 to 7 miles of spurs emanating from the foot of the snowy ranges and running mostly in a southerly direction. The average height of these spurs is about 12,000 feet above sea level; they are composed partly of stratified gneiss and partly of crystallized lime-stone, the former occurring about 4 miles towards the north and the latter about 3 miles towards the south. In consequence of the stratified nature of their formation, the spurs are, as a rule, precipitous on one side and sloping on the other. The surveyors working among them had no difficulty therefore in getting about.

"The operations of the snow party under my direction were almost entirely confined to ground in the above three zones. It may be thought perhaps that to treat similarly the remaining portion of Kumaun and Garhwál previously surveyed, would be irrelevant to this report. In order however not to leave the subject in an incomplete form, I shall proceed in a cursory manner with the description of the remaining zones.

"No. 4 Zone is by far the broadest; it averages about 50 miles, and the average height of the ranges in it is about 7,000 feet above sea level. The differences however between the heights of contiguous spurs are so trifling, that to one looking at the whole of this belt of country from a commanding point, all the ranges would appear to be nearly of one uniform height, no great contrast is to be seen anywhere. The width of this zone is greatest in Kumaun and least in Garhwál. From any point in the middle of this zone and from its southern extremities, the snowy ranges appear to rise very abruptly and seem to gird its northern limits like an immense wall, towering about 12,000 feet above it. Unlike the mountains found in most parts of the Himalayas, as far as I have seen of them, the mountains in this 4th zone appear to be much waterworn and so present very minute and intricate features. They have given topographical surveyors much hard work, entailing upon them at the same time the exercise of much judgement as to what detail should be suppressed, in order to make room for expressing the more important features. With the exception of some portions lying towards the north which is of gneiss, the principal formations are of lime-stone, slate, mica-schist and quartzose rocks.

"No. 5 Zone. This might be called the Siwalik formation of Kumaun and Garhwál. Kumaun has very little of it, the widest part in it lies to the west of Káládhúngi where it is about 8 miles. To the east of Káládhúngi this formation loses much of its Siwalik like aspect, and might be termed simply a sand-stone range, of an average height of about 4,000 feet having an average width of about 5 miles. Garhwál however has the largest share of this sand-stone formation. The widest tract of the sand-stone country in this district, consists of the Patli and Kotli Dúns, which average in breadth about 12 miles, inclusive of the outer ranges girding them. The average height of the ranges in this last or sand-stone zone, with the exception of that noted as lying in Kumaun to the east of Káládhúngi, is about 2,000 feet above sea level.

"Mr. McAFee was entrusted with the triangulation of the country about Choudans, which
Mr. McAFee.   lies at the foot of the Dharma and Byáns Valleys. He succeeded
with praiseworthy application in getting through about 600 square miles of triangulation by 24th November, when he closed work and retraced his steps to Naini Tal.

"Mr Litchfield was deputed to take up the Plane Tabling of the southern half of the Níti
Mr. Litchfield.   Valley and of the valley of the Rishiganga river, a description
of which has been already given. On completing these sections he was directed to resume work in the higher valleys of the Pindar river. He accomplished the work allotted to him in a very creditable manner but not without undergoing great exposure and privations especially in the Rishiganga Valley, the survey of which is perhaps the most formidable undertaking in the whole range of the Himalayas yet accomplished. The amount of his field work consisted in sketching an area of 837 square miles. Considering the quantity and quality of his sketching, he deserves much credit for his successful labours.

"Mr. I. Pocock was entrusted first with the sketching of the upper portion of the Mána
Mr. I. Pocock.   Valley, in sections 21, 22 and 29, which he successfully completed
by 5th October.

"Mr. Pocock's survey of this portion of the Mána Valley, was a most arduous and enterprising feat for which he deserves much commendation. On the completion of this piece of work Mr. Pocock was directed to resume the sketching of the Jowar Valley, which he had been obliged to relinquish in the beginning of July owing to the inclemency of the weather. After doing this, he completed section 68 and a portion of 62 lying on the eastern frontier of Kumaun from which he made a reconnoissance of the Nepal border. He then retraced his steps towards Rudrprayág in Garhwál, to sketch a small portion belonging to section 8, which had been inadvertently omitted when the survey of that part of the country was done. Advantage was taken of this opportunity to provide Mr. Pocock with aneroid barometers, for the determination of heights of places along his route from Almora *viá* Srinagar through Tihri-Garhwál to Landour.

"Mr. Pocock after an arduous field season closed work on 20th March and arrived at Dehra on 31st March.

"From what I could learn of the ground in the Níti Valley, I formed an opinion that the upper
Mr. McCarthy.
portion was, though very lofty, yet comparatively easy to survey; I therefore made over this portion to Mr. McCarthy, as he was the least experienced hand in the party. He accomplished the undertaking with credit, for it was accurate. His rendering of the ground, as far as giving adequate expression to the features, was however very poor.

"I have good reason to anticipate that more than ordinary difficulties will be met with in the north-eastern frontier of Kumaun in the valleys of Dharma and Byáns, the survey of which remains to be done. Their inhabitants are notorious for rascality and drunkenness, in fact they are little better than mere savages, and their proximity to the Nepal and Tibetan frontiers, renders them a very difficult people to deal with."

(27). The area topographically surveyed on the scale of 1-inch to the mile, comprises 2,176
Out-turn of work.
square miles and the portion of country triangulated covers 800 square miles. I cannot abstain from drawing particular attention to the survey of the upper part of the Mána Valley, a most difficult undertaking successfully performed by Mr. I. Pocock. In an area of 108 square miles, the average height of the ground surveyed was over 21,000 feet, the average height of the Plane Table stations was 19,500 feet and the maximum height visited by Mr. Pocock was 22,040 feet above sea level. This value was obtained differentially by observations of the boiling point at the place itself and at a trigonometrical station of known height, and approximates to the greatest height reached on any mountain by man. The Messrs. Schlagentweit in 1855, *Vide* their Vol. II, India and High Asia, ascended the flanks of this same mountain, Kamet (their Ibi Gámin), to a height of 22,259 feet, on an undefined spot, the height of which they obtained from observations with a mountain barometer, and Mr. W. H. Johnson in the report of the survey operations in Kashmir for 1863-64, is said to have visited a point "upwards of 23,000 feet above the sea". The whole of the topographical work was in very elevated regions and the ground in which Messrs. Litchfield and McCarthy were employed, was not very far below that of Mr. Pocock's in point of height. In these barren and inhospitable regions, besides the natural physical difficulties which were in themselves very trying, the commissariat arrangements were a source of much anxiety. On considering the trials of such an enterprise, the risks that must have been incurred in ascending mountains of such stupendous height and in traversing glaciers, the physical exertions in such rarefied air and the exposure to extreme cold, I think it will be admitted that these operations were of a most arduous nature and that Mr. Ryall and the Assistants employed under him are deserving of great praise for their energy and determination in overcoming such difficulties.

(28.) During the recess this portion of the party was engaged in the computations of the snow
Recess of 1875.
triangulation and in the preparation of the fair maps of the Kumaun and Garhwál Survey. The following sheets have been completed and submitted to the Photozincographic Office for publication.

Skeleton sheets Nos. VI (2nd edition) XI, XII, XIX, XX, XXI, XXII, XXIII, XXXI, XXXVIII.

Shaded sheets Nos. XII, XXII, XXXVIII.

KUMAUN AND GARHWAL SURVEY.

Tabular statement of out-turn of work.   Season 1874-75.

Details of Triangulation.

Observer's Names.	Area of triangulation in square miles.	Number of stations visited.	Number of triangles completed.	Number of intersected points fixed.	Number of points whose heights have been determined.	Average altitude in feet above sea level of stations visited.	Remarks.
Mr. E. C. Ryall, ...	200	*5	†5	0	5	13,300	* Mr. McAFee assisted Mr. Ryall by taking observations at 3 of the base stations. The area about 50 square miles embraced by these stations has been included in the out-turn shewn against Mr. McAFee.
Mr. C. H. McAFee, ...	600	21	18	56	40	11,500	† Angles observed at 2 of the forward stations during previous field season contribute towards making up this number.
Totals, ...	800	26	23	56	45	...	

Details of Topography.   Scale 1 inch = 1 mile.

Names.	Area surveyed in square miles.	Average number of Plane Table stations per square mile.	In feet above sea level.			Area of glaciers in square miles.	Remarks.
			Average height of ground surveyed.	Average height of Plane-Table stations.	Maximum height of points visited.		
Mr. E. F. Litchfield,	309	0·30	20,000	17,500	19,200	55	Very rugged and precipitous ground, principally in the Rishiganga Valley. Includes 50 square miles of reconnoissance of that valley.
	348	0·40	17,000	15,000	17,000	12	About the upper sources of the Pindar river. Ground partly very rugged.
	180	0·60	12,500	11,000	15,000	...	About the lower parts of the Pindar and Rámganga Valleys; ground easy.
„ I. S. Pocock,	108	0·60	21,200	19,500	22,040	49	Bold high ground in the upper part of the Mána Valley, culminating in some of the loftiest Himalayan peaks.
	614	0·90	12,500	11,500	14,500	11	About Jowar and Choudans; ground easy. Includes 187 square miles of reconnoissance of the Nepal border.
	2	†4·09	†2,800	†2,100	3,500	...	About Rudrprayág on the Alaknanda river ; ground easy, details very intricate.
„ J. F. McCarthy,	330	0·94	20,500	18,000	20,500	41	Bold and commanding ground about the upper parts of the Níti Valley, partly precipitous and partly undulating.
	305	1·10	18,000	12,500	15,000	...	Chiefly to the east and west of Joshimath; ground partly rugged and generally otherwise.
	2176	*0·68	*17,400	*15,000	...	168	* These averages do not include the quantities marked thus †.

Extract from the Narrative Report—dated 15th July 1875—of Captain J. R. McCULLAGH, R.E., Officiating Assistant Superintendent 1st Grade, in charge Leveling Party.

(2.) On the 30th November 1874 operations were commenced at the S. W. end of the Bangalore Base, and the point of origin to which the heights of *Movements of the party.* all the Bench-marks are referred, is the metal plate in the floor of the observatory at or about ground level. The trigonometrical value of this has been taken at 3117·775 feet.

(3.) From this the line of levels was carried *viâ* Túmkúr, Sira, Hiriyur Tallak and Rámpur to Honúr H. S. and into Bellary, continued *viâ* Alúr, Adoni, Mádawáram; and the season's work was closed at Raichore Railway Station on the 3rd April 1875.

(4.) On the 5th the return march, about 257 miles in length, was commenced and the party reached Bangalore on the 30th April.

(5.) Before commencing operations the collimation of the levels was adjusted; it was again examined on the 1st February and finally tested on completion *Conduct of the operations.* of the work, when one level was found to be almost in perfect adjustment and the other only very slightly thrown out.

(6.) The staves were compared with the portable standard bar on the 9th December, on the 1st February and finally on the 3rd April, the day on which work was closed.

(7.) Throughout the season the rules and instructions laid down for the conduct of leveling operations, were strictly adhered to.

(8.) From a short distance out of Bangalore, the general appearance of the country passed through is bare, uninteresting and far from picturesque; although it *Nature of the country.* is decidedly undulating, and might in some places be called hilly, until the neighbourhood of Bellary is approached, but from that on to Raichore there is not much to complain of in the way of impediment to leveling.

(9.) For the first 18 sections the sum of the rises and falls, passed over by the staves, gives an average of 65·7 feet per mile; up to section 42 this was slightly reduced being 60·3 feet. As far as section 59 it becomes 55·1 feet; and over the whole line the average rise and fall stands at 47·9 feet per mile.

(10.) During the operations the roads were kept to as far as possible, but the line was carried across country for a distance of about 33 miles.

(11.) The Haggri and Tungabhadra rivers were met with, and had to be crossed; the former three times, first by a bridge at Hiriyur, secondly about five miles from Honúr H. S. where there was not much water, but over a mile of deep sand, and thirdly at Moka village, where also there was little water but again about a mile and a half of very heavy sand in the river bed.

(12.) The Tungabhadra, at Mádawáram village, was a somewhat more formidable obstacle, being about half a mile across with high steep banks; the waterway was some 25 to 30 chains in width, but fortunately there were islands (of sand) which were capable of being made use of by taking a zigzag course.

(13.) During the months of December and January, the nights and early mornings were very raw and cold, and heavy mists hung about until the sun was *Weather and its influence on the health of the party.* well up. From the middle of February it began to get warm, and before the close of the working season it was decidedly hot weather.

(20.) The following is the out-turn of work for the season : 297 miles of double leveling embracing the determination of the heights of 210 Permanent Bench-*Out-turn of work.* marks, buildings, temples &c., &c; 2 Trigonometrical stations, Honúr H. S. and Bandúr Z. D. S. of the Great Arc Series; also the G. T. S. Bench-mark at the Mainwaring tank, Bellary, laid down by Lieutenant Harman, R.E., in the previous season; the "level of top of rails" at Bellary, Adoni and Raichore Railway Stations; 8 Bench-marks of the Public Works Department; and 16 Boundary pillars of the Revenue Survey.

At Raichore the usual G. T. S. Bench-mark has been engraved on the rock *in sitû*, the position being indicated by a paka pillar, in a situation, outside the Railway Station Compound, convenient for the resumption of the leveling operations at any future time.

(21.) The computations are now complete and the following table shows a comparison between the determinations of height of a few of the points connected as obtained by G. T. S. Triangulation, G. T. S. Spirit Leveling, and the Madras and G. I. P. Railway Departments.

Office duties.

Sites.	Heights.	Remarks.
S. W. end of the Bangalore Base,	3117·775	Origin of the spirit leveling operations season 1874-75, to which the values of all the Bench-marks are referred.
Bandúr Z. D. S., ...	{ 1452 1452·075	By triangulation. „ spirit leveling.
Honúr H. S., ...	{ 1583 1583·460	„ triangulation. „ spirit leveling.
Bellary, (Level of top of rails), ...	{ 1484·16 1486·879	„ Madras Railway. From sea level at Madras. „ spirit leveling.
Adoni, (Level of top of rails), ...	{ 1864·35 1866·193	„ Madras Railway. „ spirit leveling.
Raichore, (Level of top of rails),	{ 1911·21 1814·83 1815·517	„ Madras Railway. „ G. I. P. Railway. From sea level at Bombay. „ spirit leveling.

Extract from the Narrative Report—dated 4th August 1875—of Captain A. W. BAIRD, R.E., Officiating Assistant Superintendent 1st Grade, in charge Tidal and Leveling Party.

(2.) When I visited Hanstal Tidal Station in August 1874, I found that there was a considerable deposit of fine mud in the small pipe in connection with the cylinder: this caused a slight retardation in the flow of the water from the sea to the cylinder and *vice versâ*. This of course had to be rectified as soon as possible; the cleaning out of the pipe was a difficult job, and Mr. Rendell completed it in a satisfactory manner, without losing more than a day or two of the work of the Self Registering Tide Gauge. When every thing was again in thorough working order, Mr. Rendell left with his detachment for Nawanár Tidal Station to await my arrival.

The inspecting party at Hanstal Tidal Station.

(3.) Having made all preparations for commencing leveling operations, I took the field with the greater part of the Native Establishment on the 16th October and marched direct for Jorya. On my arrival there I at once engaged native boats to convey us across the Gulf to Mundra. We reached Mundra on the 21st October and camped there.

Remainder of party take the field and cross to Outch.

(4.) I visited Nawanár Tidal Station as soon as possible after my arrival at Mundra, and found Mr. Rendell engaged in the repairs of the platform round the observatory, which had suffered considerably from the heavy seas during the monsoon, since I had inspected the station in July.

Visit Nawanár Tidal Station.

(5.) Having examined the foreshore at Nawanár, I saw that nothing could be done as yet towards getting up the small iron pipe and the flexible pipe, as the sand bank had rather increased than otherwise, since I had last seen it. I could also trace a very decided difference in the configuration of the spit at the point where the creek joins the sea; so that I had hopes in 2 or 3 weeks that the bank would be washed down sufficiently for the pipe to be taken up, and moreover the wind was blowing strongly from the north which would drive the sand back along the coast. I then gave Mr. Rendell instructions for his work during the field season—that he should wait at Nawanár for a week or two and try to put the station in order as soon as possible, then take up the inspection of the observatories in turn, and generally keep the stations in working order. The daily morning reports from the stations came to my office during the whole field season. In this way Mr. Rendell was enabled to work advantageously: and at the same time I was kept informed of what was going on at each station, while I conducted the leveling operations.

Programme of work for field season.

(8.) The country between Nawanár Tidal Station and the mainland proper, is more or less a
Leveling operations. mud swamp or *Small Runn*, and is covered at the high tides of the
2 or 3 days following every new and full moon. I had therefore to
wait until the very *low high tides* which would occur about the 2 days following the "Moon's first quarter" in order to drive the levels across this treacherous bit of ground satisfactorily.

(10.) While waiting to begin work, I had several iron pegs with flat plates fixed on the top,
constructed to place the legs of the Level Stand upon, when working over shaky ground. I was in
hopes that I should then be able to isolate the instrument to a certain extent, and so lessen the tendency
of the bubble to move when reading the scale after the staff had been observed. To a certain extent
this answered, but I soon became aware how futile this plan was, for the ground was painfully difficult
to level over. I saw that I must modify the routine of working in order to obtain thoroughly good
results of the leveling and at the same time get over a respectable distance per diem.

(11.) I therefore arranged that the second leveler should read the bubble scale, after I had
observed the staff, while I actually had my eye at the instrument (for the slightest movement would have
caused the bubble to move 4 or 5 divisions and perhaps one end to disappear altogether). I read the levels
in the same way for the second leveler, while he observed with his level. Even with all this care, on this
ground, and when crossing the portions on the Runn proper, we had often to take several sets of observations before they were perfectly satisfactory.

(18.) The leveling operations were to be carried out in two sections, the first from Nawanár Tidal
Range of the leveling operations. Station along the Cutch coast, across the Runn between Shikarpúr
and Mállá, then along the Kattywar coast to Balumba, thence over
another portion of the Runn to Hanstal Tidal Station. The second series to commence at Hanstal
Tidal Station across the Runn to Jorya and thence along the Kattywar coast of the Gulf and across
the small Runn of Okhá Mandal to Okhá Tidal Station opposite the Island of Bet. Branch lines of
course were to be taken to such Trigonometrical Stations as were conveniently near the main line of
levels. The Bench-mark stones properly cut had been laid down the previous year (3 at each Tidal
Station) and the others about 10 miles apart along the route, and these had also been laid down with
reference to the Trigonometrical Stations to be connected.

(14.) From Mundra to Shikarpúr the line to be leveled over was distant from the Gulf from 5
miles at Mundra to 15 miles at Anjár; the country was tolerably
Nature of country on the Cutch side up to the Runn. flat till within a short distance of Anjár, where we met with some
steep hills and then descended again to about the same relative level
as near Mundra. From Anjár the ground continued flat for a few miles and then became undulating
almost right away to Shikarpúr. From Anjár to Shikarpúr the coast line (if I may use that expression
for the demarcation between the mainland and the Runn) was from 5 to 7 miles distant from the line
of leveling. One peculiar feature in the roads in Cutch, along which we took our levels, is that they are
as a rule 2 or 3 feet and in some cases 5 feet below the general surface of the country in the immediate
vicinity. I was more particularly struck with this when I had to visit Nawanár in the monsoon last
year, for the roads then appeared more like small canals than anything else.

(15.) The Trigonometrical Stations in Cutch which I connected were found to be in first-rate
Great Trigonometrical Stations in Cutch connected. repair, and as they had been constructed more than 20 years previous to the time we visited them, it shows that with ordinary precau-
tions on the part of the Native Authorities, our Survey marks ought
to remain in perfect preservation. The stations I visited were either on the tops of hills or of some
very high towers in the principal towns. I may mention that it took me the whole of a day and working as rapidly as possible to connect Butchow H.S., a distance of about ¼ of a mile from our main line.

(16.) Between Shikarpúr and the Runn the country is almost entirely uncultivated, and there
is a series of hillocks composed of fine black sand which are covered
Country on either side of the Runn between Shikarpúr and Mállá. with dense vegetation. These hillocks appear to be moveable; they
are dotted here and there over the plain, but the hillocks in the
immediate vicinity of the Runn here are tolerably high, and form an almost uninterrupted chain for
a mile or two to the west and running nearly parallel to the general line of the Runn.

On the Kattywar side opposite there are no hillocks but a tract of waste land for one or two miles
which is cut up by a great number of Nullahs, then we find a mile or two of cultivated fields occupied
The Meanas by the "Meanas" (who are considered a race of professional thieves).
The villages of these Meanas are scattered all over the country here, and there are some 200 of them
near the town of Mállá. Each village consists of a few straw huts surrounded by a straw hedge, and

the flag of the headman of the village, is conspicuous in each case on a long bamboo stuck into the ground in front of his hut. These Mennas are considered most troublesome people by the Officers of the Political Agency.

(17.) The Runn itself between Shikarpúr on the Cutch side and Málliá on the Kattywar side, is some 8 miles across; but of this only about 6 miles can be used for the determination of the general level of the Runn, as the ground close to the mainland on each side is from a foot to 18 inches higher.

The Runn between Málliá and Shikarpúr.

There are two Bench-marks enclosed in large blocks of masonry in the Runn itself, and situated about one mile on either side of the centre line of the Runn. These Bench-marks were laid down about 10 months before the leveling operations were commenced, and had plenty of time to settle. This part of the Runn is perfectly dry from November till the end of March, but about the end of April or beginning of May, it is covered by the water from the extraordinary high tides, and the water is also forced up by very high south-westerly winds which always prevail at that time. The Hanstal creek, being almost like a funnel at the end of the Gulf, is acted on by the full force of this wind, and the water from the Gulf is thus conveyed far up the Runn.

The ground over which we leveled was almost quite dry and has the usual appearance, blackish grey colour with here and there patches of glistening white from the salt deposited after evaporation.

(18.) I deemed it a necessary precaution in leveling over the Runn both here and afterwards that the lines should be driven in a perfectly straight direction from point to point, and also that at each point where the staff was put up, I should get an exact value of the ground immediately round that point. Accordingly starting from the Bench-mark on the Runn nearer the Cutch coast, we leveled in a direct line to a point on the sand hill close to which there is a Bench-mark on the Cutch coast, viz., Pathewalla Dhoi. Again the next line was taken directly between the two Bench-marks on the Runn, and a third section from the Bench-mark nearer the Kattywar coast direct to a point on the Kattywar mainland and closing on Bench-mark No. 2 Málliá.

Arrangements for getting a true value of the level of the Runn at each point where staff was put up. Also for fixing the line of levels so that it could be re-leveled over the same points in future.

At each point where a value of the level of the Runn was to be determined, the Muccadum was ordered to drive the pegs (very large ones) into the ground until the top was just flush with the surface; this he tested by a mason's level which he carried in his hand, the brad was then put in and he scraped away the earth all round to a depth of about ½ an inch from the surface to allow the staff to turn freely : thus the level of every point on the Runn where the staff was put up will be evaluated.

(19.) The country from Málliá to Balumba is almost entirely black soil and tolerably flat, and one or two pretty large streams had to be crossed.

Málliá to Balumba.

(20.) There are no Bench-marks between Balumba B.M. and Hanstal Tidal Station. The first 4 miles is across cultivated fields intersected by Nullahs, in most cases filled with fresh water. Having carried the line into the Runn, I made similar arrangements for determining the value of the different points where the staves were erected as before.

The Runn from Balumba to Hanstal Tidal Station.

(21.) In the very early morning the observations on the Runn are very satisfactory, everything is so very clear, but after 9 o'clock, even in the cold weather, it is almost impossible to work except at ridiculously short distances, unless perhaps on a very cloudy day; on a clear day about noon and up to 4 P.M., the atmosphere has the appearance of water boiling hard, and taking observations at that time is of course out of the question. A heliotrope seen at a short distance looks like an immense flame of fire. Even at a mile distant everything seems doubled above and reflected underneath as well. Small scrub not more than 6 inches or a foot high look immense bushes, and in one place between Hanstal and Jorya, there is a patch of this about a mile across, which may be considered as well defined a feature on the Runn as a forest on a plain.

The work on the Runn as affected by the atmosphere.

(22.) The first section of leveling operations closed on the 3rd Bench-mark at Hanstal Tidal Station and finally on the planed surface of the bed plate of the S. R. T. Gauge.

The first section closing at Hanstal Tidal Station.

(23.) Having inspected the work at Hanstal Tidal Station, which was found satisfactory, and having seen Mr. Rendell at Jorya and made arrangements for getting up some extra piping from Bombay for Nawanár Tidal Station according to your wishes in order that 2 months work might be carried out for that station, from 7th March to 7th May, I again returned to

The second section, Hanstal Tidal Station to Okhá, commenced : and the Runn from Hanstal to Jorya leveled over.

Hanstal and commenced the second section, Hanstal to Okhá. The origin was again the planed surface
of the bed plate of S. R. T. Gauge. Similar arrangements were made as formerly for the Runn and
we had some 14 miles of it to determine between Hanstal Tidal Station and Somarthal B.M. There are
also 2 Trigonometrical Stations of the net-work series of the Kattywar party on this line. These served
as closing and re-starting points for each day's work, and their heights were of course determined. From
Somarthal B.M., the ground is slightly undulating, and within 1 mile of Jorya, is cultivated. Jorya T.S.
was connected and also a Branch line of (10 miles) was taken to Haditada H.S., a principal station.

(24.) The line from Jorya to Okhá Tidal Station was taken viá Nawánagar and Khambhália to
Gúrgut which is on the Kattywar side of the Runn of Okhá Mandal.
Jorya to Gúrgut close to the Runn The country as a rule was pretty flat with the usual cotton soil up
of Okhá Mandal. to about 7 miles from Khambhália when it began to be hilly and the
ground very hard and rocky. From Khambhália also to Gúrgut it was undulating and hilly the
whole way. One or two rivers had to be crossed on this line; they were of course almost dried up at
the time we were working.

(26.) The line of levels after passing Gúrgut had to be taken across the Runn of Okhá Man-
The Runn of Okhá Mandal. dal to Topni Ness B.M. in Okhá Mandal. This Runn which is
about 2 miles broad, extends from the gulf of Cutch right away the
whole length of Okhá Mandal, and is only separated from the open sea by a strip of sand hillocks
about ¼ of a mile long and from 200 to 300 yards broad. The Runn therefore causes the Okhá Mandal to be a small peninsula joined to Kattywar by the strip of sand bank above mentioned, close to the
village of Madi.

(27.) Close to the Runn the ground is very steep and rocky. About a mile further on, it
becomes undulating and then tolerably flat right away to Okhá
From Topni Ness to Okhá Tidal Tidal Station. A great number of coral beds are exposed on the
Station. surface between Armra and Okhá Tidal Station; this evidently shows
that at a not very distant period it must have been covered by the sea. Okhá Tidal Station is situated
at the end of the peninsula and at the point where the gulf joins the sea. I have described it
in a former report.

(28.) The leveling operations were completed and closed
Closed leveling operations at Okhá on the 3 Bench-marks at Okhá Tidal Station and the S. R. T.
Tidal Station. Gauge bed plate as at Hanstal.

(30.) Having closed leveling operations I marched to Dwárka and made arrangements with
Mr. Rendell for dismantling the stations; and as you had ordered
March to Dwárka. Preparation for me to do all I could to get complete work from 7th March to 7th
dismantling the Tidal Observatories. May out of Nawanár Tidal Station, and that the instruments at
the other observatories should be kept working simultaneously, I arranged that Okhá Tidal Station
should be the first dismantled and as soon after the 7th May as possible.

(33.) Previous to dismantling Okhá Tidal Station, I sent out the Kalassies who remained and
some coolies to collect stones to build large mounds or platforms
Okhá Tidal Station dismantled. round the Bench-marks and the cylinder which you had ordered me to
leave in statu quo. By the evening of the 15th of May the whole of the instruments and all the piping,
except 50 feet in connection with the cylinder, were put on board the boat which was moved close by
for the purpose. The cylinder had been emptied of water and dried out at the bottom (there was no
sediment of any description here) and filled with clean dry sand. A thick wooden board closed the
top (being secured by bolts and nuts) and an immense mound of stones was raised over it. On the
16th Mr. Rendell sailed for Nawanár to perform the dismantling of Nawanár Tidal Station which was
done in exactly the same way as at Okhá.

(35.) On the day after Mr. Rendell sailed, I left Okhá Tidal Station for Dwárka. All that
Okhá Tidal Station as it was left. remained visible of the station being 4 immense mounds of stones.
The station was handed over to the charge of the Assistant Resi-
dent at Dwárka.

(36.) I now marched rapidly from Dwárka to Rájkot and started the office there, and a day or
Marched to Rájkot. two afterwards went out to Hanstal Tidal Station where Mr. Rendell
meanwhile had arrived to dismantle that station. I found he had
completed every thing very satisfactorily.

(37.) The duplicate sheets of the leveling operations have been completed and computed, but
Work during the recess up to date. the abstracts cannot be made out until the level of origin at Nawanár Tidal Station above mean level of sea and also that of the closing
points at Hanstal Tidal Station and Okhá Tidal Station have been determined. The Tidal diagrams

have all been carefully inked in; the time computations in duplicate have been brought up; and the correction of the diagrams for zero and for time is now in hand. Experiments for Index errors of thermometers and anemometers have also been completed.

(40.) Mr. Rendell has worked through the whole field season to my entire satisfaction. I
Personnel of the Party.   have already reported that he is most useful to me in every way
                                                 connected with the work at the tidal observatories. He has been
most painstaking in carrying out everything I wished, and it is mainly owing to his care and vigilance
that the work at Nawanár, for the 2 particular months you wished, has been successfully accomplished.

Nursing Dass has worked throughout the season the second level. He is a first rate leveler,
a very quick and careful observer and does his work generally to my entire satisfaction and fully bears
out the good name he has got from Officers under whom he has previously served.

Damoder Ramchundra, Dhondu Venayek and Shitaram Yeshwant have all worked well at the
Tidal Observatories, and give promise of being very useful.

                                                 (41.) The following statement shows the amount of leveling
Out-turn of leveling operation.   done by the party.

274½ miles on Main line by two independent levelers.
29¼   „   Branch   „   „   „
38   Bench-marks, built in masonry platforms, connected.
17   Principal stations connected.
3   Minor stations   „
45   Paka points duly inscribed and connected.

(42.) I would again beg to report that I am much indebted to the Political Agents of Cutch
Assistance rendered by Political   and Kattywar and to the Assistant Resident at Dwárka for the assis-
Officers.   tance they have uniformly rendered me.

(43.) In conclusion I think the Party may fairly be congratulated on the general success
                                              of the project in having secured both at Okhá and Hanstal Tidal
General success of the operations ;   Stations, complete sets of tidal combined with meteorological ob-
completion of one part of the project.   servations which will compare most favourably with what has been
done both in England and America, and in having so far succeeded at Nawanár Tidal Station that the
observations taken will be sufficient to evaluate (by differentiating with both Okhá and Hanstal which
were working simultaneously) the principal data required.

The leveling operations combined with the tidal observations complete the work necessary for
one part of the project and fix the level of about 30 miles of the Runn of Cutch for the season 1874-
75, and a repetition of the work some 20 years hence will effectually settle the question of Secular
Depression in this peculiar region.

Extract from the Narrative Report—dated 28th September 1875—of Captain W. M. CAMPBELL,
R.E., Officiating Deputy Superintendent 2nd Grade, G. T. Survey, in charge
Astronomical Party No. 2.

At the date of my last Annual Report, October 1873, I was employed in the reduction of the
Electro-Longitude observations, made by Captain Herschel and myself during the preceding season
1872-73.

These reductions were so far complete that I was enabled to give the results of one measurement,
that of the arc Bangalore-Mangalore, and subsequently, in time to be included in the General Report, an
approximate value of Madras-Bangalore.

(2.) The prosecution of the field operations was suspended in consequence of Captain Herschel's
taking furlough in August 1873, and the reductions were also stopped immediately after the submission
of my report, because I was unexpectedly obliged to apply for six months furlough to Europe, which
was granted.

(3.) I had some months previously been warned that my services would be placed at the disposal of Colonel Tennant for the observation of the Transit of Venus, from a date which was then
uncertain.

While I was in England, I was put on duty to assist Colonel Strange in the preparation of the instruments intended for Colonel Tennant's use during the Transit. These formed a very full and handsome equipment, consisting of a 6-inch equatorial, a transit instrument, a photoheliograph, an astronomical clock and quadruple chronograph, all, with the exception of the photoheliograph, ordered from Messrs. Cooke & Sons at so late a date that there was great doubt as to their being got ready in time. I remained on this duty as long as I thought prudent, with a view to joining Colonel Tennant in time for all necessary preparations, and when I left England, the transit instrument and a small part of the equatorial were still in the makers' hands.

(4.) I joined Colonel Tennant at Roorkee on 29th September 1874, some of the instruments had then arrived and the rest came in gradually, all reaching us before the Transit took place. In addition to the special equipment above enumerated, Colonel Tennant had the loan of the new 36-inch theodolite, designed for the Great Trigonometrical Survey by Colonel Strange, which had just arrived from England, and he put it in my charge for the Transit. Our time was very fully occupied in preparations up to the day of the Transit.

(5.) My special duty during the event, was to note the times of all the contacts, and also, while the planet was within the sun's disc, to take chronographic transits of both limbs of the sun and planet over the wires of the theodolite, using the horizontal wires during the early part of the Transit, both sets alternately for a short time about the middle, and the vertical wires afterwards. I found the observation of contact with such an instrument very difficult, because the limbs approached, especially at egress, very slowly, and as practice with the model had shown the probability of the contact being suddenly completed by the formation of the "black drop", the momentary expectation of this lasted over minutes, during the whole of which the motion of the instrument both vertical and horizontal had to be maintained by the tangent screws.

During the Transit I never left the telescope, and secured a large number of the observations of sun and planet described above, which when reduced will afford so many determinations of the relative positions of the two.

(6.) With regard to the 36-inch theodolite, I may remark that it is a magnificent instrument, elaborated in its details to an unusual degree, and as far as I can judge, its performances are excellent. A theodolite, with its large horizontal circle and comparatively short telescope, cannot be a convenient instrument for astronomical work, but I envy the surveyor who may have to use this instrument for triangulation, if his work lies in a moderately level country, *compelling him to resort neither to the tops of high hills nor towers.*

(7.) I left Colonel Tennant in April, and proceeded for a short time to Head Quarters, for the purpose of discussing with the Superintendent the programme of operations during the ensuing field season, when it is intended that I should go on with the Electro-Longitude observations with Captain Heaviside, R.E. as my colleague. I then proceeded by Calcutta and Madras to resume my proper duty at Bangalore.

(8.) At Calcutta I had several consultations with Mr. Schwendler, Electrician of the Government Telegraph Department, on the subject of the electrical arrangements of our chronographs and the electrical portion of our work generally. I found him extremely obliging, and ready to assist me in undertaking experiments as to the chronographic arrangements under discussion, to which I shall refer again. I also obtained from him some useful general information, with reference to our operations.

(9.) I was engaged for a fortnight at Madras in forwarding the determination of the difference of longitude between Roorkee and the Madras Observatory by the electric telegraph, which was required to enable Colonel Tennant to reduce his Transit of Venus observations.

(10.) After arrival at Bangalore it was a matter of some time to pick up the threads of the work, which had been in abeyance for more than a year and a half, and was of so novel a kind, that no cut and dried plan of procedure had been adopted. At first I had no assistance beyond that of my native writer and but little progress in the reduction was practicable. Since my reinforcement by Messrs. Keelan and Bond, the reductions have made rapid progress and are now nearly complete.

(11.) My own time has been very much occupied with the instrumental equipment. I would refer to my last report, and that of Captain Herschel, on this subject, which contain detailed descriptions of the equipment and the performances of its various parts. 1st, one of the transit telescopes was condemned, as being to a certain extent untrustworthy, owing to uncertainties in its line of collimation. 2nd, the electric arrangements of the chronograph were bitterly complained of by both of us, as giving endless trouble and anxiety to such a degree that up to the close of the season's work we could never safely reckon on getting through a night's observations without a hitch.

(12.) I first turned my attention to the faulty Transit, encouraged in the work by the fact that a similar failing in the Transit circle of the Cambridge Observatory, which was under investigation when I wrote my last report (*vide* para 20), had been since traced to bad soldering and corrected (*vide* Monthly Notices of Royal Astronomical Society for February 1875, page 188). The idea of such a cause, when suggested to my mind, commended itself as that which would best explain the effects we had observed, indeed it at once made clear what before was obscure. My first step was to carry out the process described as contemplated in my last report and by a little filing the reversal of the object half tube (*i.e.* revolution on its own axis through 180°) at its connection to the axis, was rendered possible.

Half an hour's observation of collimators then showed that the fault was in that part, because the errors previously observed remained identically the same, except that their signs were changed.

(13.) I then took the tube to Madras and showed it to Mr. Doderet, the Mathematical Instrument Maker to Government. When we examined it with a magnifying glass, signs of yielding round the base of the tube became apparent, and further search showed that the tube had been spliced, in order probably to make it correspond to the focal length of the object glass after the latter had been ground. The existence of such patching must be considered sufficiently discreditable to makers of the rank of Messrs. Cooke & Son, and it was also imperfectly and clumsily executed. Very little doubt remained as to our having found the seat of the mischief, and Mr. Doderet, at my request, immediately took steps to strengthen the splicing and make it effectual.

(14.) When I received the tube from Madras and put the telescope through exactly the same course of observations as before, I found that the fault, if not absolutely, was practically eliminated, as I failed to discover any certain indication of what had previously been most gross quantities.

This result must be considered very satisfactory with regard to our future observations, and moreover, having now a clear knowledge of the nature of the old fault, it may be possible to amend the method by which the collimation and level corrections for the instrument were deduced during season 1872-73.

(15.) I next attacked the arrangements of the chronograph. As already remarked I had some consultation at Calcutta with Mr. Schwendler on this subject.

My object was, 1st, to get rid of the induction coils, involving the troublesome Bunsen Batteries, and frictional electricity, and 2nd, to throw aside also if possible all chemically prepared paper. I had several alternative schemes in view.

1st.—To record by lines traced on prepared paper by means of electric currents.

2nd.—To prick holes in the paper by mechanical means put in action by electric currents.

3rd.—To use pens drawing continuous lines, the signals being recorded by sudden jerks to one side caused by electric currents.

(16.) The arguments in favor of the first were theoretically greater instantaneity of signal record, and no change being required in the parts of the chronograph for its adoption. Against it, the necessity of prepared paper, very similar to what we had already found so objectionable, and the probable necessity for strong battery power. It was to perfect this method that Mr. Schwendler so kindly undertook to execute experiments.

The second method I was familiar with, being the same as that of Colonel Tennant's chronograph, and I know it to be perfectly trustworthy and simple, but on the other hand the alteration of our chronographs to suit it would have been troublesome.

The last method I was already familiar with by description, as it is that generally used in America, and at Madras I had the opportunity of seeing it in practice in a small chronograph of Mr. Pogson's, the action of which was so very certain and satisfactory that I at once decided on adopting the principle if possible.

(17.) On examination of our chronographs I found the changes required would be very simple and easy, and our own apparatus contained the necessary parts of any importance, *viz.*, the electromagnets of the relays, which the adoption of the new method would throw out of use. I accordingly drew up a design which Mr. Doderet executed, with in some respects perfect success, and he has now in his hands an amended design, which I see no reason to doubt will prove quite satisfactory in every way.

(18.) The first attempt failed, because I was striving to obtain the double record of clock and observer (or two clocks) by means of only one pen, which would have had the great advantage of doing away with "style (or pen) equation".

After a good deal of experiment I was obliged to abandon this, finding that in order to obtain a satisfactory record, a somewhat radical change in our present means of producing the signals (breaking and making circuit) would be necessary, which I did not think the object justified me in attempting with the time and means at my disposal. The present design comprises two pens following each other on the paper, just as the styles did formerly.

My confidence in its being found to answer, is I think justified by the single record, already obtained from a similar pen, being as good as one could wish. The only change in the chronograph is, that the ebonite plate carrying the stylos has been taken off the carriage, (see my last report para. 24) and a larger plate of wood substituted, on which are fitted two electro-magnets (taken from our old relays) and the pens, which project over the barrel just as the styles did, and trace exactly similar spiral lines.

(19.) This method does away with all the objectionable features of the old arrangement, and is as simple as can be easily imagined. There may be a slight loss of accuracy, but I doubt even this, and if it does occur it must be of the irregular kind which can cause no deterioration in the final results.

It has also the advantage of economy in saving expensive chemicals, as well as by reducing the amount of apparatus carried about. Lastly, a great deal may be often gained by the two observers exchanging telegraphic information, in doing which Captain Herschel and I constantly lost time by our inability and (common to all beginners in the art of signalling) to read as fast as we could signal.

With the pen recorder the message may be written on the chronograph and read off at comparative leisure.

(20.) There is another point in the equipment which has been much improved since our last field work, viz., the collimators.

Those belonging to the Transits have only recently been received from England and are in every way superior to the ones formerly used, and they have an ingenious feature in their construction, by which any movement of the instrument on its pier (which must take place owing to difference of expansion and contraction under varying temperatures) is confined to the direction of the axis. This is likely to prove valuable, because with our field observatories the collimators are necessarily placed on pillars outside, without any adequate protection either from the heat of the sun or the cold at night.

(21.) The point is of importance chiefly with reference to the use of the collimators as meridional marks, which they never strictly are, because the deviation of the Transit instrument is determined independently every night. But if the collimators are appreciably stable, as I expect will prove to be the case (and as to which their mutual observations afford most searching evidence) they will provide the means of combining all the observations for deviation at a station, in order to get the error for each night. Our former experience shows that this, if obtainable, will prove a great advantage.

Extract from the Narrative Report—dated 23rd November 1875—of W. H. COLE, ESQ., M. A., Officiating Deputy Superintendent 3rd Grade, G. T. Survey, Officiating in charge Computing Office.

I have the honor to lay before you the report on the work performed by the Computing Office between the 1st May 1874—up to which date the last report details it—and the 1st October of this year, that is, for a period 5 months in excess of that usually reported on. This change is due to your having recently directed that Executive Officers should bring the narratives of their operations up to the end of the recess season, succeeding the field season to which they refer. I draw your attention to it, because were it not borne in mind, the out-turn of work I am about to detail would appear out of proportion to that of previous years.

CALCULATING BRANCH.

(3.) The attention of this Branch has, whenever opportunity offered, been steadily directed to the final reduction of the triangulation of India and the publication of the results, and considerable progress has now been made. Of the five large sections into which you have divided the triangulation west of the Meridian of 89° three are now in hand, and I will endeavour to give you a general idea of the progress that has been made with each before stating the work of the Office in detail.

Final Reduction of the Triangulation.

North-West Quadrilateral.

(4.) This division of the triangulation which extends over an area of about 475,000 square miles was in a very advanced state when reported on last year. All the principal triangulation had been reduced

Calculating Branch—(Continued).

and the results passed through the press, and one of the Synoptical Volumes—which give only such data of each series as are required for practical purposes—had been published, *viz.*, Volume I, or the Great Indus Series. Since that date four more Synoptical Volumes have been completed and published, *viz.*,

Vol. II. or the Great Arc Series, Section 24° to 30°.
Vol. III.   „   Karáchi Longitudinal Series.
Vol. IV.   „   Gurhágarh Meridional Series.
Vol. V.   „   Rahún Meridional Series.

There still remain three series to complete this section of the triangulation, the Jogí-Tílá Meridional, Sutlej River and North-West Himalaya. The two former are in a very advanced state and will probably together form Volume VI of the Synoptical Volumes. I hope to send them to the binder in the course of two or three more weeks. The North-West Himalaya Series is ready for the press, but has to give place to other subjects more urgently required. It will be some months before it can be published; but nothing now remains to be done in connection with it by this branch of the office further than to superintend it through the press. It will be accompanied by several charts, most of which are drawn but have not yet been photozincographed.

South-East Quadrilateral.

(5.) This section of the triangulation of India, which is contained between the Meridians of 77° and 89° and the parallels of 17° and 24°, is that which you directed should be reduced second in order. Neglecting the two short triangulations of the South Párasnáth and South Maláncha Series, which were not executed with first class instruments, the Quadrilateral contains six chains of triangles forming three mutually dependent circuits. At its north-west corner it unites with the N. W. Quadrilateral, the side Kámkhera to Bhaorása of the Sironj Base-line figure being common to both. The length and position of this side having been finally determined in the reduction of that Quadrilateral were considered invariable. At each of the other corners are base-lines, *viz.*, those of Calcutta, Vizagapatam and Bider. Its reduction necessitated finding the values of 831 unknown quantities, which should satisfy 202 equations of condition. 277 of the equations were however of such a form that an equal number of unknown quantities were readily eliminated and the undertaking was thus reduced to finding 554 unknown quantities to satisfy 15 equations, subject to the usual condition that the sum of the squares of the several quantities multiplied by their respective weights should be a minimum. Although the method of reduction was the same as that adopted for the North-West Quadrilateral, the experience gained from the latter has suggested many slight modifications in the details of the computations which have led to a considerable saving of labour. This has been further lightened to a very marked extent by the employment of Arithmometers, and I have now the satisfaction of reporting that not only has the principal triangulation been finally reduced and prepared for publication, but also that a large amount of secondary triangulation connected with it is in a far advanced state; that of the Great Arc, Section 18° to 24°, the Calcutta Longitudinal Series and the Coast Series is almost finished and only needs to be arranged for publication; that of the remaining series is in an advanced state. Thus in a few months nothing will remain but to pass the data through the press.

The following table contains the facts of computation of the Principal triangulation. In column (1) the 15 equations, which remained after the elimination of the unknown quantities above mentioned, are numbered in the order in which they were arranged for solution. Of these the first six are side equations, five of them being between base-lines, the measured lengths of which have, for the purposes of reduction, been assumed as errorless. The sixth is a circuit equation. The remaining nine are all circuit equations in Latitude (λ) Longitude (L) and Azimuth (A). The circuits are shown by the letters in column (2) which have reference to the diagram. In column (3) are the absolute terms of the equations, and the errors which had to be dispersed between the base-lines or in the circuits. It should be stated that the terms in which the linear errors, *viz.*, those of the first six equations, are here expressed differ from those employed for the N. W. Quadrilateral which will be found tabulated on page 54—a of your report for 1870-71, the former being differences in the 7th place of logs and the latter similar differences divided by *Modulus* × *sin* 1″: the change is due to a simplification in the manner of expressing the co-efficients of the unknown quantities. The simultaneous solution of the equations involved finding the values of an equal number of indeterminate factors, and column (4) exhibits the accuracy with which this solution was performed, the quantities shown in it being obtained by substituting the deduced values of these factors in the normal equations. With the aid of the indeterminate factors, values of the angular errors involved in the equations of condition were found, at first to 5 places of decimals of seconds, and afterwards reduced to 8 places. These values being substituted in the equations produce the quantities given in columns (5) and (6), and their accordance with the quantities in

Calculating Branch—(Continued).

column (3) affords the second test which was applied to the accuracy of the calculation. These tests having been considered satisfactory the angular errors to 3 places were introduced into the computations and the corresponding corrections made: the last column exhibits the residual discrepancies which then remained.

With regard to the first six equations it should be stated that the calculations of the triangles have been made with tables of logarithms to 7 places of decimals only, an 8th place being obtained by interpolation, yet the discrepancies are at most only 4 in the 8th place of logs, and two of them cancel if the triangulation is considered continuous from the side Kámkhera to Bhaorasa *viâ* Calcutta, to Vizagapatam. Furthermore, if a complete circuit is made starting from the side Kámkhera to Bhaorasa and carrying the calculation of the triangles round the whole periphery of the Quadrilateral, the value of the side of origin is reproduced identically to the eighth place of decimals of logs. The largest discrepancies in latitude and longitude still remaining are ″·005, or about 6 inches.

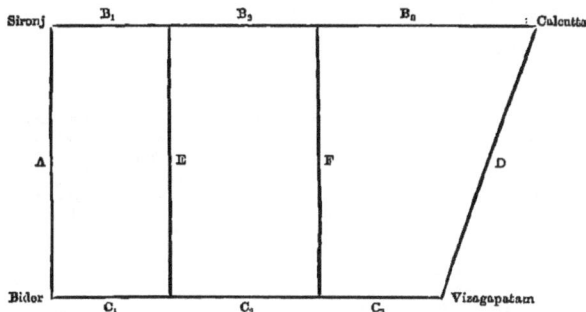

Table of the facts of computation.

No. of Equation	Triangulation involved			Before reduction	By substitution of "indeterminate factors"	As computed to 6 decimals	On contraction to 3 decimals	Residuals after correcting the angles
(1)	(2)			(3)	(4)	(5)	(6)	(7)
1	A			− 16·44	− 16·430	− 16·441	− 16·439	0·0
2	C₁−(B₁+E)			− 54·86	− 54·860	− 54·859	− 54·864	+ 0·2
3	B₁+B₂+B₃			+ 42·5	+ 42·500	+ 42·500	+ 42·501	− 0·4
4	C₁+C₂+C₃			− 21·29	− 21·291	− 21·289	− 21·292	0·0
5	D			− 6·93	− 6·932	− 6·931	− 6·932	+ 0·4
6	(E+C₂)−(B₂+F)			+ 31·9	+ 31·900	+ 31·901	+ 31·902	+ 0·2
7 in λ	(A+C₁)−(B₁+E)			+ 0·050	+ 0·0500	+ 0·0500	+ 0·0500	″·002
8 „ L	Ditto			− 0·214	− 0·2140	− 0·2140	− 0·2139	·005
9 „ A	Ditto			+ 0·212	+ 0·2120	+ 0·2119	+ 0·2117	·000
10 „ λ	(E+C₂)−(B₂+F)			− 0·216	− 0·2160	− 0·2160	− 0·2160	·004
11 „ L	Ditto			+ 0·203	+ 0·2030	+ 0·2030	+ 0·2029	·000
12 „ A	Ditto			− 4·968	− 4·9680	− 4·9682	− 4·9682	·008
13 „ λ	(F+C₃)−(B₃+D)			− 0·142	− 0·1420	− 0·1420	− 0·1419	·005
14 „ L	Ditto			+ 0·239	+ 0·2390	+ 0·2390	+ 0·2388	·000
15 „ A	Ditto			− 3·888	− 3·8880	− 3·8880	− 3·8881	·005

North-East Quadrilateral.

(6). As the reduction of the principal triangulation of the South-East Quadrilateral approached completion, I was enabled to make a commencement with the third section of the triangulation,

Calculating Branch—(Continued.)

known departmentally as the North-East Quadrilateral. It is bounded on the west by the Great Arc Series, Section 24° to 30°, on the south by the Calcutta Longitudinal Series and has in its eastern and northern periphery, the Calcutta Meridional and North-East Longitudinal Series. It contains twelve series, forming eleven circuits and its reduction will prove a more serious undertaking than that of any of the other divisions. At present only the circuit errors are in course of calculation, but this preliminary computation will shortly be complete and then the reduction itself can be taken in hand.

(7). In addition to the calculations I have already described a good deal of assistance has been given to Captain Heaviside in preparing and passing through the press the results of the Pendulum Operations. Captain Trotter has also received much aid; the computation of the entire mass of the observations made by him, while he was attached to the Yárkand Mission having been performed by this Office and the results tabulated for publication in his report. A quantity of miscellaneous work has also been performed which is briefly summed up elsewhere.

Other calculations.

(8). I noticed above the great advantage which had accrued from the use of Arithmometers, instruments which were introduced in to the office by yourself several months ago. Some of the computations which formerly occupied a pair of computers a fortnight or three weeks can with their aid be completed in four or five days. They are almost invaluable and would be quite so if more care was bestowed on their construction. They are of foreign manufacture and the several parts appear to be made in the gross, and then to be roughly put together; thus many of them soon get out of order and make mistakes. Were they carefully constructed as they would be by English mechanics, the principle on which they are designed is such that it seems impossible they should commit errors; as their manufacture is protected by a patent the desired improvement is not 1 fear likely to be effected.

Arithmometers.

Another aid to the computers, recently introduced into the office, is Crelle's Rechentafeln, a book of products of all numbers from 1 to 999. In this case foreign labour has the advantage over English; for it has produced at a cost of only sixteen shillings a most useful book, the labour of compiling which must have been enormous.

(9). The details of the ordinary calculations are as follows :—

Angle Books, indexed	467 vols.
Abstracts of Angles, copied and compared	600 angles.
Zero and general means computed	600 „

Computations in Duplicate.

	Weights computed	383
	Spherical Excesses computed	277
	Simple Quadrilaterals reduced	32
	„ Polygons „	32
	Compound Figures „	11
Principal Triangulation	Auxiliary reductions made	75
	Triangles computed	537
	Lats. Longs. Azimuths computed	750
	„ „ „ corrected (after S. E. Quadl. grinding)	140
	Heights computed	170
	„ examined, corrected and adjusted ...	680
	Traverses computed	18
	Ray Traces computed	6
Secondary Triangulation	Triangles adjusted and computed	2,400
	Heights computed	12
	Latitudes, Longitudes and Azimuths computed	1,100
Explorations	Latitudes	30
	Heights by Boiling Point	130

(10) The work performed in connection with the Typographic and Photozincographic presses, is detailed below.

Calculating Branch—(Continued).

For Typographic Office.

Synopses of the operations &c.	Pages compiled and printed.	Compiled, but not yet put to press.
Azimuth Table, Jogí-Tílá and Sutlej Series	14	
Alphabetical Lists of Gurhágarh, Rahún Sutlej and Jogí-Tílá Series	105	
Errata and Contents, Gurhágarh, Karáchi, Rahún, Great Arc (24°-30°)	11	
Note to Great Arc Final Chart	2	
Co-ordinates and Descriptions &c., of N. W. Himalaya Series, comprising 39 square degrees		The whole
Numerical and Alphabetical Lists of Principal Stations, Descriptions of Principal Stations of the Series comprised in the S. E. Quadrilateral	} 30	The remainder
Triangles Principal and Secondary of the Arc, Calcutta and Coast Series		{ About 80 pages which are half ready

For Vol. (S. E. Quadrilateral).

Lists, Descriptions of Stations, Observed Angles, Reduction of Figures and Principal Triangles

R. Calcutta Longitudinal Series ...	...	...	42 (to end of figs.)	
Great Arc (18°—24°) ...,	...	...	18 („ Δs)	
Jabalpúr ...	...	...	56 („ figs.)	
Biláspúr ...	...	...	86 („ „)	
Coast ...	...	...	4 („ lists)	
Bider ...	...	...	40 (to near end of ∠s)	

(right margin bracket: To end of heights above Mean Sea Level)

Besides the above, the auxiliary reductions of the figures of the E. Coast Series and of a portion of the Biláspúr Series, including about 20. pages of printed matter, have been compiled but not yet put to press. Some progress has also been made in setting up the azimuthal observations appertaining to the South-East Quadrilateral for the press.

Other compilations for departmental and general use.

	Compiled and printed.
Book of Routes in N.W.P., Himalayas &c., ...	34 pages
Data for Rangir Series Charts Nos. 1, 2, 3 ...	13 „
Data for Biláspúr Series Chart, (S. Section) (1872-73)	8 „
Data for E. Frontier Series „ (1873-74)	1 „
Appendices to Vol. II	23 „

For Photozincographic Office.

Final Charts.

	Compared or examined.
Karáchi Series	2
Great Arc Series (24° to 30°) ...	1
Gurhágarh „	2
Rahún „	2
N. W. Himalaya Series ...	2
Jogí-Tílá Series	1
Sutlej „	1
	Total 11

Preliminary Charts.

Madras Longitudinal and Mangalore Meridional Series (1871-73) ...	1
Biláspúr Series (S. Section) (1872-73)	1
Rangir „	3
Assam Valley Survey (1869-74)	1
„ „ „ (1873-74)	1
Bombay Island Survey	1
	Total 8

For Office use.

Triangulation of the South-East Quadrilateral ...	1

Calculating Branch—(Continued).

(11.) Observations for time were taken on 20 occasions during the year for the purpose of showing

Instrumental Work.

mean time and rating chronometers. Meteorological Observations were made in the Dehra Observatory on every day throughout the year, and the results were reduced and communicated month by month to the Reporter on Meteorology N. W. Provinces. A table of monthly means is as usual appended to this report. The large self-registering Anemometer referred to in last year's report was put into working order in January last, and a record has been since kept of the hourly velocity and direction of the wind. The winds in the Dún are so light that they often fail to turn the fans which move the direction pencil and this part of the record although it has been always tabulated, has not been made any use of at present. To do so would necessitate a careful weeding out of all hourly velocities below a certain fixed minimum. As yet only mean hourly velocities, irrespective of direction have been deduced for each month, an abstract of which follows that of the Meteorological Observations. It is remarkable how closely the curves formed from these data resemble one another.

(12.) The preservation of the Principal Stations of this Survey has been as usual steadily kept

Protection of Stations.

in view, and much correspondence has in consequence been entailed. Replies to about 350 letters on this subject were drafted by Mr. O. Wood under your direction, and about 40 letters addressed to district officers who had failed to submit their annual reports on the stations placed under their charge. Modern changes in the boundaries of districts have caused some difficulty in ascertaining what stations fall within each. Since last reporting 16 more districts have been finally settled, making in all 307 districts of which the lists are now complete. The check lists now include 2,700 stations.

(13.) Several duties of a miscellaneous character have also been performed by this branch of

Miscellaneous.

the office which may be briefly summarised as follows:—Reduction of barometer readings; computation of humidity and observed refractions on the Jogí-Tílá Series for Appendix No. 3 to Vol. 11:—Preparation of Appendices Nos. 2, 4 and 5 to Vol. 11:—Examination and arrangement of four Synoptical Vols. for the binder:—Translation of two Explorers' route survey field books:—Alphabetical lists of Indian proper names prepared for departmental issue:—New tables (Auxiliary) and a new form constructed to facilitate the computation of circumpolar star observations for azimuth:—Data collected for discussion as to the advisability of giving the observed azimuths in the S. E. Quadrilateral effect in the final reduction of the triangulation:—Circuit errors of the Kashmir triangulation and North-West Himalaya secondary triangulation determined and dispersed:—Effect of the difference in the values of the earth's axes as adopted by Everest and Clarke on differences of latitude, longitude and azimuth computed for arcs of various magnitude:—Elements of the Bombay Island Survey, executed in 1865-66, prepared for publication:—Differential latitudes and longitudes examined for the new edition of the Turkestan Map:—Captain McCullagh's and Lieutenant Harman's leveling records examined and reported on:— 'Errors of mean square' of latitude, longitude and azimuth at the terminal stations of the right and left hand branches of the circuits of the N. W. Quadrilateral, computed from the origin of each circuit. Twenty-nine officers have been supplied with data. Forms for departmental use have been issued to 96 officers, and 776 parcels containing maps, charts, &c., were booked and despatched. Four candidates for employment in the Junior Branch were examined and three instructed in departmental computations; and papers supplied for the examination of six other candidates, besides several other duties which need not be enumerated here.

TYPOGRAPHIO BRANCH.

(14.) The work performed during the 4 years ending 1st May 1874, and the 17 months, 1st May 1874 to 1st October 1875, is concisely stated thus.

	1870-71	1871-72	1872-73	1873-74	1874-75 (17 months)
Pages composed, ...	819	1,143	1,420	1,220	1,868 = 1,319 per annum.
Do. printed, ...	234,828	241,348	273,157	388,420	527,916 = 372,647 ,,

Typographic Branch—(Continued).

The total pages composed in the 17 months under report may be subdivided thus,

For volumes of the G. T. Survey,	...	...	...	...	1402
„ Route Book,	...	...	...	...	35
„ Charts, Memos, &c.,	...	...	...	...	306
„ Annual Report,	...	...	...	...	125
			Total		1868

DRAWING BRANCH.

The work executed by the Drawing Office is exhibited in the table which follows this report. Some very important maps have been prepared there during the past year; those of most general interest are the 3rd Edition of the map of Turkestan, compiled under your own superintendence; the map to illustrate the reports on Sir Douglas Forsyth's Mission to Yárkand and other maps relating to Trans Frontier explorations, the compilation of which is due to Captain Trotter.

PHOTO-ZINCOGRAPHIC BRANCH.

The work from 1st May 1874 to 30th September 1875 is shown below under the heads of Maps, Charts, Diagrams and Forms.

Maps.

SUBJECT.	When published.	No. of parts.	No. of copies printed.
Prints of maps published in former years	...	40	1,841
Guzerat, sheet No. 8	May 1874	1	118
Ditto No. 9	„ „	1	105
Index to Dehra Dún Survey	September „	1	481
Kattywar Survey, degree sheet No. VI ...	October „	1	107
Ditto No. VII ...	„ „	1	150
Index to Kattywar Survey	„ „	1	468
Route map for the W. Himalayas &c., ...	„ „	1	473
Chamba Map	November „	4	22
Index to Kumaun and Garhwál Survey	„ „	1	460
„ Guzerat Survey	„ „	1	426
Kumaun and Garhwál, sheet No. 25, skeleton ...	„ „	1	105
Dehra Dún Tea Company's Plantation, sheet No. 1 ...	„ „	1	75
Ditto No. 2 ...	„ „	1	76
Guzerat Survey, sheet 80, section 3	December „	1	135
Jaunsár Map	„ „	1	22
Eastern Turkestan ...	„ „	2	478
Plan of Landour Bazar	January 1875	1	53
Map illustrating Trans-Himalayan Explorations during 1872	„ „	1	466
Index to Mussoorie and Landour Survey	February „	1	28
Town and Cantonment of Rájkot	„ „	2	83
Map illustrating Trans-Himalayan Explorations during 1873	„ „	1	491
Kattywar Survey, sheet No. 85	March „	1	133
Guzerat „ „ 80, section 2	„ „	1	110
„ „ „ „ „ 11	April „	1	110
„ „ „ „ „ 9	„ „	1	135
„ „ „ „ „ 7	„ „	1	105
„ „ „ „ „ 1	„ „	1	127
Kattywar Survey, sheet No. 33	„ „	1	147
„ „ „ 32	May „	1	133
Mussoorie and Landour Survey, sheet No. 15, skeleton ...	„ „	1	44
Turkestan Map, sheet No. 1 (3rd edition)	„ „	1	263
„ „ 2 „	June „	1	227
„ „ 3 „	„ „	1	384
„ „ 4 „	„ „	1	278
Kattywar Survey, sheet No. 34	July „	1	154
Kumaun and Garhwál, sheet No. 38, skeleton ...	August „	1	177
„ „ „ 12 „	„ „	1	156
„ „ „ 9 „	„ „	1	156
„ „ „ 22 „	September „	1	61
„ „ „ 38 „	„ „	1	167
„ „ „ 31 „	„ „	1	159
Guzerat Survey, sheet 80, section 13	„ „	1	107
„ „ „ 8 „	„ „	1	106
„ „ „ 5 „	„ „	1	105
Dehra Dún and Siwalik No. X ⎫	„ „	1	132
„ „ „ XIX ⎬ For Forest Department	„ „	1	137
„ „ „ XX ⎭	„ „	1	108
	Total ...	92	9,974

Photo-zincographic Branch—(Continued).

Charts.

Besides the foregoing 28 Blue prints were issued and several Silver prints were prepared on the scale of the Indian Atlas for the use of the Engravers.

SUBJECT.	When published.	No. of parts.	No. of copies printed.
Madras Longitudinal and Mangalore Meridional Series (1871-78) Numerical	July 1874	2	67
Assam Valley Triangulation (1872-73) Numerical	August ,,	2	67
Karáchí Longitudinal Series, Chart No. 1 } Final	,, ,,	1	373
,, ,, 2 }	,, ,,	1	371
Rangír Meridional Series, Chart No. 3 Numerical	,, ,,	1	65
,, ,, ,, 1 ,,	September ,,	1	65
Biláspúr Series, season 1872-73 (S. section) ,,	,, ,,	1	65
Brahmaputra Series, season 1873-74 ,,	,, ,,	1	65
Great Arc Series, (Sec: 24°·30°)Final	,, ,,	1	384
Gurhágarh Meridional Series, Chart No. 1 Final	October ,,	1	367
Eastern Frontier Series, season 1873-74 Numerical	November ,,	1	65
Rangír Meridional Series, sheet No. 2 ,,	,, ,,	1	65
Gurhágarh Meridional Series, Chart No. 2 Final	December ,,	1	375
Malabar Minor Series, season 1873-74 Numerical	January 1875	1	65
Assam Valley Survey, season (1869-74) ,,	,, ,,	1	67
,, ,, (1873-74) ,,	,, ,,	1	65
Bangalore Meridional Series (Great Arc), season 1873-74 } Numerical	February ,,	1	70
Bombay Island Survey Numerical	,, ,,	1	65
Rahún Meridional Series, Chart No. 1 Final	March ,,	1	361
N. W. Himalaya Series No. 1 Final	,, ,,	1	370
,, ,, 2 ,,	,, ,,	1	372
Rahún Meridional Series, Chart No. 2 Final	April ,,	1	372
Jodhpúr Series, season 1873-74, Numerical	,, ,,		70
Total ...		25	4,271

Diagrams.

SUBJECT.	When published.	No. of copies printed.
Plates to illustrate Volumes II, III, IV, V, VI, of the G. T. Survey, and other diagrams.	July 1874	50
	August ,,	382
	October ,,	46
	November ,,	1156
	December ,,	680
	February 1875	4
	April ,,	390
	May ,,	870
	June ,,	190
	July ,,	735
	August ,,	402
	September ,,	837
Total, ...		5,243
Professional and Office Forms.	1874-75 (17 months)	34,310

Photo-zincographic Branch—(Continued.)

7,536 Maps and 4,446 Charts were issued during the year. The forms are always expended as fast as printed. Contrasting the work performed since 1870-71 we have,

Year	Maps	Charts	Diagrams	Forms
1870-71	6,465	839	18,205	10,482
1871-72	10,181	1,375	4,937	13,655
1872-73	6,910	2,206	12,055	12,549
1873-74	9,207	2,027	8,557	28,125
1874-75 (17 Months)	9,974	4,271	25,43	34,310

An abstract of the work executed during the past five years stands as follows.

SUBJECT.	Number of Prints.				
	1870-71	1871-72	1872-73	1873-74	1874-75 (17 months)
Maps, Charts and Diagrams, ...	20,509	16,443	21,171	14,791	19,488
Forms, ...	10,482	13,655	12,549	28,125	34,310

In conclusion I must express my thanks to the several members of the office for their cordial co-operation in, and conscientious discharge of its duties. Where all have worked so well it seems almost invidious to single out any for especial commendation. I cannot however refrain from doing so in one instance at least. Mr. Wood has been associated with me in the same office for nearly nine years; but I have never hitherto had an opportunity, similar to the present, for placing on record my high opinion of his services and it is with pleasure that I now avail myself of it to state that I consider them very valuable. His duties are of a nature constantly requiring the exercise of no small patience and perseverance but his energies never seem to flag and his knowledge and experience are often of the greatest service.

Mr. Todd has done excellent work while attached to this office, and while congratulating him on his restored health, I cannot but regret that it necessitates his return to field duties and thus deprives the office of his services.

Mr. Peychers has proved himself exceedingly useful and deserves every commendation. Besides taking his regular share of the work, a good deal of the final supervision of press proofs has to be entrusted to him and in this he has been of much assistance to me.

Mr. Keating has become fairly well acquainted with the processes of computation and works industriously.

Baboo Gunga Pershad has discharged his duties in the same exemplary manner he always has done and deserves that I should add my testimony to that so frequently expressed by Mr. Hennessey as to his efficiency. Baboo Cally Mohun has also gained my approbation by the intelligent interest he takes in his work. On more than one occasion he has made suggestions with reference to the calculations which have led to a diminution of labour. Baboos Kally Coomar, Gopal Chunder and Tarapodo have worked with their accustomed diligence, and the other computers have given me every reason to be satisfied with them.

In the Drawing Office Mr. Atkinson has continued to conduct his duties as successfully as heretofore, and although the loss of his two best men, Sheik Saidudeen and Goormukh Sing, has for a time considerably diminished the power of his office, he is doing his best to train up others to supply their places.

In the Photo-zincographic Office Mr. Ollenbach is as hard working as ever. I am glad to observe that he now throws more of the manual labour on his subordinates, devoting his own attention to supervision of their work, and the out-turn is very satisfactory. Mr. Dyson deserves great credit for the excellence of his negatives. I could wish that his assistants Dempster and Lloyd made more rapid progress under his instruction, but the art of Photography is not learnt in a day, and with more practice no doubt they will become more proficient.

Mr. O'Connor in the Printing Office has worked very industriously and the out-turn of work has been fully as great as the office was capable of. He was at one time somewhat lax in the discipline he maintained among his subordinates, I am glad that he has done his best to correct this fault.

Mean Velocity in miles of the winds which blew at Dehra during 8 months of 1875 for each hour of the day.

Civil Hours.	February.	March.	April.	May.	June.	July.	August.	September.
0 to 1	2·27	3·13	3·75	3·14	2·67	1·41	0·59	0·90
1 „ 2	2·19	2·68	3·00	2·71	1·97	1·52	0·66	0·74
2 „ 8	2·39	2·23	2·54	2·36	2·03	1·48	0·66	1·10
3 „ 4	2·31	2·03	2·32	1·86	1·77	1·48	0·38	0·83
4 „ 5	1·96	1·97	2·11	1·71	1·63	1·00	0·14	0·57
5 „ 6	2·58	2·10	1·86	2·07	1·70	1·07	0·28	0·50
6 „ 7	2·08	1·87	1·75	1·79	1·33	0·62	0·14	0·43
7 „ 8	1·81	1·68	1·61	1·96	1·10	1·07	0·34	0·40
8 „ 9	1·96	1·67	1·86	2·68	1·00	1·00	0·69	0·70
9 „ 10	2·19	1·90	2·78	2·78	1·43	1·38	0·79	1·20
10 „ 11	2·46	2·72	3·96	3·11	2·17	1·52	1·21	1·53
11 „ 12	2·31	2·93	4·11	3·96	2·07	1·52	1·66	1·53
12 „ 13	3·11	3·85	4·86	3·79	2·33	1·83	1·33	2·03
13 „ 14	3·07	3·88	4·93	4·18	3·07	2·07	1·90	2·40
14 „ 15	3·22	4·23	5·28	4·89	3·00	1·59	1·57	2·33
15 „ 16	3·08	3·83	4·86	4·43	2·90	1·59	1·37	1·47
16 „ 17	2·50	3·32	4·59	3·89	2·20	1·34	1·20	0·97
17 „ 18	1·50	1·98	3·34	3·68	1·30	0·90	1·07	0·57
18 „ 19	1·12	1·19	1·72	3·25	0·70	0·28	0·66	0·47
19 „ 20	1·46	2·32	2·31	3·18	1·57	0·41	0·62	0·60
20 „ 21	2·54	2·94	3·14	3·75	2·47	0·45	0·76	0·90
21 „ 22	2·08	3·00	3·72	3·36	2·27	0·69	0·55	0·77
22 „ 23	2·42	3·10	3·72	3·57	2·47	1·17	0·90	0·87
23 „ 24	2·52	3·13	3·14	3·50	2·27	1·03	0·86	1·07
Sums, ...	55·13	63·78	77·26	75·60	47·42	28·42	20·33	24·88
Averages, ...	2·30	2·66	3·22	3·15	1·98	1·18	0·85	1·04

MONTHLY Meteorological results taken from the Register kept at the Office of the Superintendent G. T. Survey of India, Dehra Dún.

YEAR & MONTH	BAROMETER At 9 30 A.M. Highest	Lowest	Monthly mean	BAROMETER At 3 30 P.M. Highest	Lowest	Monthly mean	HYGROMETER At 9 30 A.M. Dew point	Humidity	HYGROMETER At 3 30 P.M. Dew point	Humidity	THERMOMETER Max: in Sun's rays	Min: on grass	Dry Bulb Max in air	Min in air	Monthly mean in air	Wet Bulb Max wet	Min wet	Monthly mean wet	RAIN No. of days it fell	Fall in inches	WIND Average direction	CLOUD At 9 30 A.M.	At 3 30 P.M.
	in.	in.	in.	in.	in.	in.	°		°		°	°	°	°	°	°	°	°					
1874.																							
January	27·989	27·681	27·814	27·883	27·617	27·730	43·2	·716	44·3	·531	84·5	23·8	71·2	31·8	53·3	63·5	27·5	44·5	4	1·46	W.	5	5
February	·678	·417	·736	·784	·323	·656	45·4	·676	43·8	·455	87·7	34·3	77·3	37·9	57·3	64·6	25·9	46·2	6	3·77	S.	3	4
March	·832	·389	·663	·754	·389	·579	48·9	·608	47·5	·449	99·1	36·9	85·1	89·1	76·8	63·8	27·0	48·5	7	3·48	N.	4	4
April	·758	·370	·616	·677	·407	·531	53·4	·403	49·0	·252	109·8	46·7	96·7	51·3	76·8	71·5	49·5	61·2	1	0·02	W.	2	1
May	·583	·199	·450	·512	·279	·362	56·4	·365	53·7	·248	115·9	60·1	103·0	63·9	81·9	80·0	53·2	61·2	3	0·67	N.	1	1
June	·635	·279	·427	·563	·160	·350	73·3	·769	74·1	·718	113·6	65·3	101·4	69·1	84·6	82·1	59·0	72·0	21	18·73	N.&E.	7	7
July	·561	·199	·429	·473	·237	·359	75·3	·876	76·3	·846	104·8	65·3	90·3	71·8	79·0	81·4	65·0	72·9	30	34·57	S.W.	8	8
August	·663	·319	·440	·489	·270	·370	75·5	·811	76·3	·730	105·4	70·4	89·9	63·5	79·1	79·0	53·6	73·0	27	25·72	N.&W.	6	6
September	·616	·455	·541	·500	·375	·451	71·6	·715	72·7	·474	103·9	61·0	88·0	55·7	71·8	74·0	48·4	69·8	13	7·82	N.	5	7
October	·760	·510	·672	·678	·446	·582	59·1	·593	49·0	·484	100·8	62·1	86·2	45·0	71·5	66·3	31·8	60·2	0	0·00	S.	0	1
November	·688	·739	·818	·731	·671	·727	48·5	·581			94·8	40·4	82·6	38·0	68·9	59·1	34·3	51·8	0	0·00	N.	0	0
December	·900	·685	·836	·812	·604	·761	42·7	·427	43·6	·436	81·5	32·0	88·5		56·5			47·2	0	0·00		2	2
1875.																							
January	27·569	27·589	27·730	27·850	27·507	27·648	41·4	·670	41·2	·453	77·1	31·9	72·1	35·2	54·1	69·7	33·3	45·0	3	0·63	B.	2	4
February	·663	·558	·717	·781	·515	·683	47·4	·731	47·9	·546	86·0	23·5	75·4	38·5	57·6	63·2	33·2	48·9	7	6·10	W.	5	5
March	·809	·519	·649	·732	·453	·588	52·5	·513	50·1	·329	108·0	44·0	90·1	48·1	90·7	71·3	41·7	55·8	0	0·00	S.	2	3
April	·666	·410	·553	·601	·306	·465	56·2	·414	54·4	·289	109·3	66·7	97·5	60·4	79·7	75·7	46·6	60·7	1	0·01	W.	1	2
May	·662	·403	·533	·588	·318	·448	63·7	·568	62·4	·448	112·0	68·9	100·8	60·8	84·2	76·1	52·1	63·9	12	4·57	S.E.	4	5
June	·545	·255	·375	·419	·188	·292	71·4	·637	71·1	·580	115·0	61·3	99·3	69·0	79·9	81·2	53·1	70·6	10	10·39	N.	6	6
July	·523	·243	·380	·473	·207	·313	75·3	·864	77·3	·778	115·2	69·4	71·0	71·0	78·4	86·0	58·8	73·3	28	29·91	S.	8	8
August	·596	·341	·448	·520	·283	·382	74·7	·691	76·0	·838	101·4	68·8	87·6	69·3	78·4	80·4	64·3	73·1	28	22·99	B.	5	9
September	·668	·378	·555	·569	·302	·468	72·6	·837	73·5	·607	106·3	64·7	88·5	67·2	77·3	83·0	61·0	71·1	23	12·85	N.		7

NOTE.—The height of the Barometer Cistern above Mean Sea Level at Karáchi is 2332·41 feet.

Annual Return of work executed in the Drawing Branch of the Computing Office from 1st May 1874 to 1st October 1875.

DESCRIPTION OF WORK.	Finished	In hand	Scale 1 inch =	REMARKS.
Compilation.			Miles.	
Sheets Nos. 1, 2, 3 and 4 Turkestan Map, (3rd edition) with hill shading.	4		32	For Photo-zincography.
Map of Kumaun and Garhwál to illustrate Mr. E. T. Atkinson's Gazetteer of Kumaun and Garhwál, with hill shading.		1	4	ditto. Reduction to ½ scale.
Map to illustrate the report on the Trans-Himalayan Explorations in Great Tibet made during 1872, with hill shading.		1	16	ditto.
Map to illustrate the report on the Explorations Trans-Himalayan and in Nepal made during 1873, with hill shading.		1	16	ditto.
Preliminary Map of Eastern Turkestan to illustrate the reports on Sir Douglas Forsyth's Mission to Kashghar during 1873-74, with hill shading.		1	32	ditto. Reduction to ⁴⁄₅ scale.
Map to illustrate the report on the Pandit's route through Great Tibet from Ladákh to Assam viâ the Tengri Nur lake and Lhása in 1874. Sheets 1 and 2, with hill shading.		2	16	ditto.
Index Chart to the Degree Sheets of the N. W. Himalaya Series triangulation, with hill shading.		1	24	ditto. Reduction to ¼ scale.
Map of Afghanistán (by Captain Trotter).		1	16	ditto.
Sheet No. 6 of Levelled Heights.		1	2	ditto.
Do. „ 25 do.		1	2	ditto.
Revised and corrected Map of Routes in Northern India.	4		16	ditto. Reduction to ½ scale.
Sketch Map of Tihri Garhwál with adjoining states.	1		8	
Preliminary Numerical Charts.				
Rangír Series Sheet No. 1.		1	4	ditto.
Do. „ No. 2.		1	4	ditto.
Do. „ No. 3.		1	4	ditto.
Assam Valley triangulation, Seasons 1868-69 to 1872-78.		1	8	ditto.
Bombay Island triangulation,		1	½	ditto.
Final Charts.				
Great Arc Series.		2	4	ditto. Reduction to ½ scale.
Karáchí Series.		2	4	ditto. ditto.
Gurhágarh Series.		2	4	ditto. ditto.
Rahún Series.		2	4	ditto. ditto.
Jogi-Tílá Series.		1	4	ditto. ditto.
Sutlej Series.		1	4	ditto. ditto.
N. W. Himalaya Series.		2	4	ditto. ditto.
Degree Charts of the North-West Himalaya triangulation.	11	14	4	ditto.
Miscellaneous.				
Examined and reported on 19 fair Maps of Kumaun and Garhwál, Kattywar, Guzerat and Dehra Dún and Siwalika Surveys.				
Examined 143 proofs of Maps and Charts.				
Colored 7,503 Maps.				
Prepared 24 professional and Office forms on drawing and transfer paper.				For Photo-zincography and Zincography.
Prepared plans of cities of Khotan, Yárkand and Kashghar.				
Do. map to show the connection of triangulation of India and Ceylon.				
Corrected Sheet No. 14 of Mussooree and Landour Survey, and inserted numbers of boundary pillars on the several sheets of this survey.				

www.ingramcontent.com/pod-product-compliance
Lightning Source LLC
Chambersburg PA
CBHW030320270326
41926CB00010B/1443